A COMMITMENT TO EXCELLENCE

Essays in Honour of
Emeritus Professor Gabriël A. Moens

A COMMITMENT TO EXCELLENCE

Essays in Honour of
Emeritus Professor Gabriël A. Moens

Augusto Zimmermann
Editor

Connor Court Publishing

Connor Court Publishing Pty Ltd

Copyright © Augusto Zimmermann 2018

ALL RIGHTS RESERVED. This book contains material protected under International and Federal Copyright Laws and Treaties. Any unauthorised reprint or use of this material is prohibited. No part of this book may be reproduced or transmitted in any form or by any means, electronic or mechanical, including photocopying, recording, or by any information storage and retrieval system without express written permission from the publisher.

PO Box 7257
Redland Bay QLD 4165
sales@connorcourt.com
www.connorcourt.com

ISBN: 9781925826203

Cover design by Maria Giordano

Printed in Australia

Contents

Contributor Biographies   vii

1. **Essays in Honour of Professor Gabriël A. Moens: Introduction**
   Augusto Zimmermann   1

2. **Lessons from a Teacher**
   John Trone   7

3. **Constitutional Fundamentals**
   Nicholas Aroney   12

4. **The Wrongs of a Bill of Rights for Australia: A Rights-based Appraisal**
   Augusto Zimmermann   32

5. **The Spiritual Foundations of s 51(xxxi) of the Australian Constitution**
   A. Keith Thompson   70

6. **Born (Again) This Way: Why the Inherent Nature of Religiosity Requires a New Approach to Australia's Discrimination Laws**
   Michael Quinlan   96

7. **Liberal Peace and its Prospects in the Twenty First Century**
   Suri Ratnapala   148

8. **Happiness and the Law**
   Marc De Vos   176

9. **The Use of Force as a Response to Chemical Weapons Attacks – Might There Be Something Brewing in the Laboratory of International Law?**
   Jürgen Bröhmer   204

10. **Brexit, Art Loans and Frustration**
    Geoffrey Bennett   230

11. **The Finality of the Arbitral Award**
    Bruno Zeller   243

12. **Overcoming the Tyranny of Distance: Australia as an Arbitral Seat**
    Doug Jones AO   256

13. **The Joys and Challenges of (Re-)Educating Australian Jurists in International Commercial Arbitration**
    Luke Nottage and Diana Hu   281

14. **To What Degree Does Customary International Law Require Accommodation of a Source Country's Right to Tax High, Tax Low or Not Tax at All?**
    J. Clifton Fleming, Jr.   312

15. **The International Harmonization of Security Rights Law: Its Successes and Challenges**
    Henry Gabriel   322

16. **The Seven Habits of Highly Effective Mooters**
    Lorraine Finlay   349

17. **The Art and Science of Oral Advocacy: An Insider's Perspective**
    Rajesh Sharma, Harprabdeep Singh, and Eric Ng   364

18. **Security of Payment in Western Australia: The Effect of Changes Arising from the   Review of the *Construction Contracts Act 2004* (WA)**
    Philip Evans   389

    Abstracts   415

    List of Publications by Emeritus Professor Gabriël A. Moens 425

CONTRIBUTOR BIOGRAPHIES

Nicholas Aroney is Professor of Constitutional Law at The University of Queensland. He is also a Fellow of the Centre for Public, International and Comparative Law, a Research Fellow of Emmanuel College at The University of Queensland, a Fellow of the Centre for Law and Religion at Emory University and an External Member of the Islam, Law and Modernity research program at Durham University. In 2010 he received of a four-year Future Fellowship from the Australian Research Council to study comparative federalism. He has held visiting positions at Oxford, Cambridge, Edinburgh, Sydney, Emory and Tilburg universities. Most recently, he was a Visiting Professor of the Institut Michel Villey at the University of Paris II (Panthéon-Assas) and a Visiting Fellow of the Institute of Advanced Study at Durham University. Professor Aroney has published over 100 books, journal articles and book chapters in the fields of constitutional law, comparative constitutional law and legal theory. He has led several international research projects in comparative federalism, bicameralism, legal pluralism, and law & religion, and he speaks frequently at international conferences on these topics. His most notable publications in these fields include: *The Constitution of a Federal Commonwealth: The Making and Meaning of the Australian Constitution* (Cambridge University Press, 2009), *Shari'a in the West* (Oxford University Press, 2010) (edited with Rex Ahdar), *The Future of Australian Federalism* (Cambridge University Press, 2012) (edited with Gabrielle Appleby and Thomas John), *The Constitution of the Commonwealth of Australia: History, Principle and Interpretation* (Cambridge University Press, 2015) (with Peter Gerangelos, James Stellios and Sarah Murray) and *Courts in Federal Countries* (Toronto University Press, 2017) (edited with John Kincaid). Professor Aroney is a former editor of *The University of Queensland Law Journal* (2003-2005) and *International Trade and Business Law Annual* (1996-1998), and a past secretary of the Australian Society of Legal Philosophy. He is a past member of the Governing Council and the current Queensland Convenor of the Australian Association of Constitutional Law. He is also a member of the editorial advisory board of *Public Law Review* and *International Trade and Business Law Review*. He has made numerous influential submissions to government inquiries. In 2013 he undertook a review of the *Crime and Misconduct Act* for the Queensland Government with the Hon Ian Callinan AC QC and in 2018 he was appointed to an Expert Panel chaired by the Hon Philip Ruddock to advise the Commonwealth Government on whether Australian law adequately protects the human right to freedom of religion.

Geoffrey Bennett graduated in Classics and Law from Cambridge University in 1974. He was called to the Bar and has held teaching appointments at the universities of Liverpool, Leeds, Louisville, City University, London and Royal Holloway College. Between 1995 and 2016 he was Co-Director then Director of the University of Notre Dame's London Law Programme. He has taught and published in the areas of Contract, Crime, Comparative and Cultural Heritage Law. He is presently Visiting Professor in the Centre for Commercial Law Studies, Queen Mary University of London. In 2018 he was made a Senior Fellow of the Institute of Art and Law and teaches on the LL.M. in Art, Business and Law which is a collaboration between the Institute and the Centre for Commercial Law Studies at Queen Mary University of London.

Jürgen Bröhmer Ref. iur. 1989 (Mannheim University), Grad. Cert. European Integration 1991 (Europa-Institute, Saarland University), Ass. iur. 1992 (Saarbrücken), Dr. iur. 1995 (Saarland University), Habil. 2002 (Saarland University) is Professor and Dean of Law School at Murdoch University in Western Australia. Previously, he was Professor at the University of New England and Head of the Law School from 2007-11. He received his law degree from Mannheim University in Germany and his doctorate and post-doctoral Habilitation from Saarland University in Saarbrücken, Germany where worked at the Europa-Institute of Saarland University before coming to Australia. His areas of expertise are German Constitutional Law, European Union (in particular constitutional and common market issues) and Public International (international and european human rights and state immunity in particular) Law. Professor Bröhmer has authored two and co-authored one monograph in specific areas of public international, constitutional and European Union Law, edited a number of other books, and published numerous articles and book chapters.

Marc De Vos holds a Licentiate and Doctorate in Law (University of Ghent, 1993 and 2000), a Master in Social Law (Université Libre de Bruxelles, 1994), and a Master of Laws (Harvard University, 2000). His main areas of legal specialization, in which he has also practiced extensively, include Belgian and European employment and labour law (social law), EU institutional and constitutional law, fundamental rights, and the rule of law. He is also widely read in economics, sociology, and political science. About these and related topics he has authored and co-authored over twenty books and over one hundred scientific articles. He frequently publishes, teaches, lectures and debates on issues of labour and employment law, European integration, globalisation, labour market reform, pensions, ageing, healthcare, the welfare state, inequality and economic growth, both nationally and internationally, and both in academic, professional and policy circles, as well as in the media. De Vos is a professor of law at the Ghent University Law School and at Curtin University Law School, where he teaches courses on employment and labour law, EU-law, and the rule of law. He serves as Director of LLM programmes and international relations at Ghent University Law School (www.ugent.be/re/llm). He is the director of the *Itinera Institute*, an independent policy research institute, based in Brussels (www.itinerainstitute.org). Professor De Vos is a member of Belgium's High Council for Employment, of the Board of Trustees of the European Law Academy (ERA), of the Scientific Committee of ADAPT, and of various academic boards and expert committees. The recipient of several academic and educational awards, he has served as a visiting professor at universities in Europe, the United States, Australia, and Asia. He frequently has held advisory positions in various public and private organizations.

Philip Evans is Professor of Law at the University of Notre Dame Australia, Fremantle campus. He is also the Principal of PJ Evans and Associates; Lawyers, Arbitrators, Mediators and Adjudicators. He is a graded arbitrator, accredited mediator and registered adjudicator under the *Construction Contracts Act 2004* (WA). He holds a current legal practice certificate. In addition to his university teaching and research roles at the University of Notre Dame, Dr Evans conducts regular continuing professional development programs and in-house training in the areas of contract law, trade practices law, administrative law, statute law, dispute resolution, construction law, and arbitration. In 2013 he was appointed by the Western Australian government as a sessional arbitrator to resolve workers compensation disputes and in June 2014 he was appointed by the Minister of Commerce to undertake an extensive review of the operation of the *Construction Contracts Act 2004* (WA). His review has resulted in significant changes to the legislation relating to contract administration and dispute resolution in Western Australia. Before leaving to practice law full time with a national law firm in 1998, Dr Evans was the Head of the Department of Construction Management at Curtin University. In 2001 he joined the College of Law at the University of Notre Dame Australia, where he was Professor and Associate Dean of the School of Law, Director of Graduate Law Programs, and the Course Coordinator of the Graduate Certificate in Building and Construction Law. In 2010 he joined Murdoch University and was subsequently appointed Professor of Law, Deputy Dean and Dean of Law before leaving to take up a foundation professorial appointment at Curtin University Law School in July 2013. In July 2015 he left Curtin to return to private practice. He has lectured extensively in Contract Law, Torts Law, Trade Practices Law, Intellectual Property Law, Evidence, Project Management, Construction Contracts, Construction Claims and Dispute Resolution in the Construction Industry. Dr Evans has coached a number of award winning teams in international mooting competitions including the Willem C Vis International Trade Law Arbitration Moot (Vienna and Hong Kong), the International Maritime Law Moot (Australia) and the International ADR Moot (Hong Kong).

He regularly acts as a judge in each of these competitions. He has taught in a number of university twinning programs including the University of Macerata (Italy), The Lim Kok Wing University of Technology (Malaysia) and BPI International (Singapore). He is also on the editorial boards of a number of law journals and in 2016 he was appointed Research Fellow at the University Of Melbourne School Of Law. His contribution to construction law education and dispute resolution has been acknowledged through the awarding of Fellowships by the Institution of Engineers (Australia), the Australian Institute of Building, the Australian Institute of Management and the Australian Centre for International Commercial Arbitration. In 2012 Dr Evans received the Murdoch Law Students Lecturer of the Year Award and at the World Building 2013 Conference in Brisbane, received the Moray and Agnew Construction Law Award. In 2013 he received the Vice Chancellor's Award for Excellence in Teaching and the OLT Australian Award for University Teaching (Citations for Outstanding Contributions to Student Learning) for his contribution to international advocacy training. As a consequence of his contribution to the field of alternate dispute resolution, in October 2015 Dr Evans was awarded the inaugural Resolution Institute Award; *Contribution to the Professional Development of Others in ADR (Alternate Dispute Resolution)*. Dr Evans has also had a long involvement in Adult Legal Education as a regular presenter in the Professional Training Program in Arbitration Law and Practice (IAMA & WAIDM), the University of Western Australia Extension programs, Murdoch Executive Education, the Queensland Department of Main Roads, and the Chifley Business School Centre for Pavement Engineering Education Programs.

Lorraine Finlay BA (UWA), LLB (UWA), LLM (NUS), LLM (NYU) is a law lecturer at Murdoch University and adjunct senior lecturer in law at The University of Notre Dame Australia, Sydney Campus. Her research interests include criminal law, constitutional law, international criminal law and public international law. Mrs Finlay previously worked at the Office of the Director of Public Prosecutions (WA), where she worked as a State Prosecutor. She has also previously worked at the High Court of Australia, initially as the

Legal Research Officer and then as an Associate to The Hon. Justice Dyson Heydon. In 2009 she was selected as a Singapura Scholar with the NYU@NUS program. As part of this program she was awarded a dual LL.M in Law and the Global Economy (with a concentration in Justice and Human Rights) from New York University and in International & Comparative Law from the National University of Singapore. Mrs Finlay is also a Research Scholar with the Centre for Public, International & Comparative Law (The University of Queensland) and a Fellow with the Murdoch Learning Excellence Academy (LEAD). Lorraine has been awarded a number of teaching and research awards, including the OLT Citation for Outstanding Contributions to Student Learning (2013), Vice-Chancellor's Citation for Excellence in Enhancing Learning (2013), Dean's Service Award (2010 & 2011), Dean's Research Prize Commendation (2011) and MSLS Lecturer of the Year (2011 & 2014). In addition, Mrs Finlay is the Director of the Mooting Program at Murdoch. She is the Faculty Advisor to the Moot Court Bench, and is responsible for coaching a number of Murdoch's international moot teams. This includes award-winning teams in competitions such as the Philip C. Jessup Public International Law Moot (2013 International Quarter Finalists), International Maritime Law & Arbitration Moot (2011 Winning Team), INADR International Mediation Tournament (2014 H. Case Ellis Mediation Award Winners & 2011 Winning Team – Mediation Division) and FDI International Arbitration Moot (2017 International Quarter Finalists).

J. Clifton Fleming, Jr. is the Ernest L. Wilkinson Chair and Professor of Law at Brigham Young University, in Provo/UT, U.S.A. Professor Fleming joined the BYU law faculty in 1974. Fleming served as Associate Dean for Academic Affairs from 1986 to 1999 and as Associate Dean for Faculty and Curriculum from 1999 to 2004. He was appointed to the Wilkinson Chair in 1998. In 1985-86, he was Professor-in-Residence in the IRS Chief Counsel's Office in Washington, D.C. Professor Fleming's academic and teaching career has spanned the globe. He has been a Fulbright visiting professor of law at the University of Nairobi, and a visiting professor at the University of Queensland, Central European University in Budapest, Murdoch University School of Law in Western Australia, and holder of a visiting scholar chair at the University of Florida's law school. In 2011, he held the Fulbright Distinguished Chair at the Vienna University of Economics and Business, Vienna, Austria. Professor Fleming teaches courses on U.S. and International Tax Law, European Union Law, and Public International Law.

Henry Gabriel is a Professor at Elon University School of Law and an Adjunct Professor at Victoria University, Melbourne. Professor Gabriel has significant experience with international and domestic commercial law. He has spent the last three decades engaged in the development of uniform commercial laws, both domestically and globally. His recent work includes creating a legal framework with the Food and Agricultural Organization of the United Nations and other international groups to ensure food security and provide for agricultural development. The former De Vvan Daggett Professor of Law at Loyola University, Gabriel has authored nine books and more than 50 law review articles. He has been lead counsel in more than 50 federal appeals in the U.S. Supreme Court and the U.S. Courts of Appeals. He serves as a U.S. delegate to the U.N. Commission on International Trade where he works on electronic commerce and transport documents. Gabriel is a life member of the Uniform Law Commission. He was appointed a commissioner by the Louisiana Legislature, and serving the State of North Carolina for the last five by appointment of the governor. Closely involved with the Uniform Commercial Code, he was the reporter for the revisions of the sales and lease provisions of the Code as well as the chair of the committee to revise the articles governing documents of title. He also served on the drafting committee of the Uniform Electronic Transactions Act. Appointed by successive presidential administrations, Gabriel serves as a U.S. delegate to the U.N. Commission on International Trade Law where he has worked on international trade laws for electronic commerce and transport documents. He also advises the U.S. State Department as a member of the Department's Advisory Committee on Private International Law, and he is an elected member of Rome's Governing Council of the

International Institute for the Unification of Private Law (UNIDROIT). Professor Gabriel is a Fellow of the U.K.-based Chartered Institute of Arbitrators and an elected member of the American Law Institute. . He has taught international commercial law at Catholic University of Portugal, Kyushu University in Japan, University of Padua in Italy and the University of Lapland in Finland. Gabriel has also held visiting professorships at the International Islamic University of Malaysia and at Victoria University, The University of Queensland, Monash University, Murdoch University and Deakin University in Australia. He has also been a visiting professor at Tulane University and the University of the Pacific.

Diana Hu is an In-house Counsel, Regional Mergers and Acquisitions, at AIG Asia Pacific in Sydney, and previously worked as a solicitor at Corrs Chambers Westgarth. She is also a Freelance Contributor at Pearson and a former Research Assistant at the University of Sydney Law School. Ms Hu has co-authored with Professor Luke Nottage several academic works on international commercial arbitration in Australia.

Doug Jones AO, RFD, CCIArb, FIAMA, FAMINZ is a leading independent international commercial and investor-state arbitrator with over 40 years' prior experience as an international transactional and disputes project lawyer. Professor Jones is an arbitrator member at Arbitration Place in Toronto, a door tenant at Atkin Chambers London and has an office in Sydney. The arbitrations in which he has been involved include infrastructure, energy, commodities, intellectual property, commercial and joint venture, and investor-state disputes spanning over 30 jurisdictions around the world. He has extensive experience as arbitrator under the ICC, LCIA, AAA, ICDR, KCAB, AIAC (formerly KLRCA), SIAC, DIAC, ACICA, AMINZ, Resolution Institute (formerly IAMA), European Development Fund Arbitration and Conciliation Rules, as well as the ICSID and UNCITRAL Rules, in disputes of values exceeding some billions $US. Professor Jones has published and presented extensively and holds professorial appointments at Queen Mary College, University of London and Melbourne University Law School. He has held appointments at several international professional associations. He has served as the Chair of the Board of Trustees and President of the Chartered Institute of Arbitrators (CIArb), and was Chair of CIArb's Centenary Celebrations. In 2016, Professor Jones was appointed one of the four Companions of the CIArb. In 2018, he was Chair of the ICCA Congress in Sydney. Professor Jones is also serving as the President of the International Academy of Construction Lawyers (IACL) and the Immediate Past President of the Australian Centre for International Commercial Arbitration (ACICA). Finally, Professor Jones was awarded an Officer of the Order of Australia in 2012 in the Queen's Birthday Honours List for his distinguished service to the law and leadership in arbitration, alternative dispute resolution, policy reform, and national and international professional organisations.

Eric Ng is currently a Barrister-at-law at Gilt Chambers in Hong Kong, developing a practice in commercial litigation and international arbitration. He has been involved in several complex commercial and construction arbitrations since he was called to the Bar in 2014. Eric has also worked with several senior practitioners in order to develop international arbitration expertise, including working at Wilmer Hale's London arbitration group as well as with several senior counsel and arbitrators in relation to high-profile arbitration cases. Eric was previously a speaker for the 2013 City University of Hong Kong team that prevailed at the 2013 Vis Moot in Viennaand has also worked for several years as a coach for moot teams at several universities. He was also recently appointed as Adjunct Professor for the University of International Business and Economics in Beijing, China.

Luke Nottage BCA LLB (VUW) LLM (Kyoto) PhD (VUW) is Professor of Comparative and Transnational Business Law at the University of Sydney Law School, specialising in arbitration, contract law, consumer product safety law and corporate governance, with a particular interest in Japan and the Asia-Pacific. He is founding Co-Director of the Australian Network for Japanese Law (ANJeL) and Associate Director of the Centre for Asian and Pacific Law at the

University of Sydney. He is also Managing Director of Japanese Law Links Pty Ltd (www.japaneselawlinks.com). Professor Nottage has or had executive roles in the Australian Centre for International Commercial Arbitration (ACICA), and the Asia-Pacific Forum for International Arbitration. He has contributed to several looseleaf commentaries and made numerous media appearances and public Submissions to the Australian government, especially regarding arbitration and consumer law reform. He was admitted as a barrister and solicitor in New Zealand in 1994 and in NSW in 2001. He has consulted for law firms world-wide as well as ASEAN, the European Commission, OECD, UNCTAD, UNDP and the Japanese Government. He is also a Rules committee member of ACICA and on the Panel of Arbitrators for the BAC, JCAA, KCAB, KLRCA (AIAC), SCIA and TAI. Professor Nottage studied at Kyoto University (LLM) and Victoria University of Wellington (BCA, LLB, PhD), and first taught at the latter and then Kyushu University Law Faculty, before arriving at the University of Sydney in 2001. He has held fellowships at other leading institutions in Japan and Australia as well as Germany, Italy and Canada. His 14 books include *International Arbitration in Australia* (Federation Press, 2010; lead-edited with Richard Garnett), *Foreign Investment and Dispute Resolution Law and Practice in Asia* (Routledge, 2011; edited with Vivienne Bath) and *International Investment Treaties and Arbitration Across Asia* (Brill, 2018; edited with Julien Chaisse). He has also published over two hundred chapters and refereed or other articles, mainly in English and Japanese.

Michael Quinlan BA, LLB, LLM (UNSW), MA (THEO)(with H.D.)(UNDA), PLTC (CL) is Dean of the School of Law, Sydney at The University of Notre Dame Australia. Prior to taking up this role in 2013, Professor Quinlan had a distinguished career of over 23 years at the commercial law firm Allens where he was a commercial litigation partner for more than 14 years. Professor Quinlan was a long-time member of that firm's Pro Bono Committee. His pro bono practice centred around refugee and migration appeals but also involved assisting charities and individuals in need. Professor Quinlan is the Junior Vice President of the St Thomas More Society, a director of Freedom For Faith, a Board member of the Legal Profession Admissions Board (NSW), a contributing member of the Wilberforce Foundation and of Lawyers for the Preservation of the Traditional Meaning of Marriage. He has a deep interest in the relationship between law and morality and law and religion. His presentations include "How the law in Australia is used and can be used to promote or to harm the Catholic faith." (*Catholics and Law Congress*, Turon, Poland November, 2013) and "Religion, Law and Social Stability in Australia" (*22nd Annual International Law and Religion Symposium*, BYU, Provo, Utah, October 2015). His papers include:"Marriage, Tradition, Multiculturalism and the Accommodation of Difference in Australia," 18 *The University of Notre Dame Australia Law Review (2017)* 3; "When the State requires doctors to act against their conscience: the religious implications of the referral and the direction obligations of health practitioners in Victoria and New South Wales" 4 (2016) *BYU L. Rev.*7, 1237 and "'Such is Life.' Euthanasia and capital punishment in Australia: consistency or contradiction?" (2016) 6 *Solidarity: The Journal of Catholic Social Thought and Secular Ethics* 1, 6. Professor Quinlan is married to Kate and they have four children Edmund, Brigid, Sinead and Liam.

Suri Ratnapala LLB (*Sri Lanka*), LLM (*Macq*), PhD (*Qld*) is Emeritus Professor of Law at The University of Queensland and a current Fellow of the Australian Academy of Law. Professor Ratnapala's work has received international acclaim, with his book *Welfare State or Constitutional State*? being awarded a Sir Anthony Fisher International Memorial Prize by a jury chaired by Nobel Laureate James Buchanan. He is the author of *Australian Constitutional Law: Foundations and Theory* 2nd ed, 2007 and the co-author of *Australian Constitutional Law: Commentary and Cases* 2007, published by the Oxford University Press. Professor Ratnapala's latest book *Jurisprudence* 3rd ed, was published by the Cambridge University Press in 2017. He has received fellowships from the prestigious international research centres, the Institute of Humane Studies, George Mason University, Virginia, the Social Philosophy and Policy Centre of the Bowling Green State University, Ohio and the International Centre for

Economic Research, the University of Turin, Italy. In 1998, his work received further recognition when he was elected to the membership of the Mont Pelerin Society, the international grouping of liberal intellectuals. In 2000, he received a John Templeton Foundation Award for his course 'Advanced Constitutional Law and Theory', granted 'on the basis of uniqueness, innovation, and interdisciplinarity and the balance of political, economic and social theory'. In 2003 he was awarded a Centenary of Australian Federation Medal by the Governor-General of Australia for his contribution to Australian society through research in law and economics. In 2007 Professor Ratnapala was made an Alan McGregor Fellow of the Centre for Independent Studies. Professor Ratnapala has been a consultant with the World Bank, the Asian Development Bank and AusAid in institutional capacity building projects in Asia. Prior to entering the academy he was Senior State Counsel in Sri Lanka. Professor Ratnapala's main academic interests are in constitutional law and theory, legal philosophy, and constitutional political economy.

Rajesh Sharma is currently a senior lecturer at RMIT University, Melbourne, Australia. Before that he was Assistant Professor at School of Law, City University of Hong Kong. Dr Sharma has taught courses on arbitration, mediation, negotiation, foreign investment arbitration, WTO Law, international trade, banking law, foreign investment in Hong Kong, Macao, India, Australia, China and Africa (where he is associated with the Institute for Legal Excellence in Uganda). He has served as the Legal Advisor to the Macau University of Science and Technology. He has advised transnational companies on trade and investment policy in China and has done training courses with and for the WTO and UNITAR. Dr Sharma is the first Indian to hold PhD in Law from China. He holds PhD from the Chinese University of Political Science and Law, Beijing, a Master of Business Law from Monash University, Australia, an M.Phil from City University of Hong Kong and the Bachelor of Laws from the University of Delhi. He has received training for arbitrators from the World Intellectual Property Organization (WIPO), Geneva; and International Chamber of Commerce, Vienna. Dr. Sharma has received training of a mediator for community conflict resolution by the Plowshares Institute, USA and the Accord Group of Australia. He has also obtained professional training in negotiation at Harvard Law School. He has received training for teachers of WTO organized by UNU-IAS. Dr Sharma has researched extensively on the arbitration laws of China and India and other Asian countries, Investment Arbitration, Dispute Settlement in FTAs, WTO related issues, investment law and mediation. He has publications in the areas of WTO law, international trade, arbitration and dispute resolution, commercial law, and banking law. Recently he has published a book with Wolters Kluwer titled "Dispute Settlement Mechanism in the FTAs of Asia". Dr Sharma has also conducted research and provided expert comments to UNCITRAL on mediation and conciliation. These works include conducting "An Evaluation of Mediation Law in Asia", provided expert comments on "Draft Instrument on Enforcement of Settlement Agreement Across-border" and reported on "Possible Amendments in UNCITRAL Model Law on International Commercial Conciliations". At CityU, Dr Sharma was the Director of Mooting and coach of VIS Arbitration Moot at CityU. The team coached by Dr. Sharma has won the VIS (East) and VIS (Vienna) Championship in 2012 and 2013 respectively. He also designed the International ADR Moot Competition which is unique in the world because it combines arbitration and mediation where a student also takes part in as a mediator. Dr Sharma is the Associate Director of the Hong Kong WTO Research Institute, a member of Asian WTO Research Network; a panel arbitrator of Korean Commercial Arbitration Board (KCAB), a panel arbitrator at Indian Institutes of Arbitrators, a member and secretary of Hong Kong Basic Law Education Association, a member of the Centre for Global Studies and a Researcher at China-Latin America Legal Research Centre, Shanghai. Dr. Sharma is a Research Fellow of the International Academy of Belt and Road, a member of the Drafting Committee of the Dispute Resolution Rules for the Belt and Road, a member of the Working Group for the establishment of Asian Regional Mediation Organization (ARMO) and a member of the Drafting Committee for the Rules of Mediation for ARMO. He is a core member (representing

Australia) on the Committee for the Establishment of the Centre of Excellence for Dispute Resolution for Indian Ocean Regional Association. Dr Sharma has been appointed as the International Expert Mediator at the Hong Kong-Mainland Joint Mediation Centre, a panel mediator at Japan International Mediation Centre-Kyoto. Dr Sharma is an elected Associate Member of Academy of Comparative Law.

Harprabdeep Singh holds an LLB Hons. (First Class) from the City University of Hong Kong. He also has a Postgraduate Certificate in Law from the University of Hong Kong and a Bachelor of Civil Law from the University of Oxford. He is currently a Barrister at Alan Leong SC's Chambers in Hong Kong working in all forms of civil litigation and with arbitration in ADR (alternative dispute resolution). He recently prevailed in the High Court of Hong Kong dismissing a claim with costs against the largest bitcoin platform in the world (worth over US$100 billion), making it the first ever case against a bitcoin platform in Asia. In addition, Harprabdeep is an Associate member of the CIArb, a member to Hong Kong International Arbitration Centre, an institution providing alternative dispute resolution services from administered and ad hoc arbitration to mediation, adjudication and domain name dispute resolution, a member of Young ICCA, on the Special Committee on ADR, Company Law and Practice Development of the Hong Kong Bar Association and he is also a legal advisor to the US Department of Commerce on its Common Law Development Programme ("CLDP"). Though his work at CLDP, he has lectured and advised various Governments throughout the Middle East and Europe on its ADR laws and relavant arbitration rules. He is currently assisting the Government of Sri Lanka in their establishment of their newly established ADR Center with the drafting of the Center's rules and relevant amendments in the national arbitration law of Sri Lanka. His areas of expertise range from corporate law, banking, company liquidation and restructuring, bankruptcy, domestic and international arbitration to foreign exchange markets and investments. Harprabdeep has developed a predominantly civil practice and appears regularly in the High Court and District Court in a wide range of commercial litigation and arbitration disputes, with a particular focus on international trade.

His related High Court practices regularly involves cross-border disputes and he is also routinely instructed, as sole advocate or with senior counsel, in international arbitrations as counsel and tribunal secretary.

A. Keith Thompson LLB (Hons.), Dip Export, IMD (Hons.); MJur, PhD is Associate Professor and Associate Dean (Research) of the School of Law, Sydney at The University of Notre Dame Australia. Dr Thompson has enjoyed a wide and varied career in the law with experience in property, commercial, international, constitutional, criminal and human rights law. He worked for 11 years in Auckland in commercial and property law including 6 years as a partner with Fortune Manning and was then appointed as International Legal Counsel for The Church of Jesus Christ of Latter-day Saints. In that role, Dr Thompson supervised that Church's legal work throughout the Pacific Area (for 18 years) and then throughout the African continent for a further 2 years. Since returning to Australia in 2011 he has been appointed as Associate Professor and Associate Dean at The University of Notre Dame Australia's Sydney School of Law where he teaches Constitutional Law, Law and Religion and Evidence. He retains an interest in legal practice through his continuing part time role as Special Counsel at Taylor and Whitty, a regional firm with offices in south-western NSW and northern Victoria and as a consultant at the Sydney boutique firm, Stevens Vuaran. In 2010 he published a book entitled *Religious Confession Privilege and the Common Law*. He has also published on Insolvency, Vicarious Liability in Tort, Foreign Corrupt Practices and Freedom of Religion.

John Trone BA, LLB, PhD (Queensland) is the co-author with Professor Gabriël A. Moens of the 6th, 7th, 8th and 9th editions of *Lumb, Moens and Trone The Constitution of the Commonwealth of Australia Annotated* (LexisNexis Butterworths, 2001, 2007, 2012, and 2016), and *Commercial Law of the European Union* (Springer, 2010). Dr Trone has also written numerous other books and articles concerning commercial law, constitutional law and international law. Some of these publications include *Federal Constitutions and*

International Relations (University of Queensland Press, 2001), and the 29th, 30th, 31st and 32nd editions of *Australian Commercial Law* (Lawbook Co, 2013, 2015, 2016, and 2018) (with Clive Turner).

Bruno Zeller B.Com (Melbourne), B.Ed (Melbourne), Master of International Trade Law (Deakin), PhD (Melbourne), Arbitrator (AICA), and a Fellow of the Australian Institute for Commercial Arbitration, Panel of Arbitrators – MLAANZ. Dr Zeller is a Professor of Transnational Commercial Law at the University of Western Australia, specialising in International Trade and Investment Law, Maritime Law, International Arbitration Law and International Commercial and Comparative Law.. He has supervised numerous PhD students. He is an Adjunct Professor at Murdoch University, Perth, and an Adjunct Professor at the Sir Zelman Cowan Centre, Victoria University, Melbourne. He is also a Visiting Professor at La Trobe University, Melbourne, Humboldt University of Berlin., Stetson Law School, Florida, National Law University New Delhi and Aarborg University, Denmark An accomplished academic, Dr Zeller has published extensively on the CISG, arbitration law, harmonisation of contract law and carbon trading.

The Editor

Augusto Zimmermann LLB (Hon.), LLM *cum laude*, PhD (Monash) is an internationally known legal scholar and is broadly recognised as one of Australia's strongest proponents of free speech. He is Professor of Law at Sheridan College in Perth, Western Australia, and Professor of Law (adjunct) at the University of Notre Dame Australia, Sydney campus. In addition, Dr Zimmermann is a former Law Reform Commissioner with the Law Reform Commission of Western Australia (2012-2017) and a former Associate Dean (Research) at Murdoch University's School of Law (2009-2013). Professor Zimmermann is President of the Western Australian Legal Theory Association (WALTA), the Editor-in-Chief of the Western Australian Jurist law journal, an elected Fellow at the International Academy for the Study of the Jurisprudence of the Family (IASJF), and a former Vice-President of the Australasian Society of Legal Philosophy (ASLP). He is a prolific writer and his books include *Curso de Direito Constitucional* (4th edition, Lumen Jurist, 2006), *Teoria Geral do Federalismo Democratico* (2nd edition, Lumen Juris, 2006), *Western Legal Theory: History Concepts and Perspectives* (LexisNexis, 2013), *Direito Constitucional Brasileiro* (Lumen Juris, 2014, w/ Fabio Condeixa), *Global Perspectives on Subsidiarity* (Springer, 2014, with Michelle Evans), *No Offence Intended: Why 18c is Wrong* (Connor Court, 2016, with Joshua Forrester and Lorraine Finlay), and *Christian Foundations of the Common Law – Volume 1: England* (Connor Court, 2018), etc. In 2012, Professor Zimmermann was awarded the Vice-Chancellor's Award for Excellence in Research at Murdoch University, and also awarded two consecutive Murdoch School of Law Dean's Research Award, in 2010 and 2011. He has been included, together with only twelve other Australian academics and policy experts, in 'Policy Experts' – the directory of Washington-based The Heritage Foundation for locating knowledgeable authorities and leading policy institutes actively involved in a broad range of public policy issues, both in the U.S. and worldwide.

Emeritus Professor Gabriël A. Moens

Gabriël A. Moens JD (Leuven), LLM (Northwestern), PhD (Sydney), GCEd (Queensland), MBA (Murdoch), MAppL (College of Law), FCIArb, CArb, FAIM, FCL is Professor of Law, Curtin Law School. He is also Emeritus Professor of Law at the University of Queensland. Prior to his current positions he served as Pro Vice Chancellor (Law, Business and Information Technology) and as a long-serving Dean and Professor of Law at Murdoch University. He also served as Professor of Law and Head, Graduate School of Law, University of Notre Dame Australia and as Garrick Professor of Law and Director, The Australian Institute of Foreign and Comparative Law, The University of Queensland. He undertakes teaching and research in Constitutional Law, Banking Law, European Union Law, International Commercial Law, International Arbitration Law and Comparative Law. Professor Moens is a past winner of a University of Queensland Excellence in

Teaching Award. In 1999, he received the Australian Award for University Teaching in Law and Legal Studies. He is the Editor-in-Chief of *International Trade and Business Law Review*. In 2003, the Prime Minister of Australia awarded him the Australian Centenary Medal for services to education. In 1995-1996 he was a Visiting Professor of Law at J. Reuben Clark Law School, Brigham Young University, Utah. He served as a Visiting Professor of Law at Loyola University, New Orleans School of Law in 2002-2003. In 1997 and 2000 he successfully coached the T C Beirne School of Law (The University of Queensland) team to win the prestigious Willem C Vis International Commercial Arbitration Moot in Vienna, Austria. He also co-coached the winning City University of Hong Kong team in the Ninth Willem C Vis (East) Moot in 2012 and the 20th Willem C Vis Moot in Vienna in 2013. He is a Fellow (FCIArb) and Chartered Arbitrator (CArb) of the Chartered Institute of Arbitrators, London and Fellow and former Deputy Secretary General of the Australian Centre for International Commercial Arbitration (ACICA). Until 2018, he also served as the Editor-in-Chief of the *ACICA Review*. He is the co-author of a Commentary on the ACICA Arbitration Rules. Professor Moens is a *Membre Titulaire*, International Academy of Comparative Law, Paris, a Fellow of the Australian Academy of Law, a Fellow of the Australian Institute of Management (AIM WA) and a former Director and Member of the College of Law Western Australia, and the Australian Institute of Higher and Further Education. In 1998, the Asian Development Bank, Manila retained him to train officials of the Ministry of Law and Justice of his Majesty's Government of Nepal. He has taught extensively in the United Kingdom, Germany, Belgium, Italy, Austria, Australia, Indonesia, Thailand, Singapore, Hong Kong, P R China, Japan and the United States. He is co-author/co-editor of *The Constitution of the Commonwealth of Australia Annotated* (9th ed), LexisNexis Butterworths, 2016; *Arbitration and Dispute Resolution in the Resources Sector: An Australian Perspective*, Springer, 2015, *Jurisprudence of Liberty* (2nd ed), LexisNexis, 2011, *Commercial Law of the European Union*, Springer, 2010, and *International Trade and Business: Law, Policy and Ethics* (2nd ed), Routledge/Cavendish, 2006.

1

INTRODUCTION:
ESSAYS IN HONOUR OF
EMERITUS PROFESSOR GABRIËL A. MOENS

Augusto Zimmermann

It is a great pleasure to edit this collection of articles in honour of Gabriël A. Moens, who celebrated his 70th birthday this year. These articles are written by leading academics and lawyers in their fields, who share with me a profound admiration for the amazing life and legacy of Professor Moens. We have an enormous admiration for him, not only for his academic achievements but also for the fact that, indeed, he is a wonderful human being. Gabriël's legacy is nothing short of extraordinary. He acquired a solid reputation as a leading academic expert in constitutional law, legal philosophy, and business law, in particular in its international and comparative dimensions. He has also been deeply appreciated by his students and has received countless Excellence in Teaching and Research awards throughout his career. Gabriël is also a highly accomplished senior academic administrator who deeply enhanced the image and reputation of institutions that had the great privilege to make use of this competent leadership.

Gabriël Adelin Moens was born on 28 January 1948 in Ertvelde, Belgium, a village close to the Dutch border and not far from Ghent. He attended high school in Eeklo where he was a boarder and received a classical education in Latin and ancient Greek. I recall Gabriël telling me an amusing, but sad, story about his time at high school. His history teacher, who had never visited another country, told the class that they were very fortunate to be living in 'the best country in the world'. Gabriël looked around the class and saw the glowing faces of his peers, basking with pride and secure in their knowledge that they were living in the best country. However, Gabriël, rather timidly but audaciously, asked the teacher how it is possible to make such a claim, considering the teacher had not visited any other country? How is it possible to compare Belgium with any other country in this situation? His question was dismissed as irrelevant and disingenuous and he was subjected to widespread ridicule.

According to Gabriël, that episode in high school may well have affected his grades, which apparently were not very good. But this did not discourage him from pursuing greatness, and eventually achieving a remarkable career. Following high school, Gabriël attended the Catholic University of Leuven where he studied law and philosophy. Gabriël prospered at the University and enjoyed his time in Leuven. He was involved in many extracurricular activities; he even visited the United States and Canada in his second year of University and he was involved in various political and social activities. He did well and gained his law degree with Honours in 1970.

Following admission as a barrister, Gabriël practiced at the bar in Ghent for a year. In 1971, he received a scholarship to study for an LL.M. at Northwestern University in Chicago, where he developed his love and respect for the common law and the American way of teaching. Upon his return to Europe, he became a Lecturer at the Paris Lodron University in Salzburg, Austria, where he worked with Professor Ilmar Tammelo, an Estonian who had worked as an Associate Professor of Law at the University of Sydney. Tammelo, an expert in legal logic, co-authored a book on logic in German with Gabriël which was published by Springer.

On the advice of Tammelo, in 1975, Gabriël accepted a job as the last Research Assistant of Professor Julius Stone, a recognized authority on international law and jurisprudence, then working at the University of New South Wales (UNSW). Two years later, he was admitted as a PhD. student at the University of Sydney, where he completed his doctorate in 1982 which dealt with *The Quality of Equality: A Study of School Integration and Preferential Admission Programs in the United*

States. After completing his thesis Gabriël became a Lecturer in Law at the New South Wales Institute of Technology, now the University of Technology, Sydney (UTS). Whilst at UTS, he also received an invitation to work as a Jean Monnet Fellow in Law at the European University Institute in Florence which was followed, in 1987, by an appointment as a Senior Lecturer in Law at The University of Queensland.

In Australia, Gabriël has taught courses at the University of Sydney; Victoria University, Melbourne; The University of Queensland; The University of Wollongong; University of Technology, Sydney; Curtin University; Murdoch University; The University of Notre Dame Australia, among others. Beside these teaching roles in Australia, he has taught extensively in the United Kingdom, Germany, Belgium, Italy, Austria, Indonesia, Thailand, Singapore, P R China, Hong Kong, Japan and the United States. For example, he taught in the University of Notre Dame, London Law Centre Summer Program from 1991 to 2014. In 1995-1996 he was a Visiting Professor of Law at J. Reuben Clark Law School, Brigham Young University, Utah. He also served as a Visiting Professor of Law at Loyola University, New Orleans School of Law in 2002-2003.

Gabriël is not just an exceptional teacher and researcher. He is also a most efficient administrator who has served as Professor of Law and Head, Graduate School of Law, The University of Notre Dame Australia and as Garrick Professor of Law and Director, The Australian Institute of Foreign and Comparative Law, The University of Queensland. He has also served as Dean of Law at Murdoch University for nearly six years and as its Pro Vice Chancellor (Law, Business and Information Technology) for two years. When at this institution, he was a relentless builder of highly successful international programs which provided students with truly unique opportunities to experience international education. For example, he single-handedly developed summer programs in law in Macerata (Italy), Hong Kong and the United States which attracted nearly 2000 Australian students. He has also developed summer programs at the University of Ghent,

Belgium for Curtin University and led students on a study tour of London on several occasions.

When I completed my doctoral research at Monash University, Gabriël was the Law Dean at Murdoch University. I was offered by him an academic position at that School of Law. I had therefore the great honour and privilege to work under his fantastic leadership. These were the golden days of Murdoch School of Law, when Gabriël's impressive administrative skills turned a relatively obscure school into a highly regarded law school in Western Australia and beyond.

Gabriël has made extraordinary contributions to legal education, including higher and vocational education, not just in Australia but also overseas. He has done so via the teaching and mentoring of thousands of students in many countries across the globe, substantially enhancing the employment opportunities of students and relentlessly creating educational opportunities for them. Many of his activities were non-paid and went far beyond the call of duty. However, Gabriël is a very generous person and he is always willing to help students to achieve the maximum of their intellectual abilities. He is also an effective promoter of Australian Higher Education, often persuading overseas students to study in Australia. For these reasons, the Prime Minister of Australia awarded him the Australian Centenary Medal for services to education in 2003. Throughout his career, Gabriël was greatly assisted by his wife, Dr Edith Moens, who always supported his academic and professional endeavours.

Gabriël is currently an Emeritus Professor of Law at the University of Queensland. At this prestigious institution he is a past winner of an Excellence in Teaching Award. In 1999, he also received the Australian Award for University Teaching in Law and Legal Studies. He was described by his students at the University of Queensland as a 'legend' because of his exceptional teaching skills and his willingness to further the educational achievements of these students. As a coach of mooting teams, Gabriël spent hundreds of hours, on a voluntary basis (after hours and on weekends) to train his students. He is the legendary coach of victorious Willem C. Vis arbitration teams, coaching his students to absolute victory in Vienna and Hong Kong on many occasions.

At the top of all this, Gabriël has found time to author/co-author or edit/co-edit 42 books. He is co-author/co-editor of *The Constitution of the Commonwealth of Australia Annotated* (9th ed, LexisNexis Butterworths, 2016); *Arbitration and Dispute Resolution in the Resources Sector: An Australian Perspective* (Springer, 2015), *Jurisprudence of Liberty* (2nd ed, LexisNexis, 2011), *Commercial Law of the European Union* (Springer, 2010), and *International Trade and Business: Law, Policy and Ethics* (2nd ed, Routledge/Cavendish, 2006). Gabriël is also the Founder and Editor-in-Chief of *International Trade and Business Law Review*, which provides the legal and business communities with information, knowledge and understanding of recent developments in international trade, business and international commercial arbitration.

Gabriël has also made very substantial and sustained contributions to Australia's arbitration community, chambers of commerce and the media. For many years, until 2018, he generously volunteered his services to the Australian Centre for International Commercial Arbitration (ACICA) as the Editor-in-Chief of the *ACICA Review* and as its Deputy Secretary General for a decade. In such a capacity, he organised two major conferences in Perth for ACICA and the international arbitration community. In addition, Gabriël is a Fellow (FCIArb) and Chartered Arbitrator (CArb) of the *Chartered Institute of Arbitrators*, London and Fellow, Australian Centre for International Commercial Arbitration (ACICA). Gabriël is also a Fellow of the *Australian Institute of Management* (AIM WA), a Fellow of the Australian Academy of Law (FAAL), and a *Membre Titulaire* of the *International Academy of Comparative Law*, Paris. He spent hundreds of hours organizing the 16th quadrennial Conference on Comparative Law in 2002 which brought approximately 1000 people to Australia, including Chief Justices of various countries.

Despite these impressive accomplishments, Gabriël remains a friendly and humble person. The combination of competence and humility is what makes him so unique and special, so highly esteemed by his colleagues and students. National and international scholars agreed to collaborate an article for this book in his honour because he is truly a remarkable person. These leading lawyers and academics were invited by me to address one of the topics Gabriël has taught during his career, which includes constitutional law, contract law, comparative law, jurisprudence, European Union law, International commercial law, trade law, arbitration law and practice, and mooting. The result is this present collection of articles that I trust you will find a fitting tribute to Gabriël's absolutely remarkable career.

To conclude, Gabriël is a living example of great character and integrity. His colleagues, friends and admirers hope he will enjoy reading this book as much as we deeply enjoyed editing and writing it. I can only express my sincerest gratitude for everything he has done for me, for his friends, for his students, and, last but not least, for the enhancement of legal education both in Australia and overseas. Indeed, Gabriël is one of the most extraordinary individuals I have ever met in my life and this book is a much deserved celebration of his great achievements as a legal academic and academic administrator. On behalf of all his friends and colleagues, I would like to thank Professor Gabriël A. Moens for his amazing legacy. Thank you very much, indeed!

2

LESSONS FROM A TEACHER

John Trone

On many occasions Gabriël A. Moens has been recognised as an outstanding teacher, having been the recipient of numerous teaching awards. Among others, he was the co-winner of an Australian Award for University Teaching and the recipient of a University of Queensland Award for Excellence in Teaching.[1]

Another indicator of the wide recognition of his teaching abilities is that Gabriël has very extensive teaching experience across the globe. He has taught law in universities in many countries, including Australia, the United States, the United Kingdom, Germany, Austria, China, Singapore and his home country Belgium.

His teaching has covered a broad array of subjects. Thus far he has taught (among others) Australian and United States constitutional law, international trade law, comparative law, arbitration law, jurisprudence and the law of religion. He has taught both undergraduate and postgraduate classes, and both large and small group classes. He developed overseas programmes for students to study for a semester at universities on other continents. At the University of Queensland he pioneered Law School involvement in international mooting competitions, and the teams he coached had conspicuous successes.[2]

In this personal appreciation of Gabriël's merits as a teacher I write from the perspective of one of his undergraduate and doctoral students at the University of Queensland. As an undergraduate student it is easy to make comparisons between teachers because students take a large

---

[1] 'UQ Wins Two National Teaching Awards', *UQ News*, 1 December 1999, at https://www.uq.edu.au/ (accessed 28 March 2018).

2 'UQ Law School Team Ranked First in International Moot', *UQ News*, April 27, 1999, at https://www.uq.edu.au/ (accessed 28 March 2018).

number of courses with many different teachers. I find it impossible to make comparisons between thesis supervisors because Gabriël was the only supervisor with whom I had much substantive contact. Based on my experience, I felt that he was an excellent supervisor.

Gabriël was popular among students, and was consistently rated highly in teacher evaluation surveys. He had an avuncular manner with students and was regarded as very approachable. He had an open door policy and did not limit himself to two hours consultation per week. It was also clear that he carefully read student papers. Marked essays would be returned with detailed comments.

When I was taught by Gabriël law classes were invariably one or two hour lectures and tutorials, held once or twice a week. Teaching practices evolve, and since then he has often taught classes in intensive sessions, keeping his enthusiasm unflagging over many hours.

He amply communicated his enthusiasm for the subjects he taught. His hallmark was clear explanation of basic principles and concepts. Since Gabriël reiterated the key points numerous times, students came away feeling that they had actually learned something. He always spoke rather than read, for he considered that reading was "the most boring, the most inefficient form of teaching that one could possibly think of".[3] He was also no slave to Powerpoint. If he used slides they were usually restricted to a broad outline of the topics to be discussed. His popularity was due to his verbal presentation, not technology.

He combined a Socratic method with traditional lecturing. He often asked the class questions during lectures and tutorials, gently coaxing answers out of the group. He generally did not single out individual students for questioning. He often said that it was very important never to humiliate a student in class: "If you humiliate students, you lose them.".[4] He sought to encourage (rather than compel) the active involvement of students in his lectures. He was also an active presence in class, moving frequently around the lecture room while speaking through a portable microphone.

---

[3] Dorothy Illing, 'Hard Work Pays For Professor', *The Australian*, 16 February 2000, p 36.

[4] *University of Queensland Graduate Contact*, Winter 1994, p 6.

He often peppered his lectures with real world examples, so that students could appreciate the practical implications of legal rules. He also experimented with different techniques of instruction to add variety and interest to his classes. In one subject he played a video that explained the Commonwealth electoral system. In another course he brought along a guest lecturer to speak about Eastern European constitutions.

He often told amusing anecdotes in class. When he asked students to fill out teacher evaluation surveys, he said that at dinner with friends at home he often read out amusing comments from past surveys. One student had asked that in future Gabriël should deliver his lectures in the English language. That drew a big laugh from the class, which was Gabriël's intention. Of course, that student's comment was very unfair, given Gabriël's mastery of both spoken and written English. I can only ever recall Gabriël making one *slight* mispronunciation of a word in any of my classes, which is a better record than some native speakers. That word was a commercial law term that I will leave to the speculation of readers.

In Constitutional Law Gabriël outlined the key provisions and leading cases. He did not overload students with excessive detail. In his segments of the course he covered topics such as freedom of interstate trade, the corporations power, the electoral system, double dissolutions and joint sittings, and freedom of religion. His classes on the freedom of religion guarantee under the Commonwealth Constitution were notable as they included an extensive discussion of United States Supreme Court case law on the similar guarantee in the US federal Constitution.[5] Such detailed consideration of comparative law was a rare feature in our undergraduate classes.

In Commercial Law his lectures explained the law of negotiable instruments (cheques and bills of exchange), where he endeavoured to simplify a complicated area of law. He gave particular attention to the

---

[5] Including cases such as *Sherbert v Verner* 374 US 398 at 410 (1963) and *Wisconsin v Yoder* 406 US 205 at 220 (1972). See Gabriël Moens, 'The Action-Belief Dichotomy and Freedom of Religion' (1989) 12 *Sydney Law Review* 195, at 198-203, 207-210.

Sydney Wide Stores decision[6] concerning a customer's duty to fill out a cheque with reasonable care.

In Comparative Law he taught us the comparative law method. He broadened our horizons by making us aware that there were other legal systems beyond those based on English common law, since we had our first introduction to the civil law system. He used a broad brush, discussing judicial decisions from the United States, the European Union, Germany and France.

We were provided with an extensive collection of course readings, which formed the basis for class discussions. In these classes we encountered some of the classic decisions of comparative law. We were introduced to United States Supreme Court cases such as *Marbury v Madison*,[7] in which the court first exercised its power of judicial review of Congressional statutes. We discussed some of the more controversial decisions on the Bill of Rights, such as the *Smith* decision,[8] in which the court resiled from its prior case law that had mandated religious exemptions from generally applicable laws.

He also introduced us to formative decisions of the European Court of Justice such *Costa v ENEL*,[9] which asserted the supremacy of EU law over the national law of the Member States, and *Van Gend en Loos*,[10] which introduced the doctrine of the direct effect of EU primary and secondary law. Some of the abortion rulings by European constitutional courts were also discussed.[11]

---

[6] *Commonwealth Trading Bank of Australia v Sydney Wide Stores Pty Ltd* (1981) 148 CLR 304 at 317. See Gabriël Moens, 'Can You Bank on a Bank – An Examination of the Customer-Bank Relationship in Light of the Cheques and Payment Orders Act 1986 (Cth)' (1989) 15 *University of Queensland Law Journal* 183.

[7] *Marbury v Madison* 5 US (1 Cranch) 137 at 176-180 (1803).

[8] *Employment Division, Department of Human Resources of Oregon v Smith* 494 US 872 at 878-879 (1990).

[9] *Costa v ENEL* (6/64) [1964] ECR 585 at 593-594; [1964] CMLR 425 at 455-456.

[10] *NV Algemene Transport- en Expeditie Onderneming van Gend en Loos v Nederlandse Administratie der Belastingen* (26/62) [1963] ECR 1 at 12-13; [1963] CMLR 105 at 129-130.

[11] See Mauro Cappelletti & William Cohen, *Comparative Constitutional Law: Cases and Materials* (Indianapolis: Bobbs-Merrill, 1979), pp 586, 612, 615.

All of this was new for us, for we had little prior exposure to what then seemed to be quite exotic legal materials. Sometimes the topics discussed were politically controversial. Gabriël assiduously sought to keep his political views obscure in class, but occasionally hints emerged for observant students.[12]

In the light of Gabriël's success as a teacher, it is to be hoped that he will continue to teach many subjects in many locations for many years to come. If so, law students will be the beneficiaries.

---

[12] His writings and public statements have sometimes broached controversial political and social issues. See eg Warwick Bracken, 'Author of Study Critical of Human Rights Body', *Canberra Times*, 5 March 1985, p 11; Keith Scott, 'Discrimination By Any Other Name', *Canberra Times*, 13 January 1986, p 1; Gabriël A Moens, 'Mabo and Political Policy-making by the High Court, in M A Stephenson and Suri Ratnapala (eds), *Mabo: A Judicial Revolution* (St Lucia: University of Queensland Press, 1993), p 48; Gabriël A Moens, 'BA Santamaria's Contribution to Australia's Culture Wars' (Autumn 2009) 80 *National Observer* 47.

3
CONSTITUTIONAL FUNDAMENTALS

Nicholas Aroney

- **Introduction**

It is an honour to contribute to this Festschrift for Emeritus Professor Gabriël Moens. Gabriël was the supervisor of my Master of Laws thesis on the implied freedom of political communication and was kind enough to read and comment extensively on my PhD thesis on Australian federalism. Both theses addressed the role of fundamental principles and doctrines in the interpretation of the Australian Constitution. Gabriël's incisive ability to see immediately what was essential in a line of argument – as distinct from what was merely tangential to it – was exactly the kind of advice that an inquisitive graduate student like me needed. I will always be grateful to him for the sage advice and unwavering support he gave me during those formative years.

It is widely appreciated that the Australian Constitution cannot be understood without consideration of the fundamental doctrines that inform it, such as the rule of law, judicial review, parliamentary sovereignty, the separation of powers, representative democracy, responsible government and federalism.[1] But in what respects precisely, and to what extent, do each of these doctrines explain the Constitution, and in what ways to do they intersect? It is also a commonplace that these doctrines are capable of generating constitutional implications. But if these doctrines suggest contradictory conclusions, which one is to prevail?

These are related questions. No single constitutional doctrine

---
[1] See R.D. Lumb, *Australian Constitutionalism* (Butterworths, 1983).

explains the entire content of the Constitution but only particular aspects of it. Potential contradictions among doctrinal implications concern particular aspects of the Constitution. To determine how such contradictions are to be resolved requires consideration to be given to the extent to which the competing doctrines explain or are presupposed by the particular aspect of the Constitution that is in question.

In this chapter I explore the relationship between the various principles that inform the Australian Constitution and seek to identify the extent to which they respectively explain it. My focus in this chapter is on the principles. For convenience, I deliberately put aside the equally important considerations of text and history, even though I think that these should also inform our understanding of the Constitution in order to arrive at an interpretation that makes the best sense of its text, structure and intended purposes.[1]

- **A Congeries of Principles**

There are numerous cases in which conflicts between the various underlying doctrines of the Constitution have become apparent.

In *Australian Capital Television Pty Ltd v Commonwealth* the High Court of Australia famously drew the conclusion that the Constitution's provision for a system of representative democracy necessarily implies that it is beyond the Parliament's legislative power to enact a law that unjustifiably interferes with freedom of political communication.[2] It is arguable, however, that this conclusion is not warranted by the Constitution. One reason for this is that the Constitution contains only a limited range of provisions which are deliberately protective of rights because the framers considered that parliamentary institutions provide adequate safeguards. Another reason is that it is inappropriate

---

[1] For more detail, see Nicholas Aroney, 'Explanatory Power, Theory Formation and Constitutional Interpretation: Some Preliminaries' (2013) 38 *Australian Journal of Legal Philosophy* 1 and Nicholas Aroney, 'Originalism and Explanatory Power' in Lisa Burton Crawford, Patrick Emerton and Dale Smith (eds), *Law Under a Democratic Constitution: Essays in Honour of Jeffrey Goldsworthy* (Hart Publishing, forthcoming 2019).

[2] *Australian Capital Television Pty Ltd v Commonwealth* (1992) 177 CLR 106.

for courts draw multiple-stage, value-laden implications from the text and structure of the Constitution.³ The Constitution certainly provides a framework within which a system of representative and responsible government was intended to operate, but the framers deliberately chose not to include within the Constitution a protection of freedom of speech even though the United States Constitution, on which the Australian Constitution was largely modelled, of contained such a provision. Democracy is a principle that underlies the Constitution, but the particular form in which it is embedded within the Constitution suggests that it is inappropriate to attribute to the idea whatever we might consider to be appropriate or desirable. What the Constitution specifically requires is that members of Parliament are to be 'directly chosen by the people'. As Justice Dawson pointed out in *Australian Capital Television*, this properly gives rise to the implication that sufficient information must be made available to voters to enable them to exercise a 'genuine' choice when voting for members of Parliament, but it does not necessarily imply that there should be an open-ended freedom of political communication which enables the Courts to assess the legitimacy of legislation on grounds that go beyond what is necessary to ensure the genuineness of the choice made by voters.⁴ In later cases members of the High Court recognised the need to tie the assessment of legislation to the constitutionally-mandated system of representative government,⁵ but in more recent times a majority of the Court have adopted a more open-ended test that calls on the Court to assess the proportionality of legislation in an open-ended manner.⁶

In *Melbourne Corporation v Commonwealth* the High Court famously held that the federal nature of the Australian Constitution gives rise to the implication that the Commonwealth cannot single out

---

[3] Nicholas Aroney, *Freedom of Speech in the Constitution* (Centre for Independent Studies, 1998).

[4] *Australian Capital Television Pty Ltd v Commonwealth* (1992) 177 CLR 106, 187.

[5] See Nicholas Aroney, 'Justice McHugh, Representative Government and the Elimination of Balancing' (2006) 28 *Sydney Law Review* 505.

[6] *McCloy v New South Wales* (2015) 257 CLR 178, 195 (French CJ, Kiefel, Bell and Keane JJ). Note, however, continuing resistance to this among a minority of justices: eg, *Brown v Tasmania* [2017] HCA 43, [160] (Gageler J), [428]–[438] (Gordon J).

the States in a way that prevents them from exercising their essential constitutional functions.[7] It is arguable that there are good reasons for thinking that federalism is so fundamental to the Australian Constitution that such an implication is well-founded.[8] However, the exact scope of the implication is properly limited to what is necessary to ensure that the States continue to exercise the constitutional powers and functions preserved by the Constitution.[9] Consistent with this view, in the High Court's most important recent decision on this issue, a majority insisted that the essential question in such cases is 'whether the law restricts or burdens one or more of the States in the exercise of their constitutional powers'.[10]

In other cases it has been the role of potentially conflicting underlying principles that has been at stake. In the *McKinlay* and *McGinty* cases, for example, the High Court had to consider whether the principle of democracy, as implemented by the Australian Constitution, necessarily implies that each electoral district should have approximately the same population so as to ensure that the 'voting power' exercisable by each individual elector is approximately the same.[11] Support for this could be drawn from the Constitution's requirement that the number of members of the House of Representatives for each State is to be proportional to the population of the State.[12] However, the Constitution confers ultimate supervisory power to determine electoral districts upon the Commonwealth Parliament without any explicit requirement that such districts must have approximately the same population.[13] Moreover, the principle of federalism, as implemented in the Constitution, requires that the Original States, as the constituent units of the federation, are equally

---

[7] *Melbourne Corporation v Commonwealth* (1947) 74 CLR 31.
[8] See Nicholas Aroney, *The Constitution of a Federal Commonwealth: The Making and Meaning of the Australian Constitution* (Cambridge University Press, 2009).
[9] Australian Constitution, ss 106 and 107.
[10] *Austin v Commonwealth* (2003) 215 CLR 185, 258.
[11] *Attorney-General (Cth) (Ex rel McKinlay) v Commonwealth* (1975) 135 CLR 1; *McGinty v Western Australia* (1996) 186 CLR 14.
[12] Commonwealth Constitution, s 24.
[13] Commonwealth Constitution, s 29.

represented in at least one house of the Commonwealth Parliament (the Senate) notwithstanding considerable differences in their population.[14] Given these factors, the deep question in *McKinlay* and especially in *McGinty* became: does the democratic principle embedded in the Constitution imply that electoral districts must have approximately the same population so as to ensure equality of voting power or does the federal principle imply that the Parliament is free to ensure that local political communities – even if their populations vary – are adequately represented in the Parliament? One of the crucial reasons why a majority of the Court held that there is no general constitutional implication requiring electorates to be of the same size is that in the Australian Constitution the principle of democracy is adapted to the principle of federalism.[15]

Democracy, it might be said, implies that the people of the entire Commonwealth, including federal territories, should be adequately represented in the Australian Parliament, including the Senate. To this end, it seems, the Constitution provides that the Parliament may make laws allowing for the representation of territories in either house of the Parliament 'to the extent and on the terms which it thinks fit'.[16] However, as noted, the Constitution also provides that the Senate is to be composed of 'Senators for each State'.[17] Given this background: can the Parliament provide for the representation of the territories in the Senate, and can such territory senators be given full voting rights? This was the issue the High Court had to consider in the two *Territory Representation* cases.[18] A close majority held, in effect, that the democratic principle prevailed, subject to the possible proviso that the number of territory senators is kept in proportion to the number of

---

[14] Commonwealth Constitution, s 7.
[15] See *McGinty v Western Australia* (1996) 186 CLR 140, 236-40, 243-5, 266-7, 269-78, 291-2. For more detail, see Nicholas Aroney, Peter Gerangelos, James Stellios and Sarah Murray, *The Constitution of the Commonwealth of Australia: History, Principle and Interpretation* (Cambridge University Press, 2015), pp 68-73.
[16] Commonwealth Constitution, s 122.
[17] Commonwealth Constitution, s 7.
[18] *Western Australia v Commonwealth* (1975) 134 CLR 201; *Queensland v Commonwealth* (1977) 139 CLR 585.

senators representing the much more populous Original States, each of which is entitled to equal representation in the Senate.[19]

There are also several tensions in the Constitution between the separation of powers, parliamentary responsible government and federalism. The separation of powers requires that legislative, executive and judicial power are separately invested in distinct institutions of government.[20] Responsible government, however, is a system in which the executive power vested in the Queen is exercised by the Governor-General on the advice of a Prime Minister and other Ministers of State who have the confidence of a majority of the lower house of the Parliament. The constitutional crisis that occurred in 1975 when Governor-General John Kerr dismissed Prime Minister Gough Whitlam involved this tension precisely because, although the Prime Minister had the confidence of the House of Representatives, the Senate had failed to pass the annual supply bills without which a government cannot operate.[21] In a system of parliamentary responsible government, moreover, there is no strict separation of the executive and legislative branches of government. Federalism, however, involves a careful delineation of powers between the Commonwealth and the States which arguably needs to be adjudicated by a body that is independent of both the Commonwealth and the States. In almost all federations this task is undertaken by courts.[22] All three of these doctrines played an important role in the reasoning of the High Court in the *Boilermakers* case, in which it affirmed the general principle that (subject to limited exceptions) courts exercising Commonwealth judicial power cannot be invested with non-judicial power, alongside the corresponding principle that the judicial power of the Commonwealth cannot be invested in non-courts.[23] In Australia, there

---

[19] For the exact reasoning, see Aroney et al, above n 28, pp 55-57.

[20] Suri Ratnapala, *Welfare State or Constitutional State?* (Centre for Independent Studies, 1990).

[21] L J M Cooray, *Conventions, the Australian Constitution and the Future* (Legal Books, 1979).

[22] See Nicholas Aroney and John Kincaid (eds), *Courts in Federal Countries: Federalists or Unitarists?* (University of Toronto Press, 2017).

[23] *R v Kirby; Ex parte Boilermakers' Society of Australia* (1956) 94 CLR 254, 267-8,

is a strict separation of judicial power, but there is no such separation doctrine applying to executive and legislative power.

Many of the most significant decisions of the High Court have involved tensions between fundamental principles like these. Resolving them is not an easy matter. In many of the cases, the controversy arose because particular provisions of the Constitution appear to give rise to contradictory conclusions. One provision seems to allow particular action, while another seems to deny it. In such cases, working out which provision is to prevail cannot be resolved simply by interpreting the text of the Constitution in its natural meaning as Isaacs J seemed to suggest when writing the leading judgment in the *Engineers* case.[24] Explicit references in the *Engineers* joint judgment to the doctrine of responsible government and implicit references to democracy, the rule of law and other constitutional principles, suggest that more than interpretive literalism was in play.[25] But if the text is not enough in such cases, how are such contradictions to be resolved?

- **An Ordering of Principles**

The cases reviewed so far suggest that an important part of the problem concerns the respective roles to be played by the competing constitutional principles. Here much of the argument is about the extent to which each of the competing principles contributes to a rational explanation of the particular aspects of the Constitution that are especially relevant to the resolution of the case at hand. This gives rise to a general question. To what extent, and in what special respects, do principles such as the rule of law, judicial review, parliamentary sovereignty, the separation of powers, responsible government, representative democracy and federalism contribute to a rational explanation of the text and structure of the Constitution?

Logically, it would seem that an important kind of priority must

---

271-2, 275-6, 314-15. For the exact reasoning, see Aroney et al, above n 28, pp 557-9.
[24] *Amalgamated Society of Engineers v Adelaide Steamship Co Ltd* (1920) 28 CLR 129.
[25] See *Amalgamated Society of Engineers v Adelaide Steamship Co Ltd* (1920) 28 CLR 129, 142, 146-9, 152, 160.

be accorded to the rule of law.²⁶ This is because there is a sense in which the rule of law underlies every word, phrase and sentence of the Constitution. The rule of law, minimally understood, means that the actions of all holders of governmental office and the actions of all governing institutions must be subject to the law. The idea is that the law of the Constitution defines the conditions and terms on which such offices are held, confers the governmental powers that are exercised by the governing institutions and places limits and controls on them all. As AV Dicey put it, 'the rule of law is contrasted with every system of government based on the exercise by persons in authority of wide, arbitrary, or discretionary powers of constraint', for it involves the principle that 'every official, from the Prime Minister down to a constable or a collector of taxes, is under the same responsibility for every act done without legal justification as any other citizen'.²⁷

In this sense, the rule of law is a presupposition of every provision of the Constitution, for the whole point of the Constitution is to implement the rule of law according to its terms. However, while the rule of law is pervasive in this sense, it is also quite thin. Thus described it is agnostic as to the particular offices established, the particular powers conferred and the particular limits placed upon them. Only if the rule of law were to be elevated to a thicker conception of substantive political morality would it have implications beyond the fundamental proposition that what the Constitution says – whatever it says – is binding on our governing institutions. But such a larger proposition is highly questionable and has not been upheld by the High Court. The undoubted relevance of the rule of law to the Constitution consists in its thin and limited but fundamental and pervasive operation as an indispensable presupposition of the Constitution.²⁸

Judicial review is another important and closely related doctrine.

---

²⁶ See *Australian Communist Party v Commonwealth* (1951) 83 CLR 1, 193.
²⁷ AV Dicey, *Introduction to the Study of the Law of the Constitution* (London: Macmillan, 5th ed, 1897) pp 33, 180, 185.
²⁸ See Lisa Burton Crawford, *The Rule of Law and the Australian Constitution* (Federation Press, 2017); Geoffrey De Q Walker, *The Rule of Law: Foundation of Constitutional Democracy* (Melbourne University Press, 1988).

But despite its importance, it is not fundamental or pervasive in the way that the rule of law is. This, in part, is because a written constitution can exist without constitutional judicial review, or with constitutional judicial review operating only in limited circumstances. The corollary proposition that follows is this: judicial review exists in Australian constitutional law as a positive feature of the Constitution, not a necessary one. And even though it is a universally acknowledged doctrine in Australia, its specific basis in the Constitution is far from clear. Certainly, the text does not explicitly require it, even though some scholars have tried to find some textual basis for it. Rather, its place in Australian constitutional law was something intended by the framers and affirmed by the High Court as an implication of the rule of law.[29] In particular, judicial review was seen as a necessary component of a federal system in which legislative power is distributed between the Commonwealth and the States.[30]

What then of parliamentary sovereignty? This too is an important doctrine, in two respects. The first concerns the sovereignty of the British Parliament. The Australian Constitution, after all, is contained within a statute of the Parliament at Westminster.[31] According to the accepted legal position prevailing at the time of federation the British Parliament had authority to make laws for the Australian colonies. The Australian Constitution, at least at that time, became an authoritative part of the law of the Australian colonies precisely because the Parliament had the authority to enact laws operating with paramount force throughout the British Empire. According to the prevailing doctrine of the time, the Parliament was understood to be sovereign in the sense that it had the authority to make any law whatsoever and courts within the British Empire were obliged to regard its statutes as binding legislation no matter what their content.[32]

---

[29] Compare *South Australia v Commonwealth* (1942) 65 CLR 373, 408 and *Victoria v Commonwealth* (1975) 134 CLR 338, 379.

[30] Nicholas Aroney, 'The Justification of Judicial Review: Text, Structure, History and Principle' in Rosalind Dixon (ed), *Australian Constitutional Values* (Hart Publishing, 2017) 27.

[31] *Commonwealth of Australia Constitution Act 1900* (UK).

[32] Jeffrey Goldsworthy, *The Sovereignty of Parliament: History and Philosophy* (Oxford: Clarendon Press, 1999) ch 2. See also *Pickin v British Railways Board* [1974]

The second relevance of parliamentary sovereignty concerns the legislatures of the Commonwealth and the States. Because the Constitution establishes a federation none of the Australian legislatures possesses plenary legislative power in its fullest sense. The Commonwealth Parliament's power to make laws is limited to specific topics.[33] The State Parliaments' legislative powers are limited by several provisions of the Commonwealth Constitution,[34] as well as by the manner and form provisions of their own Constitutions, which are given force today by the *Australia Acts 1986* (UK and Cth).[35] However, within these constraints, the position has been that the legislative powers of the Australian Parliaments are 'as large, and of the same nature, as those of the [Imperial] Parliament itself' and 'as plenary and as ample within the limits prescribed ... as the Imperial Parliament in the plenitude of its power possessed and could bestow'.[36] Although the Australian Parliaments are thus 'restricted' as to the topics on which and the territory in respect of which they can legislate,[37] within those parameters their legislative powers are 'unrestricted'.[38]

This principle of the otherwise unrestricted powers of the Australian Parliaments has often been marshalled in response to arguments that their powers might be subject to constitutional implications of various kinds. In the *Engineers* case it was used to rebut the argument that the State governments and their instrumentalities enjoy a general

---

AC 765.

[33] Commonwealth Constitution, ss 51 52.

[34] Eg, Commonwealth Constitution, ss 90, 92.

[35] Compare *Attorney-General (NSW) v Trethowan* (1931) 44 CLR 394 and *Attorney-General (WA) v Marquet* (2003) 217 CLR 545.

[36] *R v Burah* (1878) 3 App Cas 889, 904 (India) and *Hodge v The Queen* (1883) 9 App Cas 117, 132 (Ontario). See John Quick and Robert Randolph Garran, *The Annotated Constitution of the Australian Commonwealth* (Angus and Robertson, 1901) 509-15 and, for more detail, Aroney et al, above n 28, 105-106, and 618-20.

[37] Quick and Garran, above n 49, pp 354–5, 569–72, 631–2.

[38] *Powell v Apollo Candle Company* (1885) 10 App Cas 282, 290 (New South Wales); *McCawley v The King* [1920] AC 691. For a fuller discussion, see. Nicholas Aroney, 'Politics, Law and the Constitution in McCawley's Case' (2006) 30(3) *Melbourne University Law Review* 605.

immunity against Commonwealth laws.[39] In the political communication cases it was deployed, unsuccessfully, against the proposition that the Commonwealth's legislative powers cannot be used to interfere unjustifiably with freedom of political communication.[40] In *Union Steamship Co of Australia Pty Ltd v King* it was argued that the words 'peace, order, and good government' – which are used to confer legislative power on the Australian Parliaments – might import restrictions on the scope of their powers.[41] However, the High Court rejected this on the ground that the formula is a term of art conveying 'in British constitutional language' the 'widest law-making powers appropriate to a Sovereign'.[42]

One important implication of parliamentary sovereignty is that the Australian Parliaments are not mere delegates of the British Parliament and that, accordingly, their powers are not subject to the maxim that 'a delegate may not itself delegate' (*delegatus non potest delegare*).[43] For this reason the Commonwealth Parliament is able to delegate law-making power to the Executive – which is another way in which the separation of powers is compromised in Australian constitutional law.[44] A further implication is that the Parliaments are, as a general rule, able to enact retrospective legislation.[45] And, subject to manner and form provisions operating pursuant to the *Australia Acts 1986* or the Commonwealth Constitution itself, a Parliament is not bound by

---

[39] *Amalgamated Society of Engineers v Adelaide Steamship Co Ltd* (1920) 28 CLR 129, 153.
[40] See *Australian Capital Television Pty Ltd v Commonwealth* (1992) 177 CLR 106, 181-3.
[41] See *Building Construction Employees and Builders' Labourers Federation of NSW v Minister for Industrial Relations* (1986) 7 NSWLR 372, 383–7, but also see 404–6.
[42] *Union Steamship Co of Australia Pty Ltd v King* (1988) 166 CLR 1, 9–10, citing *Ibralebbe v The Queen* [1964] AC 900, 923.
[43] *R v Burah* (1878) 3 App Cas 889, 904–6; *Hodge v The Queen* (1883) 9 App Cas 117, 132; *Powell v Apollo Candle Company* (1885) 10 App Cas 282, 290.
[44] *Victorian Stevedoring and General Contracting Co Ltd v Dignan* (1931) 46 CLR 73.
[45] *R v Kidman* (1915) 20 CLR 425, 451–2; see also 443, 455, 459–61; *Ex parte Walsh and Johnson; In re Yates* (1925) 37 CLR 36, 81, 89, 127; *University of Wollongong v Metwally* (1984) 158 CLR 447, 465, 484, 486.

the enactments of its predecessors.[46]

Parliamentary sovereignty is thus a highly significant principle of the Constitution, first because it describes the authority by which the Constitution was enacted into law by the British Parliament, and second because it informs the way in which the legislative powers of the Australian Parliaments are understood. However, as important as it is, it directly concerns only the legislative powers conferred on the Parliaments. It is not a doctrine that especially sheds light on the other two branches of government, the Executive and the Judiciary.

This brings into view the doctrine of the separation of powers, the principle that legislative, executive and judicial power ought to be separately vested in distinct institutions. As noted earlier, while important, the reach of this principle is limited in Australian constitutional law. Responsible government means that, in practice, executive power is exercised on the advice of members of the Parliament who, having the confidence of the House of Representatives, have been appointed to hold ministerial office by the Governor-General. Parliamentary sovereignty means that the Parliament is also able to delegate law-making power to the Executive, and does so frequently.[47] Notably, this occurs when the Parliament enacts a law to that effect. It does so pursuant to the legislative powers conferred upon it by the Constitution even though they are not explicit about its capacity to delegate those powers to some other institution or office holder. On the face of it, this might be thought contrary to the structure of the Constitution, which allocates legislative power to the Parliament, executive power to the Queen and judicial power to the Judicature.[48] However, the relevant provisions literally only *confer* particular kinds of government power on particular governmental institutions; they do not *prohibit* its further conferral by legislation on other institutions. To infer that they have this prohibitive effect depends on an implication,

---

[46] *McCawley v The King* [1920] AC 691. See, further, Aroney et al, above n 28, 109-111, 625-32.

[47] *Victorian Stevedoring and General Contracting Co Ltd v Dignan* (1931) 46 CLR 73, criticised in Ratnapala, above n 33.

[48] Commonwealth Constitution, chapters I, II and III; ss 1, 61 and 71.

derived from the proposition that the literary structure of the Constitution invokes the principle of the separation of powers. But it is only in respect of judicial power that the High Court has drawn this inference, concluding that as a matter of general principle federal judicial power cannot be conferred on non-judicial bodies and non-judicial power cannot be conferred upon federal judicial bodies.[49] Thus, while it could be said that the *concepts* of executive, legislative and judicial power are pervasive throughout the Constitution in the sense that virtually all of the powers conferred by the Constitution are one of these three kinds,[50] and while the *distribution* of those powers to the three branches respectively leads to the situation that each of the three powers is routinely exercised by the branch to which the power is initially allocated, the *separation* of powers in the strict sense pertains only to the conferral of judicial power upon the judiciary.

One of the most significant reasons for the High Court's rigorous insistence upon the separation of judicial power is the need, in its view, to protect the independence of the judiciary. The key institutional mechanism by which this independence is secured is the provision that federal judges cannot have their remuneration diminished and must continue to hold office until the age of 70 unless removed on an address of both Houses of Parliament for proved misbehaviour or incapacity.[51] This deliberately insulates the judges from popular opinion and parliamentary or governmental influence. Judges are not made democratically accountable in the sense that members of Parliament are held accountable through elections and Ministers of State are held accountable through parliamentary processes. This means that the

---

[49] *New South Wales v Commonwealth* (1915) 20 CLR 54; *Waterside Workers' Federation of Australia v J W Alexander Ltd* (1918) 25 CLR 434; *R v Kirby; Ex parte Boilermakers' Society of Australia* (1956) 94 CLR 254. See Aroney et al, above n 28, 557-62.

[50] Note, however, the provision for the now defunct Inter-state Commission: Commonwealth Constitution, s 101. For a discussion, see Stephen Gageler, 'Chapter IV: The Inter-State Commission and the Regulation of Trade and Commerce under the Australian Constitution' (2017) 28 *Public Law Review* 205.

[51] Commonwealth Constitution, s 72.

principle of democracy, as important as it is, applies in its fullest sense only to the executive and legislative branches of government.

What, then, is the constitutional significance of democracy? Certainly, it plays a fundamental role in several respects. In the first place, although the Constitution was enacted into law by the British Parliament, the text of the Constitution went through a process of drafting and approval that was highly democratic, at least by the standards of the time. The whole process of federating was initiated by the elected political leaders of the six colonies and given legislative form by the colonial legislatures. Most of the delegates to the federal convention who drafted the Constitution were elected by the voters in the Australian colonies (the exception being the delegates of Western Australia, who were chosen by the colonial legislature). Moreover, the Constitution was not forwarded to the British Parliament for enactment until first approved in a referendum in each of the colonies.[52] Secondly, the Constitution establishes the foundations for a democratic system of governance. It provides that the two Houses of the Parliament are directly elected by Australian voters and it is designed to enable a system of parliamentary responsible government to develop. One of the key provisions in this regard is the requirement that Ministers of State must hold seats in Parliament, at least within three months of appointment; the other is the requirement of parliamentary approval for the appropriation of money from the consolidated revenue fund for the purpose of government expenditure.[53] The Constitution also requires regular elections and regular sittings of Parliament.[54] While it gives power to the Parliament to determine electoral divisions and the scope of the franchise,[55] the High Court has held that having granted rights to vote in federal elections on the basis of universal adult franchise (with limited exceptions), the Parliament no longer has constitutional power to diminish the breadth of the franchise.[56]

---

[52] See Aroney, above n 21, ch 6.
[53] Commonwealth Constitution, ss 64, 81, 83.
[54] Commonwealth Constitution, ss 5, 6, 7, 28.
[55] Commonwealth Constitution, ss 29, 30.
[56] *Roach v Electoral Commissioner* (2007) 233 CLR 162, 173; *Rowe v Electoral Commissioner* (2010) 243 CLR 1.

Such a conclusion was controversial precisely because it involved the Court giving effect to what it understood to be an implication of the democratic principles underlying the Constitution even though the text itself gives the Parliament what appears to be unconstrained discretion to determine the scope of the franchise.[57] Thirdly, the Constitution provides, consistently with its original ratification, that formal amendments to its text can only be made by the Parliament following approval at a referendum in which Australian voters approve of the proposed change.[58]

What, then, about federalism? Federalism is as fundamental as democracy to the Constitution, but even more pervasive. It is fundamental to the Constitution for the basic reason that the essential purpose of the Constitution was to federate the Australian colonies into a 'federal commonwealth'.[59] Consistent with this, not only was the whole process of federating initiated and controlled by the colonial legislatures, but the referendums through which the Constitution was first approved were held in each of the constituent States on the premise that unless the people of a State consented to join the federation it would remain independent of the Commonwealth. The procedure for the formal amendment of the Constitution reflects its federal foundations by requiring a majority not only of the national population, but also a majority of voters in a majority of States to approve any proposed change.[60] While sometimes overlooked in this context, two other provisions of the Constitution that enable constitutional change to occur are also profoundly federal in their design and structure. The first is the provision for the referral by the State legislatures of additional legislative powers upon the Commonwealth Parliament.[61] The requirement that such transfers of

---

[57] Nicholas Aroney, 'Towards the "Best Explanation" of the Constitution: Text, Structure, History and Principle in *Roach v Electoral Commissioner*' (2011) 30 *University of Queensland Law Journal* 145.

[58] Commonwealth Constitution, s 128. On the federal aspects of this process, see below.

[59] *Commonwealth of Australia Constitution Act 1900* (UK), preamble and covering clause 3.

[60] Commonwealth Constitution, s 128.

[61] Commonwealth Constitution, s 51(xxxvii).

power apply only to those States which refer the power or adopt the referral at a later point in time reflects their fundamental constitutive role within the federation. The second provision is the power of the federal Parliament to exercise within the Commonwealth any power which at the establishment of the Constitution could be exercised only by the Parliament of the United Kingdom.[62] While of immense constitutional significance, this power can only be exercised at the request or with the concurrence of the Parliaments of all the States directly concerned, reflecting the federating compact upon which the whole Constitution is predicated.

Federalism is not only fundamental. It is also pervasive. While the Constitution treats legislative, executive and judicial power separately, in each case there is a constitutional distinction between the Commonwealth and the States. Both the Commonwealth and the States have their own independently operating institutions of government, each exercising their own discrete legislative, executive and judicial powers over distinguishable fields of operation. The scheme of the Constitution, consistent with its federal design, is that the States generally continue to possess the institutions and powers they had prior to federation, subject only to the specific powers conferred upon the federal institutions of government established by the Constitution. Thus, the Commonwealth Parliament's law-making powers are limited to particular topics,[63] the executive power of the Commonwealth extends only to the execution and maintenance of the Constitution and the laws of the Commonwealth,[64] and the jurisdiction of federal courts is limited to particular topics as well.[65] Furthermore, the Parliament itself consists of representatives of the States, distributed in proportion to population in the House of Representatives and equally in the Senate.[66] The Senate, plainly, is the

---

[62] Commonwealth Constitution, s 51(xxxviii). See *Port Macdonnell Professional Fishermen's Association Inc v South Australia* (1989) 168 CLR 340.
[63] Commonwealth Constitution, ss 51, 52.
[64] Commonwealth Constitution, s 61.
[65] Commonwealth Constitution, ss 75, 76.
[66] Commonwealth Constitution, ss 7, 24.

'states house', but even the House of Representatives is constructed in a way that reflects its federal origins.[67] Numerous other provisions of the Constitution reflect the federal foundations and purposes of the Constitution. On one hand, several provisions protect the States or the people of a particular State from discriminatory legislation or action by the Commonwealth or another State.[68] On the other hand, several other provisions either give the Commonwealth exclusive power to legislate, regulate or tax a particular field or ensure than in cases of legislative conflict the law of the Commonwealth will prevail over that of the States.[69]

Finally, it is also sometimes said that the Australian Constitution establishes a secular commonwealth.[70] This is primarily due to the provision in s 116 of the Constitution preventing the Commonwealth from making any law for the establishment of any religion and prohibiting the imposition of any religious test for the holding of public office. These provisions do require a certain kind of secularity at a Commonwealth level, although they noticeably do not apply to the States, even though this possibility was canvassed during the convention debates.[71] The Constitution also acknowledges in its preamble the dependence of the people on the blessing of Almighty God, which was inserted into the Constitution in response to an overwhelming number of petitions presented to the federal convention requesting that some such acknowledgement be made.[72]

---

[67] Note, for example, the minimum representation in the House of Representatives guaranteed to every Original State: Commonwealth Constitution, s 24. Note also that the representation of each State in the Parliament cannot be diminished except with the agreement of the people of that State: Commonwealth Constitution, s 128.

[68] Commonwealth Constitution, ss 51(ii), 99, 102, 117.

[69] Eg, Commonwealth Constitution, s 52, 90, 109. Note also the guarantee of freedom of interstate trade: Commonwealth Constitution, s 92.

[70] See Reid Mortensen, *The Secular Commonwealth: Constitutional Government, Law and Religion* (PhD Thesis, The University of Queensland, 1995).

[71] *Grace Bible Church v Reedman* (1984) 36 SASR 376. See, further, Aroney et al, above n 28, 338-341.

[72] For more detail, see Richard Ely, *Unto God and Caesar: Religious Issues in the Emerging Commonwealth 1891-1906* (Melbourne University Press, 1976).

The High Court has held that the prohibition on the establishment of any religion does not prevent the Commonwealth from providing financial support for religious schools, at least on a non-preferential basis.[73] It has also held that the prohibition on religious tests does not prevent the Commonwealth from funding the appointment of religious chaplains in public or state schools, in part because such chaplains are not officers of the Commonwealth.[74] A non-discriminatory law which is directed towards religion does not violate this s 116 provision, which is aimed at preventing Commonwealth action leading to direct involvement in and promotion of religion.[75] Unfortunately, an 'action-belief' dichotomy has influenced some of the Court's decisions in relation to the freedom of religion guaranteed by section 116.[76]

Notably the Constitution ends with a prescribed oath or affirmation of allegiance to be taken by every senator and member of the House of Representatives before taking his or her seat.[77] Similar oaths or affirmations are required of the other crucial office holders under the Constitution: the Queen herself, the Governor-General, Ministers of State and judges of federal courts.[78] While the availability of the solemn affirmation provides a secular alternative to the religious oath, such flexibility exists in order to accommodate the religious or conscientious objections of both religious believers and those who are agnostic or atheist in their beliefs.[79] The oath or affirmation plays a crucial role in the constitutional system, for it is the means by which the consciences of office holders are bound to their particular duties of office. As such, the oath or affirmation is, arguably, the existential

---

[73] *Attorney-General (Vic); Ex rel Black v Commonwealth* (1981) 146 CLR 559.

[74] *Williams v Commonwealth* (2012) 248 CLR 156.

[75] See: Gabriël A. Moens & John Trone, *The Constitution of the Commonwealth of Australia Annotated* (LexisNexis Butterworths, 9th ed., 2016), p 441.

[76] *Adelaide Company of Jehovah's Witnesses Incorporated v Commonwealth* (1943) 67 CLR 116. For criticism, see Gabriel Moens, 'The Action-Belief Dichotomy and Freedom of Religion' (1989-1990) 12 *Sydney Law Reveiw* 195.

[77] Commonwealth Constitution, s 42 and Schedule.

[78] Nicholas Aroney, *Faith in Public Office: The Meaning, Persistence and Importance of Oaths* <http://www.abc.net.au/religion/articles/2015/11/23/4358054.htm>.

[79] See, eg, *Quakers Act 1695* 7 & 8 Will 3 c 34 (UK).

basis for the rule of law, for it requires office holders to make a solemn, conscientious promise to perform their constitutional duties rather than act in their own interests or according to their own personal system of values.[80]

• Conclusions

Writing soon after the enactment of the Commonwealth Constitution, William Harrison Moore claimed that the 'predominant feature' of the Constitution was the 'prevalence of the democratic principle'.[81] Writing around the same time, John Quick and Robert Garran considered that it was the federal idea which 'pervades and largely dominates the structure of the newly-created community, its Parliamentary executive and judiciary departments'.[82] On balance, Quick and Garran had the better of these two claims. Certainly the process by which the Constitution was ratified was highly democratic by the standards of the day. But while the Constitution requires the Parliament to consist of members directly chosen by the people and is designed so that those who exercise executive power will do so in a manner that is ultimately accountable to the Parliament, other important aspects of the Constitution are not so democratic. The federal judiciary, for example, is deliberately insulated from democratic pressures and is only removable upon provided misbehaviour or incapacity. The federal principles of the Constitution, moreover, qualify the way in which the democratic principle is implemented – at the point of the Constitution's original ratification, its ordinary day to day operation and its formal amendment. Federal principles also shape the extent of the legislative, executive and judicial powers conferred on the three branches of government. In these respects, federalism is both like

---

[80] See Sir Gerard Brennan, 'Speech on Swearing in as Chief Justice', 21 April 1995, (1995) 183 CLR ix, discussed in Nicholas Aroney, 'The Rule of Law, Religious Authority, and Oaths of Office' (2018) 6 *Journal of Law, Religion and State* 195, at 208-210.

[81] Harrison Moore, *Constitution of the Commonwealth of Australia* (John Murray, 1st ed, 1902), p 329.

[82] Quick and Garran, above n 49, p 332.

and unlike the rule of law. Like the rule of law, federalism is both fundamental and pervasive; unlike the rule of law, federalism is also a highly substantive doctrine that informs much of the substantive content of the Constitution.[83]

The principles of parliamentary sovereignty and the separation of powers are also important constitutional doctrines. Like democracy, however, they are less than pervasive and their operation is limited in various ways. Sovereignty is an attribute only of the Parliament, and the kind of sovereignty it possesses is limited by the terms of the Constitution and is subject to judicial review. The separation of powers operates in full rigour with respect to the strict separation required between the judicial power, on the one hand, and the legislative and executive powers, on the other.[84] This doctrine applies rigorously only to the separation of judicial power because the principle of parliamentary responsible government has a tendency to fuse the effective control of the exercise of executive and legislative power into the hands of a Prime Minister and Cabinet who have, by definition, the support of a majority in the House of Representatives. It is only the existence of the Senate which ensures some degree of separation of executive and legislative power within the Constitution,[85] and of course the Senate's primary structural principle and rationale is a federal one.

Of the various doctrines that inform and explain the Australian Constitution, the rule of law is perhaps the most fundamental and pervasive, but only in the relatively thin sense that it is the purpose of every provision of the Constitution to define and limit the powers exercised by those who hold office under the Constitution. And it is here that the oath or affirmation of office provides the existential connection between the duties of office and the conscience of the individual office holder.

---

[83] For more detail, see Nicholas Aroney, 'Federalism: Design' in Cheryl Saunders and Adrienne Stone (eds), *Oxford Handbook of the Australian Constitution* (Oxford University Press, 2018).

[84] See: Moens & Trone, above n 88, p 271.

[85] For more detail, see Nicholas Aroney, 'Four Reasons for an Upper House: Representative Democracy, Public Deliberation, Legislative Outputs and Executive Accountability' (2008) 29(2) *Adelaide Law Review* 205.

4

THE WRONGS OF A BILL OF RIGHTS FOR AUSTRALIA: A RIGHTS-BASED APPRAISAL

Augusto Zimmermann

- **Introduction**

I am privileged to have known Professor Gabriël A. Moens for more than 11 years. Over the years I have had the opportunity to exchange numerous ideas with him. We have discussed many legal-political issues over the years, including whether or not Australia should enact a constitutionally entrenched bill of rights.

Professor Moens is a staunch advocate of constitutional government and the legal protection of individual rights. He is a defender of constitutional guarantees that ultimately protect our fundamental rights and freedoms – in particular our basic rights to life, liberty and property. And yet, he, very much like myself, does not support the enactment of a constitutionally entrenched bill of rights for Australia. Rather, he believes that, at least in Australia, such a legal document might not ever achieve these worthy goals of protecting fundamental rights satisfactorily.

In 'The Wrongs of a Constitutionally Entrenched Bill of Rights'[1], Professor Moens provides compelling reasons as to why a constitutionally entrenched bill of rights might not necessarily enhance the protection of fundamental rights in Australia. On the contrary, the in-

---

[1] Gabriël A. Moens, 'The Wrongs of a Constitutional Entrenched Bill of Rights' in M.A. Stephenson and Clive Turner (eds.), *Australia: Republic or Monarchy?: Legal and Constitutional Issues*, (St Lucia/QLD: The University of Queensland Press, 1994), p 236.

troduction of such a novelty could contribute to the elevation of a judicial philosophy that promotes activism but does not necessarily afford the levels of protection needed against legal certainty and political arbitrariness. What follows is an exposition of a few reasons as to why Australia should not have a constitutionally entrenched bill of rights.

- **Human Rights Legislation May be Unnecessary**

The tendency of governments to acquire ever increasing power has traditionally been curtailed in Western democracies such as Australia, primarily by a constitutional system of checks and balances. According to Sir Harry Gibbs, former Chief Justice of the High Court of Australia,

> The most effective way to curb political power is to divide it. A Federal Constitution, which brings about a division of power in actual practice, is a more secure protection for basic political freedoms than a bill of rights.[2]

By contrast, the effectiveness of human rights legislation to control government power is intrinsically dependent on the socio-political context in which it operates. The impressive bills of rights passed in countries such as China, Cuba, Uganda, Rwanda, Cambodia, Russia, Sudan and South Africa proved no barrier to multiple human rights abuses committed by governments of those places. Gibbs also wrote:

> Anyone who has seen the film 'The Killing Fields' will know that the fact that Khmer Republic had adopted a bill of rights did not assist the inhabitants of that unhappy country. We are all familiar with the abuses that have occurred in Uganda: that country had a bill of rights on the European model, and had judges that bravely tried to enforce it, but were unable to resist the forces of lawlessness.[3]

Governments which eschew the rule of law with its inbuilt checks and balances are prepared to use naked power to override even their own bills of rights. They may use legislative power (*per leges*) to

---

[2] Sir Harry Gibbs, 'A Constitutional Bill of Rights', *in* K. Baker (ed.), *An Australian Bill of Rights: Pro and Contra* (Melbourne, Institute of Public Affairs, 1986), p 325.
[3] Ibid., p 340.

achieve their specific aims, but will not allow themselves to be subject to constitutional checks (*sub leges*) that may curb their unrestrained power. Therefore, bills of rights can only be enforced in countries where there is already a functional constitutional framework coupled with a culture of legality that places a high value on individual rights and the idea of 'government under the law'. In such, countries rights legislation is unnecessary.

In a landmark court ruling, the then Chief Justice Sir Anthony Mason of the High Court of Australia, stated: 'The prevailing sentiment of the [Australian] framers is that there was no need to incorporate a comprehensive Bill of Rights in order to protect the rights and freedoms of citizens. That sentiment was one of the unexpressed assumptions on which the Constitution was drafted'.[4] Under the system of constitutional government created by those framers, one proceeds on the assumption of full individual rights and liberty, and then turns to the law just to see whether there might be any reasonable exception to the general rule. After comparing this constitutional model of limited government with the North-American one, the late Australian constitutional lawyer, W. Anstey Wynes, concluded:

> The performance of the Supreme Court of the United States has become embroiled in discussions of what are really and in truth political questions, from the necessity of assigning some meaning to the various 'Bill of Rights' provisions. The Australian Constitution… differs from its American counterpart in a more fundamental respect in that, as the… Chief Justice of Australia [Sir Owen Dixon] has pointed out, Australia is a 'common law' country in which the State is conceived as deriving from the law and not the law from the State.[5]

- **Human Rights Legislation May Reduce Individual Rights**

One of the main arguments by those in favour of bills of rights is that such documents are effective mechanisms to protect human rights. But

---

[4] *Australian Capital Television Pty Ltd v The Commonwealth* (1992) 177 CLR 106, at 136.

[5] W. Anstey Wynes, *Legislative, Executive and Judicial Powers in Australia* (Sydney: The Law Book Co, 1955), p vii.

this is not necessarily so. In contrast to what their advocates suggest, human-rights violations may occur regardless of the enactment of such legislation. In fact, there is even the possibility that legislation of this kind, despite all the superficial attractions they naturally achieve, may actually become a major factor in *depriving* humans of their most basic rights.[6]

In 1776, the 13 American colonies broke their ties with Britain stating that they assumed 'among the powers of the earth, the separate and equal station to which the Laws of Nature and of Nature's God entitle them'. Thus their Declaration of Independence boldly stated: 'We hold these truths to be self-evident, that all men are created equal, and that they are endowed by their Creator with certain inalienable rights, that among these are life, liberty and the pursuit of happiness. .... That wherever any form of government becomes destructive of these ends, it is the right of the people to alter or to abolish it, and to institute new government.'

For the drafters of this Declaration the whole purpose of expressing rights is to protect the citizen against excessive governmental power. What they deemed 'inalienable' are only the fundamental rights of the individual that are necessary for the legal protection of life, public security, private property, freedom of speech, etc. Of course, this is not the same as the second generation of rights that appeared in the nineteenth century. Contrary to rights of the first generation, second generation rights actually require governments to directly provide social services such as shelter, clothing, food, health care and education for their citizens.

- **Group Rights**

More recently a further generation of rights has been formed. These are the rights for such things as a healthier environment, self-determination, the preservation of cultural traditions and even a right to the unhindered practice of certain alternative lifestyles. Many of such 'rights' are called 'group rights' because they are targeted to

---

[6] Robert Dahl, 'Decision-Making in a Democracy: The Supreme Court as a National Policy-Maker' (1957), 6 *Jornal of Public Law* 279, at 291.

a specific biological, religious or ideological group. Rights of this nature are regularly evoked by the social activists who seek radical change. Some of these rights are deeply embedded in the human-rights declarations of countries such as Canada, the United Kingdom and New Zealand. Garry Furgason comments on their effect in Canada:

> Like an exploding bomb dropped in the middle of the Canadian legal system, it has destroyed a few laws, shaken up a host of other laws and generated an immense amount of activity and at least some anxiety.[7]

There are quite serious problems with the concept of 'group rights'. Since rights are not a single indivisible entity, they can and do conflict. Too much emphasis on these so-called 'group rights' may eventually result in a diminished understanding, recognition and even protection of the most fundamental rights of the individual. By granting special privileges to people on grounds of their ethnic, religious and gender affiliations, such 'rights' risk generating the marginalisation, even the persecution, of other less-favoured groups of individuals. The situation is disturbingly similar to that which occurred in Germany under National Socialism where the group was everything and the individual was nothing. As noted by U.S. sociology professor Alvin J. Schmidt,

> Political, economic and religious freedom can only exist where there is liberty and freedom of the individual. Group rights that determine a person's rights on the basis of belonging to a given ethnic or racial group, as presently advocated by multiculturalists and by affirmative action laws, nullify the rights of the individual. Group rights greatly reduce the freedom of the individual in that these rights stem only from the group; if he does not belong to the group, his rights are greatly curtailed. ...When group rights get the upper hand, gone are the 'inalienable rights' given to the individual by his Creator so admirably expressed by the American Declaration of Independence.[8]

---

[7] Garry Furgason, 'The Impact of an Entrenched Bill of Rights: The Canadian Experience' (1990) 16 *Monash Law Review* 213.

[8] Alvin Schmidt, *How Christianity changed the World* (Grand Rapids: Zondervan, 2004), p 259.

The granting of legal privileges to groups favoured by the state is what lies behind the leftist agenda for 'group rights' and its correlating focus on so-called 'affirmative action' at the workplace and other places. Such policies involve rather profound questions of equality and fairness, including whether it is ever justifiable to submerge individuals into whole groups and subject them to certain prophylactic politics which often harm their interests.[9]

Take for instance the introduction of affirmative action as applied to gender issues. In *Affirmative Action: The New Discrimination* (1985), Professor Moens explains why policies that provide special treatment and preferential hiring to women might even be considered 'an insult to those women who have succeeded in their chosen fields on the basis of their own individual qualities'.[10]

Professor Moens also says that such 'affirmative actions' may legitimise unfairness and discrimination since they appear to prioritise equal outcomes at the expense of personal merit and real opportunity. In *The Illusions of Comparable Worth* (1992), Moens and Ratnapala contend that, as a means of breaking down occupational segregation as well as the alleged earnings gap between men and women, the ongoing push for affirmative action in the workplace is fundamentally flawed not only because it assumes that the gender gap is necessarily caused by some form of unfair discrimination (whereas it may be more accurately a reflection of people's lifestyle and choices) but also because it certainly discriminates against some women (i.e., housewives) who are not the direct recipients of such legal privileges.[11]

But even if a bill of rights could be entirely free from these 'group rights', such a legislation still can be used to restrict individual rights. The example of the United States and its Bill of Rights provides a good point. Such a declaration of rights was enacted 'in an age pre-dating both the scourge of political correctness

---

[9] Ibid., p 131.
[10] Gabriël A Moens, *Affirmative Action: The New Discrimination* (Centre for Independent Studies, 1985), p 98.
[11] Gabriël A. Moens and Suri Ratnapala, *The Illusions of Comparable Worth* (Centre for Independent Studies, 1992).

and the Left's capture of the legal profession'.[12] The document is therefore free of any form of activist jargon. And yet, the country's Supreme Court has constantly relied in its abstract provision to impose their own ideological views and assumptions. In the United States, unelected judges have, among numerous other things, prohibited students from voluntary praying in public in government schools and interpreted 'due process' as incorporating an implied right to abortion on demand, thus demonstrating that even a more 'conservative' Bill of Rights remains entirely susceptible of gross abuse and manipulation.

- **Slavery**

Take also the important issue of slavery. In 1857, the U.S. Supreme Court held by a substantial 7-2 majority that black people were not really 'citizens' of the United States. As a result, the court prohibited Congress to outlaw slavery in the country. It reached such an appalling decision via an interpretation of the American Bill of Rights, and, more specifically, its Fifth Amendment's prohibition of depriving persons of their property without 'due process of law'. Such a prohibition was construed as meaning that the elected federal legislative was not authorised to remove the purported right of slaveholders to retain their human property (i.e.; slaves) if they happened to be moving into another jurisdiction within the borders of the United States. For congressmen to state that a property (slave) could not be taken with them into another State or Territory without losing it, Justice Taney stated: 'could hardly be dignified with the name of due process'.[13]

Dred Scott is broadly regarded as one of the worst decisions ever made by the Supreme Court of the United States. It is correctly credited with accelerating the American Civil War that claimed the lives of roughly 620,000 Americans. This was so because the Supreme Court, by seeking to elevate racial apartheid to the level of constitutional

---

[12] Alan Anderson, 'The Rule of Lawyers: A Bill of Rights could lead to an Elected Judiciary', *Policy*, Vol.21, No.4, Summer 2005-06, at 37.
[13] *Dred Scott v Sandford*, 60 U.S. (19 How.) 393, 407 (1957).

principle, made any constitutional solution to the matter practically impossible. Instead, the court constitutionally slavery although no such validation can be found in the document. If that wasn't bad enough, the court via its controversial ruling ended up opening a Pandora's Box that led to numerous other arbitrary rulings, including *Roe v Wade* in 1973. As law professor Stephen B. Presser points out:

> In reaching this result Taney took great pains to eschew any natural law arguments restricting slavery based on the law of nations (and English common law). 'There is no law of nations', said Taney, 'standing between the People of the United States and their Government, and interfering with their relation to each other'. In other words, no law of nations came between a property holder and his slave property. But there Taney would appear to have been wrong. At the time of the framing of the Constitution, and shortly thereafter,... the natural law and law of nations foundations for the United States Constitution... were quite clear to contemporaries. Indeed, property itself was thought to be a concept that derived, ultimately, from natural law... At the time of the framing of the Constitution the intellectual and spiritual leader of the Southern States, if not of the national itself, was Virginia. Even in that state, in the late eighteenth century, there had developed a slavery jurisprudence that circumscribed the harshest applications of slavery doctrines through adherence to the basic natural law principle of a presumption against slavery and in favor of human liberty. Thus, in several important opinions, Virginia slave holders' wishes to manumit their slaves in their wills were implemented, even though at the time the testators' deaths such manumission was not permitted by statute.[14]

- **Abortion**

Whereas in *Dred Scott* black Americans were deemed a 'property' of their slave-owners, in *Roe vs Wade* the unborn was deemed a 'property' of their parents. The legal status of the unborn was ignored, even though two years earlier pro-abortion bills had actually been defeated

---

[14] Stephen B. Presser, *Recapturing the Constitution: Race, Religion and Abortion Reconsidered* (Washington/DC: Regnery, 1994), p 132.

in 33 American States.[15] But on January 22, 1973, by a substantial 7-2 majority, the court simply struck down all the abortion laws of the 50 States of the American Federation. It did so by inhibiting the legislative regulation of abortion during the first three months of pregnancy. As for the second and third trimesters, the court held that the termination procedure was still valid if it could somehow be found to benefit the mother's mental or physical health. How aborting her unwanted child may contribute to a woman's health was not explained.

To strip the unborn from their right to life, Justice Blackmun assumed that his court was not obliged to entertain 'the difficult question of when life begins'. But if he was not entirely sure about when life begins, surely he should have opted for the lesser moral risk. And yet, he actually opted for the greater moral risk that is based on a legal opinion that, according to Francis J. Beckwith, 'has all the earmarks of a theory of life that morally segregates the unborn from full-fledged membership in the human community, for it in practice excludes the unborn from constitutional protection'.[16] Although he claimed to be taking no sides on the important discussion of when human life begins, such a ruling effectively infers that the unborn is not a human person worthy of receiving any legal protection. So the court did take sides on the issue after all.

The sort of medical procedure permitted in *Roe* is something that the court admitted it would not have allowed if it was conclusively proven that the unborn is actually a human person.[17] When the state of Texas argued in *Roe* that 'the fetus is a person within the language and meaning of the Fourteenth Amendment', Justice Blackmun replied: 'If the suggestion of personhood [of the unborn] is established, the appellant's case, of course, collapses, for the fetus' right to life is then guaranteed specifically by the [Fourteenth Amendment]'.[18] And

---

[15] Phyllis Schlafly, *The Supremacists* (Dallas/TX: Spence, 2004), p 84. On 7November 1972, pro-abortion referenda were also defeated by the citizens of North Dakota by 78 percent, and in Michigan by 61 percent.

[16] Francis J. Beckwith, *Defending Life: A Moral and Legal Case Against Abortion Choice* (New York/NY: Cambridge University Press, 2007), p 30.

[17] Ibid., p 30.

[18] *Roe v Wade* 410 U.S. 160, 157-158.

yet, the scientific evidence that human life begins at conception was ignored. Sometime prior to *Roe* the *American College of Pediatricians* had officially declared: 'Scientific and medical discoveries ... have only verified and solidified this age-old truth'.[19] According to Dr Renée Mirkes, a medical ethicist,

> At the completion of the process of fertilization when the male and female pronuclei of the human progenitors' sperm and ovum are indistinguishable and lose their nuclear envelopes, the human creature emerges as a whole, genetically distinct, individuated zygotic human organism. This individuated human organism actually has the natural capacity for the person-defining activities of reasoning, willing, desiring, and relating to others. ...The new zygote, a member of the species homo sapiens, with its particular (that is, genome-specific) bodily "matter" unified and organized, that is, formed or enlivened by means of its life principle—the soul and all of its person-defining natural powers---is a whole, living, human person. The difference between the individual in her adult stage and in her zygotic stage is not one of personhood but of development.[20]

Since it is clear that the decision in *Roe* is scientifically unsound, it is important now to consider whether such a decision is also constitutionally unsound. This particular question is not so difficult to answer since the ruling clearly rests on a misapplication of the Fifth and Fourteenth Amendments to the U.S. Constitution. The unborn has always been regarded as a 'person' within the language of the law. Of course, the constitution does not confer upon federal government any specifically enumerated power to deny anybody of their personhood. Such a power to recognize personhood to the unborn – as the holder of basic human rights – had always been exercised by the American States.[21]

---

[19] 'When Human Life Begins', *The American College of Pediatricians*, 17 March 2004, at: http://www.acpeds.org/index.

[20] Renée Mirkes, 'NBAC and Embryo Ethics' (2001) 1(2) *The National Catholic Bioethics Quartely* 163, at 187.

[21] Gregory J. Roden, 'Unborn Children as Constitutional Persons' (2010) 25 (3) *Issues on Law and Medicine* 185, at 185-86.

The Fifth and Fourteenth amendments guarantee the rights to life, liberty and property. They comprise what is generally called 'due process of law'. Nowhere in such a provision one finds the statement that 'Congress shall make no law abridging the right of privacy', and let alone a 'right' for abortion. And yet, Justice Blackmun simply *felt* that such a 'right' should be invented by the court. This abortion right would exist as a result of judicial activism designed as something to be derived from another implied right: the right to privacy.[22] Justice White certainly wasn't overstating when he argued that the majority ruling in *Roe* amounted to an 'exercise of raw judicial power'. Justice White declared:

> I find nothing in the language or history of the Constitution to support the Court's judgement. The court simply fashions and announces a new constitutional right for pregnant mothers, and with scarcely any reason or authority for its action.[23]

The second dissent in *Roe* was given by Justice Rehnquist. He reminded the majority that even if one discovers such an 'implied' right to privacy a further problem is to actually demonstrate how an invasive medical procedure conducted by a general physician and which results in the termination of an unwanted pregnancy, can ever be considered a 'private' matter. What is more, he went on to say, the trimester regulatory scheme created by the majority 'partakes more of judicial legislation than it does of a determination of the intent of the drafters of the Fourteenth Amendment... To reach its result – he concluded – the Court necessarily has to find within the scope of the Fourteenth Amendment a right that was apparently completely unknown to the drafters of the Amendment'.[24] Hence, the late Joseph P. Witherspoon, who was a distinguished professor of jurisprudence at the University of Texas, concluded:

> The failure of the Court in *Roe v. Wade*... was a failure to be

---

[22] See: Mark R. Levin, *Men in Black: How the Supreme Court is Destroying America* (Washington/DC: Regnery, 2005), p 61.

[23] *Roe v Wade* 410 U.S. 113 (1973), at 221-22.

[24] *Roe v Wade* 410 U.S. 113 (1973), at 174.

faithful to the law or to respect the legislature which framed it. Careful research of the history of these two amendments will demonstrate to any impartial investigator that there is overwhelming evidence supporting the proposition that the principal, actual purpose of their framers was to prevent any court, and especially the Supreme Court of the United States, because of its earlier performance in the Dred Scott case, or any other institution of government, whether legislative or executive, from ever again defining the concept of person so as to exclude any class of human beings from the protection of the Constitution and the safeguards it established for the fundamental rights of human beings, including slaves... and the unborn from the time of their conception.[25]

Some two decades later the creative 'interpretation' of the American Bill of Rights led the court to provide new and even more creative justifications for abortion on demand. In *Planned Parenthood v Casey* (1992) Justice Kennedy notoriously stated that it would be intolerant for an elected legislature to restrict a woman's right to terminate her pregnancy, the question whether her child lives or dies depending entirely on her voluntary will. [26] Although the drafters of the Bill of Rights believed in objective moral standards, activist judges like him 'affirm the right of a person to make up his own version of the universe'[27] One should expect such judges to know that some things are objectively wrong and therefore not permissible, because they may injure others and even the perpetrators of such actions themselves. Above all, activist judges appear to act as if they were unaware of the idea of 'inalienable rights' defined in the American Declaration of Independence, which conveys a powerful message about fundamental rights to life and dignity that nobody is legitimately competent to waive and to violate.[28]

---

[25] Joseph P. Witherspoon, *Texas Tech Law Review*, Vol. 6, 1974-1975. Quoted from Francis A. Schaeffer, *How Should We Then Live?* (Wheaton/IL: Crossway, 1983) pp. 220-21.

[26] *Planned Parenthood v Casey* 505 U.S. 833 (1992).

[27] Hadley Arkes, *Natural Rights & the Right to Choose* (New York/NY: Cambridge University Press, 2002), p 43.

[28] Ibid., p 44.

Perhaps the most remarkable statement in *Planned Parenthood* is the court's assertion that its own rulings must be cast in stone lest its legitimacy be challenged. One could ask such judges whether they think *Dred Scott* should also be cast in stone. When it comes to matters of constitutional interpretation, it is actually the written text that is ultimately binding, and not the opinion of a few unelected judges. Felix Frankfurter (1882-1992) of the U.S. Supreme Court understood it very well when he famously stated: '*Stare decisis* is a principle of policy and not a mechanical formula of adherence to the latest decision, however recent and questionable, when such adherence involves collision with a prior doctrine more embracing in its scope, intrinsically sounder, and verified by experience'.[29] Justice Frankfurter also declared: 'The ultimate touchstone of constitutionality is the Constitution itself and not what we [i.e., judges] have said about it'.[30]

But returning to abortion being elevated to a 'fundamental right'. From 1995 to 2000 anti-partial-birth abortion laws had been successfully enacted in no less than 30 American States, often by overwhelming margins. In *Stenberg v Carhart* (2000), the court held that none of such laws was valid simply because they 'criminalised' partial-birth abortion and such a criminalisation apparently amounted to violating the due-process clause as per *Roe v. Wade* and *Planned Parenthood v. Case*. Hence, Justice Breyer dictated that the court could not tolerate any law which banned partial-birth abortion, with that being so for two basic reasons: 'First, the law lacks any exception for the preservation of the...health of the mother. Second, it imposes undue burden on a woman's ability to choose'.[31] For those who are unaware of what the court had just elevated to the status of constitutional right, 'partial-birth' abortion is a gruesome procedure designed to kill a viable baby as old as nine months of gestation. It is done by the sucking out of the baby's brain soon before her birth is completed. The procedure has been described as this: 'The unborn child is turned around in the womb so that it is born feet first. Before

---

[29] *Helvering v. Hallock*, 309 U.S. 106, 119 (1940).
[30] *Graves v O'Keefe*, 306 U.S. 466 (1938), at 491-92 (concurring opinion).
[31] *Stenberg v Carhart*, 530 U.S. 914 (2000), at 930.

being completely extruded, the baby is killed so that it is not "born alive". The abortionist pierces the baby's skull and suctions out its brains, an agonising death'.[32] As can be seen, Justice Thomas was quite right when, in his dissent, he stated:

> For reading the majority's sanitized description, one would think that this case involves state regulation of widely accepted routine medical procedure. Nothing could be further from the truth. The most widely used method of abortion during this stage of pregnancy is so gruesome that its use can be traumatic even for the physicians and medical staff who perform it.[33]

- **Religious Freedom**

Let's also talk about the protection of religious freedom in the context of bills of rights. There are countless examples of the American Founding Fathers pointing to their faith as the cornerstone for their new nation and its constitutional framework. It is against this background that the opening sentence of the First Amendment to the Constitution must be interpreted: 'Congress shall make no law respecting an establishment of religion or prohibiting the free exercise thereof'. Plainly and obviously, the First Amendment explicitly prohibits the establishment of a federal church. Rather, such a provision guarantees the free exercise of religion. This is undoubtedly the most well-known and debated amendment in the American Bill of Rights.

The First Amendment combines five civil liberties so as to condense the various proposals from the state-ratifying conventions. These liberties are designed to limit the power of the central government. The first liberty protected by this amendment has received particular attention: 'Congress shall make no law respecting an establishment of religion, or prohibiting the free exercise thereof'. As can be seen, the provision limits only the federal legislature (i.e., Congress) so that the individual states were fully exempt, and they could, if

---

[32] Charles Francis, 'US Supreme Court Bans Partial-Birth Abortion', Newsweekly, 26 May 2007, at http://www.newsweekly.com.au/articles/2007may26_a.html
[33] *Stenberg v Carhart*, 530 U.S. 914 (2000) (Thomas J, dissenting).

their individual legislatures so desired, create laws establishing any official church.

The purpose of the First Amendment is to prevent the establishment of a national 'Church of the United States'. Further, its purpose is not to establish freedom *from* religion, but to create freedom *for* religion. And yet, this provision has sometimes been identified as evidence that the United States Constitution should be regarded as entirely 'secular' in nature. Since the 1990s the Supreme Court decisions have often been based on a 'neutrality principle'. According to Professor Moens, such a principle assumes that 'only a state that views itself as a "homestead for all citizens" without committing itself to... contents of [any] one religion or creed can ensure freedom for each individual citizen'.[34] As Moens points out,

> The Supreme Court first announced the neutrality principle as such in *Rosenberber v. Rector & Visitors of the University of Virginia* [515 U.S. 819 (1995)]. In *Rosenberger*, the University of Virginia (University), a state instrumentality, authorized payments from its Student Activities Fund (SAF) to outside contractors to cover the printing costs of a variety of publications issues by student groups. However, the University withheld authorization for payments to a printer for Rosenberger, of Wide Awake Productions (WAP), on the ground that, contrary to SAF guidelines, the journal had religious editorial content. In a 5-4 decision, the Supreme Court held that this action represented view point discrimination because it required University officials to scan and interpret student publications to ascertain their underlying philosophic assumption respecting religious theory and belief.[35]

Professor Moens reminds us that the rationale behind these controversial judicial rulings 'inherently trivialize' religion because they largely result in 'the removal of religious influences from American society'. Because the application of such a principle requires every

---

[34] Gabriël A. Moens, 'The Menace of Neutrality in Religion' (2004) 12 *Brigham Young University* 535, at 567.
[35] Ibid., at 544.

government to be absolutely free from religion (rather than religion to be free from government interference),[36] this inevitably leads to the degradation of religion even 'to the point of making it irrelevant'. Professor Moens concludes:

> Although, arguably, the use of the neutrality principle was developed to safeguard religious liberty, it has instead resulted in a failure to protect religion. Therefore, the Supreme Court's jurisprudence has the unfortunate consequence of facilitating the emergence of a culture of disbelief, making it difficult, if not impossible, to talk about religion in the legal context, or to talk about religion at all. Use of the neutrality principle has treated religion and religious belief as less important facets of the human personality. The recent focus on neutrality in issues between church and state, and likewise the trivialization of citizens' religious beliefs, moves counter to the philosophies upon which the United States was founded. In attempting to protect government from religion, only the latter has remained powerful in any degree.[37]

Based on a line of cases resting on the 'neutrality principle' the courts have undermined religious freedom and, ultimately, their country's long-standing religious practices and expressions. By imputing a non-historic meaning to the phrase 'establishment of religion', these unelected lawyers have, among other things, banned the centuries-old tradition of having invocations at school commencement ceremonies;[38] declared unconstitutional for the Ten Commandments to be displayed in a solitary setting at public courthouse and government buildings (despite the fact that the Ten Commandments are depicted in multiple locations throughout the U.S. Supreme Court);[39] declared unconstitutional for a nativity scene to be displayed on public property (unless surrounded by sufficient secular displays to prevent it from

---

[36] Ibid., at 567.
[37] Ibid, at 567-68.
[38] *Lee v Weisman* 505 U.S. 577 (1992).
[39] *ACLU of Tennessee v. Hamilton County*, 202 F. Supp. 2d 757 (E.D Tenn.2002); *Glassroth v. Moore*, 335 F.3d 1282 (11th Cir.2003); *Adland v. Russ*, 307 F.3d 471 (6th Cir. 2003); *ACLU of Ohio v. Ashbrook*, 375 F.3d 484 (6th Cir. 2004).

appearing religious);[40] and even declared unconstitutional for a city seal to depict any religious element, even if religion was the primary influence in the city's founding.[41]

- **Human Rights Legislation May Undermine Democracy**

The delicate balance of power between the judiciary and the legislature that is basic to a functioning democracy has been upset in many countries of the common law by human-right legislations. Indeed, the legal philosopher Jeremy Waldron believes that judicial enforcement of a bill of rights is utterly inconsistent with the ability of ordinary citizens to influence decisions through democratic political processes. Waldron says,

> If we are going to defend the idea of an entrenched Bill of Rights put effectively beyond revision by anyone other than the judges, we should...think [that]...even if you...orchestrate the support of a large number of like-minded men and women and manage to prevail in the legislature, your measure may be challenged and struck down because your view of what rights we have does not accord with the judges' views.[42]

A federal charter of rights would require Australian judges to decide questions of policy which in a democracy should be decided by the Parliament. Since this would empower the federal courts to give a final decision on important matters of social policy, these judges would be appointed not so much for their legal ability as for their political and ideological affiliations. There would be 'a great temptation to appoint judges whose views on those questions of policy are views of

---

[40] *Doe v. Santa Fe Independent School District*, No. G-95-176 (S.D. Tex. May 5, 1995); *Rubin v. City of Burbank*, 124 Cal. Rptr. 2d 869 (Cal. Ct. App. 2002); *Wyne V. Town of Great Falls*, 376 F.3d 292 (4th Cir. 2004); *Turner v. City Council*, No. 306-CV-23 (E.D. Va Aug 3, 2006).

[41] *Robinson v. City of Edmond*, 68 F.3d 1226 (10th Cir. 1995); *ACLU of Ohio v. City of Stow*, 29 F. Supp. 2d 845 (N.D. Ohio 1998); *Webb v. City of Republic*, 55 F. Supp. 2d 994 (W.D. Mo. 1999).

[42] Jeremy Waldron, 'A Rights-Based Critique of Constitutional Rights', (1993) *13 Oxford Journal of Legal Studies 18*, at 50-51.

which the executive government approves'.⁴³ According to Gibbs, 'the circumstances surrounding some judicial appointments in the United States show that it has often been impossible to resist this temptation. Thus one of the essentials of a free society -- an independent judiciary -- tends to be weakened when the judges are given what virtually amounts to political power'.⁴⁴

Naturally, the supporters of a federal charter of rights may argue that as it is enacted by a government elected by a majority of voters this makes any judicial invalidation of statutes democratic. However the establishment of what might in effect become a judicial dictatorship, even if done by democratic means, effectively weakens democracy and the rule of law. As Waldron points out, a bill of rights amounts to 'voting democracy out of existence, at least so far as a wide range of issues of political principles is concerned.' ⁴⁵ As noted by Professor Jeffrey Goldsworthy, '[g]enuine and lasting respect for one another's rights cannot be imposed by judicial fiat; it can only emerge from the dialogue and compromise that characterise politics in a democracy'. ⁴⁶ And yet, bills of rights have precisely such deleterious effect to undermine democracy, thus transferring decision making to an unelected judicial elite and particularly where there is no moral-political consensus or agreement across society. As noted by Professor James Allan,

> What a bill of rights does is to take contentious political issues – … issues over which there is reasonable disagreement between reasonable people – and it turns them into pseudo-legal issues which have to be treated as though there were eternal, timeless right answers. Even where the top judges break 5-4 or 4-3 on these issues, the judges' majority view is treated as the view that is inaccord with fundamental fundamental rights. The effect, as can easily be observed from glancing at the United States,

---

⁴³ Sir Harry Gibbs, 'Does Australia Need a Bill of Rights?', Samuel Griffith Society, Vol.6, 1995, at: http://www.samuelgriffith.org.au/papers/
⁴⁴ Idem.
⁴⁵ Waldron, above n.42, at 46.
⁴⁶ Jeffrey Goldsworthy, 'Losing Faith in Democracy: Why Judicial Supremacy is Rising and What to Do about It', *Quadrant Magazine*, May 2015, p 14.

Canada and now New Zealand and the United Kingdom, is to diminish the politics (over time) to politicize the judiciary.[47]

It is impossible to not see the irony that all such a decision-making simply reduces the size of the franchise. The decision-making rule in the top courts is simply that 5 votes beat 4. What such a process does when it comes to apply abstract declarations is to simply reduce the size of the franchise, thus affording a small committee of lawyers the ultimate power to decide on controversial moral-political issues via the invalidation or strike down of legislation. Of course, there might be a certain distrust of the elites in the capacity of their fellow citizens to make 'proper' decisions. Commenting on this problem, Goldsworthy concludes:

> My impression is that in countries such as Britain, Canada, Australia and New Zealand, a substantial proportion of the tertiary-educated, professional class has lost faith in the ability of their fellow citizens to form opinions about public policy in a sufficiently intelligent, well-informed, dispassionate and carefully reasoned manner. They may be attracted to the judicial enforcement of rights partly because it shifts power to people (judges) who are representative members of their own class, and whose educational attainments, intelligence, habits of thought and professional ethos are thought more likely to produce 'enlightened' decisions.[48]

Take for instance the ruling in *Obergefell v Hodges* ('*Obergefell*'),[49] which is undoubtedly one of the most controversial decisions ever made by the U.S. Supreme Court in all its history. The basic premise of the majority in *Obergefell* is that the right to personal choice is inherent to the concept of individual liberty.[50] Ironically, however, the majority also acknowledged that 'the Constitution contemplates that democracy is the appropriate process for change, so long as

---

[47] James Allan, 'Why Australia Does Not Have, and Does Not Need, a National Bill of Rights' (2012) 24 *Journal of Constitutional History* 35, at 40.
[48] Goldsworthy, above n.45, p 12.
[49] 566 US _ (2015).
[50] 566 US _ (2015) 13 (majority opinion).

that process does not abridge fundamental rights'.⁵¹ And yet, the court ignored what it had properly recognised and it went on to postulate that fundamental rights actually evolve as they apparently 'come not from ancient sources alone. They rise, too, from a better informed understanding of how constitutional imperatives define a liberty that remains urgent in our era'.⁵² Based on this postulation the majority candidly concluded that same-sex couples are harmed for not being allowed to marry. They need not await for popular volte or parliamentary deliberation before asserting what, in the view of the court, constitutes a fundamental right.⁵³

As can be seen, the court held in *Obergefell* that same-sex couples cannot be denied the benefits afforded to opposite-sex couples because they may not be deprived of a 'fundamental right' that is inherent to the liberty of the person under the Due Process and Equal Protection Clauses of the Fourteenth Amendment.⁵⁴ Although the 'liberty' under the Due Process Clause should be understood to protect only those rights that are 'deeply rooted in this Nation's history and tradition',⁵⁵ in *Obergefell* the majority felt entitled to redefine 'outdated' notions of liberty. In his dissent Chief Roberts convincingly asserted that '[t]he majority's decision is an act of will, not legal judgement. The right it announces has no basis in the Constitution or this Court's precedent'.⁵⁶ Since this approach offers no objective standard for the expanded latitude of how rights might 'evolve', once it is well-ingrained the swings of the ideological pendulum must allow

---

⁵¹ Ibid 24 (majority opinion).
⁵² Ibid 18-19 (majority opinion).
⁵³ See, Ibid 24 (majority opinion).
⁵⁴ Ibid 22 (majority opinion).
⁵⁵ *Obergefell v Hodges,* 566 US _ (2015) 2 (Alito J, dissenting). See also, Roberts CJ, dissenting (at 22): 'The purpose of insisting that implied fundamental rights have roots in the history and tradition of our people is to ensure that when unelected judges strike down democratically enacted laws, they do so based on something more than their own beliefs. The Court today not only overlooks out country's entire history and tradition but actively repudiates it ... [T]o blind yourself to history is both prideful and unwise'.
⁵⁶ Ibid 3 (Roberts CJ, dissenting).

the judicial elite an opportunity to go in any direction according to personal predilections.[57] By arguing that their special training in the law somehow deems them worthy of expanding the interpretation of 'rights' found to be directly derived from, or at least indirectly implied in, the U.S. Constitution, Emeritus Professor William Wagner observed:

> [J]udges gaze into jurisprudential penumbras to subjectively fashion fundamental liberty interests they personally believe require judicial protection from politically accountable expressions of the people's will (eg, the right to contraception, abortion, etc). Proponents of this approach opine that unelected judges are entitled to personally evaluate whether evolving societal customs justify the judge deeming an interest implicit in the concept of ordered liberty. When the judge concludes in the affirmative, the judge judicially anoints the interest with 'fundamental' status.[58]

Naturally, the unrepresentative character of the court would be irrelevant if judges were simply deciding according to the law. Interpreting the law is the beginning and end of judicial function. In a constitutional democracy the courts are forbidden to strike down laws unless they are clearly invalid on constitutional grounds. The courts do not control the legislature when judges interpret legislation. The term 'judicial control' is misleading for it implies that unelected judges can somehow exert discretionary power over the elected members of legislature. And yet, judges have no such power; rather, all they have to do is to discover from the enactments before them what the lawmaker intends to convey. Of course, the more general and abstract the language of the law, the more difficult the task of interpretation and so much greater the need for ability and integrity in the judges.

---

[57] Thomas Sowell, *Intellectuals and Society* (New York/NY: Basic Books, 2009), p 167.
[58] William Wagner, 'The Jurisprudential Battle over the Character of a Nation: Understanding the Emerging Threats to Unalienable Liberty in America', in Suri Ratnapala and Gabriël A Moens, *Jurisprudence of Liberty* (LexisNexis, 2nd ed, 2011), p 305.

- **Human Rights Legislation may undermine the doctrine of Separation of Powers**

Charters of Rights lead to the politicisation of the judiciary. As the generalities expressed in rights documents must be applied to particular real life situations and as rights frequently conflict with each other, there is need for judicial interpretation. After all, says Professor Mirko Bagaric, 'rights documents are always vague, aspirational creatures and give no guidance on what interests rank the highest. This leaves plenty of scope for wonky judicial interpretation.'[59]

The way judges 'interpret' these legal rights is strongly influenced by the current political environment and their own ethical values. Given that both these factors are outside their legal area of expertise, there is no good reason why a few judges should be allowed to determine for the entire community the whole hierarchy of rights and interests. For example, explains John Gava, 'judges do not have the training or skills to engage in wider debates about social or economic policy and the courts are not appropriate institutions to carry out and evaluate the research needed for such a role'.[60]

Naturally, there is an obvious potential here for a partisan administration of justice. In practice, as far as charters of rights are concerned, this potential has become fact with the supposed neutrality and moderation of judges proving illusory. Professor Moens writes,

> The possibility of attributing different meanings to provisions of bills of rights creates the potential for judges to read their own biases and philosophies into such a document, especially if the relevant precedents are themselves mutually inconsistent. Indeed, in most rights issues, the relevant decisions overseas are contradictory. For example, rulings on affirmative action, pornography, 'hate speech', homosexual sodomy, abortion, and withdrawal of life support treatment vary remarkably. These rulings indicate that the judges, when interpreting a

---

[59] Mirko Bagaric, 'Your Right to reject the Bill of Rights', *The Herald Sun*, Melbourne, November 8, 2005, p 19.

[60] John Gava, 'We Can't Trust Judges Not To Impose Their Own Ideology', *The Australian*, December 29, 2008.

paramount bill of rights, are able to select quite arbitrarily their preferred authorities... Since a bill of rights will often consist of ambiguous provisions, judges can deliberately and cynically attribute meanings to it which are different to the intentions of those who approved the bill...in Australia's case the electorate.[61]

The partisan interpretation of laws, as well as creating flawed court decisions, has the power to change pre-existing legislation to conform to these judicial rulings. This creates an unstable juridical environment, as even long-standing laws may be amended or even overruled. Professor Jeffrey Goldsworthy states:

> The traditional function of the judiciary ... does not sit altogether comfortably with the enforcement of a bill of rights. In effect, it confers on judges a power to veto legislation retrospectively on the basis of judgements of political morality. ... This involves adding to the judicial function, a kind of power traditionally associated with the legislative function, except that the unpredictability inherent in its exercise is exacerbated by its retrospective nature. That is why, on balance, it may diminish rather than enhance the rule of law.[62]

This danger has been anticipated by those who framed recent bills of rights. For example the *United Kingdom Human Rights Act 1998* allows judges to declare any previously passed legislation incompatible with the act, but not to invalidate it. Parliament must decide whether the legislation must be amended or repealed. However in practice, this well intentioned provision has proved ineffective as the Human Rights Act still has primacy and its principal interpreters are still the judiciary. The result is a shift of political power from the elected legislature to the non-elected judiciary.

The *Canadian Charter of Rights and Freedoms* is regarded as a model by most human-rights activists in Australia. However, the

---

[61] Moens, above n.1, p 236.
[62] Jeffrey Goldsworthy, 'Legislative Sovereignty and the Rule of Law', in T. Campbell, K.D. Ewing and A. Tomkins (eds.), *Sceptical Essays on Human Rights* (Oxford: Oxford University Press, 2001), at 75.

Canadian Supreme Court has found in its 'abstract' provisions 'legal' grounds to invalidate all laws against the killing of babies in utero. The court has also used the Charter to protect tobacco advertising, extend the franchise to all prisoners, make it harder to freeze judges' pay than that of other civil servants and to rewrite the marriage laws to include homosexuals. They have clearly read their own ideology into it and are now major political players. The clause in the Charter that allows judicial review of legislation if reasonable limits can be justified in a free and democratic society has proved ineffective in curbing judicial activism. As Professor Moens correctly explains:

> Since the criteria means essentially nothing in a legal sense, judges are effectively commanded by the instrument itself to give rein to their own moral sensibilities over legal criteria in deciding the validity of legislation. In such circumstances, it is not surprising in Canada the individual social and political beliefs of the judges are considered more important than the Constitution itself.[63]

In the United States, after striking out state laws against abortion, in 1992 in *Planned Parenthood vs. Casey*, the US Supreme Court stated that abortion had become a right to liberty, thus effectively giving all parents the right to murder unborn babies. Thus whether unborn babies live or die depends on the moral views of their parents.

The Supreme Court, having effectively decreed that the question of whether unborn babies lived or died was without absolute ethical significance, proceeded to deny the legal validity of any belief based on a transcendent ethic. In his majority vote Justice Kennedy defined liberty as 'the right to define one's own conceptions of existence, of meaning, of the universe, and of the mystery of life'.

In doing this Justice Kennedy rejected the idea that there is a God who requires certain standards of ethical behaviour. Law Professor Gerard Bradley commented that this is akin to establishing a 'new covenant' for the American people: 'We will be your court and you

---

[63] Moens, above n.1, p 236.

will be our people.' [64] Thus the judges and the people have obtained a right to decide for themselves what is right and wrong, providing they accept that there is no higher authority 'in heaven and on earth' than the U.S. Supreme Court.

After many controversial restrictions on the free exercise of religion by the Supreme Court, the *Religious Freedom Restoration Act 1993*, which aimed to re-establish a strict standard for protecting religious freedom and exercise, was passed unanimously by the House of Representatives, having only three dissenting votes in the Senate and was enthusiastically signed by then President Clinton. If ever a piece of legislation reflected the will of the people, this did. And yet, on June 25, 1997, in *City of Bourne vs. Flores* the court invalidated this act by considering this legislation 'majoritarian intolerance'. The Supreme Court simply denied Congress any role in offering an interpretation of the entrenched right of religious liberty that differs from the Court's interpretation.

• Human Rights Legislation may undermine the Rule of Law

The ideal of the rule of law stands in clear opposition to extemporary decisions expressing the arbitrary will of judges. Indeed, it has been suggested that the rule of law means more than the existence of clear, stable, general norms, which must apply equally to everyone regardless of social status or position. Characterised in this way, the rule of law cannot be fully developed if judges are not entirely respectful of legal rules. As the Italian political philosopher, Pasquale Pasquino, points out:

> [T]he person who judges exercises, in a sense, the most worrying power of all. In daily life it is not the legislator who renders judgement or passes sentence, but the judge... The judge protects the citizen from the caprices and arbitrary will of the legislator, just as the existence of the law protects the accused from the caprices and arbitrary will of the judge.[65]

---

[64] Quoted from Charles Colson and Nancy Pearcy, *How Now Shall We Live?* (Wheaton/IL: Tyndale House, 1999), p 409.

[65] Pasquale Pasquino, *One and Three: Separation of Powers and the Independence of the Judiciary in the Italian Constitution*, in J. Ferejohn, J.N. Rakove and J. Riley

'Unless corruption or ineptitude pervades the judiciary', argues the U.S. legal philosopher, Brian Tamanaha, 'the rogue judge will be checked by... other judges, either sitting on the same panel or at high levels of appellate review'.[66] Thus judges need to understand that nobody, not even a judge from a higher court, can ignore the law. In fact, judges who abuse their position to satisfy some personal interest cannot possibly be described as equitable upholders of the legal system. As former Australia's Chief Justice Murray Gleeson explains:

> Judges are appointed to interpret and apply the values inherent in the law. Within the limits of the legal method, they may disagree about those values. But they have no right to throw off the constraints of legal methodology. In particular, they have no right to base their decisions about the validity of legislation upon their personal approval or disapproval of the policy of the legislation. When they do so, they forfeit their legitimacy.[67]

In this sense, the power of judges to 'create' the law is not to be exercised in absolute dissonance with the existing legal rules and principles. Since judges are bound to administer justice *according to law*, including legislation of which they may disapprove, writes the English constitutionalist, Trevor Allan, '[they] must faithfully accord every Act of Parliament its full and proper application'.[68] This means that, to become an institutional support for the realisation of the rule of law, judges must be non-partisan in the political process.

Naturally, one can accept that judges may sometimes need, for reasons of ambiguity, vagueness, inconsistency, or 'gap', to complement the legal system with innovative judicial rulings. But it does not follow from this that they are authorised to ignore the positive

---

(eds.), *Constitutional Culture and Democratic Rule* (Cambridge/UK: Cambridge University Press, 2001), p 211.

[66] Brian Tamanaha, *On the Rule of Law: History, Politics, Theory* (Cambridge/UK: Cambridge University Press, 2000), p 88.

[67] Murray Gleeson, *The Rule of Law and the Constitution - 2000 Boyer Lectures* (Sydney: ABC Books, 2000), p 134.

[68] T.R.S. Allan, 'Legislative Supremacy and the Rule of Law' (1985) 44(1) *Cambridge Law Journal* 111, at 130.

law just because they may not approve its provisions. The case against such anti-legal attitude was placed in classical terms by the late Thomas M. Cooley, a celebrated U.S. constitutional law professor,

> The property or justice or policy of legislation, within the limits of the Constitution, is exclusively for the legislative department to determine; and the moment a court ventures to substitute its own judgement for that of the legislature, it passes beyond its legitimate authority, and enters a field where it would be impossible to set limits to its interference, except as should be prescribed in its own discretion.[69]

It is a breach of duty and a violation of the rule of law for judges to express their personal opinion on the merits of policy except so far as this policy does explicitly violate the written constitution. Judges may deem a specific policy pernicious to society but, if there is no sound constitutional provision preventing the elected legislature from upholding a different opinion, the courts must enforce the law accordingly. And if it be suggested that members of the judicial branch 'may overstep their duty, and may, seeking to make themselves not the exponents but the masters of the Constitution, twist and pervert it to suit their own political views', as Lord Bryce famously stated, 'the answer is that such an exercise of judicial will would rouse the distrust and displeasure of the nation, and might, if persisted in, provoke resistance to the law as laid down by the court, possibly an onslaught upon the court itself'.[70]

In this sense, advocates of the rule of law often connect this ideal of legality with a classical liberal tradition which declares the priority of the individual over the state.[71] According to the late Harvard political-science professor, the celebrated Samuel Huntington, 'it was this liberal tradition that 'laid the basis for constitutionalism and the

---

[69] Thomas Cooley, *Principles of Constitutional Law* (Boston/MA: Little, Brown & Cia, 1898), p 158.

[70] James Bryce, *The American Commonwealth* [1888] (Indianapolis/IN: Liberty Fund, 1995), p 225.

[71] Allan C. Hutchinson and Patrick Monahan, 'Democracy and the Rule of Law', in Allan C. Hutchinson and P. Monahan (eds.), *The Rule of Law: Ideal or Ideology?* (Toronto: Carswell, 1987), p 99.

protection of human rights against the exercise of arbitrary power'.[72] That so being, the rule of law is hailed as the bedrock of every constitutional government, and hence of personal freedom.[73] Because it can be interpreted in the light of 'a liberal scheme of constitutional governance', the power of the state must be subordinated to enduring (constitutional) principles that no government or public authority is authorised to abrogate.[74]

Precisely for this reason proponents of a bill of rights often assume that a judicially enforceable bill of rights might be essential for the realisation of the rule of law. But this is entirely debatable since the 'interpretation' of such abstract provisions can become indistinguishable from the moral and ideological tendencies of individual judges. As noted by Professor Moens, the experience with judicially enforceable bills of rights reveals that the premise of judicial 'neutrality' and 'moderation' is actually illusory. Instead, as Moens points out:

> The possibility of attributing different meanings to the provisions of bill of rights creates the potential for judges to read their own biases and philosophies into such a document, especially if the relevant precedents are themselves mutually inconsistent. Indeed, in most rights issues, the relevant decisions overseas are contradictory. For example, rulings on affirmative action, pornography, hate speech, homosexual sodomy, abortion, and withdrawal of life support treatment vary remarkably. These rulings indicate that judges, when interpreting a paramount bill of rights, are able to select quite arbitrarily their preferred authorities...[75]

Finally, another difficulty is that any federal charter of rights would allow existing laws to be challenged encouraging speculative

---

[72] Samuel P. Huntington, *The Clash of Civilizations and the Remaking of World Order* (New York/NY: Simon & Schuster, 1996), p 70.

[73] Suri Ratnapala, 'Securing Constitutional Government: The Perpetual Challenge', *The Independent Review*, Vol.VIII, No.1, Summer 2003, p.9.

[74] Hutchinson, above n.71, p 100. See also: Suri Ratnapala, *The Other Road to the Republic. Australia: Republic or Monarchy?*', *in* M.A. Stephenson and C. Turner (eds.), *Republic or Monarchy? Legal and Constitutional Issues* (St Lucia/QLD: University of Queensland Press, 1994), p 215.

[75] Moens, above n.1, p 236.

and frivolous legal actions. Previous legislation enacted by the democratic process generally speaking needs majority support in the community. However, human-rights legislation gives minority groups an unprecedented opportunity to impose their will on the majority. Professor Moens writes:

> those who favour a bill of rights may delight in the vagueness of these documents, for they sometimes assume that its very ambiguity will enable them to achieve through judicial decision, what they have been unable to achieve though Parliament.' This has clearly happened in Canada where 'litigious floodgates have been opened and courts have been strained by the overload.[76]

- **Human Rights Legislation May Undermine Federalism**

Professor Moens reminds us in his excellent article that '[i]t is important not to underestimate the protection of rights that is offered by the functioning of a healthy federal system'.[77] As Professor Moens correctly explains: 'A federal structure which provides for the dispersal of power among the many States significantly lessens the likelihood that there will be arbitrary government across the country. If there are infringements of individual liberty by the States, the division of powers as exists in the Australian constitutional system will tend to isolate them'.[78]

However, as Professor Moens also explains, in the act of interpreting the abstract provisions of a constitutionally entrenched bill of rights, the High Court of Australia would be able to impose uniformity and coast-to-coast dispositions on the most important areas of law, thus allowing the Court to make the right to life, or to freedom of religion or association, or to be secure against unreasonable searches, to mean exactly the same thing in every state.

According to Professor James Allan, 'a bill of rights will fall ultimately to be interpreted by the High Court, by Commonwealth

---

[76] Ibid., p 238.
[77] Moens, above n.1, p.248.
[78] Ibid., p 249.

appointed judges. So such... instruments will increase the power of centrally appointed judges, which can be thought of as a sort of centralising effect'.[79] So in that sense a federal bill of rights may engender a sort of centralising effect that could further erode the country's federal system. As Sir Harry Gibbs pointed out:

> Under the Constitution, any State legislation which was inconsistent with a Commonwealth bill of rights would be inoperative. A Commonwealth bill of rights would be likely to have the effect of imposing extensive restrictions on the exercise of State rights and powers. However much inconvenience or damage might be shown to result, a State could not remedy the situation. We have already seen how State legislation, which would have extinguished the native title successfully claimed by the plaintiffs in Mabo v. Queensland (No.2)19 was held by a majority of 4 to 3, to be inconsistent with the Racial Discrimination Act.20 If the Commonwealth Parliament enacted a bill of rights in the wide terms of some of the existing drafts, the effect on the States would be serious indeed.[80]

Here one could also evoke *Obergefell v Hodges*, the case where the U.S. Supreme Court decided that same-sex marriage was a 'fundamental right' to be protected by the Constitution. The court in *Obergefell* not only put a stop to the democracy by removing an important issue from the realm of political deliberation, but it held that their nation's federal constitution should 'evolve' in a way that is supported by neither the document's language and spirit. One of the most disturbing aspects of that ruling is its dramatic impact on the federal nature of the constitution. Federalism emphasises a decentralising principle that stimulates a 'participatory structure of government,'[81] buttressing individual liberty and eschewing political

---

[79] James Allan, 'Bills of Rights as Centralising Instruments', Samuel Griffith Society, Vol.18, 2006, at: http://www.samuelgriffith.org.au/papers/

[80] Sir Harry Gibbs, 'Does Australia Need a Bill of Rights?', Proceedings of the Sixth Conference of the Samuel Griffith Society (17-19 November 1995, Melbourne, Victoria), Vol. 6, Chapter 7, at: http://www.samuelgriffith.org.au/papers/

[81] Augusto Zimmermann, 'Subsidiarity, Democracy and Individual Liberty in Brazil', in M Evans and A Zimmermann (eds), *Global Perspectives on Subsidiarity* (Springer Netherland, 2014) 85, 88.

elitism. According to Robert Bork, federalism is an important protector of fundamental rights because,

> if another state allows the liberty you value, you can move there, and the choice of what freedom you value is yours alone, not dependent on those who made the Constitution. In this sense, federalism is the constitutional guarantee most protective of the individual's freedom to make his own choices.[82]

In drafting the American *Constitution* its framers sought to maintain a balance in the distribution of powers between the states and federal government. They designed the *Constitution* to be an instrument of government intended to distribute and limit governmental powers. By dividing political power, fundamental rights are protected through, as James Madison described, a 'double security':

> In the compound republic of America, the power surrendered by the people is first divided between two distinct governments, and then the portion allotted to each [is] subdivided among distinct and separate departments. Hence a double security arises to the rights of the people. The different governments will control each other, at the same time that each will be controlled by itself'.[83]

One of the basic characteristics of the American *Constitution* is its express limitation on federal powers. Under the Tenth Amendment to the *US Constitution*, any powers that are not the exclusive powers of the federal government, or that are not specifically denied to state governments by the *Constitution*, are the powers of the states, or of the people. Some examples of state powers include passing laws concerning marriage, divorce, contract and inheritances. Accordingly, the drafters intended to provide the states with reserved powers of local self-government, which they specifically insisted would continue under the *Constitution*, subject only to the carefully defined and limited powers specifically conferred upon the federal government. 'State reserved powers' thus ensure that the legislative powers of the states

---

[82] Robert Bork, *The Tempting of America: The Political Seduction of the Law* (New York/NY: Touchstone, 1990), p 53.

[83] James Madison, *Federalist Paper No 51* (6 February 1788).

must not be undermined by an expansive reading of federal powers. The doctrine protects the powers belonging to the states when the constitution was formed - powers which, as Thomas Cooley reminded, 'have not by that instrument been granted to the Federal government, or prohibited to the States'.[84]

The judicial act of arbitrarily creating a 'fundamental right' to same-sex marriage, via an activist interpretation of the U.S. Bill of Rights, dramatically increases the power of centrally appointed federal judges.[85] As a result, the court arbitrarily imposed federal uniformity and coast-to-coast dispositions on an important area of law that the drafters had actually reserved to the American States, thus making a legal issue to mean exactly the same thing in every jurisdiction in the United States. So, in this sense, the decision in *Obergefell* engenders a highly centralising effect that not only erodes the country's federal system but also increases social conflict and ideological polarisation. As Justice Alito dissenting points out:

> The system of federalism established by our Constitution provides a way for people with different beliefs to live together in a single nation. If the issue of same-sex marriage had been left to the people of the States, it is likely that some States would recognize same-sex marriage and others would not. It is also possible that some States would tie recognition to protection of conscience rights. The majority makes that impossible. By imposing its own views on the entire country, the majority facilitates the marginalization of the many Americans who have traditional ideas ... But if that sentiment prevails, the Nation will experience bitter and lasting wounds.[86]

Justice Alito is absolutely correct to declare in *Obergefell* that a slight majority of unelected, unaccountable lawyers have held that their nation's federal constitution should 'evolve' in a way that is supported by neither the document's language, nor its history or its authority.[87]

---

[84] Cooley, above n 69, pp 35-6.
[85] James Allan, 'Bills of Rights as Centralising Instruments', Samuel Griffith Society, Volume 18, 2006, at http://www.samuelgriffith.org.au/papers/
[86] *Obergefell v Hodges,* 566 US_ (2015) 7 (Alito J, dissenting).
[87] Curiously, Chief Justice Roberts explains how such an approach may lead to fur-

In short, they have simply imposed their own ideology on the expense of federalism and the democratic process. Justice Alito was also right to state that such an exercise of raw judicial power 'usurps the constitutional right of the people to decide whether to keep or alter the traditional understanding of marriage'. Above all, as he put it, it reveals 'the deep and perhaps irremediable corruption of [the American] legal culture's conception of constitutional interpretation'.[88]

- **Human Rights Legislation may lead to the false assumption that our basic rights are not God-given or 'inalienable', but rather State-given**

My final point is of particular relevance for those who profess to be Christian. For them, basic human rights should not be considered creations of Parliament but gifts of God. John Stott says: "We received them with our life from the hand of our Maker. They are inherent in our creation."[89] By contrast, the decline of Christianity in the West has been accompanied by a lowering of ethical standards with a consequent rise in criminal behaviour. This coupled with an increased emphasis on rights without balancing responsibilities is producing an ethical culture increasingly resistant to the respect and enforcement of our most basic individual rights to life, security and property. It is indeed very concerning that some Australian organisations pushing for more 'group rights' display little interest in the corresponding necessary individual responsibilities. Bill Muehlenberg comments:

> A Bill of Rights will certainly encourage people to demand

ther legalisation of polygamy: 'Although the majority randomly inserts the adjective "two" in various places, it offers no reason at all why the two-person element of the core definition of marriage may be preserved while the man-woman element may not. Indeed, from the standpoint of history and tradition, a leap from opposite-sex marriage is much greater than one from a two-person union to plural unions, which have deep roots in some cultures around the world. If the majority is willing to take the big leap, it is hard to see how it can say no to the shorter one': ibid 20 (Roberts CJ, dissenting).

[88] Ibid 8 (Alito J, dissenting).

[89] John Stott, *New Issues facing Christians today* (London: Harper-Collins, 1999), p 172.

rights, but will be unlikely to enjoin them to uphold obligation and responsibility. Indeed, rights claims can be used to cover almost anything, with a never-ending stream of new rights being discovered and demanded....Individual responsibility, virtue and self-control are the means by which a democracy flourishes and rights are respected.[90]

The whole common law system has been historically based on the premise which puts God, not the government, as the ultimate creator of every true right and liberty. And as our lives are a gift from God, we have no inherent right to dispose of it as we appraise but are accountable to God for all our personal choices and actions. Law Professor Gary T. Amos writes,

> Men have rights, such as the right to life. But because man has a duty to live his life for God, the right is alienable. He can defend his life against all others, but not destroy it himself. No man has the right to do harm to himself, to commit suicide or to waste his life. He has a property interest- dominium- in his own life, but not total control.[91]

In this sense, God is understood to have given us life and laws by which we should order our lives. These laws are more important than any legal right which ought not to be inconsistent with them. So when Courts deny the existence or relevance of these higher laws and by their enactments allow people to live in opposition to them, the fabric of society begins to unravel.

As mentioned above, the U.S. Supreme Court held in *Obergefell* that same-sex couples cannot be denied the benefits afforded to opposite-sex couples because they may not be deprived of a 'fundamental right' that is inherent to the liberty of the person under the Due Process and Equal Protection Clauses of the Fourteenth Amendment.[92] In his dissent Justice Alito reminds us that the majority has given to

---

[90] Muehlenberg, Bill, 'What is wrong with a Bill of Rights?' Newsweekly, Melbourne, August 13, 2005, at: http://www.newsweekly.com.au/articles/
[91] Gary T. Amos, *Defending the Declaration* (Brentwood: Wolemuth & Hyatt, 1989), p 109.
[92] Ibid 22 (majority opinion).

the Constitution a distinctively postmodern meaning. As Alito noted, '[t]he Constitution says nothing about a right to same-sex marriage, but the Court holds that the term "liberty" in the Due Process Clause of the Fourteenth Amendment encompasses this right.'[93] For this reason, according to the majority, any State law that denies same-sex couples this 'fundamental right' must be held invalid to the extent of excluding them from civil marriage on the same terms and conditions as opposite-sex couples.[94]

In his powerful dissent Chief Justice Roberts stated that '[w]hether same-sex marriage is a good idea should be of no concern to' his colleagues on the bench.[95] As the Chief Justice also pointed out, 'a State's decision to maintain the meaning of marriage that has persisted in every culture throughout human history' can hardly be considered a violation of fundamental right.[96] To declare same-sex couples to marry 'a fundamental right' is to claim to be have God-like power.

The American founding generation viewed rights as pre-existing the state. In the founding era, 'it was generally believed that rights were God-given, existing separate and apart from any human grant of power and authority'.[97] As Randy Barnett points out, '[n]atural or inherent rights were the rights persons have independent of those they are granted by government and by which the justice or property of governmental commands are to be judged'.[98] According to Professor Suzanna Sherry:

> Fundamental rights were God-given, and were rights 'which no creature can *give*, or hath a right to take away'. They were, in the language of the Declaration of Independence 'inalienable'.

---

[93] Ibid 2 (Alito J, dissenting).
[94] Ibid 23 (majority opinion).
[95] Ibid 2 (Roberts CJ, dissenting).
[96] Ibid 2 (Roberts CJ, dissenting).
[97] Lael Daniel Weinberger, 'Enforcing the Bill of Rights in the United States', in S Ratnapala and G A Moens, *Jurisprudence of Liberty* (LexisNexis, 2nd ed, 2011), p 105.
[98] Randy E Barnett, *Restoring the Lost Constitution* (Princeton University Press, 2004), p 54.

Legislators could no more rewrite these laws of nature than they could the laws of physics.[99]

Based on this principle, the enactment of a bill of rights was a matter of declaring rights already in existence. These God-given rights were deemed more important than any legal right which ought not to be inconsistent with them. Thomas Jefferson, the author of the United States *Declaration of Independence*, asked rhetorically: 'Can the liberties of a nation be secure when we have removed their only secure basis, a conviction in the minds of the people that these liberties are a gift of God?'[100]

By contrast, the artifice of the U.S. Supreme Court to create new 'fundamental rights', rather than enforcing the structural limits of the American Constitution, indicates that rights and liberties are not necessarily being protected. Indeed, when an unelected body of nine lawyers effectively becomes a 'god' unto itself, such court is enthroned as the all-powerful ruler over the life, liberty and property of the people, deciding which rights are fundamental and which are not. It is really the case of saying: 'The Supreme Court gives, the Supreme Court takes away; blessed be the name of the Supreme Court!'

- **Conclusion**

Professor Moens was the first academic to convince me that Australia should not enact a national bill of rights. This happened after I read his seminal article on the 'wrongs' of a constitutionally entrenched charter of rights for Australia. Human Rights legislation is utterly unnecessary in a constitutional democracy like Australia's and, when introduced, upsets the delicate balance of powers between the legislature and the judiciary by giving the latter far more power that it was supposed to receive according to democratic principles as well as the doctrine of separation of powers.

---

[99] Suzanna Sherry, 'The Founders' Unwritten Constitution' (1987) 54 *University of Chicago Law Review* 1127, at 1132.

[100] Quoted from Rousas John Rushdoony, *The Politics of Guilt and Pity* (Fairfax Thoburn Press, 1978), p 135.

Whereas it might be argued that in most legal systems a judicially enforceable bill of rights could improve human-rights protection, the basic question for nations like Australia is whether or not this would be desirable for that reason. As any bill of rights consists of abstract and flexible principles of political morality, the judicial 'interpretation' of such documents might eventually become indistinguishable from the moral and political philosophy of a few unelected judges. A judicially enforceable bill of rights is not an essential prerequisite for the protection of basic rights, because, as law professor Jeffrey Goldsworthy properly reminds us, such protection actually 'depends on the culture, social structure, and political organization in which each system operates'.[101]

Human rights legislation, being entirely abstract and general in nature, naturally needs some form of 'creative' interpretation. And yet, there is little legal guidance to assist in this process of abstract thinking and subjective deliberation. The outcome depends largely on the ethical views of a few unelected judges, thus providing a powerful mechanism by which a small legal elite can force its own values and beliefs on a reluctant majority of the people. That being so, human-rights legislation can upset the balance between the legislature and the judiciary, giving the latter too much power and even an arbitrary power to dictate the whole hierarchy of human rights and freedoms.

Being general in nature, human rights legislation needs more abstract or 'creative' interpretation, but there is little legal guidance to assist in this process. The outcome depends largely on the ethical and philosophical views of individual judges, thus providing an undemocratic mechanism by which a small judicial elite can force its own values on an uninterested or reluctant majority. When it comes to protecting the rights especially of the most vulnerable in our community, the result can be quite catastrophic. this could even compromise our delicate federal balance, affecting both our system of representative democracy and the rule of law, which are fundamental

---

[101] Jeffrey Goldsworthy, *The Sovereignty of Parliament: History and Philosophy* (Oxford/UK: Oxford University Press, 1999), p 279.

values which up until now have prevented the concentration of power in the hands of a few.

Furthermore, the modern emphasis on group rights at the expense of the 'inalienable' rights of the individual discriminates against non-favoured groups of individuals. It certainly diminishes the far more fundamental rights of the individual. In the community in general, such abstract provisions not just stimulates increased litigation and irresponsible/selfish behaviour, but it leads to the erroneous assumption that our basic rights are not inalienable but state-given; that is, that judges and politicians are the ultimate providers of our basic rights.

There is indeed no good reason as to why a country like Australia should ever enact a federal or constitutionally entrenched bill of rights. By contract, there is a very good reason to believe that such an enactment would very seriously compromise democracy, federalism and the rule of law in this country. This is what has occurred in countries such as Canada and the United States, where the constitutional framework has been seriously affected by the controversial actions of an unelected judicial elite.

5

The Spiritual Foundations of Section 51 (XXXI) of the Australian Constitution

A. Keith Thompson

- **Introduction**

When s 51(xxxi) of the Australian Constitution was framed, those attending the Australian constitutional conventions were alert to the issues of justice which prompted the U.S. Fifth Amendment in similar terms. But both times the Convention Debates canvassed the involuntary acquisition of private property by the federal government in Australia, the discussion was about how much power the new Commonwealth would need to do its limited business rather than about the social justice issues that were engaged.

Many commentators have concluded that the High Court's subsequent s 51(xxxi) jurisprudence is inconsistent and flawed, but to date no one has suggested that s 51(xxxi) might be applied in a principled way that fully respects the social justice issues to which it responded.

I do not expect to resolve that conundrum, but I believe that our understanding of s 51(xxxi) may be advanced by recognising that our social justice sensibilities are offended when just government compensation does not follow every Commonwealth interference with state and personal property rights. Most of us do not find Commonwealth taxation offensive or that it offends the limitation expressed in s 51(xxxi). Nor do most people consider that the forfeiture of the proceeds of crime offend this principle. But the acquisition or taking of private property by the Commonwealth without adequate compensation even when that acquisition is for a community purpose, has been offensive to human common sense since before the first version of Magna Carta was scripted.

My contribution to what I call 'a principled jurisprudence' of s 51(xxxi) in Australia, addresses some of the less satisfying High Court decisions in part by drawing upon Martin Krygier's ruminations on the Rule of Law. While I recognise that my choice of cases and rule of law standards will not satisfy all readers, I hope that any dissonance they experience will result in further examination and debate about the underlying ideas.

I have approached this task in four parts. In Part One, I trace part of the history of the idea that secular authority should not be able to appropriate or use the property of others without paying for that property or use. I trace that idea from Magna Carta to Australian federation in 1901. I acknowledge that this idea has older origins and that it is intertwined with both the philosophical idea of private property and the political idea of representation in democratic government. But I have not fully explored those intersections because my purpose is more limited. I want to suggest that if the idea of just terms and compensation are s 51 (xxxi)'s core premise, then a more detailed interrogation of what they meant at federation, may enable a more coherent jurisprudence of s 51(xxxi) in the future. In Part Two I therefore suggest what presents as unsatisfactory in s 51(xxxi) jurisprudence to date. For example, I ask why it is that the statutory abrogation of the right to sue for personal injury damages at common law should engage s 51(xxxi), when the abrogation of common law groundwater rights is not analogous if those rights had been pared back by statute in the past? In that discussion, I think I understand why the government can take away rights that it had previously given by statute. But because I do not understand why it should matter that someone receives a benefit if there is an acquisition according to vernacular understanding, I interrogate why our framers may have preferred the word 'acquisition' over 'taking' since there is no commentary on that word choice in material available to us from the Convention debates.

In Part Three, I suggest that the High Court's inconsistent s 51(xxxi) jurisprudence is also inconsistent with the Rule of Law to the extent that the Rule of Law does insist on the recompense or reimbursement of those that the Commonwealth has deprived of property according to the original ideas expressed in Magna Carta. In that discussion, I suggest following the lead of Martin Krygier, that the core ideal of the Rule of Law, is the elimination of arbitrariness and unpredictability, by any of the branches of government – executive, legislative or judicial.

In Part Four, I suggest that Australian governmental practice stands in need of improvement where s 51(xxxi) is concerned. I suggest that if the executive and legislative branches of the federal government were faithful to the ideal which is expressed in the s 51 (xxxi) guarantee, they would never take, acquire or otherwise deprive any person or entity in Australia of property without first budgeting to provide that other party with compensation that is just in every way. As stated above, I accept that taxation, forfeiture and other penalties do not offend this expression of the constitutional requirement since I believe the Australian framers did not intend that the Commonwealth's taxation and criminal enforcement powers be foreclosed by the s 51(xxxi) guarantee. But I argue that the framers intended that the power of judicial review which was afforded to the future federal courts, should abrogate the doctrine of parliamentary sovereignty when s 51(xxxi) was engaged. That is, the framers did not intend that the High Court should be at all subservient to the Parliament in s 51(xxxi) matters.

I therefore conclude with a challenge to the High Court. I challenge the members of that Court in the present and in the future, to interpret s 51(xxxi) in a manner that is fully consistent with the Rule of Law. To the extent that such an interpretation will require them to revisit the relationship between the executive, the legislature and the judiciary, I invite them to grasp that nettle. That challenge has implications for the High Court's jurisprudence concerning other sections of the Constitution including ss 81, 116 and Chapter III, but comment upon that jurisprudence is beyond the scope of this essay.

- **Part One – 'Just Terms Compensation' By Government – A Brief History**

While Lord Irvine of Lairg observed that only four chapters of the 1297 version of *Magna Carta* remain on the statute books,[1] and though he acknowledged that Sir Edward Coke had exaggerated the Great Charter's significance,[2] yet he affirmed both in the title to his paper delivered in the *Australian Parliament's* Great Hall in October 2002, and in the text of that address, that *Magna Carta* is "the foundation stone of the rule of law."[3] While it is doubtful that Stephen Langton intended to extend the protections of *Magna Carta* to the lowest classes despite the fact that modern readers are apt to think his term "free men" was universally inclusive, still *Magna Carta* "was no mere private bargain between King and barons";[4] it protected villein tenants from the abuses of their feudal lords[5] and insisted that central executive power "could no longer be employed simply in pursuit of the King's own private projects".[6] That power was supposed to be "exercised according to principle, custom and law."[7] *Magna Carta* also insisted that the trusts involved in wardship and marriage should not be exploited, and that royal punishments and fines were not to deprive the working classes of their tools of trade or livelihoods.[8] Lord Irvine summarised that *Magna Carta* "is a beacon of the rule of law" because it "proclaimed the fundamental nature of individual liberties" and access to justice.[9]

The genealogy of the Rule of Law ideas which undergird s 51(xxxi)

---

[1] 'The Legacy of Magna Carta: a Joint Commitment to the Rule of Law', Papers of the Australian Parliament No. 39, 2002, n 6 (<http://www.aph.gov.au/About_Parliament/>).
[2] Ibid, nn 1-4 and supporting text.
[3] Ibid 18.
[4] Ibid 6.
[5] Ibid.
[6] Ibid 7.
[7] Ibid 6.
[8] Ibid.
[9] Ibid 8-9.

may be seen in chapters 20-22, 28, 30-31, 39, 52 and 55 of the 1215 version of the Charter. Those same ideas remained in chapters 19, 21 and 29 of the 1225 version reissued by the guardians of the infant King Henry III.

Chapters 20-22 of the 1215 version emphasised the Rule of Law requirement that fines should only be imposed by objective and reputable men calculated to the gravity of the offence and in the case of clerics, without arbitrary reference to the value of the church property from which they received income. Chapter 39 of the 1215 version rewritten as chapter 29 of the 1225 version, famously affirmed:

> [n]o free man shall be seized or imprisoned, or stripped of his rights or possessions, or outlawed or exiled, or deprived of his standing in any way, nor will we proceed with force against him, or send others to do so, except by the lawful judgment of his equals or the law of the land.

The famous affirmation of due process before imprisonment that is implicit in this provision, often outshines the principle that a free man was not to be deprived of his rights or possessions without that same due process. But the depth of the protection of possessions guaranteed to free men in 1215 is not so easy to miss in chapters 28, 30 and 31 in that year. They state:

> 28. No constable or other royal official shall take corn or other movable goods from any man without immediate payment, unless the seller voluntarily offers postponement of this.
> 30. No sheriff, royal official, or other person shall take horses or carts for transport from any free man, without his consent.
> 31. Neither we nor any royal official will take wood for our castle, or for any other purpose, without the consent of the owner.

The Rule of Law guarantee of the sanctity of private property unmistakable in these chapters, was reiterated in chapters 52 and 55 of the 1215 version where the King promised that he would atone for past breaches of this principle by immediately restoring anything he or his officials had taken in breach of the sanctity of private property.

While that promise of retrospective government atonement backed up by a baronial oversight committee was omitted from later versions of the *Charter*, there was no dilution of the sanctity of private property at the core of the rule of the law. That principle was more fully spelled out in 1225 so that there could not be any misunderstanding:

> 19. No constable, nor his bailiff, shall take any corn or other goods of any one, who is not of that town where his castle is, without instantly paying money for them, unless he can obtain a respite from the free will of the seller; but if he be of that town wherein the castle is, he shall give him the price within forty days.
>
> 21. No sheriff nor bailiff of our's, nor of any other person, shall take the horses or carts of any, for the purpose of carriage, without paying according to the rate anciently appointed; that is to say, for a cart with two horses, tenpence by the day, and for a cart with three horses, fourteenpence by the day. No desmesne cart of any ecclesiastical person, or knight, or of any lord, shall be taken by the aforesaid bailiffs. Neither we, nor our bailiffs, nor those of another, shall take any man's wood, for our castles or for other uses, unless by consent of him to whom the wood belongs.

In his 2002 Canberra address, Lord Irvine also referenced Winston Churchill's broadcast to the United States at the end of the Second World War where he identified *Magna Carta*, the Bill of Rights, the writ of Habeas Corpus, trial by jury, and the English common law which found "their most famous expression in the American Declaration of Independence", as the repository of the "great principles of freedom and the rights of man which are the joint inheritance of the English-speaking world".[10]

But it was the American framers' capture of the *Magna Carta* guarantee of private property in the Fifth Amendment that is most relevant for the purposes of this article. The original version was

---

[10] Ibid 10 quoting from both Martin Gilbert's *Winston S. Churchill 1874–1965, volume VIII 1945–1965—Never Despair*, Heinemann, London, 1988, 200 and Churchill's own work, *A History of the English-Speaking Peoples, Volume I—The Birth of Britain*, Cassell, London, 2002, chapter VII ('Magna Carta').

drafted by the later 4th President, James Madison in 1789, and the final version ratified by the States retained his five clauses[11] though they were reordered. The Takings Clause summarises *Magna Carta*'s requirements very simply. It states that "private property [shall not] be taken for public use without just compensation". It provided the conceptual template for Richard O'Connor QC's submission on the 4th of March during the 1898 Convention debates that a new sub-section (12) should be added to s 52 of the Constitution as it was then being drafted.[12] The debate records provide no evidence of discussion save for O'Connor's explanation that questions had been raised as to whether the new Commonwealth had inherent but unexpressed power to acquire property "under just terms of compensation". To avoid the possibility that the new government might not be able to acquire property from unwilling vendors, or that it might be driven to hard bargains by those unwilling vendors, O'Connor proposed that the Commonwealth's Parliament should have power "to make laws for the peace, order and good government" of the nation "with respect to"

> The acquisition of property on just terms from any state or person for any purpose in respect of which the Parliament has power to make laws.

The language proposed by Mr O'Connor was not challenged or varied in any way after he made the proposal.[13] The only query was whether the terms of the contemplated compulsory acquisitions

---

[11] The five clauses require that all felonies be tried only on indictment by a grand jury (the Grand Jury Clause), that no one can be tried twice for the same crime (the Double Jeopardy Clause), that no one can be forced to give evidence herself (the Self-Incrimination Clause), that no one can be deprived of life, liberty or property without due process of law in terms similar to the later 14th Amendment (a Due Process Clause), and that private property cannot be taken for public use without just compensation (the Takings Clause).

[12] In March of 1898, clause 52 was the clause intended to provide the new Commonwealth with its limited powers (1898 Convention Debates, 1671 (Tuesday, 1st March 1898) per Mr Isaacs). Mr O'Connor's submission was made on Friday, 4th March 1898 (ibid, 1874).

[13] Despite the renumbering of the 'powers clause' as clause 51 in later days of the Convention, and even though the powers within that clause were also renumbered, Mr O'Connor's language was unchanged.

should be detailed in the Constitution itself, and the questioner, Mr Fraser immediately accepted Mr O'Connor's explanation that those processes would be more appropriately elaborated in an Act to be later passed by the new Parliament. While Mr O'Connor did not directly copy Madison's 1789 words, it is submitted that he intended no innovation and tailored Madison's ideas so that they fitted inside the framework already established by his colleague delegates to the 1898 Convention. While he could have followed Madison's "public use" phrase exactly, he preferred the longer "any purpose in respect of which the Parliament has power to make laws" consistent with other clauses already in the developing document and confirming that this clause would not expand the otherwise limited powers at all. The similarly enlarged reference to the property of "any state or person" again reflects the context of the Australian debates. The District of Columbia had already been established when the U.S. Fifth Amendment was drafted, but none of the Australian delegates knew where the Australian capital would be located when they did their drafting. Hence the Australian framers knew that the business of government would require the new federal Parliament to take land from one or more States and probably not just once.

It is submitted that such need was not as clear to the U.S. framers who were more focused on their recent experience with British overlords who had taken their property during the course of the War of Independence with callous disregard for Magna Carta principles. However, if any word in O'Connor's draft was innovative, it was his preference for the word 'acquisition' over Madison's 'taking'. Why that substitution? While we cannot see inside his mind, it is submitted that O'Connor made a considered choice that reflected the Australian colonial desire to preserve state power from federal encroachment. O'Connor's choice of 'acquisition' over 'taking', was not intended to expand future Australian federal power beyond what the American framers had provided. Rather, consistent with O'Connor's precisely tailored development of the American 'public purpose' phrase so that it was clear the federal government could not take property which the Constitution did not elsewhere authorise, he chose 'acquisition' so that the new federal government would have to budget to recompense state and citizens for anything it indirectly acquired as well as that property which it took directly. That is, it is submitted that the 'acquisition' word was deliberately chosen to further limit federal government power and to justly compensate everything the Commonwealth did that damaged state or citizen.

In suggesting O'Connor made deliberate policy choices when he crafted his 'acquisition' clause, I recognise that he did not exceed his White Australia mandate. That is, he did not anticipate the late 20th century jurisprudential development that has brought acquisitions of aboriginal property within the scope of s 51(xxxi). But it is submitted that O'Connor was focused on preserving the property of states and British property owners from anything the new federal government might do to deprive them of it, and not just the direct takings which were provided for in the American language from which he began his drafting exercise.

I will now discuss the High Court's s 51(xxxi) jurisprudence to date and suggest that it has not sufficiently engaged with Mr O'Connor's 1898 drafting exercise which so satisfied his co-delegates that they did not change a single word.

- **Part Two – The Troubling Aspects of The High Court's s 51(xxxi) Jurisprudence**

Most analyses of judicial consideration of s 51(xxxi) divide the clause into three parts – What constitutes 'property', 'acquisition' and 'just terms' within the meaning of the clause.

While I acknowledge that the *Racial Discrimination Act 1975* (Cth) and the aboriginal land jurisprudence that has followed in its wake, have seeded significant academic discussion as to how acquisitions of aboriginal property should be treated in future High Court jurisprudence, that analysis is beyond the scope of this paper. My purpose is to discuss what I shall call the High Court's conventional acquisition jurisprudence. That is, because I do not think the High Court's jurisprudence concerning 'property' or 'just terms' departs from Magna Carta/Rule of Law standards, I do not interrogate them.[14]

- **Acquisition cases**

Blackshield and Williams observe that the text of s 51(xxxi) "offers few textual devices for limiting its scope"[15] but that "the Court has used three main approaches"[16] to achieve that purpose. The first is to determine whether the acquisition resulted in "a corresponding benefit or advantage" to another person; the second accepts that the property

---

[14] Ever since the High Court first gave careful consideration to the nature of 'property' in *Minister of State for the Army v Dalziel* (1944) 68 CLR 261, I believe that the word has been generously interpreted consistent with the clause that O'Connor drafted which was accepted by the 1898 Convention and which became a frozen part of the Australian Constitution. While the justices in *Dalziel* could easily have found that Messrs O'Connor and Co intended that only fee simple land interests were encompassed within the constitutional wording, they generously found that Dalziel's that a "tenant in possession of an unencumbered estate in fee simple [held] the largest possible bundle" since any other interpretation would enable the legislature "to seize possession and enjoy the full fruits of possession infinitely, on any terms it chooses or upon no terms at all." That theme was continued in *Bank of New South Wales v The Commonwealth (Bank Nationalisation Case)* (1948) 76 CLR 1 when Dixon J said I take [*Dalziel*] to mean that s. 51 (xxxi) is not to be confined pedantically to the taking of title by the Commonwealth to some specific estate or interest in land recognized at law or in equity and to some specific form of property in a chattel or chose in action similarly recognized, but that it extends to innominate and anomalous interests and includes the assumption and indefinite continuance of exclusive possession and control for the purposes of the Commonwealth.

Dixon J's similarly generous approach to the interpretation of the constitutional 'just terms' phrase in *Grace Brothers Pty Ltd v Commonwealth* (1946) 72 CLR 269, has likewise guided subsequent High Court jurisprudence in a manner that accords with Magna Carta principle even in recent aboriginal cases. See for example, *Nehungaloo Pty Ltd v Commonwealth* (1948) 75 CLR 495, where Dixon J said the standard engaged by the 'just terms' words is "what is fair and just between the community and the owner of the thing taken" and *Wurridjal v Commonwealth* (2009) 237 CLR 309 where the Court found that the compensation process in the *Emergency Response Act 2007* (Cth) was sufficient to meet the just terms standard.

[15] George Williams, Sean Brennan and Andrew Lynch, *Blackshield & Williams Australian Constitutional Law & Theory, Commentary & Materials*, 6th ed., The Federation Press, Leichhardt, NSW, 2014, 1232, [27.87].

[16] Ibid [27.88].

concerned is "inherently defeasible"[17] so that it is not unjust to take it without compensation; and the third is to characterise the law as achieving some purpose other than the acquisition of property because it would be 'inconsistent, incongruous, or irrelevant' to treat it in that way.[18] While it does not seem like a contrivance to suggest that the exercise of the Commonwealth's taxation, bankruptcy or copyright powers should be an exception to the otherwise encompassing words of s 51(xxxi) since other provisions in the Constitution anticipated the exercise of these powers without just compensation at the time of federation,[19] many of the Commonwealth acquisitions which the High Court has allowed under s 51(xxxi) were not anticipated by other provisions in the Constitution.

Since the Magna Carta expressed its 'no acquisition without payment or compensation jurisprudential principle' ('the jurisprudential principle') with factual examples, in the examples that follow, I have used the facts of cases subsequently decided by the High Court to suggest that the High Court's case-by-case approach to interpretation has end-run the Magna Carta's jurisprudential principle. I submit tha jurisprudential principle was the meaning of the words of s 51(xxxi) when Mr O'Connor originally expressed them and when they were accepted by the 1898 Convention. Once again, I have suggested that O'Connor chose the word 'acquisition' over the American Fifth Amendment 'taking', to ensure that the Commonwealth could not acquire any private or state property, directly or indirectly, without just terms. That is, the Australian constitutional framers in 1898 were

---

[17] Ibid [27.89].

[18] Ibid [27.90] and [27.92].

[19] The taxation power arises under s 51(ii), the bankruptcy power under s 51(xvii) and the copyright power under s 51(xviii). Cases decided in favour of the Commonwealth under those three powers include respectively, *Commissioner of Taxation v Clyne* (1958) 100 CLR 246, *Federal Commissioner of Taxation v Barnes* (1975) 133 CLR 483, *MacCormick v Federal Commissioner of Taxation* (1984) 158 CLR 622, *Mutual Pools & Staff Pty Ltd v Commonwealth* (1994) 179 CLR 155 and *Roy Morgan Research Pty Ltd v Commissioner of Taxation* (2011) 244 CLR 97 (the taxation power); *Attorney-General v Schmidt* (1961) 105 CLR 361 (the bankruptcy power); and *Nintendo Co Ltd v Centronics Systems Pty Ltd* (1994) 181 CLR 134 and arguably *JT International SA v Commonwealth* (2012) 250 CLR 1.

concerned that the Fifth Amendment 'taking' language had already been unjustly interpreted to protect indirect U.S. federal acquisitions from the just compensation requirement, or that that might happen in the future in Australia since the new Commonwealth had yet to settle upon its seat and to acquire the land and other property necessary to establish that seat. Mr O'Connor wanted to avoid the risk that indirect acquisitions of property might fall outside the guarantee in the Australian context where significant original concern revolved around limiting the new Commonwealth's powers.

But the need to protect States and individuals from indirect acquisitions has been largely ignored. Hence a refusal to renew a lease as an exclusive dealing under the *Trade Practices Act 1974* (Cth) was not a compensable acquisition,[20] and nor was the Commonwealth's prohibition of Tasmania's right to develop the Franklin River into a hydro-electric dam system.[21] The indirect abrogation of a tobacco company's right to use its trademarks on its packaging was also unimpeached.[22] But oddly the legislative alteration of common law and statutory rights of action were compensable where they resulted in direct benefit or financial gain to another party,[23] even though the reduction or extinguishment of statutory rights or statutory rights that had previously existed as common law rights were not if they were or had become inherently susceptible to variation.[24]

My point is not to catalogue all the cases or their alleged inconsistencies. Rather, I suggest that if the jurisprudential principle undergirding our Constitution's expression of s 51(xxxi) is that the Commonwealth must always pay for what it takes, directly or indirectly,

---

[20] *Trade Practices Commission v Tooth & Co Ltd* (1979) 142 CLR 397.
[21] *Commonwealth v Tasmania (Tasmanian Dam Case)* (1983) 158 CLR 1.
[22] *JT International SA v Commonwealth* (2012) 250 CLR 1.
[23] *Georgiadis v Australian and Overseas Telecommunications Corp* (1994) 179 CLR 279; *Commonwealth v Mewett* (1997) 191 CLR 417 and *Smith v ANL Ltd* (2000) 204 CLR 493.
[24] *Health Insurance Commission v Peverill* (1994) 179 CLR 226; *Commonwealth v WMC Resources Ltd* (1998) 194 CLR 1; *Attorney-General (Northern Territory) v Chaffey* (2007) 231 CLR 651; *Telstra Corporation Ltd v Commonwealth* (2008) 234 CLR 210 and *ICM Agriculture Pty Ltd v Commonwealth* (2009) 240 CLR 140.

then significant executive, legislative and judicial re-education needs to take place in the interests of the social justice that our founders originally conceived.

However, before moving to Part Three where I will suggest that this founding jurisprudential principle is required by the Rule of Law, I pause to highlight some of the sophistry that has been used by the High Court in Australia to justify departure from what I maintain was the founding intention consistent with the Rule of Law as it has applied to governments since 1215. And note, my choices below are deliberately chosen. Though few members of the public have recoiled from the deprivation of corporate tobacco of its intellectual property, or the deprivation of farmers of groundwater rights which successive state governments had already chipped away, still there is a breach of the jurisprudential principle which I think needs to be revisited in the interests of social justice in Australia in the future.

French CJ's reasoning in *JT International SA* is a good starting point since few Australians would quibble with the finding that the Commonwealth could abrogate the intellectual property of tobacco companies since the acquisition of that property had the potential to significantly reduce tobacco consumption in this country and to reduce state and national health expenses in the future. Chief Justice French's judgment was one of five majority judgments that found that the Commonwealth's action did not engage the just terms guarantee in s 51(xxxi). He said that an acquisition was a receipt of property rights from an owner but that the complete extinguishment of those rights was not an acquisition.[25] Here there was no enhancement of the Commonwealth's proprietary rights that matched what the plaintiff had lost,[26] though one suspects the Chief Justice was well aware of the long term financial benefits that the Commonwealth was targeting. If the jurisprudential principle is that the Australian Commonwealth should never acquire anything from anyone without paying for it, then why should it matter that someone else's property

---

[25] *JT International SA v Commonwealth* (2012) 250 CLR 1, 33 [41-42].
[26] Ibid 34 [43].

was synchronistically enhanced at the same time? And how would the barons in 1215 have responded to the Chief Justice's argument that it was all right for the King to completely extinguish their property but not to merely acquire it?

For Gummow, Hayne and Bell JJ, the acquisitions power did not protect the general commercial and economic position of traders[27] even though there is a good argument that those interests were a primary concern of the barons when they negotiated the *Magna Carta* with King John. And Crennan and Kiefel JJ said that the s 51(xxxi) guarantee was not engaged because the Commonwealth had not acquired the plaintiff's intellectual property but had only limited its use.[28] In his solitary dissent, Heydon J observed that the plaintiffs had been "deprived...of everything that made their [intellectual] property worth having."[29]

There was similar sophisticated use of the benefit argument in the *ICM Agriculture* case.[30] Though common law groundwater rights had become inherently susceptible to change because of various state regulation since 1912, Hayne, Kiefel and Bell JJ found inter alia, that there could not be an acquisition within the meaning of s 51(xxxi) unless another person acquired some identifiable or measurable advantage by reason of the statutory change.[31] Laying aside the point that some of the groundwater resumed by the state in this case has since been reallocated to mining projects, the jurisprudential principle that I suggest has underlain s 51(xxxi) since its inception, would invert the principle here expressed by Hayne, Kiefel and Bell JJ. That is, the justices should not have been asking if the Commonwealth caused anyone else to benefit. They should rather have asked if a state or an individual suffered direct or indirect proprietary detriment as a consequence of the Commonwealth action whether direct or indirect.

---

[27] Ibid 35 [47] per Gummow J; 67 [167] per Hayne and Bell JJ quoting Dixon J in *British Medical Association v The Commonwealth* (1949) 79 CLR 201, 270.

[28] Ibid 99-100, 105-106 [279, 294] per Crennan J; 127 [354] per Kiefel J.

[29] Ibid 82 [216].

[30] *ICM Agriculture Pty Ltd v Commonwealth* (2009) 240 CLR 140.

[31] Ibid 201-202 [147].

And in writing this, I acknowledge that carried to its conclusion, this jurisprudential principle would obligate the Commonwealth to carry out a 'direct or indirect property audit' before it passed any legislation or took any executive action – in much the same way as it has undertaken to do in relation to the compatability of new legislation with international human rights under ss 8 & 9 of the *Human Rights (Parliamentary Scrutiny) Act 2011* (Cth).

Before I leave the *ICM Agriculture* case, I draw readers' attention to one further flaw I perceive in the reasoning of Hayne, Kiefel and Bell JJ as I measure it against the *Magna Carta* jurisprudential principle that I have outlined above. That is, that this was the first time that the Commonwealth had involved itself in the acquisition of the groundwater rights of New South Wales farmers. Up till this time, all the regulation since 1912 that had indirectly deprived New South Wales farmers of their groundwater without compensation, had been enacted by the New South Wales legislature acting alone. The High Court has recently required state governments to respect the separate judicial power of their courts in the same way as the Commonwealth is required to do since those state courts sometimes exercise Commonwealth judicial power.[32] It would not be difficult to impose federal acquisition standards on States when they are involved in partnership with the Commonwealth in cases that engage the acquisition power.[33]

---

[32] In a string of cases, the High Court has found that federal courts cannot be required to exercise power in a manner inconsistent with the independent nature of judicial power (see for example, *R v Kirby; ex parte Boilermakers' Society of Australia (Boilermakers Case)* (1956) 94 CLR 254 and *Brandy v Human Rights and Equal Opportunity Commission* (1995) 183 CLR 245). In *Kable v Director of Public Prosecutions (NSW)* (1996) 189 CLR 51, the High Court extended that rule to state courts as well when they were exercising Commonwealth judicial power.

[33] Note that in the *ICM* case, there was discussion of the 1950s High Court jurisprudence that allowed the states to avoid compliance with s 51(xxxi) if they acquired property on their own even if the Commonwealth provided the funds. The High Court confined that idea to the 'narrow principle' expressed in *Pye v Renshaw* (1951) 84 CLR 58 in seeming recognition of the moral or 'rule of law' need to prevent Commonwealth/State agreements to end-run the s 51(xxxi) guarantee of protection to non-government actors in the future (*ICM Agriculture Pty Ltd v Commonwealth*

My point in these brief examples has not been to single out egregious examples of Commonwealth-friendly s 51 (xxxi) decisions by the High Court. Indeed, I have chosen cases where the results do not seem to have concerned the public on account of perceived injustice despite my argument that the decisions are inconsistent with the jurisprudential principle that I argue underlies s 51(xxxi). I could have analysed every case decided by the High Court which found that there was no acquisition within the meaning of s 51(xxxi) despite contest by a state or person. But I have sought instead, to demonstrate how this foundational jurisprudential principle might change our future s 51(xxxi) jurisprudence if it were understood, accepted and implemented.

I shall now explain why compliance with this jurisprudential principle is required by an objective understanding of the Rule of Law.

- **Part Three – Section 51(xxxi) and the Rule of Law**

Martin Krygier has often made the point that the Rule of Law has no fixed content and that it can exist in completely different cultures.[34] But he has argued convincingly, with Locke as his primary source, that government cannot be said to be according to the Rule of Law unless its laws are "clear, stable and knowable".[35] The underlying problem to which the Rule of Law is a solution, is the moderation and control of arbitrary power. While power is necessary and should not be stifled if we seek innovation and economic growth, 'the trick' is to temper its use so that its arbitrary use does not diminish individual freedom.[36]

> Laws that conform to the rule of law are not retrospective, secret, incomprehensible, contradictory. They do not require things that

---

(2009) 240 CLR 140, 168-170 [39-46] (per French CJ, Gummow and Crennan JJ), 196-199 [133-139] (per Hayne, Kiefel and Bell JJ) and 206-207 [174] (per Heydon J).

[34] For example, see Martin Krygier, 'Fear, Hope, Politics and Law', Papers of Parliament No. 33, May 1999, Parliament of Australia, <https://www.aph.gov.au/~/~/link.aspx?_id=C6A9A0D3166348198EE463CB9E301777&_z=z> ("Krygier, Fear, Hope, Politics and Law").

[35] Ibid.

[36] Ibid, see also Martin Kyrgier, 'The Rule of Law: Pasts, Presents, and Two Possible Futures', (2016) 12 *Annual Review Law and Social Sciences*, 199, at 203.

are impossible to perform. On the basis of them, one can make plans. To the extent that a legal order approximates the rule of law ideal, citizens have or can obtain clear understanding, in advance, of their legal obligations and they can reasonably have faith that the law will constrain other citizens and officials of state in ways that, under the rule of law, they can predict.[37]

He has expressed this message in a number of ways with a number of authorities:

> [C]itizens must also be able to have reasonable faith that the interpreters and enforcers of the law will construe it with fidelity to its publicly known terms and independently of extra-legal pressures to bend or ignore it.[38]

When the Rule of Law exists in a society, its "citizens know where they stand" and their fears are reduced.[39]

Dicey would have agreed with Krygier on these points. His conception of the Rule of Law was that it meant

> the absolute supremacy or predominance of regular law as opposed to the influence of arbitrary power, and [it] excludes the existence of arbitrariness, of prerogative, or even of wide discretionary authority.[40]

And although Tamanaha believes that the English conception of law changed between Coke's 17th century idea that the common law set limits on sovereign law-makers, and Bentham's 19th century idea that "law was the product of sovereign legislative will", still there was something deep set in the English culture and society, centuries in the making: the widely shared belief and commitment, among the public and government officials, that the government operates within a limiting framework of law.[41]

---

[37] Krygier, above n.34.
[38] Ibid.
[39] Ibid.
[40] AV Dicey, *Introduction to the Study of the Law of the Constitution* (Macmillan, 1st ed, 1885; 10th ed, 1959), 202.
[41] Brian Z. Tamanaha, *On the rather: History, Politics, Theory* (Cambridge University Press, 2004), 57-58.

Even today when "the idea that the rule of law contains a blend of procedural and substantive elements",[42] the content of the Rule of Law retains the idea that "the law must be...clear and predictable" and requires that "questions of legal right and liability...be resolved by the application of the law and not the exercise of discretion."[43]

Because "[a]rbitrariness is notoriously undertheorized",[44] Kyrgier has identified different ways in which power may be improperly exercised because "legitimate interests, expectations and opinions [may not be] taken into account".[45] One of those occurs when those affected by the exercise of power "cannot know, predict or comply with the ways power comes to be wielded"[46] and such arbitrariness is not confined to executive government. Legislatures and judiciaries can be just as arbitrary as the executive when there is no accountability or "guardian of the guardians".[47]

My purpose here is not to suggest that the High Court of Australia is dangerously unaccountable or that it capriciously declines to hear the voices of citizens challenging the power that is exercised over them. But I am suggesting that unpredictability of outcome and discord with the *Magna Carta* sourced jurisprudential principle in s 51(xxxi) cases, breaches the Rule of Law according to all the accepted formulations of that principle.

To express that in another way but paraphrasing Krygier's words – the High Court's power is exercised arbitrarily and in breach of the *Magna Carta* jurisprudential principle embedded in s 51(xxxi) to the extent that it diverges from the limiting guarantee that the Australian framers intended to establish and to the extent that "those it affects cannot know, predict, understand, or comply with" it.[48]

---

[42] Williams, Brennan and Lynch, above n 15, 24 [1.45].
[43] Ibid quoting Lord Bingham, "The Rule of Law", (2007) 66 *Cambridge Law Journal* 69-72.
[44] Krygier, above n.36, at 203, citing Endicott 2014, Gowder 2016 and Sempill 2016.
[45] Ibid.
[46] Ibid.
[47] Krygier, above n.34.
[48] Krygier, above n.36, p 204.

> If one cannot know how power is to be exercised, because its grounds are…too variable to know, [or] vague beyond specification…then one has been treated arbitrarily.[49]

This understanding is more transparent when it is asked how the High Court could have allowed the Commonwealth government to take or acquire without just terms, much of the property that has gone uncompensated despite review under s 51(xxxi)? It is submitted that while High Court approval of each of these acquisitions can be justified if current community interest is the standard, under s 51(xxxi) community interest is only part of the standard. While the framers intended s 51(xxxi) to provide the Commonwealth with power to acquire property of all kinds from unwilling private and state owners for approved Commonwealth community purposes on just terms, the just terms guarantee was to be a two-way street. That is, the express power was provided so that unwilling state and private vendors could not hold the new Commonwealth government to ransom over price, but that new government would honour those vendors with just compensation in accordance with Rule of Law practice established since before *Magna Carta*. The express acquisition power removed from the States and individuals the argument that their home was a castle which could not be acquired by the Commonwealth (despite the famous movie!). But it also guaranteed to those reluctant state and individual players that they would be treated justly in accordance with high principle that can be traced back for more than 800 years. The sequitur to that Commonwealth guarantee to States and individuals was that the Commonwealth would not make any acquisition of property without budgeting and paying for that property in every case. My suggestion then is, that to the extent that the High Court has allowed the Commonwealth government to acquire state and individual property without just compensation in any case, the High Court has failed Australia. That is not to say that there have not been and will not in the future be hard cases where it is unclear whether there has been an acquisition of property within the meaning of s 51(xxxi) at all. But

---

[49] Ibid.

it does say that a failure by all three branches of the Commonwealth government to keep the Magna Carta jurisprudential principle embedded in s 51(xxxi) at the top of their minds when exercising their other limited constitutional powers, has seen many individuals suffer injustice. And this despite the federal court obligation to insist that the executive and legislative branches of government observe the guarantee of just terms to States and individuals at the heart of this particular placitum. Consider these examples:

> *1. Did the High Court have the Magna Carta jurisprudential principle at the top of its mind when it approved New South Wales' acquisition of farming land for the re-settlement of Australian soldiers in Pye v Renshaw,[50] despite finding two years earlier in PJ Magennis Pty Ltd v Commonwealth[51] that a similar written plan breached the s 51(xxxi) guarantee? No matter how one interprets that distinction, the High Court allowed the Commonwealth and New South Wales governments to breach the guarantee by the simple expedient of making the acquisition without a written agreement and because they asked twice. Sadly, the consequence of the Pye v Renshaw precedent has arguably been that the Commonwealth government thinks it can step around the s 51(xxxi) guarantee by making unwritten agreements with states.[52] That is unworthy of any High Court bench.*
>
> *2. The Tasmanian Dam case.[53] To give the underlying acquisition argument a little more life, imagine the reaction of the representatives of the future Australian states at any of the constitutional conventions during the 1890s to*

---

[50] *Pye v Renshaw* (1951) 84 CLR 58.
[51] *PJ Magennis Pty Ltd v Commonwealth* (1949) 80 CLR 382.
[52] I acknowledge however that the High Court appeared to conceptually retreat from the *Pye v Renshaw* decision in *ICM Agriculture Pty Ltd v Commonwealth* (2009) 240 CLR 140, though that retreat was not the prequel to a new and socially just interpretation of s 51(xxxi). For more detail on this retreat see my comments above at n 33.
[53] *Commonwealth v Tasmania (Tasmanian Dam Case)* (1983) 158 CLR 1.

the suggestion that the Commonwealth would prevent a colony from developing a hydro-electric dam in one of its river systems because the Commonwealth had unilaterally signed an international agreement to preserve heritage wilderness areas within its federal domain? The majority of those attending the constitutional conventions would have recoiled from that idea, and the suggestion that the Commonwealth should gain that much control of state land without a penny in compensation would have led to the drafting of further safeguarding limitations.

3. And now I return to dealings with groundwater pumping rights that the High Court denied were an acquisition of property within the meaning of s 51(xxxi) in the ICM Agriculture and Arnold[54] cases in 2009. Again, how would the Australian constitutional framers have responded to the idea that the new Commonwealth might collude with a state in the reduction of these property holder 'rights' because the state had been whittling them away for years? While that revelation in the 1890s may have led to questions about whether the states should not have more of their own powers foreclosed in the new constitution, it is inescapable that those attending the Australian constitutional conventions during the 1890s would have been disturbed by the revelation of practices to be developed in their name in the future, not least in this groundwater case, because the taking of common law property like groundwater was such an affront to the Magna Carta jurisprudential principle.

None of this denies the harder cases that would come; cases that merge questions of taxation, penalty and confiscation with the issues of taking and acquisition more clearly in the contemplation of the founders when they settled the terms of s 51(xxxi) without

---

[54] *ICM Agriculture Pty Ltd v Commonwealth* (2009) 240 CLR 140 and *Arnold v Minister Administering the Water Management Act* (2010) 240 CLR 242

demurrer.⁵⁵ But it would have disturbed the framers to see the High Court use legalism and statutory interpretation to deprive s 51(xxxi) of the spiritual effect that I believe the Australian framers intended when they agreed to Mr O'Connor's formulation of this guarantee. My argument is that it is time the High Court winds back that clock; reinstates the *Magna Carta* jurisprudential principle here outlined, and limits the powers of the Commonwealth government as was intended at federation. This interpretational adjustment will not require an unwinding of the *Engineers'* case settlement in 1920;⁵⁶ it will simply require the Commonwealth to budget and pay for all private property that it takes or acquires in the future. Even the reflection that will be required of all Ministers, Members of Parliament and their advisors in the public service to achieve this new understanding, stand to make Australia a more just society in the future.⁵⁷

- **Part Four – Best Future Practice?**

During Part Three I made reference to ss 8 & 9 of the *Human Rights (Parliamentary Scrutiny) Act 2011* (Cth). That legislation was the Commonwealth government's compromise response to the Brennan Commission's recommendation that Australia should implement a Bill or Charter of Human Rights to comply with its international commitments and to better protect its minority citizens.⁵⁸ Because of the deep divisions that Bill of Rights debates have always engendered

---

⁵⁵ For example, *Attorney-General (Commonwealth) v Schmidt* (1961) 105 CLR 361 (confiscation of enemy trading assets during and after war); *Mutual Pools & Staff Pty Ltd v Commonwealth* (1994) 179 CLR 155 (legislation preventing the refund of an invalid tax); *Re Director of Public Prosecutions; Ex parte Lawler* (1994) 179 CLR 270 (confiscation of a chartered boat being used to fish illegally in Australian waters) and *Theophanous v Commonwealth* (2006) 225 CLR 101 (forfeiture of a corrupt MP's pension entitlements).
⁵⁶ *Amalgamated Society of Engineers v Adelaide Steamship Co Ltd (Engineers' Case)* (1920) 28 CLR 129.
⁵⁷ In private electronic correspondence with Tim Wilson MP (1 August 2017), he suggested that a more just Australia was the appropriate aspirational goal of every new Member of Parliament.
⁵⁸ Williams, Brennan and Lynch, above n 15, 1148 [26.54-26.55].

in Australian politics and despite the Brennan recommendations, the Commonwealth Government retreated to a simple Act which required the Commonwealth Parliament to review all new legislation and make sure it complied with international human rights norms before it was passed into effect. The *Human Rights (Parliamentary Scrutiny) Act 2011* (Cth) was considered necessary because the Australian Constitution is light on human rights and there was no other measure in place that would focus legislators on the need to ensure compliance with underlying international commitments despite the demands of domestic legislation.

In theory, the existence of s 51(xxxi) should foreclose the need for the Commonwealth Parliament to be reminded of their obligations not to acquire state or personal property of any kind without planning and budgeting to pay for it. The creation of federal courts under the Constitution with American-style powers of constitutional review designed to keep the legislature on track despite Australia's common law inheritance, confirms that the framers were alert to the possibility that the nation's future legislators might be distracted and need to be reminded of their constitutional duties. So a non-constitutional legislative reminder like the *Human Rights (Parliamentary Scrutiny) Act 2011* (Cth) would be redundant. But can we solve this arguable Rule of Law deficit in Australian jurisprudence and practice where the High Court jurisprudence surrounding s 51(xxxi) is concerned? What would change our paradigm?

The best that commentators can do is to write academic articles, chapters in books and opinion pieces that suggest the High Court should consider its duties to citizens more seriously. In that context, perhaps an *Unjust Acquisition Reminder Act* would not be out of place since it would remind the High Court that the *Magna Carta* jurisprudential principle underlying s 51(xxxi) is a constitutional obligation rather than a passing fad of public opinion. The point is to focus the High Court on its independent role and duty as protector of state and individual rights. While the decision in the *Engineers'* case has confirmed that the new post-Gallipoli and Tobruk Australia is greater than the sum of it colonial parts, that does not mean that the High Court's role as protector of state and individual property rights under s 51(xxxi) has been subsumed into an Orwellian nation allowed to trump all other interests if there is a greater Commonwealth purpose. Section 51(xxxi) is the prototype limitation power. It is a power, but it is a bounded power. The Commonwealth can acquire state and private property for its other limited legitimate purposes, but only if it pays a just price for all it does. The Constitution was framed to allow the pursuit of collective community purpose but not at the cost of the States and individuals. The state and the individual were protected from future centralised power in the Australian federal Constitution. Though the decision in the *Engineers* case may have legitimated the supremacy of Commonwealth objectives over those of the States, it gave no license for the suppression of any individual common law right. However, the only way that this undergirding and overarching premise of the Constitution will be realised is if the High Court steps up and requires the other branches of government to respect and comply with the spirit and the letter of s 51(xxxi) in every case it reviews. It would not take many cases courageously decided against the Commonwealth, before the federal government would reconsider its bullish ways. If it had had to pay Tasmania for the loss of its sovereign rights to dam the Franklin river system, it may have reconsidered that legislation and would have counted the cost of all subsequent legislation that imposed upon state property rights. Similarly, if the High Court had insisted that the Commonwealth pay the farmers in *ICM Agriculture* and *Arnold* just terms compensation for their lost groundwater, there would have been a lot more reflection, modelling and budgeting before future legislation was passed.

- **Conclusion**

In this chapter I have suggested that a significant portion of the High Court's jurisprudence in s 51(xxxi) constitutional cases in Australia is inadequate and disrespects the purpose for which that clause was inserted in the Constitution at the instance of Richard O'Connor

QC. While that clause was modelled on the U.S. Fifth Amendment, O'Connor's choice of words in what became s 51(xxxi) was designed to expand the reach of the guarantee of state and individual property rights to include all indirect acquisitions of property by the future Commonwealth. But the guarantee was also intended to entrench the underlying government obligation which had roots at least as old as Magna Carta. That interpretive jurisprudential principle would require just compensation in all cases of Commonwealth acquisition and would prevent those acquisitions unless there was a clear purpose that could also be identified under the new Constitution. Certainly O'Connor wanted to place the Commonwealth's acquisition power beyond doubt when it had legitimate constitutional purposes so that unwilling States and individuals could not hold the new Commonwealth to ransom when it needed their property for a valid constitutional purpose. But there was to be no citizen or state financial sacrifice in that process. The Commonwealth was to pay a just price for each and every item of property it took. It was to be a government of limited rather than arbitrary or prerogative power.

    I have used the *Tasmanian Dam* and *ICM Agriculture* cases as examples of Commonwealth conduct in breach of the jurisprudential principle underlying s 51(xxxi) that would have appalled the Australian constitutional framers. In *Tasmanian Dam*, the Commonwealth deprived Tasmania of its sovereign power over the Franklin River system. In the spirit of the jurisprudential principle underlying s 51(xxxi) this was an acquisition that needed to be compensated, perhaps not in money but on terms that were just forevermore. If the High Court had said "you must pay" to the Commonwealth, the Commonwealth would have thought twice before it used its external affairs power in an acquisitive way ever again. The limited power of the Commonwealth would also have been confirmed in a manner consistent with undeniable framer intent but without breaching the *Engineers'* idea that Australia had become a nation rather than a collection of colonies by 1920. The same message by the High Court to both Commonwealth and New South Wales in the *ICM Agriculture* case, would have seen the Commonwealth government budget to pay for everything it takes from individuals and corporate individuals in the future. The decision in favour of individual property rights that the High Court should have taken in *ICM Agriculture* would not have prejudiced the Commonwealth's future sovereignty as expressed in the *Engineers'* case. It would have re-enshrined the principle of limited government upon which the new nation contemplated in *Engineers* was founded.

6

BORN (AGAIN) THIS WAY: WHY THE INHERENT NATURE OF RELIGIOSITY REQUIRES A NEW APPROACH TO AUSTRALIA'S DISCRIMINATION LAWS

Michael Quinlan

"And through the grace that I have been given, I say this to every one of you: never pride yourself on being better than you really are, but think of yourself dispassionately, recognising that God has given to each one his measure of faith". – Romans 12:3 (NJB)[1]

- **Summary**

This paper is about human rights and, in particular, the right to religious freedom in Australia. This paper does not consider the arguments most often put forward in support of religious liberty[2] or the specifics of the legislative protection which ought to be afforded to religious believers. Instead it examines recent research about the causes and benefits of religious belief. This research finds that religiosity is a natural and inherent characteristic of individuals, that there is a genetic component to religiosity and that at least for some people religion is immutable.

---

[1] *New Jerusalem Bible* (Darton, Longman & Todd, 1994) Romans 12:3. Unless expressly stated in this paper references to the Bible are to this translation. For references to other relevant passages in scripture see Rene A Lopez, "Is Faith a Gift From God or a Human Exercise," (July-Sept 2007) 164 *Bibliotheca Sacra* 259, 260 and n 139 below.

[2] See, e.g., Rex Ahdar and Ian Leigh, *Religious Freedom in the Liberal State* (Oxford University Press, 2nd ed, 2013), pp 51-84. Personal autonomy, neutrality, equality, the divide between the public and the private and public reason.

It also finds that religion benefits individuals and society. The paper provides examples to demonstrate that religious freedom is currently treated as a lesser form of human right in Australian law. It argues that, contrary to the present position, religious freedom should be treated as a particularly valuable human right. The paper concludes that as a result Australian law requires reform. Part I very briefly considers the nature of religion in Australia. Part II looks at the *Australian Constitution* and Australia's commitment to international instruments which recognise certain fundamental human rights. It identifies the piecemeal approach adopted by successive Commonwealth parliaments to human rights. As a result specific Commonwealth law protects certain characteristics but not religious liberty.[3] Part III looks at arguments for the protection of the presently protected characteristics on the basis that they, are inherent and immutable characteristics in contradistinction to religious belief which is said to be a 'voluntary life choice.' It argues that this approach is inconsistent with the evidence. Part IV considers the influence of religion on Australian society and the evidence that religious belief benefits individuals and society. Part V considers the present failings of Commonwealth law to protect the rights of Australians of faith. It considers evidence of discrimination against Australians on the basis of their religious beliefs. The paper concludes that, as a result of the inherency of religious belief and the benefits it provides to individuals and to society, it is in Australia's self-interest to adequately protect religious freedom. In the circumstances, the paper argues that there is a pressing need to re-examine Australia's approach to anti-discrimination legislation to provide more adequate and nationwide protection for persons of faith.

---

[3] Race (by the *Racial Discrimination Act 1975* (Cth), sex (by the *Sex Discrimination Act 1984* (Cth)), age (by the *Age Discrimination Act 2004* (Cth)), disability (by the *Disability Discrimination Act 1992* (Cth)) and sexual orientation, gender identity and intersex status (introduced by the Sex Discrimination Amendment (Sexual Orientation, Gender Identity and Intersex Status) Bill 2013 (Cth) which amended the *Sex Discrimination Act 1984* (Cth) to include these characteristics)). Australia has been reproached for this approach on many occasions by the United Nations Human Rights Committee. See e.g. Human Rights Committee, "121st session Concluding Observations on the sixth period report of Australia" 16 October 2017-10 November 2017 [C5]-[C6], [C17]-[C20] http://tbinternet.ohchr.org/Treaties/CCPR/

- **Introduction**

Australia has committed to a number of international instruments which recognise the importance of freedom of religion. Australian Courts have also spoken of the significance of this right.[4] Section 116 of the *Commonwealth Constitution* proscribes the Commonwealth introducing a State religion, from mandating religious tests for Commonwealth employees and from "prohibiting the free exercise of religion" but it has been narrowly interpreted.[5] It has no operation in relation to State laws.[6] Whilst the Australian Commonwealth

---

[4] *Church of The New Faith v Commissioner of Pay-Roll Tax (Vict)* [1982-1983] 154 CLR 120, 130, 150; *Canterbury Municipal Council v Moslem Alawy Society Ltd* (1985) 1 NSWLR 525, 543; *Aboriginal Legal Rights Movement Inc v State of South Australia and Iris Eliza Stevens* (1995) 64 SASR 551, 552, 555; *Aboriginal Legal Rights Movement Inc v State of South Australia and Iris Eliza Stevens* (1995) 64 SASR 551, 557; *Christian Youth Camps Ltd v Cobaw Community Health Services Limited* [2014] VSCA 75 [560]; *Evans v New South Wales* [2008] 168 FCR 576, 580. For example, they have referred to it as: 'the essence of a free society', 'a fundamental concern to the people of Australia,' 'a fundamental freedom,' 'the paradigm freedom of conscience' and as 'a fundamental right because our society tolerates pluralism and diversity and because of the value of religion to a person whose faith is a central tenet of their identity.' Australian Courts have also referred to 'the importance of the freedom of people to adhere to the religion of their choice and the beliefs of their choice and to manifest their religion or beliefs in worship, observance, practice and teaching.'

[5] *Krygger v Williams* (1912) 15 CLR 366; *Adelaide Company of Jehovah's Witnesses v Commonwealth* (1943) 67 CLR 116; *Attorney-General (Vic); Ex Rel Black v Commonwealth* (1981) 146 CLR 559; *Church of the New Faith v Commissioner of Pay-Roll Tax (Vic)* (1983) 154 CLR 120; *Williams v Commonwealth* (2012) 288 ALR 410; see Gabriel Moens, *The Constitution of the Commonwealth of Australia Annotated* (9th ed, 2016) 466—473 [795]- [804A], Denise Meyerson 'The Protection of Religious Rights Under Australian Law' (2009) 3 *Brigham Young University Law Review* 529, 538-540 and Paul Babie and Neville Rochow, 'Feels Like Déjà vu: An Australian Bill of Rights and Religious Freedom' (2010) 3 *Brigham Young University Law Review* 821, 829-832 and see discussion in Part II A and below.

[6] *The Attorney General for the State of Victoria (at the relation of Black) v The Commonwealth of Australia* [1981] HCA 2; (1981) 146 CLR 559, 605; *Grace Bible Church v Redman* (1984) 36 SASR 376; *Nationwide New Pty Ltd v Wills* (1992) 177 CLR 1 [69]-[74]; *Australian Capital Television Pty Ltd v Commonwealth Electoral Commission* (2004) 220 CLR 181, 137-146, 217, 227-233; *Williams v Threewisemonkeys and Durston* [2015] TASADT 4 (30 June 2015) (*Williams*). Given that, since those decisions, the High Court of Australia has identified an implied right of political communication under ss 7 and 24 of the *Australian Constitution* and that that implied

government has enacted legislation aimed at preventing discrimination and vilification on the basis of race,[7] sex,[8] age,[9] disability[10] and sexual orientation, gender identity and intersex status,[11] it has introduced no such legislation to provide protection from discrimination on the basis of religion. Some of this legislation contains exemptions to provide some protection to religious faiths and adherents in certain circumstances.[12] Some may argue that this difference in approach is warranted on the basis that Federal anti-discrimination legislation to date has protected inherent characteristics which are immutable. [13]It might be argued that such characteristics warrant protection more

---

right applies not only to the Commonwealth government but also to State and Territory governments, the restrictions of the religious freedom guaranteed by the *Australian Constitution* as being a fetter to the Commonwealth government but not to State governments may be an issue appropriately open to challenge before the High Court of Australia in the future. This argument was not put by the self-represented defendant in the recent decision of *Williams*, on the application of s 116 within States.

[7] *Racial Discrimination Act 1975* (Cth).

[8] *Sex Discrimination Act 1984* (Cth).

[9] *Age Discrimination Act 2004* (Cth).

[10] *Disability Discrimination Act 1992* (Cth).

[11] Sex Discrimination Amendment (Sexual Orientation, Gender Identity and Intersex Status) Bill 2013 (Cth).

[12] Some examples are that members of the clergy of any church or religious denomination are also entitled to refuse to divulge that a religious confession was made, or the contents of a religious confession made them in NSW and Victoria, (*Evidence Act 1995* (NSW) s 127; *Evidence Act* 2008 (Vic) s 127); although voting is compulsory in Australia, if an elector has a religious belief that it is his or her religious duty to abstain from voting this will constitute a reasonable excuse. of the *Electoral Act* s 245(14); *Referendum Act* s 45(13A); Australian Electoral Commission, (*Electoral Backgrounder: Compulsory voting* (12 September 2014) <http://www.aec.gov.au/About_AEC/Publications/backgrounders/compulsory-voting.htm>); exemptions are provided to religious bodies from a range of discrimination provisions to enable them to operate schools and to comply with their own doctrines in managing their own operations (*Sex Discrimination Act 1984* (Cth) ss 5, 5A,14, 21(3), 37(1)(a), 37(1)(d), 37(2); 38, *Anti-Discrimination Act 1977* (NSW) ss 8, 49ZYB, 49Y; *Equal Opportunity Act 2010* (Vic) ss 83(1)-(2); Greg Walsh, *Religious Schools And Discrimination Law* (Central Press, 2015) 1-11) and exemptions from service in the Defence Force in time of war are also now afforded to religious and other conscientious objectors (ss 61A, 61CA-61CZE of the *Defence Act, 1903* (Cth)).

[13] See Commonwealth, *Parliamentary Debates*, Senate, 18 June 2013, 3278-3279

than voluntary life choices such as religious belief.[14] Certainly evidence suggests that, in the case of same sex attraction, those who believe that characteristic to be immutable are more sympathetic to laws which protect or promote the interests of same sex attracted persons than those who see that characteristic as a choice.[15] In examining the causation of same sex sexual attraction the paper enters some ground which may be considered controversial. In doing so the author has endeavoured to apply Stein's approach to the topic namely that "all else being equal, it is better to believe things that are true than things that are false."[16] This paper does not address the legitimacy of protecting persons from harassment or discrimination because they exhibit characteristics considered to be inherent and immutable.[17] Rather it argues that Commonwealth law currently protects only certain characteristics from harassment and discrimination and that a belief in inherency and immutability appears to have been a factor in Parliament's decision to expand those protection as it did in 2013.[18] The paper argues

---

(Louise Pratt). In this speech Senator Pratt refers to inherency in support of the adoption of the Sex Discrimination Amendment (Sexual Orientation, Gender Identity and Intersex Status) Bill 2013 (Cth). This paper adopts the *Cambridge Dictionary* meaning of 'inherent' being "existing as a natural or basic part of something" <https://dictionary.cambridge.org/dictionary/english/inherent> and of 'immutable' being "not changing or unable to be changed." https://dictionary.cambridge.org/english/immutable

[14] See Rex Tauati Ahdar, 'Religious Vilification: Confused Policy, Unsound Principle and Unfortunate Law' (2007) 26 (2) *The University of Queensland Law Journal* 293, 301 and Eric Barendt, *Freedom of Speech* (Oxford University Press, 2nd ed, 2005) 190

[15] Aaron S Greenberg and J Michael Bailey, "Do Biological Explanations of Homosexuality have Moral, Legal or Policy Implications?" (Aug 1993) 30(3) *The Journal of Sex Research* 245; Edward Stein, "The Relevance of Scientific Research About Sexual Orientation to Lesbian and Gay Rights" (1004) 27:3-4 *Journal of Homosexuality* 277, 291; Jeffrey Schmalz, "Poll Finds an even Split of Homosexuality's cause." *The New York Times* 5 March 1993

[16] Stein, above n 14, 300. Stein goes on to say that "[t]ruth has a certain stability to it; arguments based on truths fare better than those based on falsehoods."

[17] See Barendt, above n 13, 190. Reliance on inherency and immutability arguments to found protections of sexual minorities has been the subject of much criticism see e.g. Lisa M Diamond and Clifford J Rosky, "Scrutinizing Immutability: Research on Sexual Orientation and US Legal Advocacy for Sexual Minorities" (2016) 53:4-5 *The Journal Of Sex Research* 363, 373-385; Greenberg and Bailey, above n 14, 245-251 esp. 247; Stein, above n 14, 277-292

[18] See Commonwealth, *Parliamentary Debates*, Senate, 18 June, esp. 3278-3279 (Louise Pratt).

that, as this approach appears to have formed part of the reasoning for protecting characteristics to date, equivalent protection of freedom of religion and belief ought to be afforded on the basis of consistency. The paper does not consider the arguments more often put forward in support of religious liberty: personal autonomy, neutrality, equality, or the divide between the public and the private and public reason.[19] Nor does it propose the form of any draft legislation or debate the specifics of legislative reform which is required.[20] Instead this paper questions the assumption that all of the other presently protected characteristics are necessarily immutable and inherent human characteristics whilst religious belief is neither. It refers to recent research which finds that religiosity is a natural and inherent characteristic of individuals that religiosity has a genetic component and that, for some people, religious faith is at least as immutable as some other presently protected characteristics. The paper argues that enacting anti-discrimination legislation to protect other characteristics but not to protect religious freedom and providing limited or no exceptions for religious persons or religious bodies, treats religious freedom as a lesser human right than the characteristics or activities which have been granted specific legislative protection. By this approach, exemptions provided to religious believers can be characterised as permitting them to engage in discrimination rather than protecting their human right to religious freedom from legislative encroachment. To demonstrate this the paper considers some examples of religious discrimination and vilification in Australia and of States and Territories preferencing interests other than religious freedom. The paper argues that it is in Australia's self-interest to protect religious freedom and that it is currently failing to do so. The paper argues for this result by reference to the inherency of religiosity,[21] the genetic role in religiosity, the significant contribution that religion has made and continues to make to Australian society

---

[19] Ahdar and Leigh, above n.2, pp 51-84.

[20] In particular the paper does not address the controversy over the current language of s18C of the *Racial Discrimination Act 1975* (Cth) see Joshua Forrester, Lorraine Finlay and Augusto Zimmermann, *No Offence Intended Why 18C is Wrong* (Connor Court, 2016).

[21] By which this paper means the inclination towards religious belief.

and the empirical evidence that religious belief benefits individuals and that it is good for society as a whole. The paper concludes that rather than being treated as a lesser human right, religious freedom ought to be treated as at least equal to other internationally recognised and protected human rights if it is not given preferential treatment. The paper concludes that on this basis there is a pressing need to revise Australia's approach to anti-discrimination legislation in order to provide more adequate and nationwide protection for persons of faith.

I The Nature of Religion in Australia

Australia's Aboriginal and Torres Strait Islander peoples have always been people of deep spirituality.[22] Today Australia is 'one of the most religiously diverse countries in the world.'[23] Whilst, since written records have been kept on the subject they have shown that most Australians have identified as Christians,[24] there has been a significant increase in those identifying with non-Christian faiths.[25] Buddhism,[26] Islam[27] and Hinduism[28] are the most common and fastest growing non-Christian religions. These changes have largely resulted from immigration and children born to immigrants rather than conversion.[29]

---

[22] G Bouma and M Mason, 'Babyboomers downunder: the case of Australia' in W Roof, J Carroll and D Roozen (eds), *The Post-War Generation and Establishment Religion: Cross-cultural Perspectives* (Westview Bolder Co, 1995) 4.

[23] Adam Possamai et al, 'Muslim Students' Religious and Cultural Experiences in the Micro-publics of University Campuses in NSW, Australia' (2016) 47 *Australian Geographer* 311, 312.

[24] Australian Bureau of Statistics, *Report 2071.0 - Reflecting a Nation: Stories from the 2011 Census, 2012–2013* (16 April 2013) <http://www.abs.gov.au/ausstats/>.
Between 2001 and 2011 the proportion of the Australian population identifying with a Christian faith tradition fell from 68% in 2001 to 61% in 2011 to 52% in 2016: Australian Bureau of Statistics *2016: Census Religion 2016 Census data reveals "no religion" is rising fast* (27 June 2017) <http://www.abs.gov.au/AUSSTATS/>

[25] Ibid (2013). From around 7.2% of the total population in 2011 (up from 4.9% in 2001) to 8.2% of the total population in 2016 (ibid 2017).

[26] Ibid (2017) 2.5% of the population in 2011 falling slightly to 2.4% in 2016.

[27] Ibid 2.2% of the population in 2011 rising to 2.6% in 2016.

[28] Ibid 1.3% of the population in 2011 rising to 1.9% in 2016.

[29] McCrindle found that only 7% of Australians who considered themselves to be

The majority of Australians continue to identify with the religious faith within which they were raised.[30] Australians who are raised in one Christian tradition who convert are most likely to do so within a Christian context.[31] Australia 'has always been a deeply spiritual place'[32] and some argue that identification with spirituality rather than religious traditions is growing.[33] Belief in an afterlife and belief in heaven and hell have remained quite stable.[34] Belief in God or some form of higher power also remained quite stable in the two decades to 2002 although it appears to have fallen somewhat this century.[35] Whilst there has been a decline in church attendances[36] and an increase

---

spiritual or religious were converts: McCrindle Research Pty Ltd, "Faith And Belief in Australia" (McCrindle Research Pty Ltd, May 2017), 15; Associate Professor Mehmet Ozalp the founding director of the Centre for Islamic Studies and Civilisation at Charles Sturt University and an executive member of Public and Contextual Theology at that University has observed in relation to Islam that "the Australian Muslim community is very young, compared to the rest of the society. This shows that it's largely driven by birth, rather than conversion." as quoted in Jason Thomas, *What's the fastest growing religion in Australia?* (15 September 2016) SBS News <http://www.sbs.com.au/news/article/2015/>.

[30] Murray Couch et al, 'The Religious Affiliation of Gay, Lesbian, Bisexual, Transgender and Intersex Australians: A Report from the Private Lives Survey' (2008) 16 *People and Place* 1, 4, 47-50; D R Evans and J Kelly, *Australian Economy and Society 2002: Religion, Morality and Public Policy in Perspective 1984-2002* (Federation Press, 2004) 48; Bouma and Mason, above n 23, 41. A comparison of the extent to which Australians continued to identify with the religious denomination which they were raised (the retention rate) relying on the 1989 National Social Sciences Survey found retention rates among Catholics of 91.9%, Anglicans of 89.9% and other Protestants of 83.9%. A comparison relying on data from 2002 found retention rates among Orthodox Christians of 80%, no religion of 77%, Catholics of 64%, nominal Christians of 46% and Anglicans of 40%.

[31] Evans and Kelly, above n 31, 47-50.

[32] Bouma and Mason, above n 23, 4.

[33] Margaret Thornton and Trish Luker, 'The Spectral Ground: Religious Belief Discrimination' (2009) 9 *Macquarie Law Journal* 77.

[34] See Evans and Kelly, above n 31, 34-38; NCLS Research, *A picture of the religious beliefs of the Australian community* (December 2011) <http://www.ncls.org.au/>. There was little change in the three decades to 2009 when the last survey was taken.

[35] Evans and Kelly, above n 31, 34, 27; NCLS Research, above n 33. It appears to have fallen from 80% in 2002 to 71%.in 2009.

[36] Evans and Kelly, above n 31,, 35-36.

in those who describe themselves in the census as of 'No Religion'[37] most Australian continue to identify with a religious faith.

II Australia's Commitment to International Instruments

- **The Australian Constitution and Relevant International Instruments**

The *Australian Constitution* says little about human rights.[38] Section 116 prevents the Commonwealth from establishing a state religion or imposing any religious test for the holding of any Commonwealth office. It also prevents the Commonwealth from prohibiting the free exercise of religion.[39] It has no application to State laws,[40] and it has been given a very narrow meaning by the Courts.[41] The Court's approach has been to focus on the purpose of an impugned law rather than to consider its effect or result on religious freedom.[42] Consider, for example *Krygger v Williams*.[43] In this case s 116 was found not

---

[37] Ibid; Bouma and Mason, above n 23, note 3. Growing from 15% of the population in 2001 to 22% in 2011 to 30.1% in 2016. It is important to note though that in the census this response is in answer to the question 'What is the person's religious denomination?' By answering this question truthfully people who are non-denominational in their religious faith as well as atheists are recorded as being of 'No Religion.'

[38] *Australian Constitution* s 51(xxxi), s 80. It does prohibit the Commonwealth from seizing property without just compensation and provides what has turned out in practice to be a limited right to trial by jury.

[39] *Australian Constitution* s 116. This section provides that 'The Commonwealth shall not make any law for establishing any religion, or for imposing any religious observance, or for prohibiting the free exercise of any religion, and no religious test shall be required as a qualification for any office or public trust under the Commonwealth.' McCrindle found that 14% of Australians identified as 'spiritual but not religious and that 36% of these people believed that there was an "ultimate purpose and meaning in life", 26% believed "in the inward journey of discovering the inner person" and 22% had spiritual beliefs drawn from a mixture of the major religions: McCrindle Research Pty Ltd, above n 30, 7.

[40] See above n 5.

[41] See above n 4.

[42] *Krygger v Williams* (1912) 15 CLR 366 369, 372-373; *Kruger v Commonwealth* [1997] HCA 27; (1997) 190 CLR 1 (Brennan J) 40, (Toohey J) 85-86, (Gummow J) 160, (Dawson J) 60-61; *Cheedy on behalf of the Yindjibarndi People v State of Western Australia* [2010] FCA 690 (2 July 2010) [73]; *Cheedy on behalf of the Yindjibarndi People v State of Western Australia* [2011] FCAFC 100 (12 August 2011) [92].

[43] (1912) 15 CLR 366.

to exempt a Jehovah's Witness, Mr Krygger, from having to attend military training despite it being contrary to his religious beliefs to do so. This demonstrates the failure of the section to provide the basic protection the law should afford to a religious believer.[44]

Australia is party to a number of relevant international agreements including the 1948 *Universal Declaration of Human Rights*[45] and the *International Covenant on Civil and Political Rights (ICCPR)*.[46] Article 18 of the *Universal Declaration of Human Rights* provides that '[e]veryone has the right to freedom of thought, conscience and religion; this right includes freedom to change his religion or belief, and freedom, either alone or in community with others and in public or private, to manifest his religion or belief in teaching, practice, worship and observance.'[47] Article 18 of the *ICCPR* provides similar protections.[48] It also requires signatories: to protect the rights of

---

[44] The fact that the Commonwealth parliament subsequently enacted specific exemptions from service in the Australian Defence Force in time of war for religious and other conscientious objectors under ss 61A, 61CA-61CZE of the *Defence Act, 1903* (Cth) may have ameliorated this specific deficiency but it does not alter the limited protection for individual believers currently provided by s116 of the *Australian Constitution*, at least, as it has been interpreted to date.

[45] *Universal Declaration of Human Rights,* GA Res 217A (III), UN GOAR, 3rd sess, 183rd plen mtg, UN Doc a/810 (10 December 1948).

[46] *International Covenant on Civil and Political Rights*, GA Res 2200A (XXI), UN GAOR, 21st sess, Supp No 16, UN Doc A/6316 (16 December 1966 adopted in March 23 1976); George Williams, 'The Victorian Charter of Human Rights and responsibilities: Origins and Scope' (2006) 30(3) *Melbourne University Law Review* 880, 892.

[47] *Universal Declaration of Human Rights,* GA Res 217A (III), UN GOAR, 3rd sess, 183rd plen mtg, UN Doc A/810 (10 December 1948) art 18.

[48] Ibid art 18. '1. Everyone shall have the right to freedom of thought, conscience and religion. This right shall include freedom to have or to adopt a religion or belief of his choice, and freedom, either individually or in community with others and in public or private, to manifest his religion or belief in worship, observance, practice and teaching. 2. No one shall be subject to coercion which would impair his freedom to have or to adopt a religion or belief of his choice. 3. Freedom to manifest one's religion or beliefs may be subject only to such limitations as are prescribed by law and are necessary to protect public safety, order, health, or morals or the fundamental rights and freedoms of others. 4. The States Parties to the present Covenant undertake to have respect for the liberty of parents and, when applicable, legal guardians to ensure the religious and moral education of their children in conformity with their own convictions.'

religious minorities 'to profess and practise their own religion';[49] to prohibit '[a]ny advocacy of national, racial or religious hatred that constitutes incitement to discrimination, hostility or violence';[50] and to 'prohibit any discrimination and guarantee to all persons equal and effective protection against discrimination on any ground such as race, colour, sex, language, religion, political or other opinion, national or social origin, property, birth or other status.'[51] Whilst Australia agreed to respect and ensure that everyone within Australia and subject to Australian jurisdiction recognises the rights set out in the *ICCPR*,[52] the Articles of the *ICCPR* have not been domesticated.[53] The same is true of the *Universal Declaration of Human Rights* and other potentially relevant international instruments.[54] As a result they do not have the force of law and they are not binding in Australia.[55]

Rather than enacting legislation to reflect the full scope of the *ICCPR*, Commonwealth law proscribes discrimination on the basis of race[56] and sex[57] (which are specifically named in the *ICCPR*) and discrimination on the basis of age[58], disability,[59] sexual orientation, gender identity and intersex status[60] (which are not specifically named

---

[49] *International Covenant on Civil and Political Rights*, GA Res 2200A (XXI), UN GAOR, 21st sess, Supp No 16, UN Doc A/6316 (16 December 1966 adopted in March 23 1976) art 27. This provides that; 'In those States in which ethnic, religious or linguistic minorities exist, persons belonging to such minorities shall not be denied the right, in community with the other members of their group, to enjoy their own culture, to profess and practise their own religion, or to use their own language.' Australia requires international obligations to be enacted into domestic law before they have domestic operation.

[50] Ibid art 20(2).

[51] Ibid art 26.

[52] Ibid art 2.

[53] In other words, they have not been made law in Australia.

[54] *Declaration on the Elimination of All Forms of Intolerance and of Discrimination Based On Religion or Belief*, GA Res 36/55, UN GAOR, 36th sess, UN Doc A/RES/36/55 (Nov 25, 1981) (Religion Declaration).

[55] *Dietrich v R* (1992) 177 CLR 292.

[56] *Racial Discrimination Act 1975* (Cth).

[57] *Sex Discrimination Act 1984* (Cth).

[58] *Age Discrimination Act 2004* (Cth).

[59] *Disability Discrimination Act 1992* (Cth).

[60] *Sex Discrimination Amendment (Sexual Orientation, Gender Identity and Intersex*

in the *ICCPR*). Although religion is specifically identified in the *ICCPR*, the Commonwealth has not enacted legislation to proscribe discrimination or vilification on the basis of religion. Nor have New South Wales or South Australia. The protections afforded in other states and territories vary considerably.[61]

- **Court Recognition of the Importance of Religious Freedom**

Whilst Australian Courts have recognised the importance of religious freedom[62] the common law has never included a fundamental guarantee of religious freedom and expression which could not be abrogated by State Parliaments.[63] Whilst the common law can be influenced by international law[64] and, where there is ambiguity, Australian courts should favour a construction of legislation which is consistent with

---

Status) Bill 2013 (Cth).

[61] *Equal Opportunity 1984*(WA) s53;*Anti-Discitmiantion Act 1998* (Tas) s16(o)-(p); *Equal Opportunity Act 1995* (Vic) s 6(j); *Anti-Discrimination Act 1991* (Qld) s 7(i); *Discrimination Act 1991* (ACT) s 7(i)(i); *Anti-Discrimination Act 1992* (NT) s 19(1)(m). For example, in Victoria, s14 of the *Victorian Charter of Human Rights and Responsibilities Act 2006* (the Charter), provides that '[e]very person has the right to freedom of thought, conscience, religion and belief' but pursuant to s 48 it does not apply to 'any law applicable to abortion or child destruction.' An example of how Victorian abortion law conflicts with religious freedom is discussed in Part V B below. Section 46(1) of the *Constitution Act, 1934* (Tas) provides that "(1) Freedom of conscience and the free profession and practice of religion are, subject to public order and morality, guaranteed to every citizen." An example of the operation of that provision is discussed in Part VB below.

[62] See above n 3.

[63] *Grace Bible Church v Reedman* (1984) 36 SASTR 376, 385; *Durham Holdings Proprietary Ltd v State of New South Wales* (2001) 205 CLR 399, [31]; *Aboriginal Legal Rights Movement Inc v State of South Australia and Iris Eliza Stevens* (1995) 64 SASR 551, 555-557; Garth Blake, 'God, Caesar and Human Rights: Freedom of Religion in Australia in the 21st century' (2009) 31 *Australian Bar Review* 279, 294-295; Meyerson, above n 4, 540-541; Neil Foster, 'Religious Freedom In Australia' (Speech delivered at the 2015 Asia Pacific J Reuben Clark Law Society Conference, The University of Notre Dame Australia, 29 May 2015) <http://works.bepress.com/neil_foster/94>.

[64] *Mabo v Qld (No 2)* (1992) 175 CLR 1; *Chow Hung Ching v the King* (1948) 77 CLR 449 citing Prof Brierley; *Jago v Judges of the District Court of NSW* (1988) 12 NSWLR 558.

Australia's obligations at international law, the Federal Parliament[65] and State Parliaments can legislate inconsistently with international law so long as they do so clearly and unambiguously.[66] As a result, the absence of any Commonwealth legislation to protect religious freedom leaves this right in a precarious position in Australia. Apart from specific legislation which protects religious freedom in limited areas, usually by way of specific exemptions from the operation of other legislation,[67] there is little substantive legislative support for religious freedom in most circumstances. Rather than being acknowledged as a human right, the extent to which religious freedom is protected depends on politics.[68] As a result, 'the Australian legal system recognises the value of religious freedom on the one hand, and on the other hand, does not place a high priority on protecting it as an existing human right.'[69]

---

[65] *Australian Constitution* s 116. Subject to the limited restriction contained in s 116 as discussed above.

[66] *Minister for Immigration and Ethnic Affairs v Teoh* (1995) 183 CLR 272

[67] *Evidence Act 1995* (NSW) s 127; *Evidence Act* 2008 (Vic) s 127; of the *Electoral Act* s 245(14); *Referendum Act* s 45(13A); Australian Electoral Commission, *Electoral Backgrounder: Compulsory voting* (12 September 2014) <http://www.aec.gov.au/About_AEC/Publications/backgrounders/compulsory-voting.htm>; *Sex Discrimination Act 1984* (Cth) ss 5, 5A,14, 21(3), 37(1)(a), 37(1)(d), 37(2); 38, *Anti-Discrimination Act 1977* (NSW) ss 8, 49ZYB, 49Y; *Equal Opportunity Act 2010* (Vic) ss 83(1)-(2); Walsh, above n 11, 1-11. For example, members of the clergy of any church or religious denomination are also entitled to refuse to divulge that a religious confession was made, or the contents of a religious confession made them in NSW and Victoria. Another exemption applies in relation to compulsory voting. Although voting is compulsory in Australia, if an elector has a religious belief that it is his or her religious duty to abstain from voting this will constitute a reasonable excuse. Exemptions are provided to religious bodies from a range of discrimination provisions to enable them to operate schools and to comply with their own doctrines in managing their own operations.

[68] Sex Discrimination Amendment (Sexual Orientation, Gender Identity and Intersex Status) Bill 2013 (Cth). For example, although as discussed in Part IV below, religious organisations are substantial providers of aged care services in Australia, there are no religious freedom exemptions for providers of those services under the Commonwealth legislation.

[69] Charlotte Baines, 'A Delicate balance: Religious Autonomy Rights and LGBTI Rights in Australia' (2015) 10 *Religion and Human Rights* 45, 50.

III Protecting Inherent and Immutable Characteristics From Discrimination

- **Are All Characteristics Presently Protected by Commonwealth Anti-Discrimination Legislation Inherent and Immutable?**

If we ignore Australia's commitment to do so through its adoption of international instruments like the *ICCPR*, it might be argued that Australian law should not protect matters of personal choice – which might be said to include religion – from discrimination and vilification, but that it should protect inherent or immutable characteristics such as race, sex, age, disability and sexual orientation, gender identity and intersex status.[70] This view appears to have been one of the motivations for the expansion of the *Sex Discrimination Act 1984* (Cth)[71] to include protections for sexual orientation,[72] gender identity[73] and intersex status.[74] In supporting that move Senator Louise Pratt observed that:

> Most Australians know gay, lesbian, bisexual, transgender and intersex people. We understand that sexuality is neither a choice nor a reason for people to be subjected to discrimination or harassment. Fewer Australians, however, have a good understanding of the issue relating to gender identity and intersex status. A person's 'gender identity' refers to their inherent sense of themselves as being male or female or perhaps even a combination of the two and this may not always align with the sex they were assigned at birth. 'Intersex status' is quite a

---

[70] See above n 13.

[71] By the passing of the Sex Discrimination Amendment (Sexual Orientation, Gender Identity and Intersex Status) Bill 2013 (Cth).

[72] *Sex Discrimination Act 1984* (Cth) s 4. This is defined in the Act to mean 'a person's sexual orientation towards persons of the same sex or persons of a different sex or persons of the same and persons of a different sex'.

[73] Ibid. This is defined in the Act to mean 'the gender-related identity, appearance or mannerisms or other gender-related characteristics of a person (whether by way of medical intervention or not), with or without regard to the person's designated sex at birth.'

[74] Ibid. This is defined in the Act to mean 'the status of having physical, hormonal or genetic features that are neither wholly female nor wholly male, or a combination of female and male or neither female nor male.'

different thing. It refers to someone whose biological make-up – the way they were biologically identified at birth – is not wholly male nor wholly female and, in fact, may be a combination of both or may be lacking some of the attributes. So there are a range of quite specific and diverse genetic and biological conditions that mean that a significant number of people have a biological intersex status. Like sexual orientation, neither gender identity nor intersex status are a choice nor are either a reason for a person to suffer discrimination or harassment.[75]

The point here is not to address the desirability of the inherency and immutability of characteristics as a legitimate basis for determining whether or not to protect people from harassment or discrimination.[76] It is simply to recognise that Commonwealth law currently protects only certain characteristics from discrimination and that a belief in inherency and immutability appears to have been a factor in Parliament's decision to expand such protection as it did in 2013.[77] If this approach forms part of the reasoning for protecting characteristics the question of whether or not any or all of these characteristics and the characteristic of religiosity are inherent or immutable warrants attention. Identifying whether particular characteristics are or are not inherent or immutable is complex. It involves considering genetics, biology and other disciplines. The paper briefly considers the characteristics of race, sexual orientation and gender identity before turning to consider the question of whether religious belief might properly be understood as an inherent or immutable characteristic. If so the paper argues that equivalent protection of freedom of religion and belief ought to be provided by the Commonwealth on the basis of consistency.

- **Race**

We are born with particular physical characteristics. To the extent to which 'race' is determined by biology – such as by skin colour for

---

[75] Commonwealth, *Parliamentary Debates*, Senate, 18 June 2013, 3278 (Louise Pratt).
[76] See above n 15.
[77] See Commonwealth, *Parliamentary Debates*, Senate, 18 June 2013, esp. 3278 – 3279 (Louise Pratt).

example - it might properly be described as an immutable or inherent characteristic. However race has long been understood in a broader cultural and social context.[78] This shift is reflected in laws which do not limit protection from discrimination to colour.[79] Scientific research, such as the Human Genome Project, has found "no meaningful genetic or biological basis for the concept of 'race'"[80] as "any two human beings are 99.9% identical genetically."[81] According to the Australian Law Reform Commission:

> It is now well-accepted among medical scientist, anthropologists and other students of humanity that 'race' and 'ethnicity' are social, cultural and political constructs, rather than matters of scientific 'fact.'[82]

In the Andrew Bolt case[83] Justice Bromberg adopted the definition of 'race' from a New Zealand case[84] as follows:

> The real test is whether the individuals or the group regard themselves and are regarded by others in the community as having a particular historical identity in terms of their colour or their racial, national or ethnic origin. That must be based on a belief shared by members of the group.[85]

As would be expected in a multi-racial society, many Australians have diverse genealogical backgrounds. They may have choices

---

[78] Thornton and Luker, above n 34, 81.

[79] Ibid; *Racial Discrimination Act 1975* (Cth) s 9; Human Rights and Equal Opportunity Commission, *'Combating the Defamation of Religions' A Report of the Australian Human Rights and Equal Opportunity Commission to the United Nations High Commissioner for Human Rights* (4 July 2008) <http://www.humanrights.gov.au>. For example, the Act prohibits discrimination on the basis of 'race, colour, descent or national or ethnic origin.' These terms have been interpreted broadly.

[80] Australian Law Reform Commission, *The Protection of Human Genetic Information*, Report No 96 (2003) 922 [36.41]-[36.42] (citation omitted) as quoted in Forrester et al, above n 19, 131.

[81] Ibid.

[82] Ibid.

[83] *Eatock v Bolt* [2011] FCA 1103; (2011) 197 FCR 261, 333-334 [310]-[313].

[84] *King-Ansell v Police* [1979] 2 NZLR 531, 542-543.

[85] Ibid. See discussion in Forrester et al, above n 19, 134-135.

about the race(s), descent(s) or national or ethnic origin(s) with which they identify For example, whilst in the past some Australians may have sought to downplay their Indigenous heritage, today many feel justifiably enriched by and embrace it. Indigeneity is now accepted to consist of a combination of community acceptance, self-identification and descent in Australia.[86] Whilst not all Australians with Indigenous heritage identify as Indigenous[87] there has been a large increase in the Indigenous population since the 1990s consequent upon this fairly wide definition and the reduction in stigma around identifying as Indigenous.[88] This means that a significant minority of Indigenous Australians today "are physically indistinguishable from white Australians."[89] Some look to recover ties to their country, culture and community.[90] In this they are not alone. The television program *Who Do You Think You Are?*[91] and websites such as *My Heritage*[92] and *Ancestry.com*[93] evidence Australians searching for a better understanding of their identity. For many Australians, questions of race, descent or national or ethnic origin are not straightforward. Answers to these questions may change over a person's lifetime as they learn more about their heritage or develop a greater appreciation and attachment to a particular part of their heritage.[94] Some Australians prefer a 'braided' identity fashioned

---

[86] Emma Kowal, "Descent, Classification and Indigeneity in Australia," in Farida Fozdar et al (ed), *Mixed Race Identities in Australia, New Zealand and the Pacific Islands* (2016, ProQuest Ebook Central) 21, 23

[87] Historian Henry Reynolds and journalist Ray Martin are two prominent examples: see Kowal, above n 87, 30, n 5.

[88] Kowal, above n 87, 23,

[89] Ibid 21

[90] Peta Stephenson, 'Indigenous Australia's Pilgrimage to Islam' (2011) 32(3) *Journal of Intercultural Studies* 3, 261.

[91] SBS, *Who Do You Think You Are?* <http://www.sbs.com.au/programs/who-do-you-think-you-are>.

[92] My Heritage, *Discover. Preserve. Share. Your Family History.* <http://www.myheritage.com>.

[93] Ancestry.com <http://www.ancestry.com.au>.

[94] For example, in the author's family there are wide differences in the importance places by each of the five siblings on their Irish heritage ranging from no attachment at all to a very high degree of attachment.

"from multiple sources to produce the outcome they desire"[95] rather than a single fixed racial identity. In short, even the characteristic of race may not be intrinsic and immutable.

- **Sexual Orientation**

Whilst claims that same sex attraction is inherent and immutable in the context of calls for additional rights and protections of sexual minorities are common[96] the causation of same-sex sexual attraction remains unclear.[97] Whilst minor differences have been detected in the brains of same sex and opposite sex attracted persons it is not known whether these differences are inherent or caused by psychological or experiential factors during their lifetime.[98] As Diamond and Rosky have observed "scientific research does not indicate that sexual orientation is uniformly biologically determined at birth or that patterns of same-sex and other-sex attractions remain fixed over the life course."[99] Whilst some twin studies have identified genetics as making a significant contribution to sexual orientation, the methodology of those studies has been criticised.[100] A particular concern has been volunteer bias which is said to have arisen because rather than participants being identified randomly they have been identified by word of mouth or

---

[95] Kowal, above n 87, 20.

[96] See discussion in Diamond and Rosky, above n 16, 364-365.

[97] Diamond and Rosky, above n 16, 364; Sergey Gavrilets and William R Rice, 'Genetic models of homosexuality: Generating testable predictions' (2006) 273 *Proceedings of the Royal Society* 3031; J Michael Bailey, Michael P Dunne and Nicholas G Martin, 'Genetic and Environmental Influences on Sexual Orientation and Its Correlates in an Australian Twin Sample' (2000) 78 *Journal of Personality and Social Psychology* 3, 524, 533-534; Jeffrey Keefe, "Homosexuality" *New Catholic Encyclopedia Supplement 2012-13: Ethics and Philosophy Volume 1* (2013, Cengage Learning) 716-719; Robert Loyd Kinney III, 'Homosexual inclinations and the passions: A Thomistic theory of the psychogenesis of same-sex attraction disorder' (2014) 81(2) *The Linacre Quarterly* 130, 132.

[98] Lawrence S Mayer and Paul R McHugh, 'Sexuality and Gender: Findings from the Biological, Psychological and Social Sciences' (2016) 50 *The New Atlantis* 7, 39-41; Jacob Felson, 'The Effect of religious Background on Sexual Orientation' (2011) 7(4) *Interdisciplinary Journal of Research on Religion* 9.

[99] Diamond and Rosky, above n 16, 364.

[100] Bailey, Dunne and Martin, above n 98, 525.

through same sex publications.[101] A large representative study by Bailey et al of Australian twins which sought to avoid participation bias found a concordance rate among identical twins of 20 per cent (in men) and 24 per cent (in women) which was about half that which had been found in some earlier twin studies.[102] Whilst Bailey et al found that "[t]he X-linked gene appears to account for only a modest amount of variance in sexual orientation' [103] and that "any major gene for strictly defined homosexuality has either low penetrance or low frequency"[104] their overall conclusion on the significance of genes in sexual orientation is heavily couched and not definitive. According to Diamond and Rosky the median concordance estimate for sexual orientation across the most reliable twin studies is .25.[105] This is substantially below the heritability estimates (from .4 to .6) that has been identified in relation to characteristics which are not widely considered to be immutable including lower back pain, smoking, divorce and body dissatisfaction.[106] There are wide fluctuations in the percentages of the population in Western counties who engage in sexual activity with persons of the same sex.[107] Studies reveal greater percentages of women reporting same sex sexual attraction in countries with higher levels of acceptance of that characteristic.[108] Education is associated with higher acceptance and higher reported incidence of same sex attraction.[109] The incidence of exclusively same sex attraction is too high a percentage to be the result of genetic mutation.[110] Environmental

---

[101] Ibid 525.

[102] Ibid 533. Other studies of identical twins have found that where one identical twin was attracted to persons of the same sex the other would be in 6 to 32 per cent of cases. Ibid 525; see also discussion in Mayer and McHugh, above n 99, 31.

[103] Bailey, Dunne and Martin, above n 98 528.

[104] Ibid 534.

[105] Diamond and Rosky, above n 16, 366.

[106] Ibid 366.

[107].Felson, above n 99, 11.

[108] Ibid 10.

[109] Ibid 10.

[110] Gavrilets and Rice, above n 98, 3031.

factors such as religious background,[111] cultural attitudes,[112] sibling relationships, fraternal birth order, adoption, peer relationships, parent-child relationships, social acceptance[113] and sexual abuse seem to play a significant causative role in same sex attraction, identities and behaviours.[114] These factors are not what would be expected if same sex orientation was determined by genes.

The view that sexual orientation is inherent and immutable is also difficult to reconcile with the evidence of significant fluidity in sexual orientation.[115] In one study up to 80 per cent of respondents who reported same sex attraction as adolescents did not report that attraction as adults.[116] It is clear that some same sex attracted people report that their sexual identity has changed over time to a heterosexual orientation.[117] A large random representative study of 12,000 found significant change in self-described sexual orientation measured when the group had an average age of 22 and measured again six years later. A different sexual orientation category was chosen by 43 per cent of the men who had described themselves as non-heterosexual and 50 per

---

[111] Felson, above n 99, 21-22, 26-27, 29.

[112] Diamond and Rosky, above n 16, 365, 367; Felson, above n 99, 10-11.

[113] Diamond and Rosky, Ibid 370-371.

[114] Kinney, above n 98, 132, 156; Gavrilets and Rice above n 98, 2, 3031–87; Elizabeth M Weiss et al, 'A Qualitative Study of Ex-Gay and Ex-Ex-gay Experiences,' (2010) 14(4) *Journal of Gay & Lesbian Mental Health* 291, 314.

[115] J Michael Bailey et al, 'Sexual Orientation, Controversy and Science' (2016) 17(2) *Psychological Science in the Public Interest* 45, 56; Mayer and McHugh, above n 99, 34, 50-57; Patrick Parkinson, 'The Controversy over the Safe Schools Program – Finding the Sensible Centre' (Research Paper, University of Sydney Law School, 14 September, 2014); Diamond and Rosky, above n 16, 368-371.

[116] Mayer and McHugh, above n 99, 7.

[117] Diamond and Rosky, above n 16, 368-369; Stanton L Jones and Mark A Yarhouse, 'Ex gays? An Extended Longitudinal Study of Attempted Religiously Mediated Change in Sexual Orientation' (Paper presented at the Sexual Orientation and Faith Tradition Symposium, APA Convention, 2009) 10; Keefe, above n 98, 717-718; Robert L Spitzer, 'Can Some Gay Men and Lesbians Change Their Sexual Orientation? 200 Participants Reporting a Change From Homosexual to Heterosexual Orientation' (2003) 32(5) *Archives of Sexual Behavior* 403, 404-405, 412-415; Kim W Schaeffer et al, 'Religiously-Motivated Sexual Orientation Change: A Follow-Up Study' (1999) 27(4) *Journal of Psychology and Theology* 329, 329-330, 333-337.

cent of the woman with two-thirds of those who changed describing themselves as 100 per cent heterosexual.[118] After reviewing multiple studies Diamond and Rosky observe that:

> Given the consistency of these findings, it is not scientifically accurate to describe same-sex sexual orientation as a uniformly immutable trait.[119]

Mayer and McHugh conclude that:

> The genetic influences affecting any complex behaviours – whether sexual behaviours or interpersonal interactions – depend in part on individuals' life experiences as they mature. Genes constitute only one of the many key influences on behaviours in addition to environmental influences, personal choices and interpersonal experiences. The weight of evidence to date strongly suggests that the contribution of genetic factors [to same sex attraction] is modest. We can say with confidence that genes are not the sole, essential cause of sexual orientation; there is evidence that genes play a modest role in contributing to the development of sexual attractions and behaviours but little evidence to support a simplistic 'born this way' narrative concerning the nature of sexual orientation.[120]

Like all human behaviours it is important not to ignore the existence of free will as genetic dispositions to particular forms of behaviour are mediated by the mind.[121] The number of same sex attracted people who themselves report that they have some choice in their sexual orientation is significant.[122] In the most rigorous work done to date 60 per cent of bisexual men, 10 per cent of same sex attracted men and 30 of same sex attracted women considered this to be the case.[123] As Stein has observed:

> [E]ven if homosexuality is biologically based, actually engaging

---

[118] Diamond and Rosky, Ibid 369.
[119] Ibid 370.
[120] Mayer and McHugh, above n 99, 34.
[121] Stein, above n 14, 274, 279.
[122] Diamond and Rosky, above n 16, 372.
[123] Ibid 371, 382.

in homosexual acts, actually identifying as lesbian or gay, and so on, are *choices,* choices that each lesbian or gay man might well not have made (that is, he or she could have decided to be abstinent and closeted).[124]

This is not to make any suggestion about how anyone who is same sex attracted should identify or act but these factors suggest that whilst genetic and inherent factors may play some role in the likelihood of a person being attracted to members of the same sex, this sexual orientation and behaviours in response to it are not immutable or determined by biology.[125]

1. Gender Identity

Scientific evidence does not support the view that gender identity is a fixed inherent characteristic which is independent of a person's biological sex.[126] Neurological studies show some correlations in brain structure of those who identify with a gender opposite to that of their biological sex but not sufficient to evidence a biological basis for cross-gender identity.[127] These differences may be the result of environmental and psychological factors, prenatal hormone exposure or genes or some combination of any or all of these factors.[128] The view that gender identity is inherent and immutable is also difficult to reconcile with the evidence that whilst some children feel an inclination to identify with the gender other than their biological gender most ultimately identify with their biological gender.[129]

In summary then, scientific evidence does not establish that sexual orientation or gender identity are determined by inherent, genetic or biological factors.[130]

---

[124] Stein, above n 14, 279; see also Greenberg and Bailey, above n 14, 250.
[125] Mayer and McHugh, above n 99, 7, 14, 26, 31-34.
[126] Ibid 8, 11.
[127] Ibid 8, 98-105.
[128] Ibid 8, 102.
[129] Ibid 6, 12, 106.
[130] Ibid 7-9, 11, 105.

- **Is religiosity simply a voluntary life choice or is it inherent or generic?**

When we think of aspects of our lives which we might consider to be voluntary life choices, the clothes you wear, the food you eat, politics, the house we live in, the music we like or the car we drive may come to mind. In life choices like this we expect to see a wide variety across and within cultures. We need to eat, we need shelter and we need clothing but, subject to our resources, we can choose, for example, whether or not to be a gourmet, to be abstemious or gluttonous or to have much or little interest in art, fashion, sport or politics. Religion is not like that.[131] Religious belief and experience have been a feature of all human societies[132] and most people have been religious believers throughout history.[133] It is no challenge to free will[134] to recognise that this suggests that religious belief and experience come naturally to us.[135] The particular religious faith that an individual follows or rejects and the fervour with which he or she does so, is no doubt 'a complex mixture of inherited cultural assumptions and attitudes and individual commitment (or lack thereof)'[136] but understanding religion as solely a matter of culture or of personal choice is a manifestly inadequate explanation for its longevity, popularity or survival despite the enlightenment and modernity.[137] This raises what may sound like a

---

[131] As Michael Stokes Paulsen has observed the position of the committed secularist is that "religious belief is irreducibly a matter of personal choice and preference (and perhaps a quaint, anti-intellectual one at that)" is a "fundamentally mistaken starting point." Michael Stokes Paulsen, "The Unconscionable War on Moral Conscience" (2016) 91 *Notre Dame Law Review* 1167, 1173.

[132] Mario Beauregard and Denyse O'Leary, *The Spiritual Brain* (Harper Collins 2008) 7; John Finnis, *Natural Law and Natural Rights* (Oxford University Press, 2nd ed 2011) 90; Candace S Alcorta and Richard Sosis, "Ritual, Emotion and Sacred Symbols" (Winter 2005) 16 *Human Nature* 4, 323, 346.

[133] Dimitrios Kapagiannis et al, 'Cognitive and Neural Foundations of Religious Belief' (2009) 106(12) *Proceedings of the National Academy of Sciences of the United States of America* 4876.

[134] Pope Paul VI, *Dignitatis Humanae* December 7, 1965 [10].

[135] Justin L Barrett, *Born Believers* (Free Press, 2012) 16; M R Trimble, *The Soul in The Brain* (John Hopkins University Press, 2009) 9-10, 17-23,178, 20.

[136] Barendt, above n 13,190.

[137] See generally Alister McGrath, *The Twilight of Atheism* (Double Day 2004); John

novel idea: that religiosity may be inherent or genetic. This idea is not so new. St Paul described faith as a gift and a grace.[138] This suggests that he considered it not to be solely a matter of personal choice. It has been recognised since at least 1917, that religious faith is not simply a matter of upbringing, culture or choice. In that year Montessori described children, brought up with no exposure to any form of religion, experiencing God and identifying God as the creator of all things.[139] Recent research, in the areas of neuroscience[140] cognitive science[141] and genetics,[142] supports the view that human beings are biologically predisposed towards religious belief and that some people may be more genetically predisposed to religious belief than others and that, at least for some people, religious beliefs are immutable.

Micklethwait and Adrian Wooldridge, *God is Back* (Allen Lane, 2009); Todd M Johnson and Brian J Grim, *World Religion Database International religious demographic statistics and sources* (2008) <http://www.worldreligiondatabase.org/wrd_default.asp>; Pew Research Center, *The Future of World Religions: Population Growth Projections, 2010-2050* (2 April 2015) <http://www.pewforum.org/2015/04/02/religious-projections-2010-2050/>.

[138] Romans 12:3, Galatians 1:15, 1 Corinthians 2:10-11, 1 Corinthians 12:8-10, Ephesians 2:8; Matthew 16:17; 11:25; *Catechism of the Catholic Church* (St. Pauls, 2nd ed, 2009) [153].

[139] Maria Montessori, *Spontaneous Activity in Education* (Frederick A Stokes Company, 1917) 352-355; see also Barrett, *Born Believers*, above n 136, 5-7, 67-68, 130-131, 176.

[140] See Andrew Newberg and Mark Robert Waldman, *Born To Believe* (Free Press, 2006) xvii-xviii; Christian Nordqvist, *What is Neuroscience?* (26 September 2014) Medical News Today <http://www.medicalnewstoday.com/articles/248680.php>. Nordqvist provides this definition of neuroscience: 'Neuroscience, also known as Neural Science, is the study of how the nervous system develops, its structure, and what it does. Neuroscientists focus on the brain and its impact on behavior and cognitive functions.'

[141] See Justin L Barrett, *Cognitive Science Religion and Theology* (Templeton Press, 2011) 5; Barrett, *Born Believers*, above n 136, 3. Barrett describes cognitive science as 'the interdisciplinary area of scholarship that considers what the human mind is and how it functions; how people think.'

[142] Jeffrey L Saver and John Rabin, 'The Neural Substrates of Religious Experience' (1997) 9 *Journal of Neuropsychiatry* 3, 498 - 499; Ananya Mandal, *What is Genetics?* (18 March 2013) Medical Life Science <http://www.news-medical.net/life-sciences/What-is-Genetics.aspx>. Mandal provides this definition of genetics: 'Genetics is the study of heredity. Heredity is a biological process where a parent passes certain genes onto their children or offspring.'

- **Believers from Birth: Religious Belief and Human Nature**

When we are born our minds are not a blank slate when it comes to religious belief.[143] Instead we are born 'with a natural propensity to believe.'[144] Belief is an essential and fundamental part of the human brain.[145] From birth we seek meaning and understanding. We look for purpose, design, function and cause in what we see around us.[146] Newberg and d'Aquili's research indicates that our minds are 'naturally calibrated to have and embrace spiritual perceptions.'[147] For example, before they turn five children are naturally likely to believe in some kind of god.[148] They are also likely to believe that the universe is created by a non-human, immortal, morally good creator with super perception, super power and super knowledge.[149] Barrett argues that these beliefs are the result of the ordinary course of human development not of indoctrination.[150] To understand why this is so involves understanding some of the basic stages of ordinary human development.

In their first year babies recognise that some things – toys, rocks and other inanimate objects - cannot move by themselves. They also

---

[143] Barrett, *Born Believers*, above n 136, 7-9, 194-195.

[144] Newberg and Waldman, *Born To Believe*, above n 141, xviii; see also Roger Trigg, 'Freedom, Toleration and the Naturalness of Religion' in Steve Clarke, Russell Powell and Julian Savalescu (eds), *Religion, Intolerance and Conflict: A Scientific and Conceptual Investigation* (Oxford Scholarship Online, 2013) 9.

[145] Newberg and Waldman, *Born To Believe*, above n 141, 8.

[146] E Margaret Evans, 'Cognitive and Contextual Factors in the Emergence of Diverse Belief Systems: Creation versus Evolution' (2001) 42 *Cognitive Psychology* 217, 253; Deborah Kelemen and Evelyn Rosset, 'The Human Function Compunction: Teleological Explanation in Adults' (2009) 1 *Cognition* 6; Richard Dawkins, *The God Delusion* (Black Swan, 2006) 210; Newberg and Waldman, *Born To Believe*, above n 141, 97; Barrett, *Born Believers*, above n 136, 44-49; Barrett, *Cognitive Science Religion and Theology*, above n 142, 70-71; Trigg, above n 145, 9; Sam Harris et al, 'The Neural Correlates of Religious and Nonreligious Belief,' (2009) 4(10) *PLOS One* 1, 4-5.

[147] Newberg and Waldman, *Born To Believe*, above n 141, 8.

[148] Harris et al, above n 147, 5.

[149] Barrett, *Born Believers*, above n 136, 3, 9, 126, 136-140, 167.

[150] Ibid 4 – 7.

recognise that human beings and animals – agents - are different.[151] Agents can act and move themselves and they can move other objects because they choose to do so. Agents can have intentions, desires and beliefs.[152] One year olds recognise that agents come in a range of shapes and sizes and that there are many types of agents. If an inanimate object has moved they know that an agent must have been involved even if they have not seen an agent.[153] Knowing that agents are required to cause things, it is natural for children to assume that someone is responsible for everything they see.[154] Young children prefer the view that the universe and the natural world was created over evolutionary explanations even when their parents are secularists who reject a creationist view.[155] From the ages of one to four children are likely to believe in supernatural beings.[156] Children can imagine intelligence – a mind - separated from a physical body.[157] The fact that up to forty per cent of children have imaginary friends when they are very young demonstrates this.[158] This also helps to explain why it is also natural for children to believe that a spirit or soul survives death.[159]

---

[151] Barrett, *Cognitive Science Religion and Theology*, above n 142, 81.

[152] Barrett, *Born Believers*, above n 136, 20-32; Justin L Barrett, Rebekah A Richert and Amanda Driesenga, 'God's Beliefs Versus Mother's: The Development of Non-human Agency Concepts' (2001) 72 *Child Development* 1, 50, 53.

[153] Barrett, *Born Believers*, above n 136, 32-33.

[154] Ibid 50-51; Harris et al, above n 147, 4-5; Evans, above n 147, 222; Barrett, *Born Believers*, above n 136, 44. As Barrett has observed: 'Very young children successfully think about agents that are not visible, and agents need not physically or otherwise resemble humans. This ability to reason about agents enables even very young children to think about gods – typically unseen human agents. Even more than having the ability to understand agents, children have a tendency to identify objects and see events as caused by agents with little provocation. This tendency to easily find agents (sometimes without large amounts of evidence) persists into adulthood and makes the discovery of gods not only possible but likely.'

[155] Evans, above n 147, 222-223; Kelemen and Rosset above n 147, 6; Newberg and Waldman, *Born To Believe*, above n 136, 97; Harris et al, above n 147, 5.

[156] Barrett, *Born Believers*, above n 136, 3, 190.

[157] Ibid 3; Dawkins, above n 147, 209; Harris et al, above n 147, 4. They have the capacity to see the invisible: Sofia Cavellletti, *The Religious Potential of the Child* (trans.) Patricia M Coulter and Julie M Coulter, (Liturgy Training Publication, 1992) 45.

[158] Barrett, above n 136, 33-34.

[159] Ibid 120.

Before they turn three or four children are likely to consider that their parents and God are both immortal[160] and that both possess super knowledge.[161] Indeed Barrett and others argue that '[t]he relative ease humans have at representing an agent with properties such as infallible beliefs could help explain why concepts of gods are so widespread and contagious.'[162] Children's reasoning develops quickly and by age four they recognise that a human being was not responsible for the natural world.[163] By four or five children are likely to recognise that humans are mortal but that God is immortal.[164] Children tend to think of spiritual matters in physical terms and so from three to eight years of age they are likely to draw God with a human face or as a human person.[165] In short, whether we grow up in an environment of faith or not our brain has a natural tendency to accept spiritual beliefs as real.[166] This tendency is so strong that children, even children of atheists, naturally become religious without any religious instruction,[167] As EO Wilson has explained:

> The predisposition to religious belief is the most complex and powerful force in the human mind and in all possibility an inerradical part of human nature.[168]

Across all cultures people seek a right relationship with the divine – with God or the gods.[169] As Robert George has observed:

---

[160] Evans, above n 147, 251; Barrett, *Born Believers*, above n 136, 116.

[161] Barrett, *Born Believers*, above n 136, 104.

[162] Barrett, Richert and Driesenga, above n 153, 62.

[163] Barrett, *Born Believers*, above n 136, 65-66.

[164] Evans, above n 147, 251; Barrett, *Born Believers*, above n 136, 116.

[165] Newberg and Waldman, *Born To Believe*, above n 141, 120-121; Andrew Newberg and Mark Robert Waldman, *How God Changes Your Brain* (Ballantine Books, 2010) 83-86. As children get older their images of God become more complex.

[166] Newberg and Waldman, *Born To Believe*, above n 141, xviii, 97.

167 Barrett, *Born Believers*, above n 136, 238; see also Trigg, above n 145, 10; Montessori, above n 140, 352-355. Barrett argues that only special personal or environmental circumstances will interrupt this natural tendency.

[168] E O Wilson, *On Human Nature* (Harvard University Press, 1978) as quoted in Thomas J Bouchard et al, "Intrinsic and extrinsic religiousness: genetic and environmental influences and personal correlates" (1999) 2 *Twin Research* 88.

[169] Robert P George as quoted in "Religious Freedom: A Conversation with Rick War-

Why do we strive like that? It is because of the way we were made; it is because of the nature of the human being. Our most immediate experience as conscious and intentional actors is our experience of our own freedom. We experience ourselves as creatures who cause things that we are not caused to cause. We experience what philosophers call free will.[170]

As human beings enjoy free will this natural tendency towards religion may result in a person remaining religious throughout their lives or in religious belief re-asserting itself later in life or in rejecting religion but as discussed below some people's beliefs are immutable.

- **Religion and Human Flourishing**

Many have argued, as Paulsen has, that "[r]eligion is of fundamental importance to human flourishing."[171] Whilst a detailed examination of the arguments for and against[172] this philosophical position is beyond the scope of this paper, this might be expected to be so if, as this paper argues, religiosity is a natural, intrinsic and integral part of human beings. It is certainly consistent with the empirical evidence of the benefits of religion examined in Part IV below.

- **Is There a Genetic Element to Religiosity?**

There appears to be a moderate to significant genetic influence in differences in spiritual and religious interests.[173] . Waller et al's 1990

---

ren, Robert George and John DiIulio" Georgetown University's Berkeley's Center for Religious Freedom. Feb 12, 2013. https://canavox.com/wp-content/uploads/2017/06/Excerpts-from-Religious-Freedom.pdf, 2.

[170] George, as quoted in "Religious Freedom: A Conversation with Rick Warren, Robert George and John DiIulio" above n 170, 2.

[171] Paulsen, above n 132, 1194, see also ibid, 3; Robert P George, *Conscience and Its Enemies – Confronting the Dogmas of Liberal Secularism* (ISI Books, 2000) 113, 115-125;Germain Grisez, Joseph Boyle and John Finnis, "Practical Principles, Moral Truth and Ultimate Ends" (1987) 32 *American Journal of Jurisprudence* 152, 135-136,141-147; Germain Grisez, "Natural Law, God, religion and Human Fulfilment"(2001) 46 *American Journal of Jurisprudence* 3, 36, 8, 14-17.

[172] See discussion in Paulsen, above n 132, 1173, n 20 and 1194 and David N Hempton, "Christianity and Human Flourishing: The Roles of Law and Politics" (2017) 32(1) *Journal of Law and Religion* 53, 53-54, 58.

[173] Brian M D'Onofrio et al, "Understanding Biological and Social Influences on

study of identical and fraternal twin pairs, raised separately, found that genetic and environmental factors both influenced differences in religious, attitudes, interests and values.[174] They identified genetics as accounting for half of the variance in religious interests and attitudes between individuals.[175] This correlation is substantially greater than that found in similar studies in connection with same-sex attraction.[176] In a later study of twins, reared apart, Bouchard et al found a modest degree of genetic influence in both intrinsic and extrinsic religiosity[177] D'Onofrio et al's study of 14,781 twins and their family members found that common religious affiliation in families was primarily cultural but that additive genetic effects as well as the shared and unshared environments of the twins sampled, influenced religious attitudes and behaviours.[178] They found, for example, that genetics played a significant role in the development of religious behaviour of adults judged by church attendance and sexual permissiveness. [179]

The brains of women and men are different in many ways including serotonin 2 chemistry.[180] Genetics account for 50 per cent of the difference in how strongly serotonin binds to serotonin 2.[181] Nelson posits that this difference may account for the higher propensity to

---

Religious Affiliation, Attitudes and Behaviours: A Behavior Genetic Perspective," (Dec.1999) 67(6) *Journal or Personality* 953,963; Andrew Newberg and Mark Robert Waldman , *Why We Believe What We Believe* (Free Press, 2006) 225-226; Newberg and Waldman, *Born To Believe*, above n 141, 225-226; Barrett, *Born Believers*, above n 136, 204-207; Saver and Rabin, above n 143, 499; Trimble, above n 136, 20; Bouchard et al, above n 169, 89, 96.

[174] Niels G Waller et al, "Genetic and Environmental Influences on religious Interests, Attitudes and Values: A Study of Twins Reared Apart and Together," (Mar 1990) 1(2) *Psychological Science* 138, 140.

[175] Ibid 140; see discussion in Saver and Rabin, above n 143, 499.

[176] See discussion in Part III above.

[177] Bouchard et al, above n 169, 89 where an intrinsically motivated person refers to a person who lives their religion whilst an extrinsically motivated person refers to a person who uses their religion.

[178] D'Onofrio et al, above n 174, 968.

[179] Ibid 970, 974.

[180] Kevin Nelson, *The God Impulse* (Simon & Schuster, 2011) 245.

[181] Ibid 245

religious experiences of some people.[182] Newberg and d'Aquili also suggest that some people may be born with a biological predisposition towards religious experience and spiritual perception. Their studies of brain scans of long-term practitioners of Buddhist meditation and of nuns, who were long-term practitioners of Christian meditation, found that the subjects of their study had a 'unique perception of reality which is continuously active whether they are meditating or not. As one of the nuns commented, "I feel God's presence every minute of the day."'[183] This research suggests that the subjects of their study were either born with this characteristic or that the regular meditation caused permanent alteration of the thalamus to make religious and spiritual experiences accessible.[184] The human brain has two hemispheres. Each seems to play a different role in relation to beliefs.[185] The left hemisphere favours the preservation of consistency whilst the right hemisphere favours changing beliefs.[186] For beliefs to change interaction between the hemispheres seems to be required.[187] The religious beliefs of those with less interaction between the cerebral hemispheres may be less susceptible to change.[188] As a result certain individuals may be

---

[182] Ibid 245

[183] Newberg and Waldman, *Born To Believe*, above n 141, 185.

[184] Andrew Newberg et al, 'The measurement of regional cerebral blood flow during the complex cognitive task of meditation: a preliminary SPECT study' (2001) 106 *Psychiatric Research: Neuroimaging* 113, 121; Antoine Lutz et al, 'Long-term meditators self-induce high-amplitude gamma synchrony during mental practice' (2004) 101(46) *Proceedings of the National Academy of the Sciences of the United States of America* 16369, 16373; Newberg and Waldman, *Born To Believe*, above n 122, 183-185.

[185] C L Niebauer et al, 'Interhemispheric interaction and beliefs on our origin: Degree of handedness predicts beliefs in creationism versus evolution (2004) 9 *Laterality* 4, 433.

[186] Ibid 435.

[187] Ibid.

[188] Ibid 443; Newberg and Waldman, *Born To Believe*, above n 141, 97; Douglas Degelman, Denée Heinrichs, and Hisashi Ishitobi, *Handedness and Religious Beliefs* Vanguard University <http://www.vanguard.edu/psychology/faculty/douglas-degelman/cv/handedness-and-religious-beliefs/>; Tabitha M Powledge, *Left-handedness: Genes and matter of chance* (29 August 2016) Genetic Literacy Project <https://www.geneticliteracyproject.org/2016/08/29/left-handedness-genes-and-a-matter-of-chance/>. Niebauer et al, above n 186, found that single handed adults were statisti-

genetically predisposed towards fundamentalism.[189]

In short, genetics appears to have a role to play in our religiosity and in the changeability of our religious beliefs. This does not mean that our genes predetermine how we behave or that our innate religious characteristics cannot be changed.[190] As Newberg and Waldman observe "as with any human trait, we each have varying predispositions and abilities. The result is that some people can feel highly spiritual while others do not."[191]

- **Developing Belief in the Specifics of a Religious Faith**

To survive from infancy human beings depend on others and must believe what others tell them – about what to eat, what is dangerous and so on.[192] Newberg and Waldman argue that, in the first few years of life, we assume that what we are told by others is true.[193] We are not born with any inherent natural inclination towards the theology of Christianity, Islam, Judaism, Hinduism or any other specific religious faith.[194] What we see and hear during our upbringing - the social norms we see around us - clearly impact on our specific beliefs.[195] Most people are 'essentially born into a religious community.'[196] Children do not

---

cally more inclined to embrace creationism and to continue to reject evolution than mixed-handed people. From this they extrapolated that there may be less interaction between the cerebral hemispheres of people who are solely left or right handed than those who are mixed-handed such that such people seem to be more resistant to changing their beliefs; note the contrary findings of Degelman, Heinrichs and Ishitobi. The question of whether and the extent to which handedness is itself genetic is itself a matter of debate.

[189] Newberg and Waldman, *Born To Believe*, above n 141, 225.
[190] Ibid 225-226.
[191] Ibid 226.
[192] Newman and Waldman, *Born To Believe*, above n 141, 24-25.
[193] Ibid xviii.
[194] Harris et al, above n 147, 5; Newberg and Waldman, *Born To Believe*, above n 141, 225; Barrett, *Born Believers*, above n 136, 141, 151, 184. In fact in Barrett's view '[b]oth the kinds of ideas that theologians develop and the intellectual practice of doing theology may be relatively unnatural.'
[195] Newberg and Waldman, *Born To Believe*, above n 141, 225.
[196] Ahdar, above n 13, 301.

however accept everything that they are told like sponges.[197] Children assimilate ideas that fit with their existing knowledge.[198] So, children are not necessarily atheists because their parents are.[199] Beliefs which develop naturally – like the predisposition towards causation and purpose – are accepted by us as true. It takes considerable effort to change those beliefs.[200] For example, to change the natural belief that the natural world suggests design and purpose is difficult and requires evidence.[201] This explains why parental beliefs about evolution are not simply adopted by their children. In fact, a creationist view continues to be preferred until early adolescence even among children taught evolutionary science in their textbooks and at school and raised by secular parents who prefer that explanation for the natural world.[202] As we naturally develop the intuition that everything is caused or designed this belief survives into adulthood such that '[e]ven among staunchly committed anti-design evolutionist, the language of purpose and design appears unavoidable. The way our brains naturally develop compels us to wonder who or what is behind the evident design and purpose in nature.'[203] Unlike atheism, which directly challenges children's natural inclination towards religious belief, this inclination is usually supplemented, rather than directly challenged, by the specific details of religious belief and practice which they are taught and absorb by watching those around them and by participating in religious experiences. These experiences are many and varied. They may include, for example, communal and regular worship, prayer, retreats, rituals, mystical or spiritual encounters with the divine, acts of charity or service or supporting moral positions in writing and by actions such as public

---

[197] Barrett, *Born Believers*, above n 136, 3, 189-191.
[198] Evans, above n 147, 222, 252.
[199] Montessori, above n 140. 353-355
[200] Barrett, *Cognitive Science, Religion and Theology*, above n 142, 155.
[201] Ibid 159.
[202] Evans, above n 147, 222, 245, 249-250; Newberg and Waldman, *Born To Believe*, above n 141, 97; Niebauer et al, above n 186, 433, 438; Barrett, *Born Believers*, above n 136, 72.
[203] Barrett, *Born Believers*, above n 136, 54-55; Kelemen and Rosset, above n 147, 5-6.

protests.[204] Some religious traditions teach that particular events cause change to a person. In some faith traditions, such as Catholicism, these events can happen in infancy without any conscious acquiescence by the person involved. That faith teaches that baptism not only cleanses the baptised person of original sin but it makes them 'a new creature.'[205] Across all cultures adolescent rites of passage are common features of religions.[206] Adolescence appears to be a neurophysiologically sensitive developmental period for learning abstract religious concepts and sacred symbols.[207] These are powerful tools to develop a sense of community and cooperation.[208] Religious rites of passage which occur late in childhood, during adolescence or as adults are matters of personal choice.[209] In traditional Protestant theology, on conversion to the faith, Christians are baptized in the Holy Spirit.[210] For many charismatics Christians receive the Holy Spirt at conversion and at 'baptism in the

---

[204] Barrett, *Cognitive Science Religion and Theology*, above n 142, 113-114.

[205] *Catechism of the Catholic Church*, above n 139, [1263], [1265], [1267], 1272], [1304]; Archdiocese of Brisbane, *Confirmation* <https://brisbanecatholic.org.au/life/confirmation/>. According to the Catechism of that Church: 'Incorporated into Christ by Baptism, the person baptised is configured to Christ. Baptism seals the Christian with the indelible spiritual mark (character) of his belonging to Christ. No sin can erase this mark even if sin prevents baptism from bearing the fruits of salvation.' The Catholic Church also teaches that baptism makes a person an adopted son of God, a 'partaker of the divine nature', a 'member of Christ and co-heir with him and a temple of the Holy Spirit,' and a member of the Body of Christ and a member of the Catholic Church.

[206] Alcorta and Sosis, above n 133, 340.

[207] Ibid 341-344, 349; see also E.M. Standing, *Maria Montessori, Her Life and Work* (Plume Books, 1998) 115-117.

[208] Alcorta and Sosis, above n 133, 349.

[209] For example, baptism, confirmation, reconciliation, bar mitzvah or bat mitzvah. For example, in the Latin rite of the Catholic Church whilst baptism is normally celebrated during infancy confirmation is celebrated later in childhood. Practise varies in Australian diocese from around the age of 7 to the ages of 12-13. The Catholic Church teaches that confirmation increases and deepens baptismal grace and causes further change to the recipient of the sacrament. It 'imprints on the soul an indelible spiritual mark, the 'character' which is the sign that Jesus Christ has marked a Christian with the seal of his Spirit by clothing him with power from on high so that he may be his witness.'

[210] Alister McGrath, *Christianity's Dangerous Idea* (HarperOne, 2007) 433.

Spirit' they receive a 'second blessing.'[211] For many of those who accept these teachings the changes which occur are permanent and real. The question of whether any or all of these changes do or do not actually occur to any or all of the people who participate in these events, is not a question that the State can resolve.[212]

Regularly repeated rituals, like religious ceremonies and prayer,[213] "lie at the heart of all religions."[214] Rituals and religious symbols, like Christmas trees and Easter eggs, give theological ideas personal meaning and imprint permanent images on the memory.[215] Repetition develops semantic memory by which participants recall the meaning of ideas and perceive certain actions as having deeper meaning.[216] It reaffirms and reinforces religious beliefs which take on increasingly real nuances and emotional importance.[217] Religious

---

[211] Ibid 425, 433.

[212] *Church of the New Faith v Commission of Pay-Roll Tax (Vic)* (1983) 154 CLR 130, 134. The High Court stated that: '[u]nder our law, the State has no prophetic role in relation to religious beliefs; the State can neither declare supernatural truth nor determine the paths through which the human mind must search in a quest for supernatural truth.' To similar effect in the United States Justice Robert Jackson in *West Virginia State Board of Education v. Barnette* 319 U.S. 624 (1943) 642 observed that "If there is any fixed star in our constitutional constellation, it is that no official, high or petty, can prescribe what shall be orthodox in politics, nationalism, religion, or other matters of opinion, or force citizens to confess by word or act their faith therein. If there are any circumstances which permit an exception, they do not now occur to us."

[213] Uffe Schjodt et al, 'Rewarding Prayers' (2008) 443 *Neuroscience Letters* 165; *Catechism of the Catholic Church*, above n 139, [2180]. For example, daily prayer, such as that practised by devout Muslims five times a day, personal or ritual prayers such as the Christian 'Our Father' or 'Hail Mary' or the Catholic mass – the Catholic Eucharistic liturgy – which occurs in churches across the world on a daily basis and which Catholics are obliged to participate in every Sunday and on holy days of obligation.

[214] Alcorta and Sosis, above n 133, 344-345.

[215] Newberg and Waldman, *How God Changes Your Brain*, above n 166, 41.

[216] Barrett, *Cognitive Science Religion and Theology*, above n 142, 142.

[217] As Newberg and Waldman observe (*Born To Believe*, above n 141, xviii): 'As Richard Dawkins aptly puts it, children are not Jewish or Christian or Muslim. Rather they are taught to believe in one set of ideas, and they are taught to disbelieve in others. With enough repetition, these beliefs and disbeliefs become neurologically embedded in memory, from which they influence future behaviours and thoughts. Thus, the more time you devote to believing in God…the more those beliefs become an integral part of your reality.' See also Newberg and Waldman, *Born To Believe*, above n 141,

traditions are also characterised by engaging, attention grabbing, memorable and abstract religious symbols such as holy water, virgin birth, transubstantiation, resurrection from the dead and incorporeal gods able to be everywhere and anywhere at the same time.[218] These beliefs which are clearly outside everyday experience and may seem to outsiders to be counter-intuitive are not only memorable, they bind religious groups together as a shared understanding and one outsiders dismiss, challenge or, in some cases, persecute.[219] As Alcorta and Sosis observe:

> [These beliefs] must be learned and since such learning has been orally transmitted throughout the vast majority of human evolution, this also implies participation in religious ritual. As a result, religious belief systems serve as both costly and reliable signals of group membership.[220]

Sosis argues that it is participation in religious ritual itself which generates religious belief. [221] Barrett suggests that the way religious believers think – how they perceive the world and how they understand events - may be reshaped through regular religious practices or by religious experiences of great intensity.[222] Newberg and Waldman have observed permanent changes to believers' brains resulting from repetition of religious practice.[223] Evidence shows that it is difficult and in some cases neurotically impossible for atheists contemplating God to experience spiritually uplifting experiences or to sense God as

---

218; Barrett, *Cognitive Science Religion and Theology*, above n 142, 119; Alcorta and Sosis, above n 133 338-339.

[218] Alcorta and Sosis, ibid 323,327-328, 331-332.

[219] Ibid 328, 332.

[220] Ibid 328.

[221] Ibid 332.

[222] Barrett, *Cognitive Science Religion and Theology*, above n 142, 117, 129.

[223] Brain scan evidence has demonstrated that prayer and meditation alter the neural activity in the parietal and frontal lobes and cause permanent neurological changes in long term practitioners (Newberg et al, above n 185, 628; Newberg and Waldman, *Born To Believe*, above n 141, 84-85, 169, 174-183; Newberg and Waldman, *How God Changes Your Brain*, above n 166, 48) and Mario Beauregard, *Brain Wars* (Harper One, 2012) 80-88; Alcorta and Sosis, above n 133, 331.

a reality.[224] It may also be difficult for non-believers to appreciate how fundamental religious belief can be to an individual.[225]

In Newberg and Waldman's view we absorb the beliefs of those around us and once our 'primary set of beliefs has been established, the brain finds it difficult to integrate opposing ideas and beliefs.'[226] This helps to explain why Christian children are more likely to draw God with a face than Jewish children[227] and why children of fundamentalist Christian parents raised with a creationist view of the universe continue to maintain that view before and after adolescence.[228] It helps to explain why those raised in families who regularly attend Church are most likely to believe in God and least likely to switch denominations, become nominal Christians or to cease to identify with any religion.[229] It also helps to explains why, as Evans and Kelley observe:

> Belief in God is not a transient or ephemeral matter, fluctuating from day to day, or month to month, or even from year to year. On the contrary, those who believe now have almost all done so for a long time, and those who do not believe now have long had their doubts.[230]

---

[224] Newberg and Waldman, *Born To Believe*, above n 141, xix, 225; Newberg and Waldman, *How God Changes Your Brain*, above n 162, 59.

[225] Newberg and Waldman, *Born To Believe*, above n 141, 19, quoting Jeremy W Hayward. Hayward explains it this way: 'As a result of a combination of innate ideas and the intimate influences of the culture and environment we grow up in, we come to have beliefs about the nature of being human. These beliefs penetrate to a very deep level of our psychosomatic systems, our minds and brains, our nervous systems, our endocrine systems, and even our blood and sinews. We act, speak and think according to these deeply held beliefs and belief systems'.

[226] Newberg and Waldman, *Born To Believe*, above n 141, xviii.

[227] Ibid 121; Deuteronomy 4:15-20, 5:8. Whilst Christianity is a monotheistic religion, in orthodox Christianity God consists of the three persons of the Trinity – Father, Son (Jesus Christ who whilst fully human is fully divine) and Holy Spirit whilst in Judaism God is never a physical being and representations of God as a physical being is prohibited by scripture.

[228] Barrett, *Born Believers*, above n 136, 73.

[229] Evans and Kelley, above n 31, 50-52. Regular church-going Christians are also very likely (89% of such people) to consider Christ's life to be extremely important to them: McCrindle Research Pty Ltd, above n 30, 43.

[230] Evans and Kelley, above n 31, 28.

Within some communities religion is so built into everyday life that the idea of living contrary to the faith let alone abandoning it, simply would not occur to many in the community. There would be difficulties in so doing if that thought did arise.[231] This does not mean that everyone raised within a faith tradition maintains their beliefs or lives them through practice, at the same level of intensity, throughout their lives. For those who do the religious impulses of childhood are likely to develop and continue to grow.[232] For others religious practice ebbs and flows.[233] Others seem unaware of religious faith until a spiritual awakening. Consistently with the view that belief in God is inherent, Muslims consider that those who embrace Islam do not convert to the faith but rather they revert or return to the belief in Allah with which they were born.[234] Similarly many Christian groups refer to those who embrace their faith for the first time or in a reinvigorated way as being 'born again.'[235]

In multi-faith, pluralist Australia, contrary to the position in some societies, conversion from one faith to another is unlikely to pose a physical risk. However it still remains comparatively rare. A 2017 report found that only 7% of Australians who identify as religious or as spiritual but not religious were converts from a different religion whilst only 12% of Australians were quite open or very interested in changing their current religious views.[236] This may be in part due to fear

---

[231] House of Lords Committee on Religious Offences in England and Wales, *Religious Offences in England and Wales – First Report* (2002-2003) Vol 1 [13]; Barendt, above n 13, 190; Ahdar above n 13, 301.

[232] Newberg and Waldman, *How God Changes Your Brain* above n 166, 130.

[233] See Newberg and Waldman, *How God Changes Your Brain*, above n 166, 127, 130. Different age groups on average have different levels of interest and engagement in religion. Possibly as autonomy and independence are particularly important to adolescence, interest in religion declines for many people in this period as the adolescent mind seeks to process competing beliefs. Interest and engagement in religion grows again from the age of twenty to the age of thirty and declines after that until another increase in involvement in organised religion from around age fifty.

[234] Stephenson, 'Indigenous Australia's Pilgrimage to Islam', above n 91, 265.

[235] John 3:1-21.

[236] McCrindle Research Pty Ltd, above n 30, 15, 17

of experiencing rejection by family or friends.[237] A better explanation is our natural propensity towards religious belief, our upbringing in a particular tradition, our participation in religious rituals and to changes to the structure of the brain as we age which make our beliefs less likely to change.[238] This helps to explain why, if they convert, Christians are more likely to convert to another faith tradition within Christianity than to a non-Christian faith.[239] It also helps to explain why, within Australia's Aboriginal peoples, conversion to Christianity and to Islam has occurred mostly among those Aboriginal communities which have seen these religions as compatible with their indigenous traditions and beliefs.[240] Similarly some Christian converts to Islam are attracted by the familiarity of the prophets, Mary and (albeit as a prophet only) Christ.[241]

Biology, upbringing, participation in religious rituals and the exercise of free will all contribute to the nature and extent of our religious beliefs. As Sam Harris and others recognise, 'some people actually believe what they say they believe.'[242] As a result, as Newberg and Waldman observe 'for many people, God is as real as anything

---

[237] Patrick Madrid, *Surprised by Truth 2* (Sophia Institute Press, 2000) xiii; Patrick Madrid, *Surprised by Truth* (Basilica Press, 1994); *Surprised by Truth 3* (Sophia Institute Press, 2002); News.com.au, *Real life: Australian woman Lydia on why she converted to Islam* (3 October 2014) <http://www.news.com.au/lifestyle/real-life>; Ben McClellan, 'Almost two Sydney women a week are converting to Islam', *The Daily Telegraph* (online) 19 January 2014 < http://www.dailytelegraph.com.au/news/nsw>. An experience which Madrid describes as 'a non-bloody martyrdom'.

[238] Newberg and Waldman, *Born To Believe*, above n 141, xviii-xix, 25.

[239] Evans and Kelley above n 31, 47-48.

[240] Stephenson, 'Indigenous Australia's Pilgrimage to Islam', above n 91, 264-266, 268-274; Peta Stephenson, 'Syncretic Spirituality: Islam in Indigenous Australia' (2013) 24(4) *Islam and Christian–Muslim Relations* 424, 432-435. In regions, such as those of the Pitjantjatjara of Central Australia's Western desert, where Christianity was considered to conflict with the assumptions behind Pitjantjatjara life, conversion to Christianity has been very low.

[241] News.com.au, above n, 238. As one convert observed: 'There was a striking similarity between Islam and my Christian upbringing. We share the prophets of Abraham, Adam, Moses, Noah, Jesus, etc.'

[242] Harris et al, above n 147, 1, 2.

else you can see or feel in the world.'[243] According to Grim and Grim, 'many, if not most people of faith, aim to conduct their affairs (to some extent, however imperfectly) guided by and inspired by their religious ideals.'[244] As an example Rick Warren has said that:

> Religion involves every single area of my life: how I make my decisions, how I spend my money, how I use my time, how I raise my children, how I educate my kids, how I build my business. If I am truly a religious person, my faith affects every area. I cannot compartmentalize it as simply worship.[245]

Whilst the latest census figures show an increase in Australians self-identifying in the "No Religion" category this does not mean that the proportion of Australians who take their religion so seriously that they consider that it defines them as persons is in decline. An Australian survey conducted in 2009 showed that 13 per cent of Australians considered that religious faith or spirituality was very important in shaping their life's decisions in areas such as lifestyle, relationships and career whilst 25 per cent thought it important, 23 per cent thought it of little importance and 38 per cent thought it was not important.[246] Surveys conducted in 2017 found that 27 per cent of Australians considered that their religion defined them as a person,[247] that 48 per cent had a strong commitment to their religious views,[248] 25 per cent would be unlikely to consider changing their religious views in the future,[249] and that 21 per cent of Australians were extremely or significantly involved in practising their religion.[250] For people

---

[243] Newberg and Waldman, *How God Changes Your Brain*, above n 166, 68.

[244] Brian J Grim and Melissa E Grim, 'The Socio-economic Contribution of Religion to American Society: An Empirical Analysis (2016) 12(3) *Interdisciplinary Journal of Research on Religion* 1, 25.

[245] Rick Warren as quoted in "Religious Freedom: A Conversation with Rick Warren, Robert George and John DiIulio" above n 170, 1.

[246] Bouma et al, 'Freedom of Religion and Belief in 21st Century Australia' (Research Report, Australian Human Rights Commission, 2011) 5.

[247] Ipsos, "2017 Global Views on Religion" (Ipsos, 2017) 4 Ipsos"2017 < http://www.tjhcouncil.org.au/media>

[248] McCrindle Research Pty Ltd, above n 30, 18.

[249] Ibid 17, 18.

[250] Ibid 16.

like this living in accordance with their religious convictions is not a matter of mere personal preference or self-will but rather a "reasoned moral duty grounded in conviction one discerns but does not invent for oneself."[251] Whilst restrictions on religious freedom are likely to impact on some people more than others for some people religious belief is no more flexible or optional than age, sex, disability, sexual orientation or gender identity. As Laycock and Berg observe:

> No religious believer can change his understanding of divine command by any act of will...Religious beliefs can change over time...But these things do not change because government says they must, or because the individual decides they should ... [T]he religious believer cannot change God's mind.[252]
>
> [C]ommitted religious believers argue that some aspects of human identity are so fundamental that they should be left to each individual, free of all nonessential regulation, even when manifested in conduct. For religious believers, the conduct at issue is to live and act consistently with the demands of the Being that they believe made us all and holds the whole world together.[253]

IV Protecting Religion is in Australia's Self-Interest?

- **The Positive Influence of Religion on Australian Society**

As a 2017 survey found that 63 per cent of Australians consider that religion does more harm than good,[254] the paper considers evidence of religion's positive influence on Australian society. Spiritual and religious belief were and remain foundational to the preservation of the unique cultures of Australia's Aboriginal and Torres Strait Islander peoples. Through emigration by those fleeing religious persecution elsewhere Australia has been the beneficiary of the failure of other

---

[251] Paulsen, above n 132, 1177.
[252] Douglas Laycock and Thomas Berg, 'Protecting Same-Sex Marriage and Religious Liberty' (2013) 99 *Virginia Law Review in Brief* 4.
[253] Ibid 13.
[254] Ipsos above n248, 4. This placed Australia 2nd in the world to Belgium (68%) and equal placed with Germany and Spain but well above Canada (55%) and the United States (39%) on this scale.

nations to afford religious freedom to their citizens. From the arrival of the First Fleet – and prior to the beginning of government provision of social services – it was the religions that provided education, welfare and other services.[255] In Australia today institutions owned or inspired by churches, religions and religious believers provide education, medical, nursing and hospice care, aged care and works of everyday charity as a standard part of life.[256] For example, the Catholic Church and organisations inspired or begun by it, provide drug, alcohol and gambling support, foster care and adoptions, mediation and counselling, accommodation, 20,000 aged care places, respite, dementia and disability care, employment, services, education to 700,000 school children and thousands of tertiary students, training and support services, children, youth and family services, family and relationship counselling and more than 10,000 hospital beds. The St Vincent de Paul and five and a half million Catholics, in 1300 parishes assist innumerable people throughout Australia every day.[257] Followers of many other faith traditions have also made and continue to make their own, many and unique contributions to the wellbeing of the nation and its people. The role of religion in humanitarian endeavours is such that some argue that 'it is only a slight exaggeration to say "no religion, no humanitarianism." These institutions exist and these contributions to society occur only through the faith commitment of their founders and of contemporary believers.'[258] Grim and Grim

---

[255] Bouma et al, above n 247, 38; Roy Williams, *Post God Nation?* (ABC Books, 2015) 1-141. A detailed examination of the role of Christianity in the provision of services in Australia and of the influence of Christianity on Australian life is well beyond the scope of this paper but a survey can be found in Williams' book.

[256] Micklethwait and Wooldridge, above n 138. Micklethwait and Wooldridge have analysed the reasons for the persistence of religious belief in the United States and, in this context, they particularly emphasise the regular acts of care and charity of ordinary Christians and their churches throughout the United States.

[257] Xt3, *Installation of Archbishop Anthony Fisher: Full Homily* (12 November 2014) <http://www.xt3.com/library/view.php?id=17926>; Michael Digges, 'Don't switch off from elections, because bigotry is alive and well' *The Catholic Weekly*, 19 June 2016, 8.

[258] Michael Barnett and Janice Gross Stein quoted in Barry W Bussey, 'The Legal Revolution Against the Place of Religion: The Case of Trinity Western University Law School' (2016) 4 *Brigham Young University Law Review* 101, 171.

have estimated the value of religious faith to the United States to be in the billions of dollars.[259] If calculated, the socio-economic impact of religion to Australian society would be likely to be as proportionately significant. This suggests that religious freedom is not only a good thing for individuals but a good thing for the Australian nation as a whole. Challenges to religious freedom not only inhibit the ability of religious people and religious institutions to continue to fulfil their mission[260] but they are bad for the economy.[261]

- **Religious Belief Benefits Individuals**

Statistically regular church goers are happier,[262] enjoy greater well-being,[263] and have lower blood pressure than the general community.[264] Even religious believers who participate irregularly live longer and are healthier.[265] Older weekly Church attendees are less likely to suffer from stroke.[266] Research also shows that statistically religious believers

---

[259] Grim and Grim, above n 245, 1, 4-13, 14-24, 25-26. They estimate the revenues of local congregational activities (US$83.8bn), religious charities (US$44.3bn), media (US$0.9bn), healthcare (US$161bn), education ($US74bn), kosher and halal food ($14.4bn), social services provided by religious congregations ($327bn), the contribution of businesses with religious roots ($438.4bn) and the incomes of religiously affiliated Americans ($4.8tr).

[260] Bussey, above n 259, 170. And around the world such institutions have closed for this reason.

[261] Brian J. Grim, Greg Clark and Robert Edward Snyder, 'Is Religious Freedom Good for Business?: A Conceptual and Empirical Analysis' (2014) 10(4) *Interdisciplinary Journal of Research on Religion* 1, 1.

[262] Evans and Kelley, above n 31, 44.

[263] Hongtu Chen et al, 'Religious Participation as a predictor of mental health status and treatment outcomes in older persons' (2007) 22 *International Journal of Geriatric Psychiatry* 144, 150-152; Izet Pajevic, Osman Sinanovic and Mevludin Hasanovic, 'Religiosity and Mental Health' (2005) 17(1-2) *Psychiatria Damubina* 84, 86; Nick Spencer et al, 'Religion and Well-being: Assessing the evidence' (Report, Theos, 2016) 10, 15.

[264] Newberg and Waldman, *How God Changes Your Brain*, above n 166, 60.

[265] Newberg and Waldman, *How God Changes Your Brain*, above n 166, 61,174, 149; Newberg and Waldman, *Born To Believe*, above n 141, 127. One long-term longitudinal US study found that those attending church at least once a month had a thirty to thirty-five per cent reduced risk of dying.

[266] Newberg and Waldman, *How God Changes Your Brain*, above n 166, 61.

achieve better academic results, enjoy higher self-esteem and better blood pressure,[267] are less likely to abuse alcohol and drugs, have suicidal thoughts or attempt or commit suicide, are psychologically healthier, deal better with emotional and health problems, recover more quickly from trauma and are more motivated to be involved in the community and to volunteer.[268] University students who engage in religious activities enjoy better social integration and emotional well-being.[269] Significantly research has shown that the decreases in psychologically distress experienced by regular Church-goers is relatively greater for those who are socioeconomically disadvantaged.[270] Studies have shown that depression and anxiety decrease as religious convictions increase[271] and that the Catholic practice of praying the rosary[272] reduces tension, stress and anxiety.[273] Statistically religious adolescents have lower testosterone levels,[274] better mental health and are less likely to suffer from depression.[275] Additionally, most religious believers consider that their religious practices and beliefs improve their relationships and their ability to cope with stress. Being involved in organised religious activities and social connections

---

[267] Alcorta and Sosis, above n 133, 336.

[268] Alcorta and Sosis, above n 133, 324; Bouchard et al, above n 169, 88;97; Alexander Moreira-Almeida, Francisco Lotufo Neto and Harold G Koenig, 'Religiousness and mental health: a review' (2006) 28(3) *Rev Bras Psiquiatr* 242, 244-245; Newberg and Waldman, *Born To Believe*, above n 141, 127; Barrett, *Born Believers*, above n 136, 225, 233-235; Grim and Grim, above n 245, 3; Greg Walsh, 'Same Sex Marriage and Religious Liberty' (2016) 35 *University of Tasmania Law Review* 2, 106.

[269] Possamai et al, above n 24, 313; Cydney J Van Dyke and Maurice J Elias, 'How forgiveness, purpose and religiosity are related to the mental health and well-being of youth: a review of the literature' (2007) 10(4) *Mental Health, Religion & Culture* 395, 409.

[270] Alcorta and Sosis, above n 133, 340

[271] Newberg and Waldman, *How God Changes Your Brain*, above n 166, 140; Van Dyke and Elias, above n 270, 410.

[272] Which involves repetition of prayer whilst counting rosary beads

[273] Newberg and Waldman, *How God Changes Your Brain*, above n 166, 155, 174.

[274] Alcorta and Sosis, above n 133, 336.

[275] Y Joel Wong, Lynn Rew and Kristina D Slaikeu, 'A Systematic Review of recent Research on Adolescent Religiosity/Spirituality and mental health' (2006) 27 *Issues in Mental Health Nursing* 161, 162; Newberg and Waldman, *Born To Believe*, above n 141, 127.

statistically improve health and longevity. As people turn 50 years of age they tend to become more involved in such religious activities.[276] The cognition and moral reasoning of religious believers is enhanced not only by the social support provided within religious communities but also by optimism about health, intellectual stimulation and higher education.[277] In times of high stress and uncontrollability, religion provides believers with a very effective coping mechanism.[278] Newberg and Waldman also observe that individuals who engage in religious and spiritual practices enjoy a wide range of emotional and physical benefits.[279] Even without the communitarian benefits of religion, those who engage in personal religious participation enjoy better well-being particularly mental health.[280]

V Does Discrimination on the Grounds of Religious Belief Occur in Australia?

If the criteria by which characteristics were considered appropriate for legal protection was solely whether those characteristics were immutable or inherent then the case for protecting religious freedom has been set out in the discussion above. However the fact of discrimination against persons with a particular characteristic may itself be a ground for considering the need for such protection. Evidence of discrimination was a key reasons for the extension of anti-discrimination legislation to protect same sex attracted, bisexual, transgender or intersex persons.[281] For this reason this Part briefly considers the evidence of discrimination on the basis of religious belief in the general community and provides some examples of State

---

[276] Newberg and Waldman, *Born To Believe*, above n 141, 130.
[277] Ibid 130-131.
[278] Van Dyke and Elias, above n 270, 408.
[279] Newberg and Waldman, *Born To Believe*, above n 141, xx; Newberg and Waldman, *How God Changes Your Brain*, above n 166, 22.
[280] Spencer et al, above n 264, 11.
[281] Explanatory Memorandum, Sex Discrimination Amendment (Sexual Orientation, Gender Identity and Intersex Status) Bill 2013 (Cth) 4; Sex Discrimination (Sexual Orientation, Gender Identity and Intersex Status) Bill 2013 (Cth).

legislation and policy discriminating against persons of faith. Whilst some argue that discrimination can be solved through education to develop a better understanding of religious faith in the community,[282] the fact that State legislation and policy discriminates against persons of faith indicates a need for a Commonwealth legislative response.

- **Religious Discrimination in the Australian Community**

Whilst the number of complaints of religious discrimination to those Commonwealth,[283] State and Territory bodies with power to hear such complaints are said to be relatively small[284] vilification, discrimination, harassment, intimidation, verbal and physical abuse, property damage and vandalism and hate crimes on the grounds of religious belief are not rare occurrences in contemporary Australia.[285] For example a study of Muslim students studying at NSW universities conducted from 2013 to 2104 found that 44 per cent had been insulted or called

---

[282] Bouma et al, above n 24, 80.

[283] *Human Rights and Equal Opportunity Commission Act 1986* (Cth). Although religious discrimination is not prohibited by Commonwealth law the Act gives this Commission power to conciliate such complaints. Given the fact that religious discrimination is not relevantly unlawful it is hardly surprising that the numbers of complaints might be small.

[284] Bouma et al, above n 24, 58-59, 80.

[285] Possamai et al, above n 24, 319-321; Joint Standing Committee on Foreign Affairs, Defence and Trade, 'Compassion: A Report on Freedom of Religion and Belief' (November 2000) [5.6], [5.7], [5.10]- [5.12], [5.19]-[5.21], [5.23]-[5.24]; Justine Kearney and Mohamed Taha, *Sydney Muslims experience discrimination at three times the rate of other Australians: study* (30 November 2015) ABC News <http://www.abc.net.au/news/2015-11-30>; International Centre for Muslim and non-Muslim Understanding, 'Islamophobia, social distance and fear of terrorism in Australia - A Preliminary report' (Report, International Centre for Muslim and non-Muslim Understanding, 2015); Abdullah Saeed, *Islam in Australia* (Allen & Unwin, 2003) 6-7, 209-212; Deepti Goel, 'Perceptions of Immigrants in Australia after 9/11' (2010) 86 *The Economic Record* 275, 596-597, 600-601, 605-608; Kristine Frederickson, *LDS World: BYU's Chris Collinsworth had angels on his left and right sides Deseret News* (16 January 2011) Deseret News http://www.deseretnews.com/article/705386994>; Julie Nathan, '2014 Report on Antisemitism in Australia' (Report, Executive Council of Australian Jewry, 9 November 2014) 6-8, 15-42; Human Rights and Equal Opportunity Commission, above n 80; Bouma and Mason, above n 23, 27-28, 44-45, 65-69, 72, 81; Thornton and Luker, above n 34, 75-84.

names because of their religion,[286] more than a quarter had experienced discrimination in accessing health services and the majority had experienced discrimination because of their religion in an education setting.[287] Studies have also found that discrimination against Muslims in Australia increased after the 11 September 2001 attacks.[288] Between September 2014 and December 2015, 243 Islamophobia Incidents were reported to *The Islamophobia Register Australia*.[289] These ranged from verbal insults (104) and threats (70), to property damage (18), to non-violent (23) and violent attacks (24).[290] These are only the reports made to the Register which are likely to constitute only a fraction of the total number of *Islamophobia Incidents in Australia*.[291] Reports of anti-Semitic physical assaults, abuse, harassment, intimidation, property damage, vandalism, graffiti and threats grew from 2013 to 2014.[292] Followers of other faith traditions in Australia also complain of discrimination.[293]

- **Religious Discrimination through State Legislation and Policies**

This section of the paper considers three examples of State legislation or policies which preference other rights or interests over religious freedom: the Christian Youth Camps case, the *Abortion Law Reform Act 2008* (Vic) and the similar NSW Policy and exclusion zone

---

[286] Possamai et al, above n 24, 319.

[287] Ibid.

[288] Goel, above n 286, 596-597, 600-601, 605-608.

[289] Derya Iner, "Islamophobia in Australia 2014-2016" (Centre for Islamic Studies and Civilisation, Charles Sturt University, 2017) 42. The report adopts Salmad Sayyis's definition of Islamophobia which is "a form of racism that includes various forms of violence, violations, discrimination and subordination that occur across multiple sites in response to the problematisation of Muslim identify."39 It defines Incident to mean "[a]n event or occurrence of an Islamophobic nature that is either physical or online event or occurrence characterised as Islamophobia/Islamophobic including physical attacks, assault, damage to property, offensive graffiti, non-verbal harassment, intimidation and online threats."

[290] Ibid 63.

[291] Ibid 42.

[292] Nathan, above n 286, 8, 17. From 231 in 2013 to 312 to 2014.

[293] Bouma et al, above n 24, 66-73.

legislation in Tasmania, Victoria, the Northern Territory and in the Australian Capital Territory.

The Christian Youth Camps Case

Christian Youth Camps (a company owned by a Trust of the Christen Brethren church and run exclusively by employees of that faith)[294] owned and operated a camp site. An organisation sought to book the site to conduct workshops and raise awareness for same sex attracted young people about the aims and beliefs of the 'WayOut Project.' These beliefs included the 'view that homosexuality or same sex attraction is a natural part of the range of human sexualities'[295] which was in conflict with the religious beliefs of the Christian Brethren. Due to this conflict the booking was declined. Christian Youth Camps was then successfully sued under the *Equal Opportunity Act 1995* (Vic) (*EO Act*). It was found that by declining the booking, Cristian Youth Camps had discriminated against those who might attend the camp on the basis of their sexual orientation. Whilst the *EO Act* provides certain exemptions for 'a body established for religious purposes' Christian Youth Camps was found not to be such a body because it was running a commercial camping site. Refusing the booking was not protected by an exemption for acts done in conformity with the doctrines of the Christian Brethren religion or necessary to avoid injury to the religious sensitivities of people of that religion. The Court found that to satisfy this defence it would be necessary to show that doctrine gave the believer no option but to act or refrain from acting in the specific circumstances.[296] The Court analysed the doctrines of the Christian Brethren faith and found that whilst it would be sinful for a believer to personally engage in same sex sexual activity, the doctrines of the faith said nothing specifically about hiring out camp sites to persons professing a contrary view. This approach gives religious believers

---

[294] *Christian Youth Camps Ltd v Cobaw Community Health Services Limited* [2014] VSCA 75 [4].
[295] Ibid [28].
[296] Ibid [287].

very little protection under the legislation and ignores the individual nature of religious belief.[297]

In this case religious freedom was found to not enable a Christian business to decline to hire its premises to facilitate an organisation teaching moral positions to children which on any fair reading were contrary to the teachings of their faith. Although the decision proceeds on the basis that it prefers the rights of same sex attracted persons who might attend such a camp not to be discriminated against on the basis of sexual orientation over the religious freedom rights of the owners and employees of a venue, it is better understood as preferring the right of an organisation to hire any venue of its choice over the religious freedom rights of the owners and employees of that venue. In either case it evidences the deference given to claims other than claims founded on religious freedom.

The Victorian Abortion Law Reform Act and the Similar NSW Policy

The Victorian *Abortion Law Reform Act 2008* (Vic)[298] (*the Act*) and a New South Wales Policy[299] require medical practitioners with a conscientious objection to abortion in Victoria to refer (and in NSW to direct) patients seeking that procedure to another medical practitioner who does not share that objection. In this way they seek to compel doctors with a conscientious objection to abortion to be complicit in that procedure. This puts Catholic doctors who seek to live by the dictates of their Church in a particularly invidious position:

---

[297] Baines, above n 70, 58. As Baines has argued '[T]he different ways that people interpret Holy Scriptures or other sources of religious tenets means that future Tribunals could find that all faithful Australians have a choice not to discriminate against others. For example, on cross-examination of the expert witnesses, the Appeal Tribunal found that the Christian Brethren faith required them to tolerate difference and to welcome and include others. Given that parliament would not have intended to allow groups to discriminate, the reasoning suggests that religious interests are not regarded as special and distinct from other interests at law.'

[298] *Abortion Law Reform Act 2008* (Vic) s 8.

[299] New South Wales Government Health 'Framework for Terminations in New South Wales Public Health Organisations' (Policy Directive No PD2014_022, New South Wales Government, 2 July 2014).

to obey is to risk automatic excommunication from their church and to disobey is to risk disciplinary action and the loss of their right to practice medicine.[300] An example is illustrative. Dr Hobart is a pro-life Catholic doctor who was reportedly approached by a couple who wished to obtain a termination of a 19 week pregnancy because they were pregnant with a girl when they wanted a boy.[301] Dr Hobart did not refer the couple, they obtained a termination elsewhere and made no complaint.[302] After Dr Hobart told the *Herald Sun* what had happened[303] the Medical Board of Victoria launched an inquiry into his 'professional conduct' and he was investigated by The Medical Board of Australia and the Australian Health Practitioner Regulation Agency.[304] Although the details of the results are not public it appears that rather than Dr Hobart's license being cancelled he was sanctioned for his conduct.[305] Although referrals or directions are not required to access terminations of pregnancy in Victoria and NSW and information about providers is readily available, the *Act* and the NSW Policy prefer a patient's ability to receive a referral or direction by any health professional they choose over the right of health professionals to act in accordance with their religious beliefs.

---

[300] Michael Quinlan, 'When the State requires doctors to act against their conscience: the religious freedom implications of the referral and the direction obligations of health practitioners in Victoria and New South Wales' (2016) 4 *Brigham Young University Law Review* 7, 101. See paper for a more detailed discussion of the religious freedom implications of the Victorian legislation and the NSW policy

[301] News.com.au *Dr Mark Hobart, who refused couple abortion for wanting a boy, believes abortion is murder* (29 April 2013) <http://www.news.com.au/national> Accessed 20 October 2015.

[302] Ibid.

[303] Andrew Smith, *Doctor refused to refer couple for sex-selective abortion: faces possible loss of his license* 7 (October 2013) Catch The Fire Ministries <http://catchthefire.com.au/2013/11>

[304] Terri M Kelleher, *VICTORIA: Melbourne GP may be struck off after refusing abortion referral* (26 October 2013) News Weekly <http://www.newsweekly.com.au/article.php?id=56391>

[305] Dan Flynn, *Victorian Premier and Opposition Leader pledge to allow conscience vote on forcing doctors to participate in abortion* (Media Release, 23 September 2014) < http://www.acl.org.au >

Exclusion Zones

The Australian Capital Territory, the Northern Territory, Victoria and Tasmania have established zones around abortion clinics within which certain conduct including silent protests are prohibited.[306] For example, in Tasmania protesting in relation to terminations within an area with a 150 metre radius of premises where terminations are conducted is illegal.[307] Some Australians are driven to protest about abortion for religious motives. This was the case for the three elderly Christian protesters (Mr and Mrs Stallard and Mr Graeme Preston) who conducted a peaceful and quiet protest outside an abortion clinic within the exclusion zone in Hobart in 2016.[308] The Magistrate described the evidence of the motivations of two of the protesters in this way:

> [Mr Preston] has been a Christian since he was 14 and he believes that human life has been created in the image of God uniquely and that human life is of absolute importance as referred to in the Scriptures. That God knows us even when we are growing in our mother's womb and in particular he believes in the incarnation of Jesus as God coming into the world born in his mother's womb and that that validates human life at every stage. Mr Preston explained that the Bible teaches people to care for one another and in particular to help those who are most vulnerable or defenceless. He considers that a child in the womb would be probably the most vulnerable category of human beings and that they are completely defenceless. He believes that it is right and necessary that people come to the aid of those who are vulnerable and defenceless which includes unborn children.[309]
>
> Essentially as I understood Mrs Stallard's evidence she regards herself as a practicing Christian, and as part of her Christian

---

[306] *The Reproductive (Acceptance to Terminations) Act 2014* (Tas) s 9(2); *Public Health And Wellbeing Amendment (Safe Access Zones) Act 2015* (Vic); *Crimes Act 1900* (ACT) ss 174 -178; *Termination of Pregnancy Law Reform Act 2017* (NT) s14.
[307] *The Reproductive (Acceptance to Terminations) Act 2014* (Tas) s 9(2).
[308] *Police v Preston and Stallard* [2016] TASMC (27 July 2016).
[309] Ibid [58].

beliefs she believes that every life is sacred, that an unborn life does not have a voice, and that as part of her Christian beliefs she needs to stand up for people without a voice which led her to protest with Mr Preston.[310]

Although the *Tasmanian Constitution,* uniquely of all Australian Constitutions, does provide protections for freedom of conscience[311] and religion and the protestors presented no physical obstacle to entrance to the facility, badgered, harangued and attacked no one and posed no threat of violence or intimidation, the religious motivations of the accused did not prevent their conviction.[312] In this case State legislation operated to prefer a person's ability to enter an abortion facility without seeing or hearing a protest over the right of religious believers to act in accordance with their beliefs.

As these examples demonstrate:

> [T]here is a tendency to treat the right to freedom of religion or belief as less important than certain other civil and political rights and this right is often treated as a 'second class citizen' in the sphere of human rights.[313]

- **Conclusion**

The discussion above demonstrates that religious belief is a natural, inherent human trait. This has significant implications for the way in which society treats religion. As Trigg argues it means that laws which merely tolerate religion are not enough.[314] In his view:

> People must be assumed free to act on all their most basic beliefs and desires unless it is shown that there is a good reason not to.

---

[310] Ibid [65].

[311] Section 46(1) of the *Constitution Act, 1934* (Tas) provides that "(1) Freedom of conscience and the free profession and practice of religion are, subject to public order and morality, guaranteed to every citizen."

[312] *Police v Preston and Stallard* [2016] TASMC (27 July 2016) [58]-[59], [64]-[65].

[313] Australia Bahi Community, Submission No 1921 to Australian Human Rights Commission, *Inquiry into Freedom of religion and Belief in 21sty Century Australia* as quoted by Bouma et al, above n 24, 30.

[314] Trigg, above n 145, 15.

> Religious neutrality, or even atheism, is not the starting point for humans, but some form of religion is. It must be accepted that, other things being equal (and we can argue if they are), humans ought to be free to indulge those impulses. They probably will insist ion doing so anyway.[315]

He also observes that:

> It could be argued that the ability and right to have free exercise of religion is as crucial for the kind of people we are as being able to be adequately fed and sheltered. Religion, for good or ill, answers a basic tendency of human nature, and we should be free to walk that path if we so wish.[316]

In the context of Australia's approach to discrimination legislation, freedom of religion issues have not arisen in competition with rights to be fed and sheltered but in competition with State and Territory laws.[317] The absence of Commonwealth laws against religious discrimination, the mistreatment of people in Australia because of their religion and the State treatment of religious freedom in the cases discussed above, demonstrate that the right to freedom of religion is treated as a lesser right to other rights and State objectives in Australia. Given human being's natural inclination to religion, the benefits of religion to Australian society and to individual believers, Australia's approach to discrimination legislation requires reform to provide more adequate and nationwide protection for persons of religious faith.

---

[315] Ibid.
[316] Trigg, above n 145, 15.
[317] Including: laws prohibiting discrimination against same sex attracted persons, laws requiring health professionals to provide referrals or directions for abortions and laws prohibiting protests outside abortion clinics.

7
LIBERAL PEACE AND ITS PROSPECTS IN THE TWENTY-FIRST CENTURY

Suri Ratnapala

- **Introduction**

It is a privilege to be invited to contribute an essay to a collection that honours the work of Gabriel A Moens, Emeritus Professor of Law of the University of Queensland. Professor Moens is a long-time colleague, friend and mentor. A man of boundless intellectual ability and energy, he was an inspiration to students and colleagues and who was extraordinarily generous with his time and resources. He was the master of the inspirational lecture with the rare quality of sustaining unwavering student engagement with the most complex of topics. It is fitting I think that the topic of this essay engages with two fields to which Professor Moens made compelling contributions: individual liberty under law and free and fair international trade.

- **The Liberal Theory of Peace**

The liberal theory of peace as first proposed by Enlightenment philosophers David Hume, Jeremy Bentham, Immanuel Kant, John Stuart Mill and later liberals holds that republican liberty within nations and free trade among nations provide the surest foundations of peace. Humanity has not, and may never achieve these conditions on a global scale. Nevertheless, in the period since the end of the Second World War, the theory has been tested and found credible in parts of the world where liberal democratic systems and cross border trade have flourished. The fall of the Berlin Wall and communism in Europe heralded a period of spreading democracy and trade liberalisation across the world that created an expanding sphere of peace among nations that embraced these values. However, liberal peace is facing serious internal and external threats. Authoritarian tendencies within new and established democracies, the rise of fascism in former communist states and the emergence of communitarian hostility to liberalism pose the most immediate but not the only challenges. This paper explains the logic of the liberal theory of peace, discusses the challenges to liberal peace and prognosticates its sustainability in the face of threats.

Liberal peace is not the same thing as the absence of war or armed conflict which can result from conquest and subjugation or fear of mutually assured destruction. It is unlike the imperial peace of the *Pax Romana* (27 BC to AD 180) or the nineteenth-century's *Pax Britannica* that were maintained by military power. It is not the same as strategic peace between rulers that serve their present convenience. Liberal peace is uncoerced and is sustained not by the interests of rulers but by the choices of people living in conditions of freedom.

Peace that results from the mutual advantage of millions of individuals and firms who trade across borders is stable. Trade allows countless numbers of total strangers living and working in different parts of the world to cooperate in producing wealth and reducing poverty. I am wearing a cotton shirt. It is not expensive, anyone can afford it. Why? Because it is the product of collaboration on a global scale among strangers. Who grew the cotton that became the textile? Who produced the chemicals that gave this shirt its colour? Who manufactured the machinery that manufactured the textile? Who designed the garment? Who sowed it? The network of cooperation is endless. Each individual that contributed to the making of this garment cooperated voluntarily for their personal advantage or profit. Their profit seeking reduced the cost of my shirt! As far as I know there was no slave labour involved. This cooperation and mutual dependence is the foundation of liberal peace.

- **Republican Liberty**

Immanuel Kant in his essay Perpetual Peace (1795) said that the 'first definitive article for perpetual peace' is that 'The Civil Constitution of Every State Should Be Republican'.[1] Republican government is one whose power is limited by checks and balances designed to suppress private vice and advance the public good (*res publica*). Its antithesis is despotism. Despots sacrifice the public interest when it clashes with their own. Kant's republicanism is grounded in the categorical moral imperative that a person should act only according to a rule that can be universalised. Thus, no individual can 'legally bind or oblige another to anything, without at the same time submitting himself to the law which ensures that he in his turn, be bound and obliged in like manner by this other'.[2] This means, in practice, that the ruler is restrained from committing the nation to war without regard to the calamitous consequences for the public. In a despotic state, 'the ruler is not a citizen, but the owner of the state, and does not lose a whit by the war, while he goes on enjoying the delights of his table or sport, or of his pleasure palaces and gala days'.[3]

But why republican, rather than simply democratic? Aristotle argued in his book *Politics* that democracy is not the best form of government. He meant by democracy the system in some city states of classical Hellas where every decision of the state was taken by a majority of citizens. This kind of democracy, he said, invariably turned into tyranny. Government according to law would give way to the momentary wishes of the majority (usually directed by demagogues) on each issue whether of public or private concern.[4] The same kind of reasoning led James Madison to devote the *Federalist Paper No 10* to the need to rescue popular government from the 'control and violence

---

[1] Immanuel Kant, *Perpetual Peace: A Philosophical Essay*, tr, M Campbell Smith (London: George Allen & Unwin, 1917), p 120.
[2] Ibid.
[3] Ibid., p 123.
[4] Aristotle, *Aristotle's Politics*, Bk IV Ch 8, B Jowett tr, (Oxford: Oxford University Press, 1916), p 57.

of faction'.⁵ He wrote that '[c]omplaints are everywhere heard from our most considerate and virtuous citizens, equally the friends of public and private faith, and of public and personal liberty, that our governments are too unstable, that the public good is disregarded in the conflicts of rival parties, and that measures are too often decided, not according to the rules of justice and the rights of the minor party, but by the superior force of an interested and overbearing majority'.⁶

This has a profound implication for peace among nations. Unrestrained majority rule enables opportunistic rulers to gain more power by exploiting nationalist sentiments of a majority. Adolf Hitler and Benito Mussolini were elected under democratic systems with ineffective checks and balances and rode to absolute power on the back of nationalism. The solution to this problem, Madison argued, was the dispersal of power both horizontally among the legislative, executive and judicial powers and geographically between the central and regional units. The theory of mixed government implemented in the Athenian Constitution and imitated by the Roman Republic, the medieval Italian city states like Florence and Vienna and by the Ancient Constitution of England were designed to prevent tyranny by distributing legislative power between popular and aristocratic assemblies.

Successful republics are sustained by a combination of both formal and informal constraints. The United Kingdom and New Zealand are constitutional monarchies without a paramount basic law. Yet they have long histories of government according to republican principles. The best crafted republican constitution will unravel without a supporting political culture, for law has no existence but in the conduct of persons.

- **Free Trade**

The second limb of the liberal theory of peace is free trade among individuals and firms across national borders. In the early seventeenth-

---

[5] James Madison, 'The Federalist No 10', *The Federalist Papers by Alexander Hamilton, James Madison and John Jay*, Garry Wills ed, (New York: Bantam Books, 1988), p 42-49.
[6] Ibid., pp 42-43.

century, when absolute monarchy and mercantilism were the order of the day in Europe, the French monk and political writer Eméric Crucé prophesied that the economic emancipation of populations and the establishment of free trade among nations would reduce the incidence of war.[7]

Mercantilism was founded on the theory that the accumulation of gold and silver makes a nation wealthier. The policy was closely linked to colonialism – the conquest and monopoly of the resources of distant lands directly or through the agency of chartered companies like the British East India Company and the Dutch *Vereenigde Oost-Indische Compagnie* (VOC). The Spanish government sponsored conquistadors to harvest precious metals from American lands and the English government sponsored privateers to plunder the treasures on their way to Spain. Mercantilism and conflict were inseparable. Colonial ambitions intensified European differences.

In 1742, David Hume published two remarkable essays in which he assailed the mercantile orthodoxy of the time. In the first essay 'On the Balance of Trade' Hume focused on contemporary monetary policy that sought to defend national economies by exchange controls. National wealth, Hume argued, is increased not by hoarding gold and silver but by art and industry.

> But there still prevails, even in nations well acquainted with commerce, a strong jealousy with regard to the balance of trade, and a fear, that all their gold and silver may be leaving them. This seems to me, almost in every case, a groundless apprehension; and I should as soon dread, that all our springs and rivers should be exhausted, as that money should abandon a kingdom where there are people and industry. Let us carefully preserve these latter advantages; and we need never be apprehensive of losing the former.[8]

Hume moreover demonstrated the futility of seeking comparative

---

[7] Edmund Silberner, *La Guerre Dans la Pensée Économique du XVIe au XVIIIe Siècle*, (Paris: Librairie du Recueil Sirey, 1939), p 133.

[8] David Hume, *Essays Moral, Political and Literary*, (Indianapolis/IN: Liberty Classics 1742/1987), p 309.

advantage by printing more money.⁹ Milton Friedman said of Hume's monetary theory: 'We have advanced beyond Hume in two respects only: first, we now have a more secure grasp on the quantitative magnitudes involved: second, we have gone one derivative beyond Hume'.[10]

In 'The Jealousy of Trade', Hume addressed the fear of the economic prosperity of neighbours, frequently the cause of war.

> It is obvious, that the domestic industry of a people cannot be hurt by the greatest prosperity of their neighbours; and as this branch of commerce is undoubtedly the most important in any extensive kingdom, we are so far removed from all reason of jealousy. But I go farther, and observe, that where an open communication is preserved among nations, it is impossible but the domestic industry of everyone must receive an encrease from the improvements of the others.[11]

The free trade theory was well understood in the nineteenth-century and espoused by the French physiocrats, the British liberals such as John Stuart Mill, Richard Cobden and John Bright, and the American liberal William Graham Sumner. Mill wrote:

> It is commerce which is rapidly rendering war obsolete, by strengthening and multiplying the personal interests which act in natural opposition to it. And it may be said without exaggerations that the great extent and rapid increase of international trade, in being the principal guarantee of the peace of the world, is the great permanent security for uninterrupted progress of the ideas the institutions and the character of the human race.[12]

Like all theories, the liberal theory of peace is true only for a given set of conditions. Commitment to domestic individual freedom and transnational free trade are the primary conditions for peace. Hence

---

[9] Ibid., pp 311-12.
[10] Quoted by cited by Thomas Mayer, 'David Hume and Monetarism', *Quarterly Journal of Economics* 95 (August 1980), p 89.
[11] Hume, above n.8, p 328.
[12] John Stuart Mill, *Principles of Political Economy*, (London: John W. Parker, 1948), p 582.

liberal peace is most likely to prevail among liberal states. Liberal states are not free of differences and disputes among themselves. Yet, history shows that they usually resolve their difference without the use of military force. In his insightful essay 'Liberal internationalism: Peace, War and Democracy' Doyle makes this point:

> The apparent absence of war between liberal states, whether adjacent or not, for almost two hundred years may therefore have significance. Similar claims cannot be made for feudal, "fascist," communist, authoritarian or totalitarian forms of rule; nor for pluralistic, or merely similar societies. More significant perhaps, is that when states are forced to decide on which side of an impending world war they will fight, liberal states wind up all on the same side, despite the complexity of the paths that take them there. These characteristics do not prove that the peace among liberals is statistically significant, nor that liberalism is the peace's sole valid explanation. But they do suggest that we consider the possibility that liberals have indeed established a separate peace – but only among themselves.[13]

Not all wars initiated by liberal states have been defensive or even justified. Democratic Britain fought many colonial wars against nations that they conquered and other colonial powers. While liberal states seem able to settle their differences with other liberal states peacefully, they seem not to be always able or willing to do so with non-liberal states. Some liberal states (Ireland, Switzerland, Sweden, Austria, Finland) have historically maintained peace with non-liberal countries by adopting neutrality.

- **Two Flawed Theories About the State of the World**

The future of liberal peace depends on the prevalence of liberal democracy among nations. There are optimistic and pessimistic views on the survival of liberal democracy. There are also opponents of liberal democracy within and outside liberal society. This has always been the case. What is perhaps new are challenges to the values and

---

[13] Michael W Doyle, 'Liberal Internationalism: Peace, War and Democracy', Nobelprize.org. 15 Jan 2011 http://nobelprize.org/nobel_prizes/peace/articles/doyle/

institutions of liberal society from nativist populism and some brands of conservative communitarianism.

The collapse of Communist Party rule in Eastern Europe and the Soviet Union generated intense speculation about the unfolding shape of the world in its geopolitical, cultural and economic dimensions. Among the most widely discussed were two papers by the American scholars Francis Fukuyama and Samuel Huntington offering opposing visions of the future. The two theses have been heavily criticised by commentators but they have provided a provocative set of ideas to enliven the debate about the future of liberal democracy.

The liberal counter revolutions in Eastern Europe and the fall of the Communist Party in the Soviet Union led some Western scholars to declare victory for liberal democracy. The most optimistic assessment was offered by Fukuyama in an essay entitled the 'End of History'. He proposed that the defeat of totalitarian communism marked the 'the end point of mankind's ideological evolution and the universalization of Western liberal democracy as the final form of human government'.[14] Huntington in his paper 'The Clash of Civilizations', argued that the world was not at the end of history but is entering a new phase of conflict the source of which is not primarily ideological or economic but cultural. He wrote:

> Nation states will remain the most powerful actors in world affairs, but the principal conflicts of global politics will occur between nations and groups of different civilizations. The clash of civilizations will dominate global politics. The fault lines between civilizations will be the battle lines of the future.[15]

These are two broad brush theories that are criticisable on many grounds, including hard evidence. However, some criticisms of Fukuyama's thesis read like obituaries of liberalism. If liberalism is dead liberal peace is also dead, at least in the practical sense. The declarations of the demise of liberalism, I contend, are as premature as Fukuyama's proclamation of its final victory.

---

[14] Francis Fukuyama, 'The End of History?', *The National Interest* (1989, Summer), pp 1-18.
[15] Samuel Huntington, 'Clash of Civilisations?' (1993) 72 (3) *Foreign Affairs* 22-49.

- **Liberalism is Not Dead and History Has Not Ended**

Many obituaries have been written of the demise of liberal democracy. Among them, are doom sayings of elected leaders, journalists and academics. In 1974, the Chancellor of the Federal Republic of Germany, Willie Brandt, gave democracy no more than 30 or 40 years in Europe.[16] U.S. Senator and diplomat Daniel Patrick Moynihan wrote that liberal democracy is 'a holdover form of government ... which has simply no relevance to the future'.[17] Philosopher Alasdair MacIntyre predicted the failure of liberalism because of its rejection of tradition (in his case, Catholic Church doctrine) on which rival claims to truth are based.[18] John Gray declared that 'the Enlightenment project' is in a state of 'world-historical collapse'.[19] In 2016 the New York Times columnist Roger Cohen declared that 'Liberalism is dead. Or at least it is on the ropes'.[20]

Liberalism that is thought to be dead or dying is really a spectrum of political theories and political action programs. At one end of this spectrum is classical liberalism that seeks to limit the role of government as far as possible to the defence of life, liberty and property. Classical liberals generally favour Mill's harm principle 'that the only purpose for which power can be rightfully exercised over any member of a civilised community, against his will, is to prevent harm to others'.[21] At the other end is welfare state liberalism that assigns to the state a wider responsibility to secure not only the basic legal rights and freedoms of citizens but the material conditions for their enjoyment. These two models are ideal types that have

---

[16] *The Economist*, 'What's Gone Wrong With Democracy' (March 2014), https://www.economist.com/news/essays

[17] Quoted in W. J. Raymond, *Dictionary of Politics: Selected American and Foreign Political and Legal Terms,* 7th ed (Lawrenceville, VA: Brunswick Publishing Corporation, 1992), 124.

[18] Alasdair MacIntyre, *Whose Justice? Which Rationality?* (Notre Dame/IN: University of Notre Dame Press, 1988), p 403.

[19] John Gray, 'After the New Liberalism' (1994) 61 (3) *Social Research* 719, p 721.

[20] 'The Death of Liberalism' (14 April 2016), https://www.nytimes.com/

[21] John Stuart Mill, *On Liberty*, People's Edition, (London, Longmans, Green & Co, 1865), p 6.

not been practically achieved in any modern state. Some sort of compromise between these two views prevails in the real politics of present-day liberal democracies. However, there is general consensus across the spectrum on the institutions of liberal society. These include non-exhaustively, representative government based on free and fair elections, toleration of peaceful dissent, the rejection of status based power, the supremacy of the law over state and citizens, basic rights and liberties of all persons, the principle of equality before the law, and the independence of the judiciary.

Liberalism in this sense is not dead or dying though it is perpetually endangered. The International Institute for Democracy and Electoral Assistance (International IDEA) in its periodic surveys of the health of democracy in the world evaluates states under the following sets of criteria: (1) Representative Government, (2) Fundamental Rights, (3) Checks on Government, (4) Impartial Administration and (5) Participatory Engagement. Its 2017 report *The Global State of Democracy* based on extensive data analysis concludes:

> There is much room for improvement in virtually all dimensions of democracy. However, the situation is better than suggested by increasingly pessimistic views regarding the prevalence and resilience of contemporary democracy. The trends since 1975 suggest that most aspects of democracy have improved, and that most democracies have been resilient over time. Moreover, current democratic regressions are generally short lived and followed by recovery when internal democracy-friendly forces cooperate and resist leaders with authoritarian tendencies.[22]

These findings are confirmed by the data collected by evolutionary psychologist and social philosopher Steven Pinker in his book *Enlightenment Now*.[23] Pinker relies on the annual time series published by the Polity Project that assigns scores for every country in every year in relation to the citizen's ability to express political

---

[22] International IDEA, *The Global State of Democracy: Exploring Democracy's Resilience* (Stockholm: International IDEA, 2017), p 2.
[23] Steven Pinker, *Enlightenment Now: The Case for Reason, Science, Humanism and Progress*, (New York: Viking, 2018), pp 199-213.

preferences, constraints on power and the guarantee of civil liberties. The study shows three waves of democratisation since the beginning of the nineteenth-century with the third and current wave continuing despite setbacks.[24] Nevertheless new threats to liberal democracy have emerged and their causes need to be understood and addressed by those who care about its survival. The peaceful democratic change of government in Malaysia at the General Election of 9 May 2018, the first since the nation's independence in 1957, is heartening. There are other bright spots for democracy but also red lights flashing elsewhere.

History has not ended and is not about to end. It is a continual contest of ideas and programs that date back to the beginning of society.

- **The true clash is between liberal democracy and fascist ambition**

Samuel Huntington argued that since the Cold War ended it is far more meaningful to see the nature of international conflict as a clash of civilizations rather than ideological blocs:

> Civilization identity will be increasingly important in the future, and the world will be shaped in large measure by the interactions among seven or eight major civilizations. These include Western, Confucian, Japanese, Islamic, Hindu, Slavic-Orthodox, Latin American and possibly African civilization. The most important conflicts of the future will occur along the cultural fault lines separating these civilizations from one another.[25]

This is a grossly oversimplified thesis. There are obvious cultural, linguistic and spiritual, affinities among peoples that Huntington identifies as civilizations. Civilisational differences can be a cause of conflict especially if one civilization seeks hegemony over another. There are two main reasons why this thesis is misleading. The first is the overlap of cultures and civilizations. The second is the adaptive evolutionary character of societies.

---

[24] Ibid., pp 202-03.
[25] Huntington, above n.15, p 23.

First, as John Rawls pointed out, in many communities there is overlapping consensus across cultural boundaries with respect to justice by which he means the fundamental principles of the political system.[26] We can see this happening among nations. Japan, South Korea, Singapore and Taiwan, despite their Confucian heritage are electoral democracies with free market economies that are strongly integrated with the West. India, the spiritual and cultural home of the Hindu civilisation is the largest functioning democracy in the world with an economy locked into the capitalist system and whose diaspora plays an increasingly important role in commercial, industrial, scientific and service sectors of Western economies. Further, there is no monolithic Islamic civilisation that is clashing with the liberal democratic West although, naturally, the despotic rulers of many Islamic nations reject Western ideas of democracy and human rights. Liberal democracy has been growing in Latin America[27] where people have strong religious, linguistic and cultural connections to Europe and North America. Many of the Slavic nations of Eastern Europe are members of the European Union who have subscribed to the constitutional norms, individual human rights and the market economy of that regional community.

Second, cultures are not static but complex evolving systems. They borrow ideas and institutions and imitate good (and sometimes bad) practice. They also change through endogenous forces. In an ideal world of zero transaction costs we might expect societies to converge to the model of economic and social organisation that is most efficient in satisfying the diverse aspirations of individuals that form each society.[28] If so, we may expect the causes of conflict to diminish over time. The real world unfortunately is a world of heavy, though diminishing, transaction costs. Some of these are information,

---

[26] John Rawls, *Political Liberalism* (New York/NY: Colombia University Press, 1991), pp 134-49.
[27] International IDEA, note 6 above, p 4.
[28] Douglass C North. *Institutions, Institutional Change and Economic Performance*, (Cambridge: Cambridge University Press, 1990), 93.

communication and transportation costs.[29] Some flow from the constraints of tradition, often enforced by dominant sections of society defined by criteria such as caste, gender or faith. But the greatest costs are those imposed by rulers in their own private interests or in pursuit of misguided notions of the public good.

These costs are heaviest and most visible in countries ruled by dictators. Dictatorships routinely censor information, violate basic rights and freedoms including free expression, association and movement, discriminate against selected persons and groups, jail or eliminate opponents, disallow political dissent, prevent political reform and perpetuate their power at the expense of the public good. The cost of achieving change under these conditions is prohibitive. Dictatorial actions of rulers are invariably taken in the name of patriotism, national security, culture, indigenous values, public interest and on supposed popular choice. Yet rarely, if ever, does a dictatorship consult the public on these matters through free and fair elections or referenda.

Huntington's thesis was always empirically suspect. Ronald Inglehart and Pippa Norris point to the World Values Surveys conducted in 1995-96 and 2000-02 to refute Huntington's claim of a clash between Western and Islamic civilisations.

> These results represent a dramatic change from the 1930s and 1940s, when fascist regimes won overwhelming mass approval in many societies; and for many decades, Communist regimes had widespread support. But in the last decade, democracy became virtually the only political model with global appeal, no matter what the culture. With the exception of Pakistan, most of the Muslim countries surveyed think highly of democracy: In Albania, Egypt, Bangladesh, Azerbaijan, Indonesia, Morocco, and Turkey, 92 to 99 percent of the public endorsed democratic institutions – a higher proportion than in the United States (89 percent).[30]

---

[29] Anderson, J. and E. van Wincoop 'Gravity with Gravitas: A Solution to the Border Puzzle,' 93:1 (2003) *American Econ. Review*, pp 170-192.

[30] Ronald Inglehart and Pippa Norris, 'The True Clash of Civilizations', *Foreign Policy*, No. 135 (Mar- April, 2003), 62-70, p 66

- **Post War International Order and Liberal Peace**

Following the defeat of fascist Germany and Imperial Japan and the worldwide devastation caused by the war, the liberal-democratic Western Powers embarked on an ambitious programme to reshape the international order according to liberal principles. They sought to establish what came to be known as the 'Rules Based International Order' (RBIO).

Their first aim was to pacify and liberalise the vanquished nations. West Germany and Japan received liberal democratic constitutions with guaranteed basic rights and freedoms for citizens. Western Europe, beginning with the European Coal and Steel Community evolved into the present day European Union, an economic and political partnership of 28 nations. It is built on the two pillars of the liberal theory of peace: liberal democracy within member nations and free trade among them. Today, it is hard to imagine conflict in Central and Western Europe, a region of the world riven by war over two thousand years. Japanese society under the US imposed liberal democratic constitution has become a deeply pacifist nation relying on trade, not conquest, for its rapid progress.

The Rules Based International Order is founded on a large number of multilateral conventions and treaties. There are three major planks of RBIO as it has grown over the post-war decades: Promoting civil and political rights and liberties of persons wherever they live, fostering free trade among nations and reducing armed conflict.

- **Civil and political rights and liberties**

The Charter of the United Nations, the Universal Declaration of Human Rights, the International Covenant on Civil and Political Rights (ICCPR), and associated covenants, commit member nations (in effect all sovereign states) to the promotion of the rights and liberties essential to the liberal democratic form of governance. There are judicially enforceable bills of rights in most liberal democracies today. Regional institutions such as the European Court of Human

Rights (ECHR) and the Inter-American Court of Human Rights (IACHR) have provided important restraints on abusive governments. None of this means that the system is an effective global guarantee of human rights. Totalitarian socialist states give their own illiberal interpretations of their treaty commitments. Human rights violations continue unchecked in parts of the world and have got worse in many countries. However, the progress of human rights in the world overall has been positive as Christopher Farriss's mathematical modelling of human rights in the period 1949-2014 suggests.[31]

- **Free trade**

The greatest progress towards the Rules Based International Order has been in the field of international trade. On August 14, 1941, in darkest hour of the Second World War, President Franklin D Roosevelt and Prime Minister Winston Churchill met at a secret location to sign the *Atlantic Charter* as a vision of a post war peaceful world made of a community of independent, secure and prosperous nations. In Clause 4, the leaders agreed that:

> They will endeavour, with due respect for their existing obligations, to further the enjoyment by all States, great or small, victor or vanquished, of access on equal terms, to the trade and to the raw materials of the world which are needed for their economic prosperity.[32]

History records that victors routinely wreaked vengeance on the vanquished and exacted reparations. The victorious Western Alliance did the opposite, reconstructing the defeated nations under the Marshall Plan and other aid programs and helping them to establish liberal democratic systems in place of fascist regimes. On a global scale, the U.S. initiated the economic agreements at Bretton Woods, San Francisco and Havana which set up an institutional framework for a world-wide liberal economic order. Starting with the General

---

[31] Cited by Pinker, above n. 23, 207-8

[32] http://www.un.org/en/sections/history-united-nations-charter/1941-atlantic-charter/index.html

Agreement on Tariffs and Trade (GATT) in 1948, the community of nations progressively by tortuous negotiations built the current framework of liberalised international trade in goods and services overseen by the World Trade Organisation (WTO).

World trade during the seventy years since GATT has coincided with unprecedented rates of economic growth with Third World countries being major beneficiaries. There is also evidence that international trade promotes institutional improvement and the rule of law in emerging economies.[33] Early liberals perhaps did not foresee the extent to which the economic interests of nations commingle in a global economy that allows capital mobility, foreign direct investment, arbitrage, cross-border supply chains, electronic commerce, floating currencies and open stock markets. The new international economic order is one where nationalistic economic policies are difficult to sustain and conflict with trading partners self-defeating.

Nevertheless, U.S. President Donald Trump has launched a frontal assault on the multilateral free trade system by his imposition of tariffs on steel, aluminium and a range of other products imported from China and other countries including allied nations leading to retaliation by China in like measure. Mr Trump who is a critic of the WTO avoided its procedures in taking this action by claiming threats to national security. He has also sought to scuttle the WTO's appellate body by withholding support for judges nominated to the panel.[34] Mr Trump's preference is to abandon general rules of the international trading system in favour of bilateral deals that he believes would benefit U.S. producers. If the U.S. is successful in dismantling the current trading system, it would seriously threaten free trade, a key element of the current liberal peace.

---

[33] D Rodrik, A Subramanian and F Trebbi, (2004), 'Institutions rule: the primacy of institutions over geography and integration in economic development', *Journal of Economic Growth*, (2004) 9(2), 131-165; F Alcalá and A Ciccone, 'Trade and productivity', *Quarterly Journal of Economics* (2004) 119 (2), 613–646.

[34] *Wall Street Journal* July 11, 2018, https://www.wsj.com/articles/

- **The Long Peace**

There has been no armed conflict between great powers since the end of World War II, a period some call the 'The Long Peace'. War between lesser nations and internal civil war persist but less frequently. Armed conflict anywhere produces human tragedy. The Middle-East is a theatre of war. Russia's territorial ambitions in Eastern Europe, the Indo-Pakistani confrontation over the Kashmir, the belligerence on the Korean Peninsula, and Chinese intrusions in the South China Sea are potential flashpoints. Yet, the decline in the occurrence of war is an undeniable statistical fact despite an upturn of political violence since 2014 mainly involving radical Islamic movements.[35]

The trend towards peace happened with a little help from the U.N. Indeed, the Security Council (SC) whose authorisation a nation requires for legal military action or economic sanctions and who alone may establish Peace Keeping Forces tends to be paralysed when its intervention is needed most. The two authoritarian permanent members of the SC Russia and China are frequently at odds with liberal states and do not hesitate to veto collective action proposed by western powers. The nuclear deterrent, economic realities and *realpolitik*, were factors that contributed to peace. But the greatest impetus was generated by spreading democracy and international trade.

- **Current Threats to Liberal Peace**

Republican liberty and free trade, despite compelling evidence of their pacific effects, remain under serious attack from four directions: violence by anti-liberal forces such as Islamic terror groups, intellectual criticism of liberal values, nativist populism in democracies, and re-emergence of powerful fascist states.

- **Terrorist attacks on liberal democracy**

Terrorist attacks on liberal democracy is not a new phenomenon. In the post WWII era, so-called people's liberation movements were endemic in newly independent states lacking stable democratic institutions.

---
[35] Pinker, note 33, 158-59

Stable, free and prosperous democracies were also targeted in the 1970s by extreme left youth organisations, some of whom embraced terrorism as the means to revolution. The most notorious and destructive among them were the Red Army Faction of West Germany (the Baader-Meinhof Gang), Italy's Red Brigade, Japan's Red Army, India's Naxalite-Maoist Movement and the Symbionese Liberation Army of the U.S. These movements ended without popular support.

The current Islamic Jihadist movement poses a much greater threat for the simple reason that it appeals to significant minorities in Muslim majority nations and within Muslim migrant communities elsewhere. Jihadism bears a close resemblance to Marxism. Like Marxism it is driven by global ambition. Jihadists will not be appeased by the destruction of the State of Israel or by the creation of a Caliphate of all Islamic countries. Liberal commitments to individual freedom, equality before the law, representative democracy and the subjection of rulers to the governance of general laws are at odds with dictatorship of a communist party or an Islamic theocracy. Liberal institutions are not subject to an ideological manifesto or a holy book however interpreted. Jihadists, like the Marxists, regard liberal ideas and institutions as deadly threats to the religious social order that they seek to create. For Marxists and Jihadists co-existence with liberalism is impossible. Marxists and Jihadists regard themselves naturally at war with liberalism. Marx and Engels realised that socialism in one country was impossible in the long term. Likewise, Jihadists know that a theocracy that denies freedom and human aspirations cannot withstand the flow of goods, services and ideas.[36]

One of the great costs that terrorism inflicts on liberal states is the extraordinary powers that it allows governments to acquire in the cause of national security and public safety. Most Western countries enacted special counter-terrorism laws in the aftermath of the 9/11 attacks. The first of these was the *Patriot Act* passed overwhelmingly with little discussion by the two houses of the US Congress. It was followed

---

[36] Friedrich Engels, *The Principles of Communism* (1847), at http://www.marxists. org/archive/marx/works/1847/11/prin-com.htm

by the *Anti-Terrorism Act 2001 (Canada), Terrorism Suppression Act 2002 (NZ), Anti-Terrorism Act 2005 (Cth), Counter-Terrorism Act 2008 (UK)* and similar legislation in other OECD countries. These statutes typically provide for extraordinary surveillance procedures, long term detention, disclosure of private information and communications, and departures from traditional procedural and evidentiary safeguards. Many of these measures may be considered unavoidable given the nature and gravity of the threats posed by terrorist organisations some of whom are backed by states with nuclear potential. How these powers are contained both legally and politically and limited to their legitimate ends is a true test of liberal credentials.

- **Anti-Liberalism in Western Philosophy**

The liberal democratic system has been under virulent attack by Marxist, neo-Marxist and postmodernist academics and commentators for many decades. The common themes in their critiques are: (1) individual freedom under liberal democracy atomises society and alienates persons from each other;[37] (2) liberal belief in scientific inquiry and objective knowledge is false as all knowledge and truths are subjective;[38] and (3) liberalism is a system of concealed power operating under the guise of freedom.[39] These theories hold sway in university humanities departments but have little traction among the general population that trusts the evidence of their senses and their own rationality, however imperfect.

Some conservatives and communitarians have, wittingly or not, lent their voices to the critical chorus. Many obituaries have been written of the demise of the Enlightenment and its most treasured legacy, liberal democracy and individual freedom. As mentioned, in

---

[37] P Gable, 'Reification in legal reasoning' (1980) 3 *Research in Law and Sociology*, p 281.

[38] B H Smith, *Contingencies of Value*, (Cambridge, MA: Harvard University Press, 1988), 149; M Poster, 'Why not to read Foucault' (1989) 31 *Critical Review* 155, p 159.

[39] M Foucault, *Archaeology of Knowledge and the Discourse on Language*, (New York: Pantheon Books, 1972), pp 220-227.

1974 the then Chancellor of the Federal Republic of Germany gave democracy no more than 30 or 40 years in Europe.[40] In 1992, an American diplomat wrote that liberal democracy is 'a holdover form of government . . . which has simply no relevance to the future',[41] and in about that same period a well-known American philosopher predicted the failure of liberalism because of its rejection of tradition on which rival claims to truth are based.[42] If these prophecies come true liberal peace will end to be replaced by growing conflict mitigated only by less stable forms of strategic peace between rulers.

Many authoritarian rulers agree with the communitarian argument. The 'Asian Values Doctrine' is frequently invoked by Asian leaders to justify undemocratic rule. I have never understood this argument because of its circularity.

- The community does not favour liberal-democracy.
- The community opinion has not been tested by a democratic process.
- Why? Because the community does not favour liberal-democracy.

Circularity aside, this argument ignores the fact that liberal political systems allow more room for individual and collective dissent than any previous political or moral system. The liberal tradition is a tradition of toleration. As Brian Barry says, 'For though liberalism does presuppose a theory of the good, it is one in which freedom plays a central role, and this includes the freedom to create a community based upon non-liberal principles'[43] Liberal societies do not practice ex-communication and inquisition or prevent exit. Pre-liberal societ-

---

[40] *The Economist*, 'What's Gone Wrong with Democracy' (March 2014), at https://www.economist.com/news/essays/

[41] Quoted in W. J. Raymond, *Dictionary of Politics: Selected American and Foreign Political and Legal Terms*, 7th ed (Lawrenceville/VA: Brunswick Publishing Corporation, 1992), 124

[42] Alasdair MacIntyre, *Whose Justice? Which Rationality?* (Notre Dame/IN: University of Notre Dame Press, 1988), p 403

[43] Brian Barry, 'The Light That Failed?' (1989) 100 (1) *Ethics* 160, p 168.

ies did. Liberalism's pre-eminent value is the freedom of choice which every other system denies. There is mass demand for permanent migration to liberal societies—hardly any to the dictatorships. This must tell us something.

- ## Perversions of Democracy – The Pathways to Fascism
- ### Liberal Democracy and Majority Rule

There is a critical difference between majority rule and liberal democracy. It is impossible to maintain majority rule in the long term without checks and balances. History has shown that an elected majority government unrestrained by limits on power inevitably becomes a minority government without opposition. It is not sufficient to have checks in a written constitution. There must be institutions rooted in a political culture that can withstand executive assaults. The United Kingdom and New Zealand have no enforceable written constitutions but have robust institutions that have been effective barriers to despotism. The judiciary, the media and the electoral system are early targets for intimidation and corruption by popularly elected governments with authoritarian ambitions – as the world has seen in Russia, Turkey, Venezuela, Nicaragua and is now distressingly witnessing in Poland and Hungary.

Liberal democracy is republican democracy. It exists where the basic civil rights and liberties of people are beyond the reach of even popularly elected governments. The presence of a bill of rights in a constitution does not secure these entitlements in the absence of a sustaining political culture.

- ### Populism – good and bad

The term populism has been at the centre of current discussions about the state of liberal democracy in the West. 'Populism' is an undefined expression that has been appropriated by parties of the left and the right who oppose what they call 'the establishment', another imprecise label which usually means the status quo with respect to the norms and practices of governance. Populism can be good or bad for liberal democracy. Likewise, so can the 'establishment'. An 'establishment' which is unresponsive and uncaring and serves special interests at the expense of the general interest of society is bad. Populism that seeks to reform such an establishment is good.

However, we need to bear in mind two facts. First, there will always be a governing establishment in a functioning state. The alternative, in the absence of an anarcho-libertarian utopia, is social and economic chaos. Hitler and Mussolini, who rode to power on waves of public disenchantment with the status quo, created monstrous establishments that caused human tragedy on an apocalyptic scale. The Bolsheviks who overthrew the Czarist establishment replaced it with the most pervasive and invasive system of government ever devised. Mao Tse Tung's Cultural Revolution that sought to destroy for ever the establishment, by some estimates, cost two million lives. Robert Mugabe of Zimbabwe and Hugo Chavez of Venezuela who gained power by anti-establishment promises created their own which enriched the rulers and impoverished the people. The list is as long as the political history of our race. The second pertinent fact is that establishments being human can never be perfect. Since there will always be an establishment, the constitutional task of a liberal democracy is to tame it and direct it to the public good. The dangerous sort of populism is founded on nativism that identifies a race or religion with the nation and the nation with the state and the state with a charismatic national saviour. Populist leaders usually arise in times of discontent with promises of restoring the nation to greatness. No society can eliminate discontent and those that tried it, like the communist states, fared the worst. Dissatisfaction is part of being human and is a driver of change and growth. Happiness depends on what a person expects of life and expectations change with the state of the world. Our ancestors did not desire fast food, smart phones, Facebook friends and instant entertainment for they were not of their world. They had other unfulfilled wants.

It is easy to take the prosperity of liberal democracies for granted and to magnify every problem as a crisis needing a radical response. As

Pinker warns: 'When we fail to acknowledge our hard-won progress, we may come to believe that every problem is an outrage that calls for blaming evildoers, wrecking institutions, and empowering a leader who will restore the country to its rightful greatness'.[44] Among these villains are invariably foreigners and minorities, international traders, mainstream politicians, bureaucrats and experts who Donald Trump calls the swamp that needs to be drained. Trump perhaps did not know that '*Drenare la palude*' or 'drain the swamp' was an early catch cry of fascist dictator Benito Mussolini in his surge to power. Surely his advisors Stephen Bannon and Michael Anton knew.

- **Undermining of Liberal Democracy by Misguided Liberals**

Constitutions and laws do not exist by the magical force of the words that express them but because of a culture of reverence that they command among officials and citizens. This fidelity can be eroded if the system betrays the legitimate expectations of the community and threatens the very culture that sustains the system. This has happened in a number of ways in Western democracies.

- **Loss of Control of the Law-Making Process**

A community lives by generally known and accepted rules of conduct. The immense growth of the administrative state has relocated effective legislative power to the hands of an unelected and unresponsive bureaucracy. The European Commission is the most prominent example of democratic deficit. But executive legislation pervades Western democracies. Rights and duties of citizens are increasingly determined by non-judicial bodies with licence to depart from due process and interpret vague legislative standards in pursuit of policy goals rather than clear entitlements. The ordinary citizen may not comprehend the complexities of administrative law but the cumulative effect of the drift of power to unaccountable bureaucratic structures is widely felt in the community.

---

[44] Pinker, above n. 23, p 452.

7.13.2. Political Correctness – Informal System of Social Control

In most liberal democracies, acts such as racial vilification and incitement to violence are punishable offences. In Australia acts that cause offense are sufficient to attract penalties. Under s18C of the *Racial Discrimination Act* it is unlawful for a person to commit an act that 'is reasonably likely, in all the circumstances, to offend, insult, humiliate or intimidate another person or a group of people ... because of the race, colour or national or ethnic origin of the other person'.[45] The vagueness of the expression 'reasonably likely, in all the circumstances, to offend' leaves the Human Rights Commission, in the first instance, an enormously wide power to stifle free speech.

A person's freedom in Western liberal democracies is limited not only by formal legislation but also by the rules of organisations. One of the great achievements of liberal democracy, equality before the law, has been eclipsed by the notion of diversity pursued mindlessly by Universities, governments and even national sports bodies and commercial entities that stand to benefit by taking the correct line. Universities demand politically correct language, impose diversity at the cost of merit and banish from campuses speakers that student unions dislike.

- **Uncontrolled Immigration**

It is hardly surprising that the movement of people seeking permanent migration today is one way – from dysfunctional illiberal states to prosperous liberal states. Migration of people across nations is a historical phenomenon. It has produced enormous economic and cultural benefits to host countries and helped to alleviate poverty in many parts of the world. Immigration enriches culture. Rome could not have attained its grandeur without harnessing and integrating the human riches of its conquered provinces on whose natives the Empire bestowed Roman citizenship. The greatness of the United States is built on the genius and industry of immigrants. Apart from economic

---

[45] Section 18(C) of the *Racial Discrimination Act* (Cth).

benefits, liberal ideals do not favour shutting the door on those fleeing oppression. However, a liberal democracy cannot accept unlimited or uncontrolled migration without endangering its institutional foundations. This is a cold hard fact.

Liberal institutions comprise formal and informal constitutional arrangements, the basic laws of the land, the traditions of toleration and the acceptance of the democratic ways of governance. Not all migrants sign up to the liberal rules of the game as we have seen from the terrorist events of the recent past. Even if these are dismissed as inconsequential or manageable the general sense of insecurity that rises with mass migration will cause popular reactions that nativist demagogues will use to discredit liberal institutions and advance their authoritarian ambitions. The far-right parties in Europe owe their recent successes to precisely these concerns. Key elements of Donald Trump's winning strategy were the promises of a great wall on the Mexican border and a halt to Muslim immigration to the US. Liberals who dismiss these concerns as racial prejudice commit a serious error and undermine their own cause. I cannot help thinking that policies of multiculturalism and diversity have done little to unite local and migrant communities.

- **Fascism: The Ultimate Challenge**

While it is important to address the challenges arising within liberal democratic societies, it would be folly to neglect the growing threat from what the U.S. Secretary of Defence James Mattis says are 'revisionist powers that seek to create a world consistent with their authoritarian models'.[46] Mattis regards Russia and China as posing greater threats to the U.S. than terrorists movements across the world.

The classic fascist regime as epitomised by the Mussolini and Hitler dictatorships consists of a one-party authoritarian government led by a charismatic leader. In the fascist state the party and government are difficult to separate. The nation is identified with race and the state becomes the ultimate good. Individualism is suppressed

---

[46] ABC News (20 January 2018), http://www.abc.net.au/news/

for the communal good, knowledge is censored, and civil liberties are extinguished. The fascist state favours mercantilism against free trade, rejects both liberalism and socialism, adopts capitalist means of production under state control and displaces the rule of law with the will of the regime.

Few states today display all these features but many are trending towards the archetype. Hitler and Mussolini rose to power within democracy. Putin of Russia, Mugabe of Zimbabwe, Chavez of Venezuela, Ortega of Nicaragua, Erdogan of Turkey, and the theocracy of Iran used or are using democratic pathways to consolidate one party rule. The Prime Minister of Hungary Viktor Orbán believes that democracy need not be liberal. He also believes, wrongly, that a democracy organised on liberal principles is unsustainable.[47] Many fear that Orbán is treading a familiar path to authoritarian rule.

There are easier paths to fascism for leaders who inherit the authoritarian apparatus of failed communist states and military dictatorships. The rulers of China and Russia continue to be the avowed foes of free societies. Russia is working overtly and covertly to reabsorb East European nations into its empire and subvert the democratic processes of Western nations. China's President for life, Xi Jinping, has ambitions of world domination. As David Martin Jones says the 'China dream is, then, more than a regional vision. It envisages Eurasian hegemony based on China's market heft and capital investment'.[48]

- **New Mercantilism the Chinese Way**

Beginning in the 1980s China progressively embraced capitalist modes of production and exchange with spectacular results. China became a member of the World Trade Organisation on 11 December

---

[47] Speech at the XXV Bálványos Free Summer University and Youth Camp on 26 July 2014, *The Budapest Beacon*, https://budapestbeacon.com/full-text-of-viktor-orbans-speech-at-baile-tusnad-tusnadfurdo-of-26-july-2014/

[48] David Martin Jones, 'Between Declarations and Dreams: China, US Foreign Policy and Southeast Asia', *Policy* 34:1 (Autumn 2018), p 45

2001. Today it is second largest economy in the world. The Chinese government loudly proclaims its commitment to free trade and is a leading critic of the Trump administration's protectionist policies. Despite this rhetoric, China is a mercantilist state that threatens free trade and therefore the liberal peace. We must remember that France, Spain, Portugal, and initially the Netherlands and Britain, became dominant powers through mercantilism backed by military power. The Chinese are not pursuing their modernised version of mercantilism with battleships and gunboats – or are they?

The Chinese economy even in the privatised sector is ultimately state directed. It would be a suicidal company that disregards the wishes of the state. Economic actors have no recourse against the actions of the all-powerful state. The Chinese government directly owns giant corporations including banks that are key players in the nation's 'Belt and Road Initiative' (BRI) that is seeking to establish Chinese controlled trade routes across Asia and into Africa and Europe. China is militarising the South China Sea and is working to establish naval bases along its trade routes. China seeks a trading system which it can dominate through sharp power.

China's Asia strategy is plain. Chinese state-owned banks give loans to poor countries to fund unaffordable infrastructure (often of doubtful value) to be built by Chinese state-owned corporations with Chinese labour. In Sri Lanka, the Chinese built a cricket stadium in the wilderness, a little used airport, a harbour now virtually owned by the Chinese under long lease and are currently building a 'Port City' on Colombo's waterfront. Lack of transparency in these transactions breed corruption and cause institutional debasement.

- **Concluding Thoughts**

The post-World War liberal peace has not eliminated armed conflict. However, in regions of the world where republican government and free trade prevail there has been a dramatic reduction of war and consequently unprecedented economic growth. It has enabled millions of people to escape from poverty and bestowed affordable goods and services unimaginable at the beginning of the Twentieth Century.

There were hopes that Russia and China would eventually join the liberal democratic family as their people have much more to gain by freedom and free exchange with the West. Sadly, the interest of the people does not necessarily coincide with the interest of a fascist regime. The more prosperous the people, the less they are likely to accept state control of their lives. Moreover, fascists need enemies to galvanise nationalists, a key part of their base.

The liberal peace depends on the prevalence of liberal democracy. Threats to the latter equally threaten the former. I have sought to draw attention to several such threats. Three threats loom above all else: nascent fascism, the new mercantilism of China and the potential of a US initiated new trade war.

8

Happiness and the Law

Marc De Vos

- **Introduction**

Contributions to a *Festschrift* ideally reflect the interests and personality of the celebrated colleague. In this spirit, my contribution addresses a topic that sets the law in a broad societal context and practices critical interdisciplinary analysis, qualities I have appreciated in the scholarship and teachings of Professor Moens.

Happiness has been one of man's deepest desires throughout the ages, and philosophers have grappled with the idea of happiness since the dawn of civilization. From the 18th century onwards, happiness has been broadly equated with pleasure and well-being, a subjectivist and sometimes hedonistic understanding that departs from the more austere and transcendent ideals of earlier times.[1] The Enlightenment also elevated the promotion of happiness to the level of public policy. A famous passage in the American Declaration of Independence classifies "the pursuit of happiness" as an unalienable human right. The revolutionary French Constitution of 1793 declared general happiness to be the goal of society. Utilitarian thinkers of the late 18th and early 19th century defined "the greatest happiness for the greatest number" as the overall yardstick for public policy choice.[2]

Happiness did not figure prominently in mankind's most recent and most predominant societal experiment to promote well-being: the welfare state. The traditional welfare state is primarily an engine for

---

[1] D. McMahon, *Happiness: A History* (Atlantic Monthly Press, 2006).
[2] J. Bentham, *Introduction to the Principles of Morals and Legislation*, first published in 1789.

insurance against life's tribulations. Its underlying drive is material redistribution in search of fairness and justice. Its programme is essentially protective in nature and paternalistic in purpose, aiming to provide material security for entire populations. Personal well-being was part of the equation, but only as an expected natural by-product of the essential welfare goals of munificent income security and/or material support. Much of the welfare state was and remains fundamentally materialistic, not hedonistic.

This is changing. The pursuit of happiness is back in vogue. Across academe – in economics, in political science, in psychology, and in epidemiology – the exploration of happiness or generic "subjective well-being" is booming. Reams of new research, a string of recent books, and the conference circuit have turned happiness into arguably one of the hottest topics of contemporary social sciences.

There is much to be said for this rediscovery of happiness. It can add a quality dimension to our prominent quantitative measures of human development, such as economic growth, income evolution, employment figures, poverty rates, education scores, and the like. In the field of economics, it is part of a useful evolution to broaden the understanding of human action and nuance the stereotype of human beings as self-interested, rational, utility-maximizing agents. Personal happiness is unquestionably important in life and therefore relevant as a topic of public concern. Improving our understanding of happiness will improve our understanding of societies. Adding happiness to the array of perspectives on policy issues, can insert a human angle and force us to ponder effects that would otherwise remain ignored.

But can and should the actual promotion of happiness be a purpose or subject of policymaking as such? Should the pursuit of happiness become politics? Some of the towering figures of the happiness revival advocate nothing less than a radical happiness agenda. We are told that "We need a revolution in government. Happiness should become the goal of policy, and the progress of national happiness should be measured and analysed."[3] Economics could equally be

---

[3] R. Layard, *Happiness: Lessons from a new science* (London: Penguin Books, 2005), 147-147; see also: R. Layard, *Happiness is Back* (Prospect, 2005), 108.

revolutionized and become *happynomics*: "it is – or should be – about personal happiness".[4] A comprehensive monograph on happiness politics is available.[5] Politicians are paying attention and have entered the happiness game. Official indexes and programmes to define and measure happiness or well-being, pioneered by several international governmental organisations, are trickling down to the national level, resulting in an annual 'Global Happiness Policy Report'.[6]

This paper challenges some of the underlying assumptions of the burgeoning happiness agenda. I first tackle the assumption, entertained by the more extreme happiness revivalists, that happiness is a desirable alternative for, or a needed correction of, economic growth and its traditional measure of Gross Domestic Product or GDP (Section 8.2). I then address the three core arguments that support the promotion of happiness as a political agenda: that more economic growth is not the way to promote more happiness (Section 8.3), that "happiness" or "subjective well-being" can be sufficiently defined and measured as to make it a reliable policy instrument (Section 8.4), and that its promotion is morally desirable (Section 8.5). I use this critical analysis to briefly describe the potential tension between happiness policy and the rule of law (Section 8.6). Finally, I warn against the inevitable politicization of 'happiness as policy' (Section 8.7). I conclude by repositioning the relevance of happiness, arguing for a policy of facilitation rather than determination (Section 8.8).

- **Beyond GDP, and Back**

From an academic perspective, happiness is an idea whose time has come, especially in the field of economics. Economics as a profession is going through a period of soul searching and experimentation, provoked by its collective failure to predict and prevent the US subprime debacle and the ensuing GFC. The hour of the *behavioural economist*, who puts irrationality and human fallibility at the centre

---

[4] B. Frey e.a., *Happiness. A Revolution in Economics* (MIT Press, 2008), Chapter 1.
[5] D. Bok, *The Politics of Happiness* (Princeton University Press, 2010).
[6] First published in 2018.

of his analytic universe, has struck. With it has come an increasing openness for proactive policies, of which happiness policy is an example.

The mildest shift – the only one to be officially embraced by governments as yet – operates under the assumption that GDP alone is not a reliable measure of progress, but it does not dump GDP altogether. A stronger version abandons GDP-growth because it supposedly fails to improve well-being overall and happiness in particular. More growth, it is argued, does not produce more well-being or happiness beyond a certain point that has already been reached by nearly all developed countries. With growth thus becoming a zero-sum game, the next step is to abandon it or at least to focus instead on increasing well-being by other means, particularly through more redistribution.[7] Finally, the most extreme version exhumes a veritable growth phobia, identifying economic growth as the mother of evils social and environmental in a finite world perilously close to its limits, with the logical conclusion that one should aim to achieve "prosperity without growth".[8]

"Gross Domestic Product" or GDP is the market value of all final goods and services produced by an economy in a given year. For decades the annual growth rate of GDP has been the key instrument to measure economic development within and among countries. GDP is based on a clear methodology that, however dependent on nationally produced statistics that are not always equally reliable, allows for straightforward comparisons over time and between countries. It is thus a useful, reliable and transparent instrument to gauge the evolution of macro-economic activity in a given setting. In the public parlance and perception, GDP is easily associated with overall economic progress.

---

[7] The most popular work here is R. Wilkinson and K. Pickett, *The Spirit Level. Why greater equality makes societies stronger* (New York: Bloomsbury Press, 2009). Similar analyses are made by R. Layard, *above n.3*.

[8] The most popular work here is T. Jackson, 'Prosperity Without Growth?', *Sustainable Development Commission, 2009*. Similar analyses are made in A. Simms, V. Johnson and P. Chowla, *Growth Isn't Possible. Why we need a new economic direction* (London: New Economics Foundation, 2010).

However, no serious researcher has ever failed to recognize the intrinsic limitations of "GDP" as a statistical measure of progress. GDP and its forerunner, Gross National Product (GNP), have been downplayed as measures of total economic welfare from the day of their invention.[9] GDP has no consideration for the origin or impact of the output it measures. Deficit spending countries can boost their GDP-output artificially by going ever deeper into the red, even while they burry themselves under mountains of public debt that may eventually trigger total collapse. Similarly, serial private consumption by a shopaholic population can lift a country's GDP while its flipside of private debt remains in the shadows until it too spooks the markets or saps the banks. More generally, GDP reflects changes in annual output while ignoring changes in underlying stock or assets such as roads, buildings, machinery, factories, the environment, or natural resources. In the words of the late Robert Kennedy:

> . . . Gross National Product counts air pollution and cigarette advertising, and ambulances to clear our highways of carnage... It counts the destruction of the redwood and the loss of our natural wonder in chaotic sprawl . . . Yet the gross national product does not allow for the health of our children, the quality of their education or the joy of their play. It does not include the beauty of our poetry or the strength of our marriages, the intelligence of our public debate or the integrity of our public officials . . . it measures everything, in short, except that which makes life worthwhile.[10]

GDP thus measures progress that is not the essential progress of mankind. It has endured nonetheless because economic growth, while it is not the end, is the essential means to the end. Growth is the great enabler, both of public policy and of personal choice. In poor countries, economic growth is the precondition for tackling the dismal curses of underdevelopment: malnutrition, infant mortality, illiteracy, diseases, and low life expectancy. Of course, growth alone is never enough. Its

---

[9] For an overview, see A. Tarasofsky, *GDP and its derivatives as welfare measures: a selective look at the literature*, Centre for the Study of Living Standards, 1998.
[10] 1968 speech at the University of Kansas.

fruits must be adequately used through policy. But without growth, such policies become impossible. In the developed world, our recent period of economic distress should remind us all of how essential growth remains to fund our ever increasing and returning societal needs, from law enforcement to national defence, from infrastructure to education, from healthcare to pensions, and far beyond.

We therefore focus on annual growth of economic output because it offers a measurable and verifiable snapshot of that great enabler of all things essential. We value GDP because we know that any slowdown in its development implies unemployment, poverty and hardship for millions, reduces our society's capacity to address these, and undermines our ability to invest in our future and in our security. It is no accident that, for all the buzz about well-being and "post-GDP", it turns out that most of the desired indicators of subjective well-being are actually adequately mirrored by the objective parameters of GDP-evolution and the unemployment rate. Whatever its undeniable limitations, GDP remains an important gauge, not only of economic development, but also of overall societal well-being.[11]

GDP-growth also means much more to overall society than a mere improvement of material living standards of its citizens. Living standards affect the social, political, and ultimately the moral character of a people. Economic growth fosters greater opportunity, tolerance of diversity, social mobility, commitment to fairness, and dedication to democracy. Conversely, these fundamental societal values typically suffer in times of stagnating or declining living standards. Economic growth cements and strengthens a society and its social fabric, while economic decline erodes and frays it from within. There are therefore powerful moral benefits to economic growth, well beyond the realm of the material or its empowerment of the immaterial.[12] We may obviously

---

[11] See S.C. Kassenböhmer and Ch.M. Schmidt, *Beyond GDP and Back: What is the Value-Added by Additional Components of Welfare Measurement?*, IZA DP No. 5453, 2011; in the same vein: R. Boarini, A. Johansson, and M. Mira d'Ercole, 'Alternative Measures of Well-Being', *OECD Social, Employment and Migration Working Papers*, no. 33, 2006.

[12] B.M. Friedman, *The Moral Consequences of Economic Growth* (New York: Alfred Knopf, 2005).

question whether economic opportunities are sufficiently available to all, whether the fruits of progress are sufficiently shared throughout society, or whether growth does not jeopardize our environment and natural resources for the future. But these are essentially redistributive or organizational concerns.

Then there is the environment. Mankind has an inevitable ecological footprint beyond the direct impact of billions of human beings on this planet's resources. But decades of uneven economic progress around the world have shown us that a cleaner environment everywhere comes with increased affluence. Richer countries gradually shift from materialist to post-materialist values, with quality of life and the environment gaining in importance as incomes rise.[13] More wealth then liberates more resources for environmental protection. Richer countries thus have better air quality, better water quality, more forests, and more overall environmental protection.[14] Our planet will never see a post-carbon economy without major shifts in technology, energy, infrastructure, and transportation, all of which require massive investment and huge markets which only economic growth can deliver. Moving beyond GDP will not move us beyond carbon. If we value GDP, therefore, it is also because we believe that sustainable environmental protection can best be achieved through channelling economic development and applying its proceeds according to the shifting needs of environmental programmes.

The maximization of GDP per se, is not and has never been a proper objective of public policy. But we do value GDP per se, as a measurement of the quantifiable economic growth that underpins and enables much of our entire human existence, and particularly those policies that seek to address the myriad of societal concerns at any given time in history. We value GDP per se, because it is an objective and aggregate yardstick while other parameters of progress are more

---

[13] R. Inglehart and C. Welzel, *Modernization, Cultural Change, and Democracy: The Human Development Sequence*, (New York: Cambridge University Press, 2005).
[14] G. Grossman and A. Krueger, *Economic Growth and the Environment*, NBER Working Paper No. 4634, 1994; B. Lomborg, *The Skeptical Environmentalist*, (Cambridge: Cambridge University Press, 2001).

political, subjective and/or personal. Economic growth is an acceptable common denominator because it can allow and mean different things to different people and at different times. GDP is not about happiness or the quality of life directly because – as we shall see – these are largely subjective notions that belong more to the realm of personal preference than of public policy. The coarseness of GDP is therefore more than statistical imperfection. It reflects an implicit understanding of the limits of public policy. What we do not measure, we do not qualify as a static and permanent object of necessary government action.

GDP focuses on economic output and leaves its destination to either public or private decisions. It is the means to an end that leaves the end open to the dynamics of political and personal choice. A reformed measure that integrates various criteria of social or societal progress can become an end in itself: it chooses, codifies and imposes what can otherwise remain debatable, open and voluntary. When subjective well-being and happiness are to be incorporated into an annual measure of progress, we risk committing ourselves to defining and prescribing an agenda for what once remained mostly outside the sphere of politics. We risk not only putting happiness back on the radar of policy interest, but moving our entire model of development towards a more happiness-driven growth model. Measures of well-being, rather than GDP, should then be our guide.[15] Maximizing happiness, rather than income, should then be the goal of government policy. Fostering security and stability, instead of economic dynamism and change, then becomes essential.[16] Happiness, it seems, is in growing less.[17]

Our rediscovery of happiness therefore indeed comes with a true paradigm shift. A previous age, inspired by the liberal mind-set of Western Enlightenment, required the state to get out of the way and allow its citizens to freely pursue their personal happiness. Our age is turning to the state to define happiness and to organize it for us.

---

[15] Layard, above n.3.
[16] Layard, above n.3, Chapters 9 and 11.
[17] C. Caresche, G. Guibert and D. Szynkier, *Le bonheur est-il dans la décroissance?*, Paris, Fondation Jean Jaurès, 2011.

This begs two fundamental questions: are we right in assuming that the pursuit of happiness differs from the pursuit of economic growth, and can we safely rely on governments to determine the pursuit of happiness for its populations?

- **Economic Growth Does (Not) Promote Happiness**

The political agenda to complement, adjust or even replace economic growth with happiness rests upon the cardinal assumption that more growth and wealth do not produce more happiness. Throughout the developed world people have gotten richer and richer: average living standards have more than doubled since 1950. But people on average are nonetheless no happier or only marginally so.[18] Since more wealth apparently does not generate more happiness, a society more concerned with the latter than with the former should adopt specific policies in support of happiness. If economic growth does little to improve well-being, then it should not be a primary goal of government policy. We need an alternative criterion for progress. Case closed.

Thus the happiness logic in its undiluted form.[19] But does it hold up to scrutiny? The assumption that more wealth does not produce more happiness is commonly known as the "Easterlin Paradox". In a number of statistical papers starting in the early 1970s economist Richard Easterlin registered an apparent anomaly. On the one hand, within a given country wealthier people on average are clearly happier than poorer ones. On the other hand, *over time* there appeared to be very little, if any, relationship between increases in income and happiness levels.[20] The Easterlin Paradox was born and many a study since has strived to explain it as human nature. It appears that we are all stuck on a "hedonic treadmill". As incomes rise, we grow accustomed to our higher standard of living and eventually derive no lasting satisfaction from it. After a certain level of comfort is reached, additional wealth

---

[18] Bok, above n.5, Chapter 1; Layard, above n.3, 29-31.
[19] Essentially advocated by Layard, above n.3, Chapter 14.
[20] R. Easterlin, *Does Economic Growth Improve the Human Lot? Some Empirical Evidence*, in *Nations and Households in Economic Growth* (New York: Academia Press, 1974).

thus fails to achieve enduring happiness benefits. Some of this may be due to personal desire and some of it may be sociological, as we perennially compare ourselves with fortunate neighbours or friends with whom we want to keep up. Another explanation for the paradox is the psychologist's "set point" theory of happiness, in which every individual is presumed to have a default personal happiness level that he or she falls back to over time, irrespective of positive or negative life developments.

Does the Easterlin Paradox justify the claim that happiness should topple growth as a main goal of government policy? I believe it does not, for a number of reasons. First off, the validity of Easterlin's paradox itself is far from being beyond any reasonable doubt. More recent statistical work has indeed demonstrated a clear relationship between per capita income and average happiness levels, with no sign that the correlation weakens as income levels increase or over time.[21] Extensive time-series comparisons now show those enjoying materially better circumstances also enjoying durably greater subjective well-being, with higher living standards delivering higher subjective well-being.[22] In short: the Easterlin Paradox may actually not exist at all. At least the jury is still out, and the academic controversy is raging.[23] *'A simple, but unhelpful answer, is that more research is needed'*, dixit... Richard Easterlin.[24]

No matter how significant or insignificant Easterlin's Paradox may turn out to be, a number of findings are beyond question. The Paradox applies only to *longitudinal effects*: tracing the happiness of

---

[21] A. Deaton, 'Income, Health, and Well-Being Around the World: Evidence From the Gallup World Poll' (2008) (2) *Journal of Economic Perspectives* 22.

[22] B. Stevenson and J. Wolfers, 'Economic Growth and Subjective Well-Being: Reassessing the Easterlin Paradox', *IZA DP* No. 3654, 2008; B. Stevenson and J. Wolfers, 'Subjective Well-Being and Income: Is There Any Evidence of Satiation?', *NBER Working Paper* No. 18992, 2013.

[23] See R. Easterlin et al., 'The Happiness-Income Paradox Revisited', *IZA DP* No. 5799, 2011; C. Graham, 'The Challenges of Incorporating Empowerment into HDI: Some Lessons from Happiness Economics and Quality of Life Research', *U.N. Development Programme*, Research Paper 2010/13.

[24] Easterlin, above n.23.

a sample of people in prosperous nations over a long period of time shows that life satisfaction tends to change very little with the rise and fall of their income as they progress through life and career. At any specific moment in time, however, average levels of happiness are higher as one moves up the income scale. International surveys also show differences in average happiness among nations to be closely correlated with differences in average income per capita. Wealthier countries thus have happier populations than poorer ones.[25]

Furthermore, the Easterlin Paradox relies on aggregate happiness data for an entire population. It does not track the evolution of happiness across *sub-groups within that population*. When this is done, it turns out that historically disadvantaged groups – such as women and African Americans in the United States – have seen their happiness levels improve substantially over time.[26] There can be little doubt that their improvement is closely connected to increased educational and economic opportunities, both of which would not have existed but for an undercurrent of economic growth and the revenues it generated. As long as there will be societal needs, as long as there will be people on the lower range of the ladder yarning to move up, growth and wealth will clearly continue to be crucial for raising living standards and happiness in sync.

My point is more fundamental, however. The Paradox does not claim that economic growth is not supportive of happiness. It only claims that, over time, people adapt their expectations to their increased wealth. That does not support the conclusion that growth does not matter for happiness. It does not imply that less economic growth would leave happiness untouched. This is the crux of the debate: not whether more economic growth and prosperity produce durably more happiness, but whether less economic growth and prosperity would help happiness. To put it more bluntly in different terms: the key issue is not whether the public overall is no happier than it was half a century ago; it is whether the public would be willing to return to the living

---

[25] See the overview by Bok, above n.5, Chapter 1.
[26] B. Stevenson and J. Wolfers, 'Happiness Inequality in the United States', *IZA DP* No. 3624, 2008.

standards of that epoch – with few cars, no colour TV, no computer, internet or cell phones – and be equally happy.[27]

I know of no studies examining this premise, or for that matter confirming it. All the available indications are certainly against it. We know all too well that underperforming economies fail their citizens in job creation and deliver insufficient resources to fuel the perennial innovation in healthcare, the insatiable needs for care and welfare, or the schooling needs of the deprived. Joblessness, lack of economic or educational opportunities, eroding healthcare, poor pensions: those are the tokens of economic stagnation and they most certainly undermine happiness instead of promoting it. Easterlin himself is keen to point out that unemployment consistently has one of the most negative impacts on happiness.[28] That material aspirations escalate with economic growth, reducing and eventually levelling happiness effects, simply does not imply that reducing or freezing growth would generate more happiness.

Money, work, health, family relationships, community, and friends are universally valued as major happiness factors.[29] Few among us would expect government to provide for a satisfying marital life or a community of friends. That leaves money and work, both of which directly depend on the economic growth that is equally required to protect public health and provide healthcare. For all the major happiness factors that reasonably fall within the ambit of government policy, economic growth is thus the common underlying facilitator. There is little intrinsic trade-off between economic growth as a public policy aim and personal happiness. Obviously, this does not mean that general and personal welfare are not legitimate concerns that can be politically separate from economic growth as such. Indeed, much of today's economic regulation in the broadest sense, covering issues such as consumer law, environmental law and employment law, has been developed to ensure a match between economics and welfare.

---

[27] In the same vein: S. Lebergott, S. Lebergott, *Pursuing Happiness: American Consumers in the Twentieth Century* (Princeton University Press, 1993), 15.

[28] Easterlin et al., above n.23.

[29] Stevenson and Wolfers, 'Economic Growth', above n. 21, 4; Layard, above n.3, 63.

However, a government that prioritizes happiness over economic growth is a government that is ready to accept a lower standard of living for its citizens. Human adaption indeed works both ways: we can adjust to misery as well as to wealth. Which dimension of happiness matters to a particular person, depends on that person's ability to pursue a meaningful and active life. When prospects are meagre, people place more value on simple, day-to-day experiences such as friendship or religion.[30] In other words: when a society fails to offer economic opportunity and jobs, people derive more well-being from non-economic factors. Making happiness the overriding aim of public policy would bring us to accept and even justify hardship and decline. This could not be called a moral policy on any grounds. Amartya Sen has made this point very powerfully:

> The *hopeless beggar, the precarious* landless labourer, the dominated housewife, the hardened unemployed or the over-exhausted coolie may all take pleasures in small mercies, and manage to suppress intense suffering for the necessity of continuing survival, but it would be ethically deeply mistaken to attach a correspondingly small value to the loss of their well-being because of this survival strategy.[31]

Material progress enables life satisfaction. Increasing wealth may also bring a degree of satisfaction which is hard to measure by polls of personal happiness. And many of us undoubtedly strive for wealth because it enables us to achieve other goals – for ourselves, our families and our communities – that happiness meters simply do not register. The focus on happiness over growth could curtail our ability to use material prosperity for non-material goals. With this potential perverse effect in mind, we can now turn to the fundamental operational question and the central mission of the happiness revival: can we safely rely on government policy to promote personal happiness?

- **Measuring Happiness Measurement**

Switching from the private pursuit of happiness to the public promotion of happiness requires a determination of what happiness actually is, and

---

[30] C. Graham, *The Pursuit of Happiness: An Economy of Wellbeing* (Brookings, 2011).
[31] A. Sen, *On Ethics and Economics* (Blackwell Publishing, 1987), 45-46.

the ability to organize its promotion collectively. From a methodological perspective, no defensible happiness policy can really be considered without a clear understanding of its subject. Happiness is labelled as a "new science" rooted in empirical observation.[32] It is claimed we now know, at long last, what really makes people happy. But a neutral observer who encounters happiness studies for the first time cannot help but being struck by how unsophisticated they actually are.

Empirical happiness research to date is mostly based on surveys that ask individuals how happy or how satisfied they are with their lives. These surveys typically involve general questions probing happiness or life satisfaction: *"taken altogether how would you say that things are these days?" Do you think of yourself as very happy, pretty happy or not too happy?" "Have you lost much sleep over worry?"; "Been able to concentrate on things?"; "Felt you are playing a useful part in things?"; "Felt capable of making decisions about things?"; "Felt constantly under strain?"; "Felt you could not overcome your difficulties?"; "Been able to enjoy your normal day-to-day activities"; "Been able to face up to your problems"; "Been feeling unhappy and depressed?"; "Been losing confidence in yourself?"; "Been thinking of yourself as a worthless person?"; "Been feeling reasonably happy all things considered?"*. The World Values Survey, for example, asks, *"Taking all things together, would you say you are: very happy; quite happy; not very happy; not at all happy?"* and, *"All things considered, how satisfied are you with your life as a whole these days?"* Other variants, such as the Gallup World Poll, employ a ladder analogy: interviewees are asked to imagine a ladder with each rung representing a successively better life. Respondents then report the "step" on the ladder that best represents their life. Such lines of questioning remind one more of the shrink's sofa than of meticulous data mining. But they are nonetheless invoked to "scientifically" diagnose the state of the human condition.[33]

---

[32] R. Layard has titled his seminal book *Happiness: Lessons from a New Science*. Comp. A. E. Clark et al., *The Origins of Happiness: The Science of Well-Being over the Life Course* (Princeton University Press, 2018).

[33] See A. Oswald, 'Emotional Prosperity and the Stiglitz Commission', *IZA Discussion Paper* No. 5390, 2010.

The immediate conclusion is that happiness data are a collection of tentative happiness gauges, summarily offered by fallible respondents, in response to rather crude questions, and interpreted by fallible researchers, some of whom admit to a policy agenda.[34] It is widely recognized that responses to happiness surveys are *inherently subjective and relative*. Feelings of personal well-being are influenced by infinite personal and cultural biases. Each and every individual faces life's predicaments differently. Our biological and neurological make-up differs: happiness and unhappiness, at the end of the day, are about brain waves. Education and cultural norms vary. Societal attitudes and expectations differ. All of these affect the way different people judge similar situations on their personal happiness scale. One records *subjective* well-being and therefore by definition accepts that responses will be subjective. But should we really use subjective individual data as scientific intelligence to determine public policy?

Happiness measurements are also to some extent *inherently unreliable*. People may be motivated to manipulate reports of their own well-being, either downplaying or exaggerating well-being according to the context and the purpose of the inquiry. If Gross National Happiness would be used to measure well-being, citizens could strategically adapt their life satisfaction responses in order to influence policies to their liking. It also recognized that respondents to happiness surveys tend to be unduly susceptible to fluctuations of moment-to-moment mood. Subjective reports of well-being moreover suffer from our tendency to conform our responses to implicit standards of assessment or comparison we acquire through culture and society.[35] These standards also evolve in time, making the entire exercise of comparing happiness over time inherently problematic.

Furthermore, the standard of judgment people use when reporting their level of happiness is contextual and malleable. For instance,

---

[34] For a pedagogical and descriptive overview, see Bok, above n.5, Chapter 2.

[35] G. Loewenstein and P.A. Ubel, 'Hedonic Adaptation and the Role of Decision and Experience Utility in Public Policy', (2008) 92 *Journal of Public Economics* 1795, 1799-1800; W. Wilkinson, 'In Pursuit of Happiness Research. Is It Reliable? What Does It Imply for Policy?', *Cato Policy Analysis* No. 590, 2007, 6-9.

when people are asked to report how well they were doing *relative to their own and their parents' past*, self-reported levels of happiness rise dramatically.[36] The whole mechanism of grading happiness in relation to wealth – *the* key statistic fuelling the "beyond-GDP" logic – suffers from the flaw that no respondent can keep on increasing his/her personal happiness level beyond "very happy", whereas income continues to rise over time. The purported disconnect between increased wealth and increased happiness is thus partly organized by the very statistical mechanism that is supposed to report it.

The perennial Achilles heel of all statistical inquiries is the distinction between correlation and causation. It is not enough to fathom the connection or disconnection between wealth and happiness. For any judgment to be scientifically admissible, one also needs to establish the causes of the observed relationship. Happiness surveys are mostly unable to link the recorded sentiments to a comprehensive set of possible sources of happiness or distress. There are some recognized categories of correlation, linking happiness to money, work, health, family relationships, community, and friends. But beyond these broad generalizations, many possible factors that influence subjective well-being still await exploration. Although there is some evidence that the link between wealth and happiness is direct and causal, i.e. not dependent on other factors besides increasing wealth,[37] we simply do not know enough of what drives (un)happiness in a given society.

Happiness surveys are obviously not entirely random. They cannot be discarded as irrelevant. Some studies have tried to verify recordings of subjective happiness, through repetitions or by connecting them to more objective factors. They have found relevant degrees of reliability.[38] As time progresses, happiness methodology

---

[36] See M.R. Hagerty, 'Was Life Better in the 'Good Old Days'? Intertemporal Judgments of Life Satisfaction', (2003) 2 Journal of Happiness Studies 4.

[37] J.-S. Pischke, 'Money and Happiness: Evidence from the Industry Wage Structure', *NBER WP* 17056, 2011.

[38] A. Krueger and D. Schkade, 'The Reliability of Subjective Well-Being Measures', *CEPS Working Paper* No. 138, 2007; A. Oswald and S. Wu, 'Objective Confirmation of Subjective Measures of Well-being: Evidence from the USA', *IZA Discussion Paper* No. 4695, 2010.

should improve.[39] But for now, happiness research essentially relies on rudimentary surveys because it has nothing better. People are reckoned to be the best available judges of their own happiness.[40] If people's words on ephemeral feelings are to be taken for granted, then why question the much more reliable and verifiable source of their actions as revealed preferences? Why question people's consumer decisions and desire for prosperity, but accept their version of happiness?[41]

Happiness surveys are a collection of snapshot impressions, asking respondents to commit their immediate feelings to paper. However, we all know that true meaning and value in life only transpires over time and in retrospect. Available happiness estimates are about instant and real-time sensations, not about sustained contentment. This is a crucial caveat. Happiness measurement risks steering happiness policy towards short-term satisfaction, begging the question whether this is truly the kind of happiness our society should seek to foster. While happiness policy questions GDP or wealth for a supposed lack of happiness effect in the long run, it is based on an understanding of happiness as an instantaneous and real-time phenomenon.

Other research demonstrates that circumstances and events often have a surprisingly small impact when happiness is instead measured over time. By and large, happiness levels appear remarkably impervious to changes in the external environment. People both report and experience approximately the same level of happiness regardless of their social or personal well-being. For example, numerous studies have found that people with severe chronic health conditions report happiness levels that are close to those reported by healthy persons, and that are much better than healthy people believe their moods would be if they had those conditions. Such gradual adaptation of our feelings of well-being to different circumstances is neither universal nor complete, but it is strong.[42] Circumstances that we can change through actions

---

[39] See Clark et al., above n.32.
[40] Frey et al, above n.4, Chapter 1.
[41] A. Wolfe, 'Hedonic Man. The new economics and the pursuit of happiness', *The New Republic*, July 2008.
[42] See the overview in D. Gilbert, *Stumbling on Happiness* (New York: Alfred Knopf, 2006), 153; Loewenstein and Ubel, above n.35, 1799.

or policy thus have a smaller lasting influence on our subjective happiness than given factors such as genetic disposition. That begs an uncomfortable question: if we should care less about economic growth because people adapt to wealth, why should we care more about happiness when people adapt to fortune and misfortune alike?

- **Happiness and Morality**

There are roughly two types of happiness. So-called *eudaimonic* well-being (from the Greek *daimon* - true nature), harks back to Aristotle and his conviction that true happiness is found by leading a virtuous life and doing what is worth doing, with the realisation of our human potential as the ultimate goal. Then there is the happiness that Aristotle found vulgar: the *hedonic* well-being derived from mere personal pleasure and contentment, traditionally associated with Jeremy Bentham and his strictly utilitarian approach to life.

What kind of happiness do we seek as a contemporary policy aim? One of the leading happiness protagonists puts it this way: 'By happiness I mean feeling good – enjoying life and wanting the feeling to be maintained. By unhappiness I mean feeling bad and wishing things to be different.'[43] The dean of American happiness scholars describes a happy person as one that 'experiences life satisfaction and frequent joy, and only infrequently experiences unpleasant emotions such as sadness or anger.'[44] This approach is hedonistic. The happiness surveys, with their focus on personal sentiment and instant sensations, are also biased towards the hedonic side. The overwhelming inclination of contemporary happiness research is towards the hedonic-subjective idea of happiness.

If hedonic pleasures are to constitute the bedrock of public policy, we risk committing our societies to a course of instant and often superficial gratification, instead of real fulfilment and progress. If hedonic contentment is to be its goal, then the burgeoning happiness revolution may prove to be conservative: it will end up promoting the

---

[43] Layard, above n.3, 12.
[44] Ed Diener, quoted in Bok, above n.5, 9.

very materialism and consumerism their proponents associate with the GDP-addiction they seek to undo. Relaxing, shopping, watching TV, socializing, and having sex: these are activities that typically generate a high level of hedonic happiness. Household work, professional work, and commuting are associated with low average levels of happiness.[45] Are we to promote an empty lifestyle of transient pleasures?

Whatever the orientation, one thing is clear: *no happiness policy can be considered without a prior normative and moral choice on the type of happiness we want to promote*. Are we to promote hedonistic contentment, notwithstanding its short-term and fleeting nature, or do we instead seek true happiness over the longer term, even if that requires short-term sacrifices and even unhappiness? Should we promote pleasant feelings and to minimize painful feelings, or instead distinguish bad pleasures from good ones, and bad pain from good pain? This requires a reflection which the happiness literature has largely ignored so far.[46] The claim that happiness is self-evidently good and therefore by definition the right guide for public policy and private decisions alike[47], does not cut it. John Stuart Mill's famous aphorism on 19th century utilitarianism applies to its present-day reincarnation: 'Better to be Socrates dissatisfied than a fool satisfied'.

What matters for individuals, impacts society at large. Irrespective of whether we favour hedonic or austere happiness as the standard for personal well-being, we should take into consideration its *potential aggregate effect for society* and mankind in general. Few among us would favour deliberately organizing hardship for the sake of promoting greatness. But we cannot ignore the fact that the active public promotion of hedonic happiness is bound to undermine some of the melancholy and dissatisfaction of the human condition that has so often spurred creativity and progress in many fields. We cannot fail to recognize that individuals who reach the highest level of happiness typically do not possess that nagging sense of unfulfilled ambition

---

[45] Layard, above n.3, 15.
[46] For an overture, see M. Nussbaum, '*Who is the happy warrior? Philosophy poses questions to psychology*', (2008) 37 *Journal of Legal Studies* 81-112.
[47] Layard, above n.3, 113 and 115.

that pushes others to heights of innovation and worldly success.⁴⁸ We should not forget that the success story of capitalistic innovation is rooted into a culture of hard work, personal sacrifice, and delayed gratification.⁴⁹

Puritans may deplore the erosion of progress – whether material, scientific or artistic – that is bound to arise when we cover humanity under a warm blanket of happiness.⁵⁰ But we should at least consider the dilemma many of us will recognize as parents in raising children. Do we indulge them in the latest fashion, TV-show and video-game, or do we instead install discipline, stimulate hard work, teach the limits of money, and the value of earned success? Do we embrace the Chinese "Tiger Mother" (in)famously portrayed in a current bestseller, pushing our children to the limits of their ability in iron discipline, hoping they will appreciate and value it later in life?⁵¹ Or do we accept failure and take off the pressure, even when it undermines their future potential? Similarly in education: do we emphasize discipline, learning and the transfer of knowledge, or are schools there to make children happy and assertive?⁵² Hedonic contentment may be the easy ride and the more pleasurable one while it lasts, but it may also end up eroding overall progress and leave the individual frustrated in later life.⁵³

Beyond societal progress, there is the issue of *societal cohesion*. Turning individual happiness into a policy goal implies an individualistic policy orientation. It may remove us from a narrow-minded obsession with individual interest, but only to replace it by a focus on individual pleasure. Happiness policy echoes the world-

---

⁴⁸ Bok, above n.5, 51.
⁴⁹ D. McCloskey, *The Bourgeois Virtues*, University of Chicago Press, 2006; M. Weber, *The Protestant Ethic and the Spirit of Capitalism*, first published in German in 1904-05.
⁵⁰ E. Wilson, *Against Happiness: In Praise of Melancholy*, Farrar, Straus and Giroux, 2008.
⁵¹ A. Chua, *Battle Hymn of the Tiger Mother*, Penguin Press, 2011.
⁵² T. Loveless, *How well are American students learning?*, Brown Center Report on American Education, October 2006, Volume II, Number 1.
⁵³ R. Epstein, *Happiness and Revealed Preferences in Evolutionary Perspective*, 33 Vt. L. Rev. 559 2008-2009, 570-571.

view of their 19th century utilitarian predecessors. Jeremy Bentham famously stated that "the community is a fictitious body" and that the interest of the community is "the sum of the interests of the several members who compose it".[54] This atomic approach to society is the philosophical prerequisite for the utilitarian agenda of happiness promotion: you cannot posit individual happiness as the aim without accepting the individual as the yardstick. However, any society rests upon a moral order – whether articulated or unspoken – that balances freedom and coercion, and settles the relation between personal impulses and community requirements.[55] By focusing on personal happiness, we ignore societal cohesion and its moral foundation. Our societal contract contrasts self-interest with public interest. We inevitably will have to limit the promotion of happiness to what is accepted as proper and desirable. Here again, the happiness programme necessitates a normative and moral inquiry.

This brings me to *societal fairness*. Is our key societal objective to produce happiness, or justice? Are the policy implications of a happiness agenda compatible with our understanding of justice and fairness, or not? Those who associate justice with the welfare state's redistributionist programme may well prefer *Justland* over *Happyland*.[56] Most American happiness preachers write of happiness but imply welfare and redistribution, as if the two are one and the same.[57] However, subjective well-being depends more on living standards than on state welfare[58], rising income inequality has coincided with declining happiness inequality[59], and the effect of inequality on the poor's happiness depends much more on a society's

---

[54] Bentham, above n.2.

[55] D. Bell, *The Cultural Contradictions of Capitalism*, (Twentieth Anniversary Edition, Basic Books, 1996), Chapter 6.

[56] F. Vandenbroucke, *Geluk als doelstelling, doelstelling als geluk. Een pleidooi voor vitaliteit*, Redenaarsconcert "De Triomf van de Menselijkheid", 2011.

[57] See the list and the quotes in Wilkinson, above n.35, 2-4.

[58] R. Veenhoven, 'Well-Being in the Welfare State: Level Not Higher, Distribution Not More Equitable' (2000) 2 *Journal of Comparative Policy Analysis* 91-125.

[59] Stevenson and Wolfers, above n.26.

cultural attitude towards inequality than on inequality per se.[60] The basic assumption that wealth does not bring everlasting happiness suggests that happiness policies will be less materialistic in emphasis. Choices will undoubtedly have to be made. The more conservative or libertarian minded will point out that more happiness is closely related to more economic and political freedom, and that the opportunity for merited success beats any welfare programme on the happiness scale.[61]

The moral case for a deliberate happiness agenda is therefore not straightforward. Any happiness policy – no matter how shaky or solid its statistics, no matter how sound or foolish its economics – will face a difficult moral trade-off. More fundamentally, however, we cannot escape the fact that it will always fail to capture a wide range of values and dimensions that people legitimately care about. If life is about much more than money, as most of us will readily admit, it is also about much more than mere personal happiness. Any happiness policy by definition succumbs to an egotistic bias that ignores other fundamentals of the human condition, not only on the personal level but also in the context of marriage, family and society at large. From an ethical point of view, society should clearly not only be concerned with having its citizens living the good life, but also a life that is good. At the end of the day, happiness policy becomes the political determination of happiness, to which we now turn.

- **Happiness and the Rule of Law**

Whatever it takes to achieve genuine personal happiness exists within individuals and not within the powers of politicians or public officials. There are too many personal, family, genetic, cultural or societal

---

[60] The effect of inequality on the poor is statistically insignificant in the United States but larger in Europe, due to different societal attitudes towards inequality: A. Alesina, R. Di Tella and R. MacCulloch, 'Inequality and Happiness: Are Europeans and Americans Different?', (2004) 88 *Journal of Public Economics* 2009-2042.

[61] A. Brooks, *The Battle. How the Fight Between Free Enterprise and Big Government Will Shape America's Future* (New York: Basic Books, 2010), Chapter Three; Wilkinson, above n.35.

factors, and too many plain idiosyncrasies that will forever remain beyond the grasp of public policy and public servants, no matter how enlightened and determined.

Furthermore, no single policy is able to instil happiness directly into a person's heart. The best a policy maker can do is to approximate by offering a context which he understands to be amenable to happiness. For that he will have to select what instruments to use and what criteria to apply. Any happiness policy will have to limit its aim and standardize its method. It will focus on income redistribution, interfere in education, ensure water supply, provide housing, regulate advertising, invest in public transportation, mandate parental leave, recalibrate working conditions for well-being, or offer accessible healthcare for all; to name a number of the policy solutions proposed in the happiness literature.

The pursuit of happiness by policy thus boils down to having politics and public choice prioritize a version of happiness. The inevitable outcome is an agenda of organizing what politically qualifies as happiness. By seeking to promote happiness we end up prescribing it. When the promotion of well-being becomes a policy goal, the policy maker always imposes values by deciding what kind of well-being is taken into consideration. A focus on happiness as the overriding common good leaves little room for a debate on other or ultimate goals, and may end up in an agenda that denies people the possibility to choose between goals for themselves.[62]

Moreover, any happiness policy by definition assumes the desirability of the happiness it promotes. Embracing happiness as a political agenda thus requires governments to separate desirable from undesirable happiness.[63] It is not just happiness as such that is politically defined, but also the *morality of happiness*. This gets the happiness agenda into hot philosophical waters. A system of government rooted in the respect of personal liberty, cannot justifiably

---

[62] In the same vein: P. Barrotta, 'Why Economists Should Be Unhappy with the Economics of Happiness' (2008) 24 *Economics and Philosophy* 145-165.

[63] R. Layard recognizes this explicitly in *Happiness is back*.

interfere with its members' liberty by legislating morality, unless it serves a sufficiently important and legitimate social objective.[64] The rule of law is a system of government that puts personal liberty at the heart of the polity.[65] Rule of law countries are distinguishable from other systems by their lack of *predestination*. They provide platforms for participatory decision making without fixing its direction or destination beforehand. The political promotion of hedonic pleasure therefore sits uncomfortable with the constitutional tradition of liberty that lies at the heart of Western legal theory and the rule of law. That tension need not necessarily always yield conflict, but it is there and it should be duly considered.

From the perspective of legal theory embracing happiness essentially implies using the law as an instrument for welfare or utility maximisation, enlightened perhaps, but inevitably one that politicises society and lives.[66] In this regard, happiness policy relates to the law as does a paternalistic policy that interferes with a person's liberty of action for reasons of politically defined welfare goals.[67]

Do we want the state to frame our state of happiness, or do we want the state to allow and enable us to strive for personal happiness ourselves? That, at the end of the day, is the key political and philosophical question which the happiness movement forces us to confront. In the worst scenario, the politics of happiness have an illiberal undertone, exemplified by the current embrace of happiness policy by authoritarian regimes. In the best scenario, they open a new dimension in the expanding universe of the welfare state, paving the way to what could be called *hedonic welfarism*. Indeed, the politics of happiness are essentially a collection of well-intended programmes that institutionalize the search

---

[64] For an overview of this age-old issue, see J.L. Hill, *The Constitutional Status of Morals Legislation* (2009) 98 (1) *Kentucky Law Journal* 1-66.

[65] For an overview, see B. Tamanaha, *On the Rule of Law* (Cambridge University Press, 2004).

[66] Comp. J. McConvill, 'Happiness and the Law: Original Thinking for Legal Scholarship' (2005) 1 *Original Law Review* 58.

[67] See and comp. R. Dworkin, 'Paternalism', in Wasserstrom (ed.), *Morality and the Law* (Wadsworth Publishing Co., 1971).

for happiness through an updated welfare state. The happiness revolution starts with the individual expression of individual happiness emotions and ends in standardized collective provisions. Like our GDP-addiction, it too reduces and stereotypes societal evolution through fixed and general formulas that may eventually narrow and impoverish our understanding of human progress.

We need to understand the *determining factors behind emotions of happiness*. Personal freedom and control are powerful predictors of personal happiness. Economic freedom, political freedom, perceived societal tolerance, autonomy and self-determination, are all decisively correlated to personal happiness.[68] Happiness starts with the freedom to determine your happiness yourself. If not carefully focused, a happiness agenda can thus fail its own purpose on three accounts. *First*, by putting happiness before growth, it may reduce for entire populations the possibility of self-realisation which rising living standards enable, as we have seen. *Second*, by favouring happiness as the ultimate goal, it may reduce the possibility for people to choose other ultimate ends instead. *Third*, by promoting happiness through entitlements, it may well support the happiness at the expense of reducing the autonomy and self-determination that can support happiness overall.

- **Conclusion**

For every human being, indeed for most living creatures, well-being and happiness matter tremendously. The pursuit of happiness is a natural and crucial part of the human existence, as philosophers have recognized for many centuries. A state of personal happiness clearly can benefit society as well. Happy people on average have more productive and successful careers[69], are more willing to engage

---

[68] See, among others, M. Benz and B. Frey, 'Being Independent is a Great Thing: Subjective Evaluations of Self-Employment and Hierarchy' (2008) 75 *Economica* 362-383; R. Inglehart et al., 'Development, Freedom, and Rising Happiness. A Global Perspective' (2008) 3(4) *Perspectives on Psychological Science* 264-282. See also, for a more political perspective, Brooks, above n.61.

[69] A. Oswald, E. Proto, and D. Sgroi, 'Happiness and Productivity', *IZA DP* No. 4645, 2009.

in the risk-taking of the successful entrepreneur[70], live longer and healthier lives[71], and even drive more safely.[72] There is thus a strong case for integrating a happiness perspective into policy reflection. Valuing happiness also brings us closer to the essentials of life, and may thus help to supersede some of the materialistic biases of existing policies. Fostering a public debate about happiness can help us address modern societal phenomena such as stress, loneliness, lack of hope and trust, and the like. In short: the happiness perspective can help us realize and understand societal ills that are worthy of public policy concern.[73]

However, if happiness is promoted as a key societal aim we risk returning to a utilitarian past, defending the greatest happiness of mankind as the ultimate common good and its promotion as the overarching goal of public policy. I have argued that such an agenda would come with dangerous assumptions, weak credentials, unclear motives, and doubtful goals. Dangerous assumptions that unduly question the validity of economic growth as an instrument for well-being (section 2). Weak credentials that rely on limited or inaccurate statistics (sections 3 and 4). Unclear motives lacking a coherent ethical framework and sitting uncomfortably with the ethical foundations of the rule of law (sections 5-6). Doubtful goals offering little more than an open-ended entitlement spree (section 7).

Nobody has ever torn the pursuit of happiness out of the almanac of human progress. But we should not switch from a perceived obedience to GDP to a real obedience to coarse emotional indicators. We need to recognize the inherent fallibility of happiness meters and consider their limits as reliable instruments. Happiness can be added

---

[70] R. Bosman and F. van Winden, *Global Risk, Investment and Emotions*, Center for Economic Policy Rsearch, DP 5451, 2006.

[71] E. Diener and M.Y. Chan, 'Happy People Live Longer: Subjective Well-Being Contributes to Health and Longevity' (2011) 3 *Applied Psychology: Health and Well-Being* 1-43.

[72] R. Goudie e.a., *Happiness as a Driver of Risk-Avoiding Behavior*, CESifo WP Series No. 3451, 2011.

[73] C. Graham, *Happiness for All? Unequal Hopes and Lives in Pursuit of the American Dream*, (Princeton University Press, 2017).

to the list of qualitative criteria that allow us to better judge and value quantitative economic development, enabling our economies to mature further towards a reality of economic growth that is both high-quantity and high-quality. We need growth that is sustainable. Human well-being is an important part of that legitimate concern, even if we should be mindful of pursuing it where we lack genuinely reliable and objective standards.

Let's not get carried away. The happiness agenda is big on promise but small on delivery. It promises to overhaul our entire policy make-up towards the common good of personal happiness. It ends up with a pretty random but rather predictable collection of 'hedonic' welfare prescriptions. This should not surprise us. Making the promotion of happiness the pinnacle of policy priorities is as easy in principle as it is hard in practice. The problem of the happiness agenda lies not so much in its aim as in the inherent fallibility and arbitrariness of its implementation. There is only so much one can know about subjective well-being and only so much one can do about it through policy. At the point of action, the politics of happiness will be more about the preference of its authors than of its subjects.

Government can and must play an important part in the promotion of happiness for its citizens. We do not need to reinvent the wheel and revolutionize our economic model for it. All available research shows lasting happiness to be primarily dependent on personal temperament, marriage, social relationships, employment, perceived health, religion, and the quality of government. Government should therefore evidently get its own house in order, allowing its citizens to have trust in rulers, rules, and ruled alike. It should favour a strong economy capable of providing many employment opportunities. It should promote public health and healthcare, even if that does not condemn it to any particular healthcare model a priori. It should give due attention to environmental standards and to the overall quality of life in urban development. It can consider specific measures in support of family life, social activities, or the freedom of religion.

All of this is already acquired in much of the developed world, even if we do not label it as happiness policies. There is a thin line between facilitating the individual pursuit of happiness and prescribing it for all of us. That line will make the difference between an open society that maximizes the opportunity for prosperity and the possibility of happiness, and a compulsive system that potentially reduces the scope for both.

9

THE USE OF FORCE AS A RESPONSE TO CHEMICAL WEAPONS ATTACKS – MIGHT THERE BE SOMETHING BREWING IN THE LABORATORY OF INTERNATIONAL LAW?

Jürgen Bröhmer

- **Introduction**

The law regulating the use of force is one of the most important cornerstones of international law. The willingness of states to give due regard to the law governing the use of force is literally of existential significance for those affected by the actions of states involving the use of or abstention from the use of military force. This becomes paramount in situations when the traditional framework of rules regarding the use of force suggests that force cannot be legally employed in conflicts with a strong moral impetus to react to perceived gross atrocities regardless of the legalities involved and if only to more or less symbolically communicate one's outrage and frustration. The long-standing discussion about humanitarian intervention as a potential justification for the use of force is in essence driven by this legal-moral conflict.

This little contribution to honour Gabriël A Moens cannot attempt to recap the debate on humanitarian intervention. Instead what is attempted here is to undertake a closer look at the recent military strikes by the USA, France and Great-Britain in response to the use of chemical weapons against civilians by the Syrian government and to ask whether the response of the international community could indicate the possibility of a (beginning) development or shift in international law.

- **The Prohibition of the Use of Force**

The prohibition of the use of force is a cornerstone of the coexistence of nations on the planet. Military force inherently leads to death and destruction and death and destruction are not conducive to development and the welfare of humans and their communities. It is therefore not even disputed that the use of military force is generally massively disadvantageous regardless of the realistic assessment that there are scenarios in which the use of force is the only means to avert even more disadvantageous consequences. The allied response in World War II to the blatant aggression of the German Reich in Europe and elsewhere and Japan in the Asia-Pacific is a good example. There is evil that can only be repelled by force even if one were to argue from a pacifist perspective that, in the long run, any violent response will have its steep price. The prohibition of the use of force in international law is an attempt to achieve for the community of states on this planet that which has been fought for and which is the defining value of the nation-state: the centralisation and monopolisation of the use of force to achieve peace. Peace is the precondition for people in a society to be able to develop and prosper and the same is true for the multiple state-based societies that make up the international community. The notion of the failed state and the example of states who are not (yet) failed states but have severe problems with the monopolization of the use of force amply demonstrate that even after several centuries the construct of the nation-state still has not completely succeeded in this quest. It is not in the least surprising that the ongoing process to achieve a similar monopolization of the use of force by legally prohibiting states to resort to force – with narrowly defined exceptions - which only commenced with the creation of the United Nations in 1945, is still an unfinished. The High-Level Panel on Threats, Challenges and Change convened by the UN Secretary-General noted:

> For the first 44 years of the United Nations, Member States often violated these rules and used military force literally hundreds of times, with a paralysed Security Council passing very few Chapter VII resolutions and Article 51 only rarely providing

credible cover. Since the end of the cold war, however, the yearning for an international system governed by the rule of law has grown.[1]

But despite this somewhat dire finding the Report also states:

> The cold war shaped much of global politics for the next 45 years. The rivalry between the United States and the former Soviet Union blocked the Security Council from playing a dominant role in maintaining international peace and security. Nearly all armed conflicts and struggles for liberation were viewed through the prism of East-West rivalry until the historic collapse of the former Soviet Union and the end of communist rule in Eastern Europe.
>
> Nonetheless, without the United Nations the post-1945 world would very probably have been a bloodier place. There were fewer inter-State wars in the last half of the twentieth century than in the first half. Given that during the same period the number of States grew almost fourfold, one might have expected to see a marked rise in inter-State wars. Yet that did not occur and the United Nations contributed to that result. The United Nations diminished the threat of inter-State war in several ways. Peace was furthered by the invention of peacekeeping; diplomacy was carried out by the Secretary-General; disputes were remedied under the International Court of Justice; and a strong norm was upheld against aggressive war.[2]

However, whereas the number of interstate wars has remained relatively small the number of domestic civil wars has increased significantly.[3]

---

[1] Report of the UN Secretary-General's High-Level Panel on Threats, Challenges and Change, A More Secure World: Our Shared Responsibility, 2 December 2004, A/59/565, para 186.

[2] Report of the UN Secretary-General's High-Level Panel on Threats, Challenges and Change, A More Secure World: Our Shared Responsibility, 2 December 2004, A/59/565, para 10 and 11.

[3] See, for example, http://www.un.org/pga/70/wp-content/uploads/sites/10/2016/01/Conflict-and-violence-in-the-21st-century/ (last accessed on 10 October 2017); for conflict data see also the Uppsala Conflict Data Program, Department of Peace and Conflict Research (UCDP), http://ucdp.uu.se/ and the Peace Research Institute Oslo (PRIO), https://www.prio.org/.

World War II was the most violent outbreak of military conflict in human history both militarily and with regard to massive violations of even the most basic rules of humanity in conducting the war and beyond the actual conduct of and unrelated to the war (especially the Holocaust in Germany). The military activities culminated in the first use of nuclear bombs against the Japanese cities of Hiroshima and Nagasaki and thus the first use of weapons of mass destruction. On 27 May 2016, US President Barrack Obama spoke about war in general and the nuclear bombing at the Hiroshima Peace Memorial Park:

> Seventy-one years ago, on a bright, cloudless morning, death fell from the sky and the world was changed. A flash of light and a wall of fire destroyed a city and demonstrated that mankind possessed the means to destroy itself.
>
> Why do we come to this place, to Hiroshima? We come to ponder a terrible force unleashed in a not so distant past. We come to mourn the dead, including over 100,000 Japanese men, women and children; thousands of Koreans; a dozen Americans held prisoner. Their souls speak to us. They ask us to look inward, to take stock of who we are and what we might become. [...]
>
> The World War that reached its brutal end in Hiroshima and Nagasaki was fought among the wealthiest and most powerful of nations. Their civilizations had given the world great cities and magnificent art. Their thinkers had advanced ideas of justice and harmony and truth. And yet, the war grew out of the same base instinct for domination or conquest that had caused conflicts among the simplest tribes; an old pattern amplified by new capabilities and without new constraints. In the span of a few years, some 60 million people would die—men, women, children no different than us, shot, beaten, marched, bombed, jailed, starved, gassed to death.[4]

The attempts to outlaw war in the first half of the century failed. However, World War II and especially the events at Hiroshima and Nagasaki made it clear that humanity must continue its efforts to ban

---

[4] Barrack Obama, Address at the Hiroshima Peace Memorial, 27 May 2016. Text and audio available at http://www.americanrhetoric.com/speeches/barackobama/barackobamahiroshimaspeech.htm (last accessed on 29 December 2017.

the use of force as a means to resolve disputes. In the past, the price of war - in almost inverse proportionality to the creation and mishandling of the political causes leading to these wars - was often mainly paid by the general populations of the respective states and not so much by the rich and powerful. From the day of the explosion of the "Little Boy" nuclear device over Hiroshima on 6 August 1945 and the "Fat Man" bomb three days later over Nagasaki it had become painfully obvious that war could henceforth literally spell the end of humanity, rich and poor, powerful or powerless. Since then the spectre of total destruction has grown exponentially with the invention of even more destructive fusion bombs ("hydrogen bombs"), the development of delivery systems on a large scale, and the proliferation of nuclear arms beyond the "traditional" nuclear powers. Fission or fusion bombs may well not be the endpoint in the development of weapons of mass destruction when one considers advances in biochemistry, genetics or in the digital world. It has never been more imperative to find a different and better way to dispute settlement than the use of force.

- **Article 2(4) United Nations Charter**

Only three months after the dropping of the nuclear bombs and the end of WW II in the Pacific theatre and less than six months after the war's end in the European theatre, the United Nations was founded on 24 October 1945. The founding treaty, the Charter of the United Nations (UNC), tackled the use of force problem with a mix of substantive and institutional measures aimed at creating a system of collective security, which was to prevail over unilateral decisions of using force as just another element from the political toolbox. The substantive centrepiece is the general prohibition of the use of force in Article 2(4) UNC and this provision is the starting point for any legal consideration of the use of force. The general prohibition of the use of force operates in conjunction with two exceptions stipulated in the UNC. The first one is the collective response through the United Nations Security Council who has the power to authorize the use of force under certain circumstances (Chapter VII UNC, Articles 39-51, especially Articles 39 and 42). The second exception is the recourse to the "inherent right of self-defence" of states against an "armed attack" by an aggressor (Article 51 UNC). This right can be exercised unilaterally or in conjunction with other states who are willing to exercise self-defence collectively with the attacked state. The right to self-defence ends when the Security Council has taken the measures necessary to maintain international peace and security, i.e. when the collective system has kicked in effectively. The UN system pertaining to the use of force is thus similar to the system in place within states. In principle the use of force is monopolized by the state and individuals may exercise force only under limited circumstances, one of which is self-defence.

The substantive rules pertaining to the use of force are embedded in an institutional framework in an attempt to give it the greatest possible legitimacy. The cornerstone of that institutional framework is the Security Council of the United Nations (UNSC) and within it the special status of the five permanent members of the UNSC (P5)[5] and their special right of veto under Article 27 UNC. It ensures that, in addition to self-defence, force can only be used legally if the UNSC votes in favour of authorizing such force and if the majority includes "the concurring votes of the permanent members" (Article 27(3)).

However, the legitimacy benefit of this institutional embedding comes at the price of the efficacy of the system. The UNSC is unable to act if only one of the P5 disagrees with the majority view. Especially during the so-called "Cold War" between the western states and the Communist states under the leadership of the Soviet-Union the UNSC was in essence paralysed with regard to decisions regarding the use of force. The notable exception was the Korean War, which arose from the invasion from communist North Korea into South Korea and the subsequent UNSC Resolution 83 of 27 June 1950 calling upon

---

[5] The UNSC has 15 members of which ten are elected by the General Assembly and another five are permanent members. The five permanent members, often referred to as the P5, are the Republic of China (now the People's Republic of China), France, the Union of Soviet Socialist Republics (USSR, now Russia), the United Kingdom of Great Britain and Northern Ireland, and the United States of America, Article 23 (1) UNC.

and authorizing UN member states "to furnish such assistance to the Republic of Korea as may be necessary to repel the armed attack [...]".[6] It was not until 1991 when the UNSC again authorized the use of force as a collective reaction to the invasion of Kuwait by Iraqi forces seeking to annex Kuwait as a province of Iraq.[7]

Authorizing the use of force, in other words authorizing war as a reaction to the breach of the peace by an aggressor is, of course, always a difficult proposition. It works best if the breach of the peace happened on a small(er) scale and involves only smaller military powers. It cannot work once a major power is directly militarily involved and determined to continue its aggressive military actions because the price of military counter-measures quickly becomes too steep both in economic and in human cost. That is not only but especially true if the P5 themselves are involved in military activities. It is hard to imagine a scenario where the Security Council would authorise the use of military force against the USA, China or Russia.

The fact that in many instances only non-military options are realistic options is, of course, not to be lamented at all. The upside is the preservation of peace and the avoidance of what could fast become a major conflict. The downside is that malicious resolve could be seen as prevailing thus undermining the authority of the international legal order. For example, the annexation of the Crimea by Russia at the expense of Ukraine is an unlawful *fait accompli* and for the time being it is hard to see how this could ever be reversed. But one has to be realistic: it is sometimes preferable to accept an unlawful state of

---

[6] UNSC-Resolution 83 of 27 June 1950, http://www.un.org/en/ga/search/view_doc.asp?symbol=S/RES/83(1950) (last accessed 31 December 2017). The resolution could only pass because the Soviet-Union boycotted the UNSC at the time, i.e. did not participate in any procedures or voting and the Chinese vote was at the time still exercised by the (Taiwanese) Republic of China and not (yet) by the People's Republic of China on the mainland. Coincidentally this fact was also the reason for the Soviet boycott in the first place. In the light of the wording of Article 27(3) one could think that a boycott would amount to a veto because it speaks of "concurring votes" of the P5 but that was not the view that prevailed.

[7] UNSC-Resolution 678 (1990) of 29 November 1990 (the vote was 12:2, with Yemen and Cuba against; China abstained).

reality than to try to change it at all cost. It is downright mandatory to accept an unlawful state if rectifying the situation would create more suffering than the unlawful state creates. A second problem lies in a possible appearance of inequality or discrimination between the more powerful and less powerful nations. An aggression by a small state might trigger an international military reaction through the Security Council whereas the same behaviour by a large power might not. That is, of course, the direct consequence of the fact that military countermeasures by the international community can deliver a positive outcome only in the context of smaller scale aggressions of similar behaviour found to threaten or breach international peace and security. From a legal perspective this "inequality" is of no consequence – there is no equality in illegality.

Finally, it should be noted that Article 2(4) is part of the United Nations Charter, which constitutes an international treaty. The prohibition of the use of force is thus a treaty obligation. Given that all states currently in existence are members of the United Nations one may conclude that the prohibition is universal treaty law. Despite this, the ICJ has repeatedly held that the prohibition is also and separately a norm of customary international law. The ICJ went even further and stated that the prohibition of the use of force is not only a "regular" norm of customary international law but that it is also regarded as having the status of a so-called *jus cogens* or peremptory norm of general international law, i.e. fundamental norms from which states cannot derogate by treaty:[8]

> 190. A further confirmation of the validity as customary international law of the principle of the prohibition of the use of force expressed in Article 2, paragraph 4, of the Charter of the United Nations may be found in the fact that it is frequently referred to in statements by State representatives as being not only a principle of customary international law but also a fundamental or cardinal principle of such law. The International Law Commission, in the course of its work on the codification of

---

[8] See Article 53 Vienna Convention on the Law of Treaties, https://treaties.un.org/ (last accessed on 4 January 2018).

the law of treaties, expressed the view that "the law of the Charter concerning the prohibition of the use of force in itself constitutes a conspicuous example of a rule in international law having the character of jus cogens" (paragraph (1) of the commentary of the Commission to Article 50 of its draft Articles on the Law of Treaties, ILC Yearbook, 1966-11, p. 247). Nicaragua in its Memorial on the Merits submitted in the present case States that the principle prohibiting the use of force embodied in Article 2, paragraph 4, of the Charter of the United Nations "has come to be recognized as jus cogens". The United States, in its Counter-Memorial on the questions of jurisdiction and admissibility, found it material to quote the views of scholars that this principle is a "universal norm", a "universal international law", a "universally recognized principle of international law", and a "principle of jus cogens".[9]

- **Exceptions to the Prohibition of the Use of Force**

The exceptions to the prohibition of the use of force are contained in Chapter VII (Articles 39-51) UNC. The UNC provides for only two exceptions from the prohibition of the use of force. The first exception is the possible collective response and authorisation of force by the Security Council ("collective security") and the second is the right to – individual or collective – self-defence as stipulated in Article 51 UNC at the end of Chapter VII UNC. The UNC aims to monopolize the use of force just as the newly developing nations states in a century long-struggle strove to monopolize the use of force in domestic societies.

These two exceptions, the collective security exception exercised by the Security Council and the right to (individually or collectively exercised) self-defence differ considerably. Yoram Dinstein has summarized the differences as follows:

> Collective security postulates the institutionalisation of the lawful use of force in the international community. What is required is a multilateral treaty, whereby Contracting Parties

---

[9] *Case Concerning Military and Paramilitary Activities in and Against Nicaragua (Nicaragua v. United States of America* (merits) [27 June 1986], ICJ 1986, 14 available at http://www.icj-cij.org/ (last accessed 17 May 2018), paras 188-9.

create an international agency vested with the power to employ force against aggressors (and perhaps other law-breakers). Such an instrument is basically "introverted" in character (designed against the potential future aggressor from among the Contracting Parties), unlike a collective self-defence treaty [...] which is "extroverted" (envisaging aggression from outside the system). Collective security shares with collective self-defence the fundamental premise that recourse to force against aggression can (and perhaps must) be made by those who are not the immediate and direct victims. But self-defence, either individual or collective, is exercised at the discretion of a single State or a group of States acting unilaterally. Collective security operates on the strength of an authoritative decision made by an organ of the international community.[10]

Collective self-defence, i.e. one or more states coming to the aid of an attacked state can be exercised ad hoc in reaction to the aggression, or it can be based on a collective security treaty where the member states enter legal obligations to assist each other when attacked. One such example with Australian participation is the so-called ANZUS-Treaty which stipulates in Article IV(1) that

Each Party recognizes that an armed attack in the Pacific Area on any of the Parties would be dangerous to its own peace and safety and declares that it would act to meet the common danger in accordance with its constitutional processes.[11]

Probably the most important such treaty so far, certainly the one which has been the most relevant since its creation is the North Atlantic Treaty Organization (NATO), which regards itself as a "crises management organization" that currently has 18,000 military personnel serving in missions around the globe.[12] Its core function is

---

10 Y Dinstein, *War, Aggression and Self-Defence* (4th ed. 2005) at 278.
11 Security Treaty between Australia, New Zealand and the United States of America (ANZUS), 1 September 1951, in force 29 April 1952, Australian Treaty Series 1952 No. 2, available at https://www.austlii.edu.au/au/other/dfat/treaties/1952/2.html (last accessed on 13 January 2018).
12 See https://www.nato.int/cps/en/natohq/topics_52060.htm (last accessed on 13 January 2018). The site also contains a list of the many missions NATO undertook since the end of the Cold War.

still that of a collective self-defence organization and Article 5(1) of the NATO-Treaty consequently states:

> The Parties agree that an armed attack against one or more of them in Europe or North America shall be considered an attack against them all and consequently they agree that, if such an armed attack occurs, each of them, in exercise of the right of individual or collective self-defence recognised by Article 51 of the Charter of the United Nations, will assist the Party or Parties so attacked by taking forthwith, individually and in concert with the other Parties, such action as it deems necessary, including the use of armed force, to restore and maintain the security of the North Atlantic area.[13]

Until today Article 5 was only invoked once on 12 September 2001 as a reaction to the terrorist attacks on the US in New York on 11 September 2001. Today, there are many collective security treaties effective around the globe.

The question of whether there are other legal justifications for using military force outside of (Chapter VII of) the UNC is one of the most controversial questions in international law. To say that such justification could exist firstly requires a determination of the scope of the UNC. If the UNC were regarded as the comprehensive and exhaustive legal instrument with regard to the use of force, if in other words the UNC were regarded as a self-contained regime allowing no recourse to other norms of (customary) international law, then the two exceptions stipulated in Chapter VII UNC would have to be regarded as the only possible legal justifications for using military force. If one does not regard the UNC as comprehensive and exhaustive with regard to the regulation and justification of the use of force, if in other words one does not regard the UNC as a self-contained regime, then other exceptions for the use of military force are least conceivable. However, being conceivable does not mean that such further exceptions to the use of force outside of the UNC actually exist. Any claim to such

---

[13] North Atlantic Treaty, 4 April 1949, in force 24 August 1949, 34 UNTS 243, text available at https://www.nato.int/cps/ic/natohq/official_texts_17120.htm (last accessed on 11 May 2018).

exceptions as being part - in the absence of treaties – of customary international law will have to demonstrate that there is settled state practice and the complementing *opinio juris* to support any further exception(s) as part of customary international law. The most contentious further justification discussed in this context is military humanitarian intervention to combat gross violations of human rights.

- **The Strikes against Syria by the USA, Great-Britain and France on 13 April 2018**

The immediate cause for the missile strikes by the three permanent members of the UN Security Council was the alleged and, though disputed, highly probable use of chemical agents as part of the campaign by Syrian government forces to recapture the town of Douma (Eastern Ghouta) just outside of Damascus. According to a statement by the World Health Organization (WHO) these attacks appeared to have affected several hundred people with 43 deaths "related to symptoms consistent with exposure to highly toxic chemicals".[14]

Everything to do with chemical weapons, from their development to their use, is comprehensively prohibited by the Chemical Weapons Convention (CWC) which was concluded in 1992 and came into force in 1997. It not only prohibits development, production and stockpiling of chemical weapons but also explicitly bans the use of such weapons (Article 1).[15]

The use of chemical weapons in the Syrian civil war is not new. Large-scale use of chemical weapons (in the same area as the April 13 attacks) was first determined in August 2013 and led to diplomatic

---

[14] "WHO concerned about suspected chemical attacks in Syria", Statement by the World Health Organization of 11 April 2018, http://www.who.int/mediacentre/news/statements/2018/chemical-attacks-syria/en/ (last accessed on 11 May 2018).

[15] Convention on the Prohibition of the Development, Production, Stockpiling and Use of Chemical Weapons and on their Destruction (CWC), http://disarmament.un.org/treaties/t/cwc/text (last accessed on 11 May 2018). The CWC was concluded in 1992, opened for signature in January 1993, entered into force on 29 April 1997 and currently has 192 member states including all five permanent members of the Security Council. India, Israel is a notable absence and has not ratified the treaty. The Syrian Arab Republic acceded in September 2013.

efforts to eliminate these weapons in Syria. The first major success in this regard resulted from a joint effort of the USA and Russia which culminated in the "Framework for Elimination of Syrian Chemical Weapons, dated 14 September 2013" prepared by the two nations.[16] The Syrian Arab Republic subsequently deposited with the United Nations Secretary-General its instruments of accession to the Chemical Weapons Convention. That, in turn, made it possible for the Executive Council of the OPCW on 27 September 2013 to issue a "Decision" regarding the "Destruction of Syrian Chemical Weapons"[17] setting out the pathway to the elimination of chemical weapons by the Syrian Arab Republic as envisaged in the US/Russia Framework. An OPCW-UN Joint Mission in Syria was formally established on 16 October 2013 to implement the elimination of these weapons.[18] This Joint Mission completed its task by the end of September 2014 and the view was that all chemical weapons had been destroyed.[19] However, this conclusion appears to have been overly optimistic and wrong.

Between March 2013 and March 2017, 25 incidents of chemical weapons use targeted primarily against civilians in the Syrian Arab Republic were documented, of which 20 were attributed to Syrian government forces.[20] Almost exactly one year before the April 2018 attacks in Douma, a very similar scenario had unfolded in April 2017.[21] On 4 April 2017, an airstrike by Syrian government forces

---

[16] Joint National Paper by the Russian Federation and the United States of America, Framework for Elimination of Syrian Chemical Weapons, communicated to the Members of the Executive Council of the OPCW for the 33rd Meeting 27 September 2013, EC-M-33/NAT.1, https://www.opcw.org/fileadmin/ (last accessed on 11 May 2018).
[17] OPCW, Executive Council, 33rd Meeting 27 September 2013, EC-M-33/DEC.1, https://www.opcw.org/fileadmin/OPCW/ (last accessed on 11 May 2018).
[18] See https://opcw.unmissions.org/ (last accessed on 11 May 2018).
[19] See https://opcw.unmissions.org/un-chief-commends-special-coordinator-and-her-team-successful-completion-opcw-un-joint-mission (last accessed on 11 May 2018).
[20] UN General Assembly, Human Rights Council, Thirty-Sixth Session, 11-29 September 2017, Report of the Independent International Commission of Inquiry on the Syrian Arab Republic, A/HRC/36/55, 8 August 2017, https://documents-dds-ny.un.org/doc/ (last accessed on 12 May 2018).
[21] Ibid. (fn. 20), Annex II - Inquiry into allegations of chemical weapons used in Khan Shaykhun, Idlib, on 4 April 2017, p. 21 et seq.

against the town of Khan Shaykun held by Al-Nusra forces led to massive civilian poisoning symptoms and casualties including at least 83 people killed.[22] President Trump responded to this transgression by launching a missile strike on Shayrat Airbase in Syria only three days later.[23]

- **The Response of the International Community to the Joint Military Action by the USA, France and Great-Britain**

Simplistically put one could summarize the response of the international community to the military strikes in traditional fashion: the "West" largely in favour, Russia and her allies and China against and other states more or less leaning one way or the other with what one might describe as an overarching objective to avoid being drawn into the debate. However, it is nonetheless helpful to have a closer look at some of these responses.[24]

The states involved in carrying out the attack used different approaches to justify their actions. The President of the French Republic issued the following statement:

> Dozens of men, women and children were massacred in Douma on Saturday, 7 April using chemical weapons, in total violation of international law and United Nations Security Council resolutions. There is no doubt as to the facts and to the responsibility of the Syrian regime. The red line declared by France in May 2017 has been crossed. Tonight, I have therefore ordered the French armed forces to intervene, as part of an international operation conducted in coalition with the United States of America and the United Kingdom against the clandestine chemical weapons arsenal of the Syrian regime. Our response has been limited to the Syrian regime's facilities enabling the production and employment of chemical weapons.

---

[22] Ibid. (fn. 20), Annex II - Inquiry into allegations of chemical weapons used in Khan Shaykhun, Idlib, on 4 April 2017, p. 21 et seq., para 11, 32 (casualties), para 30 et seq., 33-4 for attribution of attack to Syrian government forces.

[23] For more information see BBC coverage, for example, http://www.bbc.com/news/ (last accessed 12 May 2018).

[24] Obviously this can only be a cursory overview rather than a comprehensive analysis.

> We cannot tolerate the normalization of the employment of chemical weapons, which is an immediate danger to the Syrian people and to our collective security. That is the meaning of the initiatives constantly promoted by France at the United Nations Security Council. France and its partners will today continue their efforts at the United Nations to enable the creation of an international mechanism to establish responsibility, prevent impunity and obstruct any temptation on the part of the Syrian regime to repeat these acts.[25]

The statement is rather weak on legal justification. It mentions the limited scope of the attack, uses strong words to describe the atrocities and emphasises the extent of the violation of international law caused by the use of chemical weapons by using the attribute "total". It also mentions that a "red line" set by France has been crossed by the Syrian government. The unilateral setting of red lines is, of course, not a category of international law. Hence the only plausible meaning of this could be that France has reacted to the recurring use of chemical weapons, had announced that it would not tolerate further use and would, if it so chooses, use force to make that point. It is as if to say that the use of chemical weapons is so much outside the scope of acceptable behaviour that, with proper warning, states can even use force in a measured way.

The British representative in the Security Council emphasized:

> Our action was a limited, targeted and effective strike. There were clear boundaries that expressly sought to avoid escalation, and we did everything possible, including rigorous planning, before any action was undertaken to ensure that we mitigated and minimized the impact on civilians. Together, our action will significantly degrade the Syrian regime's ability to research, develop and deploy chemical weapons and deter their future use.[26]

---

[25] Press statement by the President of the French Republic on the intervention of the French armed forces in response to the use of chemical weapons in Syria, 14 April 2018, http://www.elysee.fr/communiques-de-presse/article/ (last accessed on 10 May 2018)..

[26] Security Council, Seventy-third year, 8233rd meeting, 14 April 2018, S/PV.8233, https://documents-dds-ny.un.org/doc/(last accessed on 12 May 2018), p. 6.

The emphasis is on the chemical weapons, on reducing the potential for repeated uses of such weapons in the future, and on the proportionality of the attacks to avoid collateral damage. What follows is even more interesting as only the United Kingdom referred to humanitarian intervention as the principal justification for the use of force in this instance:

> The Syrian regime has been killing its own people for seven years. Its use of chemical weapons, which has exacerbated the human suffering, is a serious crime of international concern as a breach of the customary international law prohibition on the use of chemical weapons, and that amounts to a war crime and a crime against humanity. Any State is permitted under international law, on an exceptional basis, to take measures in order to alleviate overwhelming humanitarian suffering. The legal basis for the use of force for the United Kingdom is humanitarian intervention, which requires that three conditions to be met."
>
> First, there must be convincing evidence, generally accepted by the international community as a whole, of extreme humanitarian distress on a large scale, requiring immediate and urgent relief. I think that the debates in the Council and the briefings we have had from the Office for the Coordination of Humanitarian Affairs and others have proved that. Secondly, it must be objectively clear that there is no practicable alternative to the use of force if lives are to be saved. I think that the vetoes have shown us that. Thirdly, the proposed use of force must be necessary and proportionate to the aim of relief of humanitarian suffering. It must be strictly limited in time and in scope to this aim. I think we have heard both in my intervention in Ambassador Haley's how that has also been met.[27]

This line of argument is interesting because it potentially broadens the scope of what is usually considered humanitarian intervention. The chemical attacks have been happening many times since 2013. The missile strikes could at best have achieved a reduction of the stockpile of available chemical weapons and could possibly deter

---

[27] Ibid. at p. 6-7.

their future use. However, that is all speculation and in essence points to the notion of a kind of preventive humanitarian intervention, in contrast to, for example, removing a terror regime such as the Pol Pot regime in Cambodia or creating a security zone and thus immediately stopping or mitigating ongoing gross violations of human rights. And indeed, the intervention could not and did not claim to do anything to halt the ongoing civil war and the toll on civilians who are suffering incredibly and in many cases no less even in the absence of the use of these specifically and particularly abhorrent weapons. The question therefore arises whether chemical weapons are regarded as so atrocious that they warrant a forceful response even if traditional legality thresholds, i.e. the assent of the Security Council, cannot be overcome?

Ambassador Haley of the USA also used some noteworthy language:

> We are here today because three permanent members of the Security Council acted. The United Kingdom, France, and the United States acted not in revenge, not in punishment and not in a symbolic show of force. We acted to deter the future use of chemical weapons by holding the Syrian regime responsible for its crimes against humanity.[28]

One would have to conclude from this statement that, firstly, the use of force to deter the future use of chemical weapons can be a justification for using military force. One would have to conclude secondly that using force as a countermeasure to the use of chemical weapons could be regarded as holding a regime responsible for the crime against humanity which the use of chemical weapons constitutes, at least if these weapons were used in a similar context as in Syria, i.e. with a history of condemnation by the international community, with various SC resolutions addressing the situation and even with concrete steps that should actually have taken away any and all chemical weapons and left none to use.

In addition and very much in line with the UK's response, the US emphasized the proportionality of the response and the fact that the

---

[28] Ibid. at p. 5.

Security Council cannot fulfil its task because of Russia's blockade politics:

> Our action was a limited, targeted and effective strike. There were clear boundaries that expressly sought to avoid escalation, and we did everything possible, including rigorous planning, before any action was undertaken to ensure that we mitigated and minimized the impact on civilians. Together, our action will significantly degrade the Syrian regime's ability to research, develop and deploy chemical weapons and deter their future use.[29]

India, through an Official Spokesperson of the Ministry of External Affairs, communicated a rather indifferent note:

> We have taken note of the recent strikes in Syria. India is closely following the situation. The alleged use of chemical weapons, if true, is deplorable. We call for an impartial and objective investigation by the OPCW to establish the facts. In the meantime, we urge all Parties to show restraint and to avoid any further escalation in the situation. The matter should be resolved through dialogue and negotiations, and on the basis of the principles of the UN Charter and in accordance with international law. We hope that the long drawn suffering of the people of Syria would come to an end soon.[30]

In essence India appears to try to avoid any clear positioning. The use of chemical weapons is referred to as "deplorable" but the actual use of chemical weapons in this case is cast in factual doubt. The explanation that such conflicts should be resolved "on the basis of the principles of the UN Charter and in accordance with international law" could be interpreted as an indirect hint that the missile strikes did not live up to this test. This is certainly more a statement of "neutral caution" than a strong condemnation of the actions taken.

The Prime Minister of Japan issued the following statement:

---

[29] Ibid. at p. 6.

[30] Indian Official Spokesperson's response to queries regarding the recent strikes in Syria, 14 April 2014, http://www.mea.gov.in/media-briefings (last accessed on 10 May 2018).

> The use of chemical weapons is extremely inhumane and Japan cannot tolerate it. The Government of Japan supports the determination of the United States, the United Kingdom, and France to never allow the proliferation and use of chemical weapons. On this basis, we understand that the countries took the action in order to avoid further aggravation of the situation. In East Asia as well, weapons of mass destruction such as nuclear, biological, and chemical weapons pose an increasingly serious threat. Under the robust Japan-U.S. Alliance, Japan will continue to fulfill its role for the maintenance of peace and stability in the region while collaborating and cooperating with the international community.[31]

The choice of words is noteworthy. Japan does not state support for the strikes Japan merely "understands" why this action was taken. However, the use of chemical weapons is decried in the strongest terms as "extremely inhumane" and impossible to tolerate.

The statement issued by the President of the European Commission, Jean-Claude Juncker almost avoids any comment on the strikes as such and concentrates on the repeated chemical attacks of the Syrian regime and the needs for accountability for such wrong doing:

> Last night, France, the United Kingdom and the United States responded in a coordinated military action to the heinous chemical weapons attack carried out by the Syrian regime against civilians in Douma on 7 April. As the European Commission has stated, the use of chemical weapons is unacceptable in any circumstances and must be condemned in the strongest terms. The international community has the responsibility to identify and hold accountable those responsible of any attack with chemical weapons. This was not the first time that the Syrian regime has used chemical weapons against civilians but it must be the last. As it enters its 8th year of conflict, Syria desperately needs a lasting ceasefire respected by all parties that paves the way for achieving a negotiated political solution through the United Nations-led Geneva process, to bring peace to the

---

[31] The Prime Minister of Japan and His Cabinet, The Prime Minister in Action, Press Occasion on the Attack on Syria by the United States, the United Kingdom, and France (2), 14 April 2018, https://japan.kantei.go.jp/ (last accessed on 10 May 2018).

country once and for all. After the suffering they have endured, Syrians deserve nothing less.[32]

The new German Foreign Minister Heiko Maas, by contrast, issued a very strong statement:

> War has been raging in Syria for seven years. Time and again, we have seen that the Assad regime has committed war crimes and also used chemical weapons against civilians, as all available information indicates was recently the case in Douma, too. Chemical weapons are banned internationally. Their use is a war crime that must lead to consequences in order to ensure that these terrible events are not repeated. The United Nations Security Council has already been blocked for months on Syria, including on the issue of the use of chemical weapons, by Russia's actions. In the current case, too, the Security Council was unable to fulfil its role. In this situation, the limited attack on Syrian regime military structures by France, the United Kingdom and the United States as permanent members of the Security Council sent an appropriate and necessary message, which will help to make it more difficult for suffering of this kind to be caused again in the future.[33]

The German Foreign Minister emphasises the blockade by the Security Council by Russia and in that respect follows the line of argument employed by the USA. It should be noted that this line of argument overlooks China, which also consistently supports the traditional view on the use of force which would require a Security Council authorization. But the German Foreign Minister goes one step further and, in the light of the Security Council's inability to act, refers to the strikes not only as appropriate but necessary. Chancellor Merkel in her own response underlined this and said:

---

[32] Statement by President Jean-Claude Juncker on the situation in Syria, 14 April 2018, http://europa.eu/rapid/press-release_STATEMENT-18-3346_en.htm (last accessed on 10 May 2018).

[33] Statement by German Foreign Minister Heiko Maas on the airstrikes in Syria, Press Release of 14 April 2018, https://www.auswaertiges-amt.de/ (last accessed on 10 May 2018).

> We support our American, British and French allies having taken responsibility as permanent members of the Security Council in this fashion. The military action was appropriate and necessary to maintain the effectiveness of the ban of chemical weapons and to warn the Syrian regime to abstain from further violations.[34]

This can only be interpreted as stipulating two avenues of justification for the strikes. One, to deter the Syrian regime from repeating the use of chemical weapons and, two, to more generally defend the prohibition of chemical weapons.

Finally, the leaders of the G7 nations jointly issued a separate statement:

> We, the G7 Leaders of Canada, France, Germany, Italy, Japan, the United Kingdom, the United States of America and the European Union, are united in condemning, in the strongest possible terms, the use of chemical weapons in the April 7 attack in Eastern Ghouta, Syria. We fully support all efforts made by the United States, the United Kingdom and France to degrade the Assad regime's ability to use chemical weapons and to deter any future use, demonstrated by their action taken on April 13. This response was limited, proportionate and necessary – and taken only after exhausting every possible diplomatic option to uphold the international norm against the use of chemical weapons. Use of chemical weapons is a breach of the Chemical Weapons Convention and constitutes a threat to international peace and security. The repeated and morally reprehensible use of chemical weapons by the Assad regime in the past has been confirmed by independent international investigators. We condemn this deliberate strategy of terrorizing local populations and forcing them into submission. Syria's possession of chemical weapons and their means of delivery are illegal under UN Security Council Resolution 2118 and the Chemical Weapons Convention. We stand together against impunity for those who

---

[34] German Chancellor Angela Merkel's official statement regarding the military strikes conducted by the USA, Great-Britain and France in Syria, Press release 112, 14 April 2018, https://www.bundesregierung.de/Content/DE/ [translation by the author] (last accessed on 10 May 2018).

develop or use these weapons, anywhere, anytime, under any circumstances.[35]

Again, the line of argument to justify the actions taken pivot around the egregious use of chemical weapons, the need to degrade the arsenal and deter future use of these weapons and the limited and proportionate and carefully planned nature of the force used.

If one attempts to contextualise these various statements in a plausible way one cannot avoid the conclusion that all actors are aware of the problematic nature of unilateral, i.e. non Security Council mandated, military action. If one accepts this premise then there are only two logical conclusions. Either the acting states and the states voicing support for the missile strikes do not care about international law at all and prefer to act solely out of political expediency and perhaps only because they can. However, there is little evidence for this conclusion. It is hard to see much evidence for such a motivation. Or, secondly, one would have to conclude that these states, and even those states urging caution and pointing to the UN Charter, are driven by the believe that the use of chemical weapons is particularly egregious and sufficiently distinct from other causes of intense suffering that the traditional rules addressing the use of force do not apply and therefore "unilateral" actions are possible under certain circumstances, e.g. as explained by the British delegate in the Security Council.

This line of argument is not altogether different from the lines of argument employed in the longstanding debate on humanitarian intervention but the subject matter is restricted to a particular kind of violation – the use of chemical weapons. The difference lies in the fact that there is no conceivable reason to use these weapons whatever the circumstances. There is therefore no avenue to defend their use. That would explain the apparent significance placed, for example by Russia, on the factual side, i.e. on whether such weapons had indeed been used by the Syrian regime. From the perspective of the traditional

---

[35] G7 Leaders' Statement on Syria, published separately by the states forming this group but explicitly including the European Union, 17 April 2018, http://www.consilium.europa.eu/en/press/press-releases/2018/04/17/ (last accessed 10 May 2018).

and restrictive use of force rules it does not matter who is responsible for the use of chemical weapons as the military response to it is illegal anyway. That would explain why there is little debate on the extent of the damage caused by the use of these weapons, which, as deplorable as the use of these weapons is, pales in comparison to the harm, suffering and casualties caused in this conflict by conventional weapons.

In other words, limiting the scope of a potential third exception to the prohibition of the use of force to incidents involving the use of chemical weapons circumvents questions discussed in the context of general humanitarian intervention e.g. what extent of human rights violations are sufficiently "gross" to justify intervention with force. The number of casualties caused by the crime becomes – notwithstanding the still applicable principle of proportionality - irrelevant in the determination of possible military counteractions, The use of chemical weapons alone and per se could render an additional justification for using force with the only possible defence being a denial of the crime or responsibility for it.

- **Russia's Draft Security Council Resolution**

Russia reacted to the strikes with strong opposition and a draft resolution that was put to the Security Council for voting:

> The Security Council,
>
> Appalled by the aggression against the Syrian Arab Republic by the US and its allies in violation of international law and the UN Charter,
>
> Expressing grave concern that the aggression against the sovereign territory of the Syrian Arab Republic took place at the moment when the Organization for the Prohibition of Chemical Weapons Fact-Finding Mission team has just begun its work to collect evidence of the alleged use of chemical weapons in Douma and urging to provide all necessary conditions for the completion of this investigation,
>
> 1. Condemns the aggression against the Syrian Arab Republic by the US and its allies in violation of international law and the UN Charter,

> 2. Demands that the US and its allies immediately and without delay cease the aggression against the Syrian Arab Republic and demands also to refrain from any further use of force in violation of international law and the UN Charter,
>
> 3. Decides to remain further seized on this matter.[36]

From a strictly legal perspective this resolution reflects the "traditional" and restrictive state of the law regarding the use of force. There was no "armed attack" in the sense of Article 51 UNC and there was no mandate by the Security Council to use force in this situation. Hence, from the basis of this "traditional" view, i.e. a view that either regards the United Nations Charter as a self-contained regime which comprehensively addresses all matters related to the use of force or, even if not self-contained, denies that there is any evidence of settled state practice in customary international law that would point to a further exception from the prohibition of the use of force, the strikes undertaken by France, the UK and the USA were indeed illegal.

Whether that justifies using the term aggression is yet another question. What constitutes an aggression has now been defined in the context of the International Criminal Court (ICC) in the 2010 amendment of the Statute of Rome and the newly added Article 8*bis*.[37] According to Article 8*bis* the strikes on Syria would constitute an aggression only if they could be regarded as a "manifest" violation of the United Nations Charter. In other words the crime of aggression distinguishes between regular breaches of the Charter and those that are manifest. The reason for this distinction reflects the ongoing discussion on whether there must not be some space for a third category of the use of force, i.e. one that does not fit into the "traditional" and restrictively understood UNC system but that one does not constitute aggression either.

What is striking in this case is that the Russian draft resolution

---

[36] Russian Federation Draft Resolution, Security Council, S/2018/355, 14 April 2018, https://documents-dds-ny.un.org/doc/ (last accessed on 11 May 2018).

[37] See https://www.icc-cpi.int/NR/rdonlyres/ (last accessed on 9 May 2018).

was voted down in the Security Council and how it was voted down[38]:

> In favour: Bolivia (Plurinational State of), China, Russian Federation
>
> Against: Côte d'Ivoire, France, Kuwait, Netherlands, Poland, Sweden, United Kingdom of Great Britain and Northern Ireland, United States of America
>
> Abstaining: Equatorial Guinea, Ethiopia, Kazakhstan, Peru.

The Russian draft found only 2 supporters, China and Bolivia. Eight members of the Security Council voted against and a further four members abstained. One must be careful not to over-interpret this voting pattern. It is not far-fetched to say that the no-vote consisted largely of states that are politically closer to the western permanent members of the Security Council. But that said this certainly does not lend itself as support for the notion that the strikes against Syria constituted a "manifest" violation of the Charter. Together with some of the responses by individual states shown above this voting pattern could be construed as evidence for a degree of support among a significant part of the community of states for a third category of uses of force perhaps (not yet) justifiable under the UNC-system but regarded as a tolerable reaction to behaviour commonly – and with no visible exception – regarded as utterly egregious and absolutely indefensible.

- **Conclusion**

This study does not pertain to be comprehensive, not even with regard to the incident at issue here. But it does shed light on legally relevant behaviour of various states that requires explanation. Of course, one could cynically claim that the missile strikes are evidence for the demise of international law and the primacy of international power politics. States do what they do because they can. They regard their actions as reflecting their political interest at the time and they do not

---

[38] Security Council, Seventy-third year, 8233rd meeting, 14 April 2018, S/PV.8233, https://documents-dds-ny.un.org/doc/ (last accessed on 11 May 2018), p. 22-3.

care about any legal framework that restricts them. But that approach to state action is too superficial. There is genuine concern precisely out of fear that the international law framework might suffer fatal blows in core areas. There is a concern that even the use of chemical weapons could become just another transgression, just another "parking offense" in the realm of international law. There is the concern that the moral imperative and the legal framework drift apart. And there is the fact that the development of international law includes its breach as one inherent instrument. That goes for the development of customary international law but to some degree it also goes for the development of treaty law through authentic treaty interpretation by the states as masters of the treaties they conclude. International law moves like a glacier, slowly but surely. One cannot know what the outcome will be. Perhaps the "traditional" restrictive regime around the use of force will prevail. But it is conceivable that the notion of a third category of justified uses of force will gain further traction. If that were the case the use of chemical weapons could be the nucleus because it is a much narrower and thus better definable category of egregious behaviour than what might generally qualify as "gross" violations of human rights.

10

BREXIT, ART LOANS AND FRUSTRATION

Geoffrey Bennett[1]

- **Introduction: The EU Background of Support for Art Loans**

It may not be as widely appreciated as it should be that loans of art within the European Union (the EU) are not simply a fortuitous product of the fact that the EU has led to closer relationships, both economic and political, between its member states. It could be said that they are integral to the cultural policy of the EU. Article 167 of the Lisbon Treaty states that: 'The Union shall contribute to the flowering of the cultures of the Member States, while respecting their national and regional diversity...' and that action shall be aimed at supporting, 'non-commercial cultural exchanges'. A commitment to the mobility of art within Europe is therefore expressly articulated as an important EU objective. The uncertainties inherent in Brexit, and the enormous range of contingencies and difficulties likely to be encountered in the next few years, and probably well beyond, make it difficult to predict with any accuracy what the eventual impact will be of Brexit on art loans, and much else besides. What follows, therefore, is necessarily tentative. Perhaps the best that can be done at this stage

---

[1] This is a revised version of an article originally published in (2017) XXII *Art Antiquity and Law* 118. I am grateful for the helpful observations made by those attending an event to mark the launch of the Art, Business and Law LL.M. hosted by Clyde & Co, London, in January 2017, and also those participating in the British Institute of International and Comparative Law HEURIGHT Workshop on The Human Right to Access and enjoy Cultural Heritage held in May 2018. The authoritative text on art loans is, Norman Palmer, *Art Loans*, (Kluwer 1997). It is anticipated that a second edition will be published in 2018. Although an art loan may well be a bailment of goods I have assumed throughout that art loans are likely to be governed predominantly by contractual considerations.

is to consider what issues might arise although, even so, any list is likely to be incomplete as well as leading to anxiety about problems which ultimately may not arise as acutely as is currently feared in some quarters.[2]

Obviously the general law of the EU has as one of its core principles the free movement of goods and people. In addition there have over the years been a number of targeted initiatives which relate more specifically to matters that could have an impact on art loans. For example, in 2006 the Action Plan for the EU Promotion of Museum Collections Mobility and Loan Standards sought to promote loan administration, develop trust and co-operation between institutions and lower costs. This has led to the development through the Network of Museum Organisations (NEMO) of a standard loan agreement accessible via an online toolkit.[3] This resource deserves to be better known amongst those dealing with the administration of loans between museums and galleries. Although not sufficiently comprehensive for a large, complex or commercially significant arrangement it is clearly written with ample scope for including alternative wording to fit individual needs. At the very least it provides a useful checklist of the essential issues that need to be clarified in advance of any loan. For example, a choice of law clause may be particularly important in a loan between entities in different EU jurisdictions. An arbitration clause may reduce further the risk of formal litigation. A final clause suggested is that, 'Should individual terms of this contract become invalid or inapplicable... the remainder of this contract remains untouched'. Although rather colloquially expressed, and perhaps none the worse for that, such a clause reduces the uncertainty consequent upon the discovery that a discrete clause within the contract is inappropriate, or even nonsensical, with the potential, without such a clause, to taint and invalidate [4] the rest of the agreement. Given

---

[2] I am particularly grateful to Jane Knowles, Head of Exhibitions the National Gallery, London, for alerting me to many of the practical considerations.

[3] Located at: http://www.ne-mo.org/fileadmin/Dateien/public/NEMO_Standard_Loan_Agreement/NEMO_Standard_Loan_Agreement.pdf

[4] Of course in English law the same result might be reached a s a matter of the construction of the contact, see *Nicolene Ltd v Simmons* [1953] 1 Q.B. 543, but there is

that many agreements between institutions can be very informal and arrived at under time pressures it is useful to have an aide memoire which covers the essential points in a standard loan. It all amounts to a recognition by the EU of the need to put in place practical initiatives and support to advance what would otherwise sound like the rather aspirational rhetoric of Article 167.

Whilst the focus of this article is to deal with legal issues consequent upon Brexit it would seem unrealistic in assessing its impact not at least to make some mention of the economic support which is derived from EU membership which in the future may not be available either on the same scale as in the past, or at all.[5] The extent of the EU's support as a major source of funds for cultural activities, which includes museums and galleries, is highlighted in a recent House of Lords Library briefing.[6] Creative Europe, established by the EU in 2014, is the European Commission's vehicle to support the EU cultural and audio-visual sectors. It has a €1.46 billion budget for the period 2014-20. The United Kingdom received €40 million from the period 2014-15. Of this money 31% is earmarked for cultural activities. The Regulation which brings all of this into effect states that it is: 'to promote the transnational circulation of cultural and creative works... to improve access to cultural works in the Union and beyond'.[7] Of importance in the future will be the meaning attached to "and beyond" since after 2019 this term will embrace the UK.[8] It is currently completely unclear how the UK will fare within this category but, at the very least, it will not have access to the same priority and level of resources available to an EU member. As mentioned, these are all

---

much to be said for expressly anticipating a problem rather than hoping a court will subsequently find its way to a sensible conclusion.

[5] On this point, see further Kristin Hausler and Richard Mackenzie-Gray Scott, 'Outside the Debate: The Potential Impact of Brexit for Cultural Heritage in the UK' (2017) XXII *Art Antiquity and Law* 101.

[6] http://researchbriefings.parliament.uk/ResearchBriefing/Summary/LLN-2017-0003

[7] Regulation (EU) No 1295/2013 of the European Parliament and of the Council of 11 December 2013.

[8] Countries within that category are: Iceland, Norway, Albania, Bosnia and Herzegovina, Macedonia, Montenegro, Serbia, Georgia, Moldova and Ukraine.

economic considerations, albeit implemented by European legislation, but likely to be of significant impact. At the very least, it seems likely the loss in financial support from the EU may adversely affect the climate in which many international partnerships in the arts operate, and that will include loans of art. A striking recent example[9] is the grant in 2016 of more than £10 million of investment from the EU Regional Development Fund to National Museums Liverpool. This in turn apparently unlocked a further £70 million in additional funding. The reassurance of EU funding may therefore have what one might call a 'multiplier' effect which means that looking merely at the direct amount of the EU contribution may seriously underestimate the actual impact of such funding. The absence of such a level of funding in the future, and the catalyst that it provides, especially when combined with the current difficulty and uncertainty relating to corporate involvement in sponsoring events and projects, is surely likely to have a significant negative impact. Of course an objection could be made that money made available from the UK's contribution to the EU budget could fund the shortfall. The difficulty with this argument is that there appears to be no evidence that the arts will become a pressing government priority area for expenditure amongst the competing claims to public funds in an immediately post-Brexit UK.

- **More Specific Legal Issues Affecting Loans**

In considering the largely legal issues affecting museums and galleries arising out of Brexit a useful starting point is the EU Exit Impact Statement prepared by the UK Registrars Group which comprehensively seeks to identify major sources of concern.[10] For example, what will happen to long-term contracts already in place and concluded before Brexit was instigated? There could be changes to export and import legislation which mean that loans are imported back into the UK under a different import system to that which governed their export. How long will the law be in a state of

---

[9] See the Museums Association website www.museumsassociation.org.uk
[10] 'EU Exit: Impact Statement', *UK Registrars Group*, October 15, 2016, at http://www.ne-mo.org/fileadmin/Dateien/

limbo? How will this affect long term planning particularly of loans which involve a significant commercial element?[11] Will lending and borrowing costs increase? If so, will that make the UK less attractive as an exhibition partner, whether to borrowers or to lenders? If export/import requirements become more onerous, as seems probable, are there likely to be road transport delays, for example, to those using the Eurotunnel route? Will that make airfreight shipments more attractive or necessary so inevitably increasing costs and environmental impact? How will it affect guarantees? What will be the impact on V.A.T.? How will export licensing be affected?[12] What will be the impact on the staff needed to operate loans? For example, what regulations will govern those who accompany cultural goods in transit or oversee their installation or removal? What regime will govern truck drivers who deliver loans from other EU countries? Will they now require visas and, if so, how onerous will be the processing of such paperwork? What is the future of the European Health Insurance Card (EHIC) which gives reciprocal health benefits to EU nationals? If the UK ceased to be a participant will there inevitably be increased health insurance costs? A major concern underlying all of these questions is that costs may increase as a consequence of Brexit at the very time that funding for museums and galleries is under pressure.

It is perhaps unduly pessimistic to think that all of these concerns will lead to serious problems. The difficulty, however, is that, at present, it is completely unclear what the final answer to any of these questions will be. For example, as regards professionals entering the UK to carry out limited professional duties, there already exists

---

[11] Although not mentioned in the Statement, and in the absence of hard evidence it is speculative, is there already a degree of 'planning blight' affecting museums and galleries? The author is aware of anecdotal evidence that, for example, smaller museums with restricted budgets and less ability to absorb disruption to cross-border operations are sensitive to this issue.

[12] A concise account of the complex issue of the UK's export controls, as they currently stand, and how they relate to EU law and international conventions, is to be found in, Handbook on the Law of Cultural Heritage and International Trade, EE Publishing 2014, pp. 460-505 by Kevin Chamberlain and Kristin Hausler.

the immigration category of 'Standard Visitor visa'.[13] This applies to a non-EU national such as, for example, an American university professor accompanying students on a short course in the UK. This does not necessarily require an application for a visa in advance from a British consulate. On the other hand it does require some foresight from the receiving UK institution, a need for some resident expertise in immigration matters and the inevitable risk that something will go wrong, if only because of human error in administering a more cumbersome set of procedures, when previously there was no difficulty at all.

- **Legal Disaster**

Assuming there is a contract in place and a problem arises, a paradigm case would be a situation where something goes seriously wrong between the formation of the contract and the dispatch of the loan, what would be the legal outcome? What would be a disaster that could lead to a state of limbo? Obviously if the parties have provided for the eventuality in their contract then, all things being equal, the contract will determine the outcome. It might be said that the general law of contract only comes into play when the parties have not made their own provision to cover an eventuality. What amounts to a disaster in legal terms is only limited by the scope of one's imagination but it is easy to see that it could become an issue in a post-Brexit world.

The classic case which still underlies the modern law, is *Taylor v Caldwell*.[14] This concerned the hire of a music hall which was destroyed by fire after the contract was concluded but before the first

---

[13] This new enlarged category replaces the previous category of "Business Visitor', see https://www.gov.uk/standard-visitor-visa/overview. The complexity of the current immigration legislation, and the frequency with which the details change, regardless of Brexit, is not to be underrated.

[14] (1863) 32 L.J. Q.B. 164. The doctrine of Frustration is well known to lawyers and no attempt is made here to give a general account of the law. A concise summary can be found in, J. C. Smith, *The Law of Contract*, Oxford University Press, 2016. The principles are remarkably stable perhaps because the threshold to trigger the doctrine is high and case law is thereby limited.

concert was due to be performed. The hirer sued on the basis that he had contacted for a benefit which he had not received, and lost. The court held that the unforeseen destruction of the subject matter, without fault, meant that both parties were excused from further performance under the contract.[15] If therefore some event renders the contract impossible or illegal then the parties may be able to invoke the doctrine of frustration.

What would be realistic examples in the case of museums and galleries? An example might be the destruction of the museum by fire before the object of the loan had been delivered, or indeed the theft or destruction of the object itself. Another topical example might be loss or damage caused to objects or institutions through earthquakes of the kind that have recently affected sites in central Italy. Finding cases where the doctrine of frustration has arisen in the world of art is not easy but a report which raises interesting and difficult issues about its application is suggested by an incident involving damage to a painting by Pablo Picasso, *Le Reve*.[16] The painting was bought by a Las Vegas casino magnate for $48.4 million in 1997. He subsequently entered into a contact to sell it to a hedge fund mogul for $139 million. Before the painting was delivered the seller, whilst gesturing to friends explaining the painting's history, tore a coin-sized hole in the painting with his elbow. This apparently wiped $54 million off the value of the painting. Although professionally repaired the damage was apparently still visible under certain conditions. Had the contract been frustrated?[17] Could the buyer or indeed the seller have enforced the contact of sale, albeit at a reduced price? In the event the parties mutually agreed to rescind the contract so the case never reached a court for determination. If it had it is far from clear what the result

---

[15] The remedies have been refined by subsequent case law and most notably the Law Reform (Frustrated Contracts) Act 1943 which seeks to ensure that loss and benefit are shared fairly between the parties.

[16] Discussed in Davis & Ludlam, 'Wynn or Lose? A Frustrating Case' (2007) XII *Art Antiquity and Law*, 171.

[17] Assuming the application of English law. The general principles of American contract law are comparable.

would have been. Could it have been regarded as so-called self-induced frustration and so not frustration at all? The problem is that it is arguable that not every careless act by a party necessarily rises to that level. Had the painting 'perished' so as to trigger frustration?[18] Again, it is not entirely clear how a court would have construed this concept. The upshot of this and other caselaw is that in order to animate the doctrine of frustration the frustrating event has to be calamitous not merely costly, inconvenient or unfortunate.[19] In a transaction involving art, as with anything else, this puts a premium on trying to anticipate and allow for the unforeseen in a contract so as to reduce the risks consequent upon being thrown back on a rather restrictive doctrine. Allowing for the contingency in the contract obviously produces a more predictable and easily managed outcome agreed in advance by the parties.

The difficulties in establishing frustration is one reason for having a *force majeure* clause in a contract. This often covers similar ground to what might come under frustration but can be something that spreads the net of mishap rather wider and may cover incidents which would not have risen to the level of a frustrating event. In other words, it can embrace a serious problem which might be encountered and then provide an agreed contractual remedy. Strikes, delays and lockouts are standard candidates in commercial contracts.

How might any of this be sensibly applied to the sorts of problems that arise in the art world? An example drawn to my attention is an agreement between a major national gallery for the loan of a painting which contained a strict condition that only a curator from the lending museum would be allowed to handle the painting. At the end of the

---

18 The term used in s. 7 of the Sale of Goods Act 1979.
19 A case which could be said to be concerned with cultural property and illustrates the restrictive scope of the doctrine is *Amalgamated Investment and Property Co Ltd v John Walker & Sons Ltd* [1977] 1 W.L.R. 164. Here developers agreed to pay £1.7 million for an old whiskey warehouse. A couple of days afterwards the building was listed which effectively killed any development potential and slashing the value of the property to £210,000. The court held that mere economic hardship did not frustrate the contract.

exhibition the major eruption of an Icelandic volcano in 2010 blocked air travel preventing the curator from flying. What might have happened if this event had occurred at the beginning of the loan and time was sensitive, as it might be because of other exhibition commitments? Would this constitute frustration? Perhaps so, although in fact the parties sensibly agreed in the actual case to vary the contractual term and allow the gallery's own staff to package the picture.

Of course it may be simplistic to think of an exhibition being frustrated by the loss or unavailability of one item. A modern exhibition might well draw on thirty or forty different institutions or individuals so that the loss of one item will not necessarily jeopardise the whole enterprise. It should also be remembered that there is no such thing as partial frustration. It is an all or nothing decision. This lack of flexibility again underlines the advantages of the parties to a transaction making their own provision for what is to happen in the event of disaster or mishap.

- **The Impact of Brexit**

How is all of this relevant to Brexit? As individual examples they are clearly unrelated but the underlying principles could easily become relevant. An obvious possibility is that a contract becomes illegal after it has been concluded. Typical examples from earlier caselaw involve, for example a contract to do something perfectly legal, such as build a reservoir, which as a result of wartime regulations becomes unlawful , prohibited and therefore frustrated. Can one imagine a realistic scenario of this kind involving an art loan? It is not impossible but one wonders how likely it is. One aspect of Brexit is that it is not expected to result in the UK actually leaving the EU until 2019. Contracts to be performed in the immediate future seem unlikely to be affected. It would be possible, but surprising, if legislation was passed which renders a loan agreement quite unforeseeably illegal. It is not like a sudden outbreak of war, which is what lies behind many frustration cases; it is more likely that it will simply render the agreement more burdensome or expensive to perform. That is a good reason for making allowance for such a contingency. That could include, in the last resort, an understanding that the arrangement will be cancelled.

Of course it is in the current climate uncertain but it is hard to believe that Brexit will place museums and galleries in any worse legal position that they currently encounter when dealing with another non-EU country, such as the United States. There is a long history of loan agreements with that country albeit that the legal framework in which such agreements operate have a long and relatively settled history. On the other hand, it has to be conceded that the United States is distinctive in having a sophisticated history of developing art law and, not a negligible factor, it is more common for American museums and galleries to employ professional in-house lawyers so better equipping such institutions to deal with shifting legal requirements.

- **What Can or Should be Done to Manage the Legal Difficulties Posed by Brexit in Advance?**

Is this an unwelcome bid by lawyers to make more technical and legalistic than it needs to be something that gets along without elaborate legal input? Of course one answer to this question is that the problems posed by the UK leaving the EU present a new order of uncertainty which needs to be addressed. The more fundamental underlying objection was something Professor Norman Palmer was well aware of.[20] He draws attention to the fact that loan agreements between museums are never litigated and there appears to be no example of such a case in the UK. One comment on lawyers noted,[21] 'They have a role to play but the tail must not wag the dog'. Professor Palmer observed,[22] "No observer, schooled in the adversarial rights of the common law, can fail to be impressed by the village atmosphere in which art loans are conducted, by the sense of common purpose and the prevalence of trust and goodwill". One museum official is quoted as

---

[20] See 'Art Loans as Legal Animals', (1996) I *Art Antiquity and Law* 251.
[21] Ibid at 252.
[22] Ibid at 252

saying,[23] '[A] great number of loans take place between Art Galleries and Museums worldwide ... [T]hese institutions are, however diverse their geographical situations, all very like each other. The staff in them have common professional goals, and speak a common professional language. Over and above the rules laid down on pieces of paper - loan forms etc. - all these people understand very well how the system works, what is expected of a loan or exhibition and what it is all about'. Professor Palmer's observation was, 'A reluctance to litigate is, of course, sound policy; a refusal to contemplate it may not be'.[24] Brexit may throw up new problems which, whatever one's previous position may have been on paying attention to the legal ingredients of art loans, at least should sharpen concern about the possibility of future disputes. Legal analysis is almost invariably laced with pessimism but that may be better than trying later on to unravel the consequences of issues that have never been articulated.

- **Some Specific Practical Considerations**

Examples of clauses which might be even more important to include and agree than hitherto are arbitration and choice of law clauses.[25] The political climate surrounding Brexit makes these arguably more problematic than they once were. Recent comments by government ministers show the controversial nature of jurisdictional issues, in particular the stated aim in some quarters to have nothing to do with the Court of Justice of the European Union.[26] It is looking some way ahead, but if the UK does indeed go down this road how will EU museums and institutions view the UK's legal system? Will there be a perception, regardless of limited legal considerations, that the English courts are no longer sufficiently in tune with European mores? At least one possibility, although not one that so far appears

---

[23] Ibid at 252
[24] Ibid at 253
[25] See Hetty Gleave, 'Art Disputes and Procedural Matters Post-Brexit' (2017) XXII *Art Antiquity and Law* 152.
[26] Formerly the European Court of Justice, the name still more often used in political discourse.

to have been heavily canvassed, is that the Irish courts may be a more attractive place than hitherto for resolving legal disputes between a UK and EU institution. They would constitute an English speaking forum but one in which the law routinely applied in EU states is fully recognized.

A recent development following the Brexit vote has been a collapse in the value of sterling. It might be anticipated that the currency will remain volatile for the foreseeable future, indeed for as long as the outcome of negotiations with the EU remains uncertain. Where an exhibition with a significant commercial element is planned, possibly several years ahead, this could have a critical impact on costs and revenue. Accordingly it may now be prudent in such a case to include a clause to agree in advance how currency fluctuations are to be dealt with, a policy already adopted by at least one major gallery.[27]

- **Conclusion – Looking Beyond the Immediate Post-Brexit World**

Looking further ahead, if one cannot meet a legal challenge head on the next best thing may be to circumvent it. It is possible that an effect of Brexit will be to change the spirit and atmosphere in which museums and galleries have hitherto operated. In an article written in 2006 Professor Palmer makes the point that, 'the practice of loaning between museums, whether long term or otherwise, is only one way

---

[27] An example of the difficulty in anticipating all the legal permutations of Brexit, and a consideration that could affect any non-UK litigant, is the impact of currency fluctuations on an order for costs. In *Elkamet Kunststoffechnik GmbH v Saint-Gobain Glass France S.A.* [2016] EWHC 3421 the court awarded £20,000 in additional costs to allow for Sterling's depreciation in the aftermath of Brexit. Currency fluctuation is not a new problem as it affects costs but the recent extent of it could be considered so with implications for the attractiveness of using English law in major commercial disputes. It would be surprising if there were not further caselaw on this issue. The subject is considered in detail in Michael Howard and John Knott, 'The Impact of Currency Fluctuations in the World of Art and Antiquities' (2017) XXII *Art Antiquity and Law* 285.

of causing art to circulate'.[28] As an example reference is made to the acquisition of the Cassel collection of silver which brought together eleven co-acquirers led by the Ashmolean and Victoria and Albert Museums. The question is raised of whether it is only a matter of time before we have cross border, as opposed to purely domestic, syndicates to acquire ownership? Might it one day become acceptable to consider floating and mobilizing existing museum collections into collective ownership? Even if it did not directly solve problems related to cross-border movements of goods would it impact beneficially on the climate in which European loans operate? At present there appears to be no evidence of, or appetite for, this happening but in a post-Brexit world might it appear more attractive? As Professor Palmer observes,[29] 'Property, like truth, is a jewel of many facets'. Originally Professor Palmer's suggestion was anchored within an EU context which assumed free movement of goods and services and a European legal system which, if not uniform, at least gestured in the direction of some degree of convergence. It would be ironic, but perfectly plausible, if the catalyst to make a move in this direction now worth considering was in fact the UK's departure from the EU.

---

[28] Itinerant Art in the European Community, (2006) XI *Art Antiquity and Law*, 275. The article is a revised version of a paper presented at a conference, Encouraging the Mobility of Collections, organized by Finland's EU Presidency in co-operation with the European Commission.
[29] Ibid at 284.

11

THE FINALITY OF THE ARBITRAL AWARD

Bruno Zeller

- **Introduction**

This paper has been written in honour of Professor Gabriël A. Moens – a scholar and a gentleman – as a gift for his 70th's birthday. In the 1990s I met Gabriël at a conference in Brisbane and then again in Vienna on the occasion of the Vis Moot and we stayed connected ever since. Gabriël has always been interested in arbitration and hence it is obvious that the topic must deal with arbitration. Three recent cases are of interest for different reasons and are worth noting.

In general, an arbitral award is binding and final pursuant to article 35 of the Model Law as well as confidential. It is also established that the award can be set aside under article 34 of the Model Law or a court can refuse to recognise or enforce an award under article 36 of the Model Law or article V of the New York Convention.

- **The Role of the Seat**

Setting aside an award pursuant to Article 34 is said to be usually taking place in the court of the seat.[1] There is no dispute that the choice of a seat is crucial. Chief Justice Allsop did comment that

> The quality and legal culture of the court of the seat of any arbitration is critical. The court of the seat has a crucial role in the supervision of the procedural conduct of the reference and thus of its fairness.[2]

---

[1] A. Redfern, C. Partasides, M. Hunter, and N. Blackaby, *Redfern and Hunter on International Arbitration* (6th ed, Kluwer Law International, 2015), Chapter 10, para 10.04 and 10.05.

[2] Chief Justice Allsop of the Full Court of the Federal Court of Australia was surely

The role of the seat has been shaped by two theories namely territorialism and delocalization.³ The point of the debate is to answer the question where and how arbitrators derive their powers to perform what might be termed a quasi-judicial function. In brief under the territorialism theory arbitrators derive their power from the place where they perform their duties. The procedural laws and the choice of law rules of the seat therefore govern the process.

The delocalization theory on the other hand proposed that international arbitration tribunals are detached from the control of the seat of arbitration. Parties under this theory will hold their arbitrations at a common convenient place⁴ and hence derive their power from the international legal community.⁵ The end effect is that an award set aside in one country can be enforced in another one - as an example - demonstrated by the French practise. This issue is not confined to civil law countries but rather depends on the facts of the case.

- **Enforcing an Annulled Award**

However, what is not disputed is that courts will not revisit the award - that is - they will not rehear the dispute but rather confine themselves to the stated rules of setting aside or not enforcing the award pursuant to the reasons in the above-mentioned articles. Simply put the facts and the reasoning of the arbitration tribunal is not questioned by courts. This has been demonstrated recently in an English High Court decision. In *Nikolay Viktorovich Maximov v. Open Joint Stock Company "Novolipetsky Metallurgichesky Kombinat"*⁶ The claimant asked the court to enforce an annulled agreement. Despite the fact

---

right to stress the above point in his Keynote Speech to the 2nd Annual Global Arbitration Review in Sydney in November 2014.

³ For a detailed discussion see Jean Francois Poudret & Sebastien Besson, *Comparative Law of International Arbitration* (2nd. Ed., Sweet & Maxwell, 2007).

⁴ M.L. Moses, Principles and Practice of International Commercial Arbitration (Cambridge University Press, 2008), p 56.

⁵ E. Gaillard & John Savage (eds.), Fouchard, Gaillard & Goldman's On International Commercial Arbitration (Emmanuel Gaillard & John Savage eds., 1999), p 3.

⁶ [2017] EWHC 1911 (Comm).

that the annulment of the award by the Moscow Arbitration Court was based on the wrong application of Russian law the English High court – though critical - was not persuaded that the errors were so severe as to deprive the claimant of natural justice. However, of interest is that the claimant sought to enforce the award also in France and the Netherlands. The French courts did enforce the award whereas the Dutch decision – after an initial refusal to enforce – is still pending. This case again indicates that a selection of a seat must be a careful decision and not merely one of convenience.

Another issue which occupied the courts recently is the attempt of a party to an arbitration to litigate again later using the same facts. Generally, this is not possible as - based upon the contractual obligation - the disputes must be arbitrated and not litigated and hence litigation is blocked as noted in article 8 of the Model Law and in article 6 has restricted the interference of courts to well defined functions.

- **The Litigation Issue – A New Problem**

Despite the fact that litigation is excluded when the contract mandates arbitration two issues have recently been decided which deal with the "twilight zone" between arbitration and litigation. The Victorian Supreme[7] court was asked to decide whether an award can be set aside when not all issues referred to arbitration have been decided and how corrections can be applied to an issue which the arbitrator expressly did not determine. In effect, the question of the extent to which the arbitrators mandate subsists had occupied the court. This decision is also of interest as the Victorian *Commercial Arbitration Act 2011* follows closely the Model Law specifically article 34. Indeed, Croft J noted:

> ... in light of the authorities it now almost goes without saying, it is vital to interpret the CAA in light of its status as a domestic application of an international model law—the UNCITRAL Model Law on International Commercial Arbitration ("the Model Law"). Notwithstanding the fact that the CAA is a

---

[7] *Blanalko Pty Ltd v Lysaght Building Solutions Pty Ltd*, [2017] VSC 97, (Blanalko).

domestic statute in the State of Victoria, it should be interpreted in conformity with international norms with respect to the Model Law, "so far as practicable".[8]

The court relied on the ruling by the court of appeal in Subway[9] where it was noted that certainty and uniformity of application are paramount because the international agreement is addressed to a much wider and more varied judicial audience than an act of a domestic legislature, the interpretation of the domestic enactment should be unconstrained by technical rules of interpretation and should instead be informed by "broad principles of general acceptation.

The second similar issue recently occupied the English Court of Appeal.[10] The question was whether a central allegation which has already been determined by a tribunal can be litigated against a person who was not a party but was involved in the arbitration as a witness and financier of the respondent.

This paper will demonstrate that the two decisions have clarified a point of law which assist in determining where arbitration and litigation in effect are inter-twined. In effect, the lesson is that arbitration clauses must be carefully drafted in order to bind all parties which are potentially tied up in a transaction. Non-parties to an arbitration – but involved as a witness or connected to the facts at issue- need to take advice whether they can be joined. Arguably the problem of potentially litigating as well as having arbitrated the same fact situation needs to be linked to a careful selection of the seat in order to minimise problems in the enforcement process.

The first part will explain the English decision followed by the decision of Croft J in the Victorian Supreme court.

- **The English Court of Appeal**

In brief, the English Court of Appel[11] conclude that "a subsequent

---

[8] Ibid., para 10.
[9] *Subway Systems Australia Pty Ltd v Ireland* (2014) 46 VR 49, para [29].
[10] *Michael Wilson & Partners v Sinclair* [2017] EWCA Civ 3
[11] Ibid.

litigation is not an abuse of process for being a collateral attack against a previous arbitral award, where the respondent to the litigation was not a party [but involved] to the earlier arbitration. "[12]

- **The Admissibility of the Award Under the Test of Abuse of Process**

There is always an interplay between litigation and arbitration as noted by the Court of Appeal which overturned the High Court's decision. The interesting point was that the party in the original arbitration and the party in the litigation were connected. The facts are simple. *Michael Wilson & Partners* (MWP) brought arbitral proceedings against one of their former directors (Mr Emmott) of breaching a fiduciary duty of accepting shares and funds after a completion of certain transactions. Mr Emmott in his defence in the arbitration claimed that he was merely holding the funds in trust for Mr Sinclair. The tribunal dismissed the claims by MWP. MWP then commenced proceedings against Mr Sinclair in the High Court of England and Wales. Mr Sinclair's defence applied to strike out the action as an abuse of process on the bases that the matter had already been decided in the arbitration and was therefore "entirely inconsistent with, and contrary to the findings made in, the award to which MWP had been a party."[13]

The High Court found that the abuse of power doctrine also did apply "where the decision under collateral attack was an arbitration award."[14]

Abuse of power has been defined as:

> *The abuse of process which the instant case exemplifies is the initiation of proceedings in a court of justice for the purpose of mounting a collateral attack upon a final*

---

[12] Debevoise and Plimpton, Client update, at http://www.debevoise.com/~/media/files/insights/publications/2017/02/20170228_english_court_of_appeal_clarifies_test_for_abuse_of_process_in_subsequent_litigation_collaterally_challenging_an_arbitral_award.pdf

[13] Above n 10, para [10].

[14] Ibid para [37].

> *decision against the intending plaintiff which has been made by another court of competent jurisdiction in previous proceedings in which the intending plaintiff had a full opportunity of contesting the decision in the court by which it was made.*[15]

The courts have also explained where the abuse of power is not applicable. Sir Andrew Morritt V-C noted that it is not a collateral attack on an earlier decision of a court of competent jurisdiction:

> If the parties to the later civil proceedings were not parties to or privies of those who were parties to the earlier proceedings, then it will only be an abuse of the process of the court to challenge the factual findings and conclusions of the judge or jury in the earlier action[16]

As far as litigation is concerned the law is clear. However, there are important differences between litigation and arbitration. The latter is consensual whereas the former is subject to a courts coercive power.

The court – noting this difference - agreed with the decision in *Art & Antiques Limited v Richards*[17] where Hamblen J stated that it would be a rare case "where an action in this court against a non-party to an arbitration can be said to be an abuse of the process of this court"[18] and "the defeat of the claim in arbitration will not usually prevent him from pursuing his claim against the other person in litigation."[19]

The issue which was not expressly addressed by the court was the potential breach of the confidentiality issue in an arbitration. However, this was overcome by the tribunal allowing access to a redacted copy of the award to Mr Sinclair. [20]

This is not surprising nor unusual as soon as an arbitral matter is either enforced or set aside the confidentially issue is not applicable

---

[15] *Hunter v. Chief Constable of the West Midlands* [1982] AC 529, t p 541B-C
[16] *Secretary of State for Trade and Industry v. Bairstow* [2004] Ch 1, at para [38].
[17] [2013] EWHC 3361 (Comm) at [23].
[18] Ibid at para [24].
[19] Ibid.
[20] MWP above n 10 at para 31.

anymore. However, the question of the admissibility of the award for the purpose of the litigation was tested by the court. The defence argued that factual findings made in one case are not admissible in subsequent proceedings.[21] The court noted that a court is permitted to "consider the contents of either an earlier judgment or an earlier arbitration award in order to see whether a later claim amounts to an abuse of its process."[22]

Specifically, the Court of Appeal explained why the High Court was wrong because the primary judge did not consider the fact that Mr Sinclair refused to be a party to the arbitration and that the Commercial Court action was therefore the only forum in which MWP could advance its claim against him. This was sufficient to prevent the claim amounting to an abuse of process, particularly since a breach of fiduciary duty alleged against Mr Emmott was a necessary pre-condition of MWP's claim against Mr Sinclair.[23] The high threshold has not been reached and the following factors were emphasised.

First the[24] only means for MWP to pursue Mr Sinclair is through the courts as there was never a prior claim against Mr. Sinclair. Besides Mr Emmott is not being vexed twice. Secondly – an importantly – because MWP was inviting the court to come to a different view to the arbitration it was not mounting an illegitimate collateral attack on the award.[25] Thirdly the court noted that the facts that Mr Sinclair was a witness and funded Mr Emmott does not have any bearing on the issue of abuse of process. In addition, the tribunal could not grant any relief between MWP and Mr Sinclair.[26]

Fourthly Mr Sinclair was not a part to the arbitral proceedings, as matter of fact he refused to join the arbitration and maintained "that

---

[21] Ibid para [71].
[22] Ibid para [73].
[23] Ibid para [83].
[24] Ibid para [93].
[25] Ibid para [94].
[26] Ibid para [97].

the outcome of the arbitration was 'totally irrelevant to the dispute' between MWP and him."[27]

The court in the end left the question as to the admissibility of the award in the litigation for the Commercial Court to decide. This point was not raised in this matter by the court of appeal. As the appeal from MWP was allowed it clearly establishes that a person must be a party to an arbitration otherwise that person is capable of being sued in a litigation even if an arbitral award has already been decided on the same matter.

- **The Victorian Decision**

A litigation dealing with a breach of a design and construction contract were partially settled the remainder was sent to arbitration. The arbitrator delivered an interim award which resolved the majority of the issue and invited the parties to make submissions on - among other things - costs.[28] The problem was that the arbitrators' decision was termed the final award. However, the arbitrator did not decide the issue of Blanalko's Supreme Court costs because he decided that he lacked the necessary information.[29] The case turns on the application and interpretation of article 33 of the CAA or Model law in conjunction with the setting aside of the award namely article 34. The reason advance by the parties was that as the arbitrator did not make a decision the award must be set aside.

- **The setting side argument**

To begin with the court correctly noted that if the arbitrator did not make a decision at all recourse to article 34(2)(a)(iii) will fail.[30] This article states:

> *(2) An arbitral award may be set aside by the court specified in article 6 only if:*

---
[27] Ibid para [89].
[28] Blanalko, above n. 7, para [2] to [3].
[29] Ibid para [4].
[30] Ibid para [48].

(a) the party making the application furnishes proof that:

(iii) the award deals with a dispute not contemplated by or not falling within the terms of the submission to arbitration, or contains decisions on matters beyond the scope of the submission to arbitration, provided that, if the decisions on matters submitted to arbitration can be separated from those not so submitted, only that part of the award which contains decisions on matters not submitted to arbitration may be set aside;

It must be remembered that the parties did ask the arbitrator to rule on the cost issues hence the decision when made will fall within the submission to arbitrate. The court came to the conclusion – examining the critical part in the decision – that the arbitrator considered the answer to the question whether to make an award on the Supreme Courts costs. Croft J noted:

> All the arbitrator has done is not discharge his whole mandate; he has not gone beyond it. As to the latter, particularly, there is no delegation to, or direction to, the parties to take the Supreme Court Costs claim to a "third party" decision maker; namely the Court in this instance.[31]

Croft J consulted previous conventions namely the predecessor of the New York Convention, the Geneva Convention on the Execution of Foreign Arbitral Awards[32] where the word "That the award *does not deal with the differences contemplated by or falling within the terms of the submission to arbitration*"[33] were deleted in article 34 and article V of the New York convention hence "a decision not to make a decision" is not a decision that may be set aside under s 34(2)(a)(iii).[34]

It is obvious that an arbitrator is not allowed or should not make

---

[31] Ibid.
[32] *Geneva Convention on the Execution of Foreign Arbitral Awards* (1927), Art 2(c) ("the Geneva Convention")
[33] Ibid article 2(c).
[34] Blanalko above n 10, para [49].

a decision without sufficient evidence hence he should never merely guess or act on assumptions. However, the question is whether it is within the power of an arbitrator not to make a decision. If it is not then the arbitrator exceeded his power and hence the award can be set aside.

On this issue the Singapore Court of Appeal in *CRW Joint Operation v PT Perusahaan Gas Negara (Persero) TBK*[35] pointed out;

> It is useful, at this juncture, to set out some of the legal principles underlying the application of Art 34(2)(a)(iii) of the Model Law... [I]t applies where the arbitral tribunal improperly decided matters that had not been submitted to it or failed to decide matters that had been submitted to it. In other words, Art 34(2)(a)(iii) addresses the situation where the arbitral tribunal exceeded (or failed to exercise) the authority that the parties granted to it.

However an important proviso does apply namely:

> [I]t must be noted that a failure by an arbitral tribunal to deal with every issue referred to it will not ordinarily render its arbitral award liable to be set aside. The crucial question in every case is whether there has been *real or actual prejudice* to either (or both) of the parties to the dispute.[36]

Croft J and the Singapore Supreme Court demonstrated clearly that it is the fact that an arbitrator did not deal with the issue is decisive but the crucial question is: has there been "real or actual prejudice" to each party in the arbitral process? Importantly article 34 only applies to a final award. Hence the court addressed the issue whether the award is final or not.

- **Proper Characterisation of an Award**

Article 34 can only be invoked if the award is final. The court – quoting Mustill and Boyd[37] – made the points that an award isn't

---

[35] [2011] 4 SLR 305., para [31].
[36] Ibid para [32].
[37] Sir M. J. Mustill and S.C. Boyd, *The Law and Practice of Commercial Arbitration*

final if the arbitrator leaves certain issues to another party to decide. The exception is that if an arbitrator reserves certain matters for future decisions then he only issued an interim award. After carefully considering the jurisprudence underpinning Mustill and Boyd Croft J concluded that:

> I find that, in spite of its labelling, it was clearly not a final award. The Award did not decide all issues put to the arbitrator within the arbitrator's mandate and did not involve an order or direction that might be characterised as an invalid delegation of power to a third party.[38]

The result was that the arbitrator only delivered an interim award and until this is resolved access to article 34 is barred.

- **Interplay Between Article 33 and 34**

Blanalko is an important decision in the analysis of the interplay between articles 33 and 34. Article 33 states:

> - Within thirty days of receipt of the award, unless another period of time has been agreed upon by the parties:
>
> (a) a party, with notice to the other party, may request the arbitral tribunal to correct in the award any errors in computation, any clerical or typographical errors or any errors of similar nature;

It is obvious that article 33 only applies to an award and not an interim award and it only applies to correct errors which do not go to the core of the dispute. In other words, article 33 deals with the correction of minor issue which will not change the outcome fundamentally.

Setting aside of an award pursuant to article 34 is at a point where an arbitration has come to an end that is the final award has been issued. However, – in addition to article 33 – a court can suspend the setting aside process under article 34(4) where they find that the arbitral tribunal might correct or can overcome the grounds for setting aside an award.

---

in England (2nd ed, Butterworths, 1989), 387.
[38] Blanalko above n 10, para [66].

A similar remedy is available under article 33(3) which notes:

> *(3) Unless otherwise agreed by the parties, a party, with notice to the other party, may request, within thirty days of receipt of the award, the arbitral tribunal to make an additional award as to claims presented in the arbitral proceedings but omitted from the award. If the arbitral tribunal considers the request to be justified, it shall make the additional award within sixty days.*

The difference between articles 33(3) and 34(4) is simply addressing the mechanism of the request. In article 33 it is the parties and in article 34 it a discretionary power given by the Model law to the court.

Importantly the Singapore court of Appeal in *BLC v BLB*[39] succinctly stated that:

> It is clear that the Model Law supports the principle of minimal curial intervention. To this end, as long as the parties do not agree otherwise, the Model Law provides via Art 33(3) a mechanism for a party to seek redress from the arbitrator first before turning to the courts when he believes that the arbitrator had omitted to deal with a stand-alone claim presented to him. In such circumstances, should a party be entitled to ignore Art 33(3) and instead apply to set aside the entire award under Art 34, knowing that the court may in appropriate circumstances fall back on its powers to remit part of the award back to the tribunal under Art 34(4) if it decides that setting aside the entire award is not the appropriate remedy?

The point the Singapore Supreme court made was that if a party omits to resort to article 33(3) first it might impact on the courts discretion to set aside an award under article 34.[40]

- **Conclusion**

Blanalko and *MWP* are important decision in narrowing and explaining the "twilight zone" between arbitration and litigation. The problem of

---

[39] [2014] 4 SLR 79, [109].
[40] Ibid, para [117].

the inter-relationship affects important principles in both arbitration and litigation. Firstly, the point of confidentiality of arbitration is always challenged when it moves into the court system as public policy mandates that litigation is not confidential. Secondly the relationship between articles 33 and 34 of the Model Law has been clarified.

Importantly the courts in both jurisdictions correctly noted that setting aside an arbitration award required that the award is final and that corrections pursuant to article 33 are not possible. In *MWP* the issue of abuse of power has finally been resolved and will guide courts in future decisions where an award is attacked though litigation. The interesting point is that the litigation can attack an award if one of the parties was not connected to the original award but the subject matter is the same.

12
OVERCOMING THE TYRANNY OF DISTANCE: AUSTRALIA AS AN ARBITRAL SEAT

Doug Jones AO[1]

- **Introduction**

It was not so long ago that international arbitration was confined to a select few seats within Europe and North America. The concentration of business within these regions gave birth to well-established arbitral seats including London, Paris and New York. Indeed, Europe was home to the very first arbitral institutions, the London Court of International Arbitration (LCIA) established in 1892,[2] and later, The Hague's Permanent Court of Arbitration (PCA) in 1899.[3] Historically, many would argue that international arbitration is restricted to these few seats. However, international arbitration is moving away from its Eurocentric roots. The past century has witnessed the growth of an interconnected global economy, the product of accessible transport, technological development and free trade. Transactions are becoming increasingly cross border, and inevitably, as are the ensuing disputes. Asia is now a rapidly growing commercial centre, resulting in the demand for effective dispute resolution mechanisms in the Asia-Pacific region. To accommodate this, arbitration diversified and parties

---
[1] I gratefully acknowledge the assistance provided in the preparation of this paper by my legal assistant, Sara Pacey. This paper is an adaptation of my earlier published speech, 'Australia as a Global Hub' (Speech delivered at LCIA Symposium, Sydney, 8 October 2017) <https://disputescentre.com.au/wp-content/uploads/2017/10/LCIA-Keynote-Address-.pdf>.

[2] Tomas Kennedy-Grant, 'Transnational Litigation and Arbitration' (1998) 7 *New Zealand Law Journal*.

[3] Permanent Court of Arbitration, *History* (2013) <https://pca-cpa.org/en/about/introduction/history/>.

are now offered a greater array of developed arbitral seats than ever before. Thus, as arbitration has flourished across the globe, much of its recent development has occurred in close proximity to Asia's booming economies.

Nestled within this Asia-Pacific region is Australia, a nation that has emerged as a competitive commercial centre. According to the 22nd Global Financial Centres Index, the competitiveness of Sydney as a commercial centre is ranked eighth in the world. In March 2017, Australia took the record for the longest run of uninterrupted GDP growth in the developed world, enjoying 26 years or 104 financial quarters since its last technical recession.[4] Australia's growth as a global commercial hub has inevitably driven the need for advanced commercial dispute resolution mechanisms. Foremost among these is international arbitration, an effective means of resolving disputes that is efficient, discrete, flexible, and importantly, legally binding. In catering to the growing demand for arbitration, Australia has developed into a sophisticated seat. While the factors to consider in electing an arbitral seat are numerous and different parties will have different priorities, some needs are universal. Robust legislation, a supportive judiciary, and effective institutions are often the key to the success of arbitration and in many respects, Australia is at the leading edge.

Many would agree that the growing significance of Australia in the international business and legal world is unprecedented given its roots as a convict settlement whose survival was nearly entirely dependent on England for the majority of its early history. One cannot forget the 'tyranny of distance'[5] which has so characterised Australian history, the phrase itself coined in 1966 by the renowned Australian historian Geoffrey Blainey. In light of Australia's growing position within the international commercial sphere, the validity of Blainey's phrase today should be questioned.

---

[4] Australian Bureau of Statistics, *5206.0 – Australian National Accounts: National Income, Expenditure and Product, Sep 2017* (2017) <http://www.abs.gov.au/ausstats/abs@.nsf/mf/5206.0>.

[5] Geoffrey Blainey, *The Tyranny of Distance: How Distance Shaped Australia's History* (Macmillan Publishers, 1966).

In celebration of Professor Gabriël Moens' 70th birthday, I am therefore delighted to share this paper advocating for the rising prominence of Australia as a seat for international commercial arbitration. The current trajectory of arbitration in Australia is positive, aided by recent developments in both arbitration laws and facilities. To echo the sentiments of Professor Moens, the widespread adoption of the *New York Convention* and *Model Law* principles into domestic law has provided 'a strong foundation for international commercial arbitration in Australia'.[6] I join with the authors of this book to commemorate Professor Moens' outstanding contributions to the field through his role as an arbitrator, lawyer, academic and the Deputy Secretary General of ACICA.

This paper is structured as follows:

- First, I will begin with a discussion of the Australian context, starting with a brief note on Geoffrey Blainey's seminal history, 'The Tyranny of Distance',[7] followed by a discussion of Australia's arbitration origins.

- Second, I will continue by highlighting the many practical benefits which make Australia a favourable venue for international arbitration.

- Third, I will examine the existing legislative framework by which international arbitration has become embedded in the Australian legal system.

- Fourth, I will analyse the commendable judicial support for arbitration which has characterised the non-interventionalist, pro-enforcement approach to recognising arbitral awards.

- Finally, I will conclude with a discussion of Australia's excellent arbitration institutions and their rules, which serve to ensure commercial parties are provided with the very best service.

---

[6] Gabriël Moens and John Trone, 'The International Arbitration Act 1974 (Cth) as a Foundation for International Commercial Arbitration in Australia' (2007) 4, *Macquarie Journal of Business Law* 295.

[7] Blainey, above n 5.

- **Background**

- **Historical Origins**

Blainey's book 'The Tyranny of Distance'[8] recently turned fifty, and despite its age remains a vivid and unique insight into Australia's history, mainly due to its focus on distance, an often accepted but unexplored part of Australian life. Distance has shaped Australian history in the movement, communication, and economy of its peoples.

For Blainey, it was Australia's remoteness, combined with a lack of attractive trade goods that left the European imperial powers disinterested throughout much of the 18th century.[9] Australia's early colonial history was characterised by its inherent isolation from the rest of the world. This isolation was exacerbated by supply voyages and journeys that took months and were often beset by icebergs, wild seas, and scurvy.[10]

Not only is Australia distant from many regions of the world, but its urban centres are also distant from one another. Early settlers were confined to the east coast by the wall of mountains and immense harsh inland that lay to their west.[11] The distance inland made domestic and international exporting of commodities such as wheat and wool a time-consuming and expensive task, rendering these Australian products uncompetitive until the railroad was built, itself an arduous task given the distance to cover.[12]

To return to arbitration, the same brush that provides this grim recount of Australian history often paints a similarly pessimistic outlook of present-day Australia as a place inaccessible to the rest of the world, and an unlikely choice for an arbitral seat. The writer respectfully disagrees. Unbeknownst to many, the use of arbitration in Australia has a rich history. Australia's relationship with arbitration

---

[8] Ibid.
[9] Ibid.
[10] Ibid 40-45.
[11] Ibid 121-123.
[12] Ibid 125, 129.

pre-dates Western civilisation. Indigenous Australians have, for many millennia, implemented their own dispute resolution system that closely resembled arbitration to resolve disputes between members within a community.[13] As noted by Dr Diane Bell, indigenous customary law is comprised of 'rules backed by sanctions and a set of dispute resolution mechanisms'.[14] The arbitrators in these disputes were the elders of the communities. This practice has survived the passages of both culture and time. Mirroring Australia's customary law practices, Australia's common law system also has developed effective dispute resolution mechanisms. Today, arbitration is widely used to solve disputes of a commercial nature, enabled by Australia's pro-arbitration legislation and supportive judiciary.

Australia's struggles, plagued by the tyranny of distance, therefore seem to be concerns of the past. Today, travel is swifter. Markets are better connected. Communication is immediate, and business between Sydney, London, New York, Beijing, Tokyo and many other commercial hubs has never been more convenient.[15] What was tyrannical in the days of yore has become a lot less, attributable to technological developments such as the introduction of the A380 aeroplane and access to state of the art teleconferencing. Emerging from this commercial climate is the growth of interconnected and interdependent economies, particularly within the Asia-Pacific region, giving Australia access to Asia's rapidly growing market.

- **Practical Benefits**

Overcoming the challenges posed by distance, Australia has developed itself as an attractive seat for international arbitration with many practical benefits to compliment the pro-arbitration legal framework.

First, with the emergence of the economies of Asia, Australia is

---

[13] Australia Law Reform Commission, *Traditional Aboriginal Society and Its Law*, Dispute Resolution in Australia 2nd ed (2002) 11.

[14] Diane Bell, 'Aboriginal Women and the Recognition of Customary Law in Australia' (1983) 1 *Papers of the Symposium on Folk Law and Legal Pluralism* 491, 503.

[15] Blainey, above n 5, 350.

geographically well-positioned as a regional seat. The recognition of Asia as home to the world's fastest growing economies has catalysed a shift in trade and commerce patterns.[16] Asia is currently enjoying unprecedented influence in international markets, which is set to increase with trade arrangements such as the ASEAN alliance and the latest form of the Trans-Pacific Partnership.[17] This increase in cross-border transactions[18] will inevitably result in greater demand for arbitration as an effective means of resolving commercial disputes between parties residing in different legal jurisdictions.[19] Australia's geographical proximity to the Asia-Pacific region gives this country a distinct advantage as a seat compared to its European counterparts.

In 2016, parties from India, China and Singapore featured significantly in the caseload of the prominent Asian arbitral institutions of SIAC and HKIAC,[20] while Asian countries were featured in over 10% of the LCIA's caseload.[21] In 2016, the International Chamber of Commerce (ICC) saw a 22% increase in parties from South and East Asia.[22] While a party or legal representative in Hong Kong would face a seven-hour time difference to reach London, a hearing in Sydney would be only two or three hours ahead (and the same time zone in

---

[16] Akrur Barua, 'Packing a mightier punch: Asia's economic growth among global markets continues' *Deloitte Insights* (online), 18 December 2015, <https://www2.deloitte.com/insights/us/en/economy/>

[17] Ibid.

[18] Marilyn Warren, 'Australia as a 'safe and neutral' arbitration seat' (Speech delivered at ACICA's 'The Australian Option' Chinese Tour, People's Republic of China, 6 June 2012).

[19] Justice Steven Rares, 'The Modern Place of Arbitration - Celebration of the Centenary of the Chartered Institute of Arbitrators' (Speech delivered at the Chartered Institute of Arbitrators, Sydney, 22 April 2015), 17.

[20] Singapore International Arbitration Centre, 'SIAC Annual Report 2016' (Annual Report, Singapore International Arbitration Centre, 2016) 14; Hong Kong International Arbitration Centre, 'HKIAC Annual Report 2015' (Annual Report, Hong Kong International Arbitration Centre, 2015) 8.

[21] London Court of International Arbitration, 'LCIA Annual Report 2016' (Annual Report, London Court of International Arbitration, 2016) 8.

[22] International Chamber of Commerce, 'ICC Reveals Record Number of New Cases filed in 2016', *International Chamber of Commerce* (online) 18 January 2017 <https://iccwbo.org/media-wall/news-speeches/>

Perth). Similarly, the flight from Singapore to Sydney is shorter than the flight from Singapore to London. The growth of the arbitration industry in Asia has gifted Australia with the advantage of geographic proximity to many parties and to flourishing arbitration practices.

Australia's proximity to the Asia-Pacific also provides parties with access to a myriad of high quality arbitration practices across the region. Nearly all major international firms have developed arbitration practices in Asia and many have highly experienced and specialised teams operating in the region.[23] Many of these firms have also expanded their arbitration practices to Australia, bringing with them the experience and expertise accrued from practice in many jurisdictions. Further, numerous Australian law firms have established arbitration practices and some have formed international partnerships, facilitating the growth and development of their local teams.

However, these practical benefits would mean nothing in the absence of a strong legal framework for arbitration. Accordingly, the remainder of this paper will discuss Australia's appeal as a seat with reference to the existing legal features that make Australia well-suited to respond to the growing demand for arbitration in the Asia-Pacific region.

- **Legal Framework**

When deciding upon an arbitral seat, a country's legal framework will often inform the party's decision. Echoing the sentiments of Justice Clyde Croft, the success of arbitration is dependent on the legislature passing laws that create a favourable environment for arbitration.[24] Relevantly, an article[25] co-authored by Professor Moens cited *HIH Casualty & General Insurance Ltd (in Liq) v Wallace*,[26] noting that:

---

[23] The Legal 500, 'Asia Pacific: Regional International Arbitration' *The Legal 500* (online) 2018 <http://www.legal500.com>

[24] Justice Clyde Croft 'Commercial Arbitration in Australia: the Past, the Present and the Future' (2011) 59 *VicJSchol* 1, 3.

[25] Moens and Trone, above n 6.

[26] (2006) 204 FLR 297.

[T]he enforceability of the arbitration agreement is determined in light of applicable state and federal legislation and the common law...the court's power to order such measures derives from its domestic law...[27]

It is therefore essential to turn to the applicable laws governing arbitration in Australia, an examination of which clearly demonstrates this nation's commitment to respecting party autonomy and the right to arbitrate.

- **Current Legislation**

Australia's pro-arbitration stance is evident in the laws regulating international and domestic arbitration. Through legislative reform, the principles arising from leading international instruments have been given the force of law in Australia.[28] The laws governing arbitration incorporate the *UNCITRAL Model Law*,[29] the result of which is uniformity and consistency of arbitration laws the nation over, in line with international best practice. A product of this uniformity has been the development of consistent Australia-wide jurisprudence and precedent. Australian arbitrators and counsel have become familiar with the *Model Law,* equipping them to compete for arbitration work, internationally and locally. The expertise of local judges and support from the Australian judiciary is equally impressive.

Australia's modern arbitration laws are, of course, the product of centuries of reform since English colonisation in 1788. Like most Commonwealth nations, Australia derived many of its initial arbitration laws and general laws from those enacted in England. Starting with the English *Act for Determining Differences by Arbitration 1698*,[30] the

---

[27] Ibid 2-5, citing *HIH Casualty & General Insurance Ltd (in liq) v Wallace* (2006) 204 FLR 297 [44].

[28] Justice Steven Rares, 'The Role of Courts in Arbitration' (Speech delivered at the 2012 ADR in Australia and Beyond, the New South Wales Bar Association and ACICA Seminar, The Westin Hotel Sydney, 4 August 2012).

[29] *Model Law on International Commercial Arbitration of the United Nations Commission on International Trade Law,* GA Res 40/72, UN GAOR, 40th sess, 112th plen mtg, Supp No 17, UN Doc (A/40/17) (21 June 1985) (amended on 7 July 2006).

[30] 9 & 10 Wm 3, c 15.

first *Arbitration Act* was passed by the New South Wales Parliament in 1867, regulating domestic arbitration. More recently, *Uniform Commercial Arbitration Acts*[31] have been adopted by every state and territory, and they now incorporate the 2006 Amended *Model Law* after undergoing substantial reform in the 2010. This reform was championed by the New South Wales Supreme Court, bringing Australia in line with international best practice, and is illustrative of the Australian commitment to continual refinement of its arbitral mechanisms.

The life of the federal *International Arbitration Act*[32] *(IAA)* which governs Australian international arbitration law is much shorter by comparison. Upon its enactment in 1974, this Act incorporated both the 1958 *New York Convention*[33] and the 1965 *ICSID Convention*,[34] and in 1989 it was amended to incorporate the *Model Law*. In 2010, it was reformed again to incorporate the 2006 Amended *Model Law*, along with a repeal of provisions that had previously allowed parties to opt out of the *Model Law*. The amended *IAA*[35] goes so far as to give primacy to the *Model Law* in international arbitration matters,[36] bringing Australia in line with the leading international arbitral procedure adopted by 78 states in 109 jurisdictions.[37] Parliament's express intention to promote and enforce international arbitral awards is evident in the object of the *IAA*. Section 2D stipulates that the object of the Act is to encourage the use of arbitration, to facilitate

---

[31] *Commercial Arbitration Act 2010* (NSW); *Commercial Arbitration Act 2011* (VIC); *Commercial Arbitration Act 2011* (SA); *Commercial Arbitration Act 2012* (WA; *Commercia Arbitration (National Uniform Legslation Act 2011* (NT); *Commercial Arbitration Act 2011* (TAS); *Commercial Arbitration Act 2013* (QLD); *Commercial Arbitration Act 2017* (ACT).

[32] *International Arbitration Act 1974* (Cth).

[33] *New York Convention*, opened for signature 10 June 1958, 330 UNTS 38 (entered into force 7 June 1959).

[34] *ICSID Convention,* opened for signature 18 March 1965 (entered into force 14 October 1966).

[35] *International Arbitration Act 1974* (Cth).

[36] Ibid s 21.

[37] UNICTRAL, *Status, UNCITRAL Model Law on International Commercial Arbitration (1985), with amendments as adopted in 2006* (2018) <http://www.uncitral.org>

the use of arbitration agreements and to recognise and enforce arbitral awards, while giving effect to Australia's obligations under the *New York Convention* and *Model Law*.[38] Parliament's willingness to amend domestic law to reflect changing international standards and *Model Law* emphasises the pro-arbitration position adopted by the Australian legal system.

- **Legislation Features**

These enactments have brought Australia's domestic and international arbitration regimes in line with international best practice, and provide a strongly supportive environment for arbitration.

To quote the Hon Marilyn Warren AC, (Former Chief Justice of the Supreme Court of Victoria):

> The Australian Legislative Architecture is now one which has been significantly enhanced so as to be more effective and facilitative to International Arbitration.[39]

The accuracy of this statement is made obvious by an analysis of the latest amendments to the *IAA*. The Act supplements and goes beyond the *Model Law* in many respects. Division 3, for example, contains several provisions that mandatorily apply on an 'opt out' basis that aim to improve the arbitral process.[40] These provisions allow parties to obtain subpoenas from the court,[41] apply to the court for orders compelling persons to attend examination before the arbitral tribunal,[42] and provide that confidentiality of information in proceedings must be observed.[43] They also give tribunals the power to continue proceedings and make an award where a party fails to assist the tribunal after being ordered to do so,[44] the power to order a party

---
[38] *International Arbitration Act 1974* (Cth) s 2D.
[39] Warren, above n 18.
[40] *International Arbitration Act 1974* (Cth) s 22(2).
[41] Ibid s 23.
[42] Ibid s 23A.
[43] Ibid s 23C.
[44] Ibid s 23B.

to provide security for costs,[45] to award interest up to the making of an award[46] and on award debts,[47] and to award costs with orders in respect of their taxation.[48] A very robust and detailed provision dealing with the consolidation of proceedings applies on an 'opt in' basis,[49] providing multiple grounds which may give rise to a consolidation of proceedings or an alternative action,[50] such as a joint hearing[51] or stay of proceedings.[52] Importantly, the *International Arbitration Act*[53] restricts the meaning of 'public policy' for the purpose of articles 34 and 36 of the *Model Law* to situations where the relevant interim measure or award was affected by fraud,[54] corruption,[55] or a breach of natural justice.[56]

Thus in review, arbitration legislation in Australia has clearly followed a narrative of pro-arbitration guided reform. This narrative, however, is not limited to legislation alone.

- **Judicial Support**

- **Generally**

It is well established that the success of international arbitration requires unwavering judicial support. An advantage of selecting Australia as a seat is the state and federal courts' willingness to adopt an arbitration-friendly approach. Indeed, the Federal Court in *Elders International Australia Pty Ltd v Beijing BE Green Import & Export*

---

[45] Ibid s 23K.
[46] Ibid s 25.
[47] Ibid s 26.
[48] Ibid s 27.
[49] Ibid s 22(5); s 24.
[50] Ibid s 24(1); 24(2)(a).
[51] Ibid s 24(2)(b).
[52] Ibid s 24(2)(c).
[53] Ibid.
[54] Ibid s 19(a).
[55] Ibid s 19(a).
[56] Ibid s 19(b).

Co Ltd[57] interpreted the role of courts under the *IAA* as to facilitate the encouragement and enforcement of international arbitral awards in a manner that is proper, efficient and impartial.[58]

A key feature of Australia's judicial system is the emphasis placed on ensuring consistency across state and federal jurisdictions. Presently, state and federal courts have concurrent jurisdiction over matters arising from the *International Arbitration Act*. This facilitates the consistent enforcement of arbitral awards, the result of which is the creation of a uniform body of arbitration jurisprudence over time.[59]

While the Federal Court of Australia has jurisdiction over international arbitration matters, the Supreme Courts preside over both domestic and international arbitration disputes.[60] A court that has played a leading role in catalysing positive reform is the Supreme Court of New South Wales. The Court championed reform to the *Uniform Commercial Arbitration Acts,* and offers parties a specialist Commercial Arbitration List in its Equity Division. This specialist list assures parties that their commercial arbitration matters will be dealt with efficiently and fairly by arbitration-experienced Judges. The Victorian Supreme Court offers a similarly specialised practice through its Arbitration List in the Commercial Court.[61] Many judges are in support of these Arbitration Lists. Indeed, the Hon Justice Croft, the Judge responsible for the Victorian Supreme Court List, stated:

> One of the benefits of the Arbitration List is that a consistent body of arbitration related decisions will be developed by a single judge or a group of judges. This should provide parties with greater certainty when judicial intervention or support is required.[62]

---

[57] [2014] FCAFC 185.
[58] Ibid 197 [14].
[59] Warren, above n 18, 3.
[60] Ibid 5.
[61] Ibid.
[62] Justice Clyde Croft, 'Arbitration Reform in Australia and the Arbitration List (List G) in the Commercial Court - Supreme Court of Victoria' (Speech delivered at the Seminar of the Commercial Bar Association of the Victorian Bar, Victoria, 24 May 2010), 5.

Extra-curially, senior Australian judges have also noticed increasing judicial support for arbitration in general. The Hon James Spigelman AC wrote, in his time as Chief Justice of New South Wales, that:

> the longstanding tension between judges and arbitrators has disappeared. Most judges no longer consider arbitration as some kind of trade rival. Courts now generally exercise their statutory powers with respect to commercial arbitration by a light touch of supervisory jurisdiction directed to maintaining the integrity of the system.[63]

His successor, The Hon Thomas Bathurst AC, noted the same in his opening address to the *4th International Arbitration Conference* in 2016.[64] Similarly, in the Federal Court case of *Uganda Telecom v Hi-Tech Telecom*,[65] Foster J delivered this passage in support of international arbitration in Australia:

> The whole rationale of the [International Arbitration] Act, and thus the public policy of Australia, is to enforce such awards wherever possible in order to uphold contractual arrangements entered into in the course of international trade, in order to support certainty and finality in international dispute resolution.[66]

These comments demonstrate the judiciary's clear support for arbitration, positioning Australia as an ideal seat with a favourable climate for international arbitration.

- **Non-Interventionist Approach**

Critical to the success of arbitration is respect for the arbitral process, and a non-interventionist approach to enforcing arbitral awards. Drawing on Professor Moens' reading of *Model Law* provisions,

---

[63] James Spigelman AC, 'Foreword' in L Nottage and R Garnett (ed), *International Arbitration in Australia* (The Federation Press, 2010) viii.

[64] Tom Bathurst AC, 'Opening Address at the 4th International Arbitration Conference' (Speech delivered at the 4th International Arbitration Conference, Sydney, 22 November 2016) [27].

[65] *Uganda Telecom Ltd v Hi-Tech Telecom Pty Ltd* [2011] FCA 131.

[66] Ibid [126].

'judicial intervention should be exceptional'.[67] These principles lie at the heart of the *New York Convention* and the *Model Law*.[68] The ever-increasing body of case law that has developed since Australia's modern arbitration laws were reformed demonstrates that these are principles that the Australian courts understand and abide by.

A cornerstone principle of international arbitration is the need to preserve party autonomy and the freedom to contract. The judiciary in Australia understand this principle, exemplified by *Comandate Marine Corp v Pan Australia Shipping Pty Ltd*,[69] where the Federal Court of Australia found that arbitration clauses must be construed liberally, giving proper regard to the 'broad and flexible meaning'[70] of the agreement. Their Honours gave consideration to the significance of the parties' agreement to submit to arbitration[71] and the need to respect party autonomy.[72]

Several years later, this non-interventionist approach to enforcement was affirmed by the High Court of Australia in its landmark 2013 decision *TCL Air Conditioner v The Judges of the Federal Court of Australia*.[73] In this case, the Court cemented in law that the final and conclusive nature of an arbitral award is a consequence of the parties' agreement to have their dispute referred to arbitration.[74] A non-interventionist approach to the enforcement of awards was therefore warranted, and importantly, the Court confirmed that the grounds of appeal of awards are limited to those provided for in the *Model Law*. This application of the law is consistent with Parliament's legislative

---

[67] Moens and Trone, above n 6.
[68] Paul Friedland and Professor Loukas Mistelis, '2015 International Arbitration Survey: Improvements and Innovations in International Arbitration' (Research Report, White & Case and Queen Mary University of London, 6 October 2015) 6.
[69] (2006) 157 FCR 45.
[70] Ibid [165].
[71] Ibid [164].
[72] Ibid [165].
[73] *TCL Air Conditioner (Zhongshan) Co Ltd v The Judges of the Federal Court of Australia* [2013] HCA 5.
[74] *TCL Air Conditioner (Zhongshan) Co Ltd v The Judges of the Federal Court of Australia* [2013] HCA 5 [40], [111].

intention that courts should give weighting to the existence of an arbitration agreement, and subsequently, the parties' choice to refer their dispute to arbitration.[75]

Pro-Enforcement Bias

A feature which contributes to the appeal of arbitration is the finality of awards. Article III of the *New York Convention* asserts that member states must recognise foreign arbitral awards as binding, and enforce them accordingly. Consistent with international arbitration law, Australian law provides limited grounds for arbitral awards to be appealed.[76] In an Australian case considering an appeal for breaches of natural justice, the Full Court of the Federal Court set a high threshold for setting aside or denying enforcement of arbitral awards under the *Model Law*.[77] Not only is a breach of the rules of natural justice required, but it must also result in real unfairness or real practical injustice in the conduct of the dispute resolution process.[78]

This decision is one of many Australian decisions that confirms the limitations on the appeal and review of arbitral awards. An error in fact or law is insufficient grounds for a Court to set aside an award.[79] There is also no general discretion to refuse enforcement in Australia, and the public policy ground for refusing enforcement under the *IAA* is to be interpreted narrowly without residual discretion.[80] To quote Foster J of the Federal Court of Australia, the 'pro-enforcement bias'[81] of the *New York Convention* is mirrored in Australia's *IAA*. In *Traxys Europe SA v Balaji Coke*,[82] Foster J recognised the importance of restricting public policy grounds, warning:

---

[75] Rares, above n 28.
[76] Ibid 15.
[77] *TCL Air Conditioner (Zhongstan) Co Ltd v Castel Electornics Pty Ltd* [2014] FCAFC 83.
[78] Ibid.
[79] Moens and Trone, above n 6, 8.
[80] *Uganda Telecom Limited v Hi-Tech Telecom Pty Ltd* [2011] FCA 131.
[81] *Traxys Europe SA v Balaji Coke Industry Pvt Ltd (No 2)* [2012] FCA 276 [90] (Foster J).
[82] *Traxys Europe SA v Balaji Coke Industry Pvt Ltd (No 2)* [2012] FCA 276.

If the enforcement of awards is to be subjected to the vagaries of the entire domestic public policy of the enforcement jurisdiction, there is the potential to lose all of the benefits of certainty and efficiency that arbitration provides and which international traders seek.[83]

Aside from sitting as a Judge in the Federal Court of Australia, Foster J is the Arbitration Co-ordinating Judge in the New South Wales Registry of the Federal Court.[84] The Federal Court plays a large role in the enforcement of international arbitral awards. For instance, the Court encourages parties to include 'pre-litigation protocols' in contracts that direct parties to arbitration or other forms of alternative dispute resolution. On an institutional level, the Federal Court's inclusion of international arbitration as a National Practice Area within the National Court Framework is in itself indicative of the Australian judiciary's high regard for international arbitration.[85]

On a state level, the New South Wales Supreme Court goes so far as allowing specific parts of awards infected by a breach of natural justice to be severed from the balance of the award.[86] The *IAA*[87] does not restrict the circumstances in which an award can be severed. Therefore, Australian courts have powers to partially enforce an award, even where part of the award is void. This prevents the award from being declared void altogether if the void portion is separate and divisible.[88] This application of the Act was confirmed in the 2015 case *Aircraft Support Industries Pty Ltd v William Hare UAE LLC*.[89]

By narrowing the grounds on which arbitral awards can be appealed, Australian courts provide international commercial parties

---

[83] Ibid [90] (Foster J).
[84] Federal Court of Australia, *The Hon Lindsay Graeme FOSTER* (2017) FedCourt <http://www.fedcourt.gov.au>.
[85] Rares, above n 28.
[86] *William Hare UAE LLC v Aircraft Support Industries Pty Ltd* [2014] NSWSC 1403, affirmed on appeal in [2015] NSWCA 229.
[87] *International Arbitration Act 1974* (Cth) s 8(7A).
[88] *Aircraft Support Industries Pty Ltd v William Hare UAE LLC* [2015] NSWCA 229 [57] [60] (Bathurst CJ).
[89] Ibid.

with efficiency and finality, benefits which encourage many to turn to arbitration as a means of resolving disputes.[90]

- **Arbitration Agreements**

Australia's pro-arbitration stance can also be seen in the drafting of arbitration agreements. The *IAA*[91] requires a stay where parties have undertaken to submit to arbitration any or all differences that have arisen or that may arise between them in respect of a defined legal relationship, whether contractual or not.[92] The definition of an arbitration agreement under the *IAA*[93] accords with Article II of the New York Convention, thus ensuring that Australian courts are construing agreements in a manner consistent with international law. Further, the use of ambiguous terminology such as 'may' as opposed to 'must' or 'shall' in arbitration agreements are common sources of disputes over the validity of the agreement, not only in Australia, but the world over. However, Australian courts will enforce arbitration agreements containing the word 'may' where a proper interpretation of the clause demonstrates that the parties intended that arbitration be mandatory.[94] By broadly construing the language of arbitration agreements, Australian courts give effect to parties' intention to arbitrate, again demonstrating the pro-arbitration attitudes of the Australian legal system.

Arbitrability

Arbitrability, being whether a dispute is capable of settlement by arbitration,[95] is another area often subject to dispute. Admittedly it is an issue not fully resolved, with general jurisprudence being that

---

[90] *Traxys Europe SA v Balaji Coke Industry Pvt Ltd (No 2)* (2012) 201 FCR [63] [90].
[91] *International Arbitration Act 1974* (Cth).
[92] *International Arbitration Act 1974* (Cth) s 3(1) (definition of 'arbitration agreement').
[93] Ibid.
[94] *PMT Partners Pty Ltd (in liq) v Australian National Parks and Wildlife Service* (1995) 184 CLR 301.
[95] Doug Jones, *Commercial Arbitration in Australia* (Thomson Reuters, 2nd ed, 2013) 161.

some commercial matters warrant the kind of close public scrutiny that only courts can provide.[96] Broadly speaking, matters deemed non-arbitrable include anti-trust and competition disputes, securities transactions,[97] insolvency, taxation,[98] insurance,[99] workplace[100] and domestic building disputes.[101] However, the courts have refrained from taking a categorical approach. Instead, the question of arbitrability is first considered with reference to domestic law and public interest, and secondly, as a matter of construction.[102] The courts will give regard to the construction of the arbitration agreement, considering whether the scope of the agreement is broad enough to include such disputes. Notably, disputes arising from private contractual interaction between two commercial entities are more likely to be considered arbitrable.[103] The balance of case law suggests that courts are increasingly treating disputes as arbitrable, showing a liberal approach to arbitrability in Australia.[104]

Thus, overall, Australian courts have a strong history of promoting and supporting the autonomy of arbitral proceedings, limiting their involvement to those situations in which they have been specifically

---

[96] *Siemens Ltd v Origin Energy Uranquinty Power Pty Ltd* (2011) 279 ALR 759; Michael Mustill and Stewart Boyd, *Commercial Arbitration* (Butterworths, 2nd ed, 1989) 149.

[97] *Comandate Marine Corp v Pan Australia Shipping Pty Ltd* (2006) 157 FCR 45 [97]-[98] (Allsop J) (concerning an international commercial arbitration governed by the Model Law); *Nicola v Ideal Image Development Corporation Inc* (2009) 261 ALR 1.

[98] *AED Oil v Puffin FPSO Ltd* [2009] VSC 534 [45].

[99] *Insurance Contracts Act 1984* (Cth) s 43(1).

[100] *Metrocall Inc (Successor by Merger to Pronet In) v Electronic Tracking Systems Pty Ltd* (2000) 52 NSWLR 1.

[101] Some domestic building disputes are barred from arbitration by statute, see for example *Home Building Act 1989* (NSW) s 7C. See generally Jones, above n 95, 152-161.

[102] Warren, above n 18.

[103] See, *inter alia*, *Comandate Marine Corp v Pan Australia Shipping Pty Ltd* (2006) 157 FCR 45; *Nicola v Ideal Image Development Corporation Inc* (2009) 261 ALR 1; *ACD Tridon Inc v Tridon Australia Pty Ltd* [2002] NSWSC 896; *IBM Australia Ltd v National Distribution Services Ltd* (1991) 22 NSWLR 466; *Rinehart v Welker* [2012] NSWCA 95.

[104] Jones above n 95, 162.

requested to do so by parties or tribunals, and to the limit provided by the applicable laws.

Arbitral Institutions

Australia's appeal as a seat is enhanced by the existence of the premier international arbitration institution, the Australian Centre for International Commercial Arbitration (ACICA). The effectiveness of arbitral institutions can be measured by two primary factors: first, modern institutional rules that deal with complex contemporary arbitration issues, and second, world class facilities that ensure the smooth conduct of proceedings.

Arbitration Rules

ACICA plays a pivotal role in maintaining the high standard of arbitrations in Australia, enabled by its sophisticated Arbitration Rules. In 2005, ACICA introduced official Arbitration Rules designed to bring Australia in line with international best practice.[105] Notably, Professor Moens played a significant role in the release of the 2005 ACICA Rules, by providing official commentary on the Rules in collaboration with Dr Samuel Luttrell. The ACICA Rules were inspired by long-standing international arbitration laws and practices, combined with the rules of leading international arbitration institutions.[106] The 2005 Rules also included provisions specifically tailored to the needs of Australia as a seat.[107] For example, Article 17.3 authorised any member of the tribunal to make procedural decisions alone, providing the parties with greater efficiency by eliminating the delay arising from arbitrators needing to consult with one-another on procedural questions.[108] It is this flexibility that has allowed ACICA to effectively support and facilitate international arbitrations in Australia.

---

[105] Professor Doug Jones, 'The Australian Centre for International Commercial Arbitration (ACICA) and its Rules' (2009) *Dusseldorf International Arbitration School*, 1.
[106] Ibid.
[107] Ibid.
[108] Australian Centre for International Commercial Arbitration, *ACICA Rules* (At 1 August 2005) Article 17.

While the 2005 Rules have since been superseded by the 2016 Rules, many provisions from the 2005 Rules, including Article 17.3, are still reflected in the Rules today.

The ACICA Rules have undergone significant reform to ensure arbitration in Australia remains consistent with international best practice. Following the emergence of the amended UNCITRAL Arbitration Rules in 2010, ACICA released revised Arbitration Rules in 2011 and 2016 respectively. The main feature of the 2011 revision was incorporating emergency arbitrator provisions. The introduction of these provisions differentiated ACICA from many international institutions, as it was one of the first institutions to introduce such provisions.[109] These revisions gave parties greater flexibility, such as the ability to seek emergency interim measures of protection from an emergency arbitrator prior to the creation of the tribunal.[110] Emergency arbitration has, in recent years, become a topical point of discussion for the international arbitration community, and the ACICA Rules provide a solid emergency arbitration framework dealing with matters such as emergency arbitrator appointment, emergency interim measures, and the binding and enforceable effect of emergency decisions.[111] 2011 also witnessed the introduction of the Appointment of Arbitrator Rules, providing parties with greater ease when applying for arbitrator appointments for disputes seated in Australia.[112] These rules have also been superseded by the 2016 Rules, however many key features of the 2011 Rules, including the emergency arbitrator provisions, remain an important aspect of ACICA's current rules.

The current ACICA Arbitration Rules incorporating the Emergency Arbitrator Provisions came into force on 1 January 2016. One of the major objectives of the 2016 revisions has been to address increasingly vocal public concern over the time and cost of international arbitrations. Thus the ACICA Rules include an 'overriding objective' to conduct

---

[109] ACICA, *ACICA Rules 2011* (2011) <https://acica.org.au/acica-rules-2011/>
[110] ACICA, *ACICA Rules (Incorporating Clauses for Arbitration and Mediation)* (At 1 August 2011).
[111] Ibid Sch 1.
[112] Ibid.

proceedings with fairness and efficiency in proportion with the value and complexity of a given dispute.[113] The 2016 Rules place greater emphasis on party and tribunal autonomy.[114] Under these Rules, arbitrators are mandated to adopt certain case management practices, such as case management conferencing, and to encourage settlement by the parties.[115] ACICA has also sought to facilitate effective consolidation and joinder,[116] and to protect arbitrators in the discharge of their functions through a robust immunity.[117]

ACICA also provides a separate set of Expedited Arbitration Rules that operate on an opt-in basis to manage arbitration in a quick, cost effective and fair manner where time is of the essence. These were initially introduced in 2008 to maximise cost efficiency and minimise delay, giving consideration to the scope and complexity of the dispute itself.[118] In 2016, ACICA released revised Expedited Arbitration Rules, ensuring Australian standards remain consistent with international best practice. Further, ACICA's commitment to demonstrating leadership in the field can be seen with the publication of its Tribunal Secretary Panel and Guidelines, which came into effect on 1 January 2017. The object of the Guidelines is 'to encourage transparency with respect to the appointment, duties and remuneration of tribunal secretaries'.[119] Evidently, the conception of the ACICA Rules represents a landmark event in ACICA's history as a leading institution.

---

[113] ACICA, *ACICA Arbitration Rules Incorporating the Emergency Arbitrator Provisions* 2016 (At 1 January 2016) Article 3 ('*ACICA Rules*').
[114] Malcolm Holmes et al, 'The 2016 Rules of the Australian Centre for International Commercial Arbitration: Towards Further Cultural Reform' (2016) *Asian International Arbitration Journal* 211, 212.
[115] ACICA, *ACICA Rules 2016* (At 1 January 2016) Article 21.3.
[116] Ibid art 14.
[117] Ibid art 49.
[118] Ibid.
[119] ACICA, *ACICA Guideline on the Use of Tribunal Secretaries* (1 January 2017) Australian Centre for International Commercial Arbitration <https://acica.org.au/acicaguidelineontheuseoftribunalsecretaries/>.

- **Features and Facilities**

The development of excellent infrastructure to support international arbitration has set Australia apart as a regional seat. In Australia, international firms have a clear right to practice domestic litigation, which cannot be said for other seats, such as Singapore or Hong Kong. Australia is also home to institutions which offer high-quality administrative services including custom-designed ADR venues, world-class technology, complimentary refreshments, security access and translation services.[120] In addition to ACICA, Australia has numerous arbitration institutions and centres, including the Chartered Institute of Arbitrators (CIArb), the Resolution Institute, Australian Maritime and Transport Arbitration Commission (AMTAC), Australian International Disputes Centre (AIDC) and the Australian Disputes Centre (ADC).[121]

The Australian Disputes Centre, established in 2010, is the centrepiece of Sydney's local arbitration framework and provides world class dispute resolution services. This custom designed venue for arbitration is located in the heart of Sydney's central business district, in close proximity to counsel chambers, most of Australia's largest (and in many cases international) law firms, state and federal government offices, and first class accommodation. It offers all the features of the best dispute resolution centres, including conference rooms, breakout rooms, and excellent interpretation services and can be customised to the needs of the arbitration to maximise cost effectiveness for the parties. It should be noted that ACICA has a close relationship with ADC, allowing the two organisations to promote arbitration together whilst offering an extensive range of commercial dispute resolution services.[122] The shared objective of these organisations, that being to further arbitration within Australia, has resulted in high-quality service and facilities for use by commercial parties.

---

[120] ACICA, *Australian Disputes Centre International* <https://acica.org.au/australian-disputes-centre/>.
[121] Doug Jones and Bjorn Gehle, 'Australian Centre for International Commercial Arbitration (ACICA) (2010) *World Arbitration Reporter.*
[122] Ibid.

A cornerstone feature of arbitration institutions such as ACICA is their role in implementing initiatives designed to promote and improve arbitration practices in Australia. A prime example of this is ACICA's collaboration with the judiciary to form the ACICA Judicial Liaison Committee. The committee, currently chaired by Chief Justice of the Federal Court James Allsop, was established in 2010 with the objective of creating consistency in arbitration-related court proceedings.[123] In terms of members, the committee is comprised of ACICA representatives and judges from the Federal and Supreme Courts of Australia. Through cooperation with the judiciary and other arbitral organisations, ACICA has played an integral role in the continuing success of international arbitration in Australia.

The facilities of Australian arbitral institutions are enhanced by the use of leading technology. In August 2016, ACICA published their 'Draft Procedural Order for the Use of Online Dispute Resolution Technologies,' which provides a framework for using new technologies for arbitration in accordance with the ACICA rules.[124] In the introduction to the Draft Procedural Order, ACICA outlines video conferencing and WebEx Meeting Centre Online Product as examples of tools that can assist in cross-border arbitration, particularly during preliminary conferences.[125] Similarly, in Australian domestic courts, the Federal Court of Australia has provided for the use of electronic filing, hearings and virtual courtrooms for case management.[126] The Victorian Supreme Court has also adopted a Practice Note favouring the use of predictive coding to streamline the process of

---

[123] ACICA, *Judicial Liaison Committee* (2018) Australian Centre for International Commercial Arbitration <https://acica.org.au/judicial-liaison-committee/>

[124] ACICA, *Draft Procedural Order for the Use of Online Dispute Resolution Technologies in ACICA Rules Arbitrations* (2016) ACICA <https://acica.org.au/wp-content/uploads/2016/08>

[125] Ibid.

[126] Federal Court of Australia, *General Practice Note – Technology and the Court*, 25 October 2016. See also Damian Sturzaker, 'Technical Innovations in International Arbitration – Why Australia needs to move to Arbitration 2.0' (2014) *CIArb* <https://www.ciarb.net.au/resources/international-arbitration/>

discovery of large volumes of electronically stored information.[127] The appearance of witnesses in arbitration by video-conference is also now commonplace.[128] With the growing acceptance of technology by the courts and ACICA, it is likely that the technology capabilities of Australia will continue at the leading edge of international best practice.

Australian arbitration institutions have also developed a focus on diversity in arbitration, which is increasingly important today.[129] In terms of gender diversity, ACICA has demonstrated real leadership. Between 2011 and 2016 a quarter of ACICA's appointments have been female arbitrators,[130] and in 2016 its president signed the Equal Representation in Arbitration Pledge committing to encouraging greater female representation and diversity in arbitration.[131]

Evidently, arbitration institutions have played a large role in promoting, regulating and enabling international arbitration in Australia. The continual development of arbitration rules and facilities has positioned Australia as a leading arbitral seat in the Asia-Pacific region.

- **Conclusion**

Australia's legal framework supporting international arbitration is world-leading, characterised by a willingness to adapt to meet, and frequently, to lead international best practice.

Australia's appeal as a seat is well summarised by the Hon Marilyn Warren AC's comment that:

---

[127] Supreme Court of Victoria, *Practice Note General No 5 – Technology in Civil Litigation Practice Note*, 30 January 2017, 8.9.

[128] Damian Sturzaker, 'Technical Innovations in International Arbitration - Why Australia needs to move to Arbitration 2.0' Chartered Institute of Arbitrators (online) 2014, <https://www.ciarb.net.au/resources/international-arbitration/>

[129] Berwein Leighton Paisner, 'International Arbitration Survey: Diversity on Arbitral Tribunals: Are We Getting There' (Research Report, Berwein Leighton Paisner, 10 January 2017) 7.

[130] Lara Bullock, 'ACICA aims for equality in arbitration', *Lawyers Weekly* (online) 27 June 2016, <https://www.lawyersweekly.com.au/news/>

[131] ACICA, *Media Release Equal Representation in Arbitration Pledge* (20 June 2016) ACICA <https://acica.org.au/wp-content/uploads/>

> [o]ur Australian brand of arbitration is one that looks to reduce transaction costs, ensure certainty and efficiency [for] parties, and one that provides a neutral and safe seat to dispute resolution.[132]

The combination of a pro-arbitration legislature, an independent and supportive judiciary, and effective arbitral institutions and centres makes Australia an ideal option for both domestic and international arbitration. Having a stable political landscape and being cost effective, culturally sensitive, and proximate to many of the Asia Pacific's economic hubs supports the notion that the tyranny of distance no longer plagues Australia in the commercial context. Rather, Australia is in a prime position to lead international arbitration in the Asia Pacific given all of these qualities. Thus, the tyranny of distance now appears to be outmatched by the real capabilities provided by Australian arbitration, as commercial parties look to Australia as a seat of arbitration, safe in the knowledge of its numerous practical and legal benefits.

---

[132] Warren, above n 18, 17.

13

THE JOYS AND CHALLENGES OF (RE-)EDUCATING AUSTRALIAN JURISTS IN INTERNATIONAL COMMERCIAL ARBITRATION[1]

Luke Nottage[2] *and Diana Hu*[3]

- **Introduction**

The expertise of Professor Gabriel Moens lies mainly in business law, but extends to constitutional law and jurisprudence, with a strong emphasis on international and comparative dimensions.[4] He has also had a long academic and professional engagement with the vibrant

---

[1] This chapter draws on support from an Australian Research Council Discovery Project grant over 2014-7 (DP1401025226). We thank Kirsten Gan for excellent research and assistance. Others are thanked below, but we retain sole responsibility for any misconceptions or errors. A version of sections of this chapter was published the Resolution Institute journal, (December 2016) *The Arbitrator & Mediator* 91-104, with a manuscript version (adding an online Appendix of the analysed judgments) available at <https://ssrn.com/abstract=2862256>.

[2] Professor of Comparative and Transnational Business Law, University of Sydney; ACICA Special Associate.

[3] In-house Counsel, Regional Mergers and Acquisitions, AIG Asia Pacific, Sydney. The views of the authors in this chapter do not necessarily reflect the views of AIG Asia Pacific.

[4] He is one of very few Australia-based titular (full) members elected to the venerable International Academy of Comparative Law (see Titular Members (2015) <http://iuscomparatum.info/members/titular-members/>); another is the recently appointed Chief Justice of Australia, Susan Kiefel. Most are associate members, including Nottage who serves with Justice James Douglas and Professor Cheryl Saunders on a de facto national committee for Australia. Prof Moens also organised in 2002, at the University of Queensland, the large four-yearly Congress of the Academy. He also is the Editor-in-Chief of the annual *International Trade and Business Law Review* (now published by LexisNexis Butterworths), for which Nottage joined the Editorial Board from 2014.

world of international commercial arbitration, before it expanded dramatically throughout much of the Asian region particularly over the last 10-15 years.[5] He has long been one of only two full-time professors on the Board of the Australian Centre of International Commercial Arbitration (ACICA), serving also as an honorary Deputy Secretary-General. As such, Prof Moens provided input into the ACICA Arbitration Rules, developed first in 2005 and with significant revisions in 2016,[6] co-authoring an important commentary on the original Rules with a former doctoral student (and now leading mid-career international arbitration counsel).[7] Through its Board, ACICA has also provided submissions on arbitration law reforms and as *amicus curiae* in a (fortunately unsuccessful) constitutional challenge to the regime for enforcing international arbitration awards with the seat in Australia.[8] In addition, Prof Moens has edited a revamped and twice-yearly *ACICA Review*, as well as organising the first-ever ACICA conference in Perth that resulted (unlike other ACICA annual conferences) in a major edited book.[9]

---

[5] See generally Luke Nottage, 'A Weather Map for International Arbitration: Mainly Sunny, Some Cloud, Possible Thunderstorms' (2015) 26 *American Review of International Arbitration* 495.

[6] See, by some then members of the ACICA's drafting committee, Simon Greenberg, Luke Nottage and Romesh Weeramantry, 'The 2005 Rules of the Australian Centre for International Commercial Arbitration – Revisited' in Luke Nottage and Richard Garnett (eds), *International Arbitration in Australia* (Federation Press, 2010) 79; Malcolm Holmes, Luke Nottage and Robert Tang, 'The 2016 Rules of the Australian Centre for International Commercial Arbitration: Towards Further "Cultural Reform"' (2016) 12 *Asian International Arbitration Journal* 211-34, also at <http://ssrn.com/abstract=2786839>.

[7] Samuel Ross Luttrell and Gabriël Adelin Moens, *Commentary on the Arbitration Rules of the Australian Centre for International Commercial Arbitration* (2009) <https://acica.org.au/wp-content/uploads/Rules/Commentary/Commentary-on-the-Arbitration-Rules-of-ACICA-G-Moens-S-Luttrell.pdf>.

[8] *TCL Air Conditioner (Zhongshan) Co Ltd (TCL) v The Judges of the Federal Court of Australia* (2013) 251 CLR 533.

[9] Prof Moens also kindly involved Nottage in that conference and book project: Luke Nottage and Simon Butt, 'Recent International Commercial Arbitration and Investor-State Arbitration Developments Impacting on Australia's Investments in the Resources Sector' in Philip Evans and Gabriel Moens (eds), *Arbitration and Dispute Resolution in the Resources Sector: An Australian Perspective* (Springer, 2015) 153-79.

Prof Moens has also been a dedicated instructor in international commercial arbitration for many institutions. Sometimes these have been part of broader courses such as International Business Law, taught since 2015 for the LLM program of the University of Sydney (where he had also completed a PhD in 1982[10]). He is perhaps best known for his early and consistent coaching and support for the Vis Moot competition, first organised by Prof Eric Bergsten and Pace University from 1994 in Vienna. As shown by Figure 1.1 below,[11] this competition to hone students' skills in international commercial law and arbitration has grown enormously since.

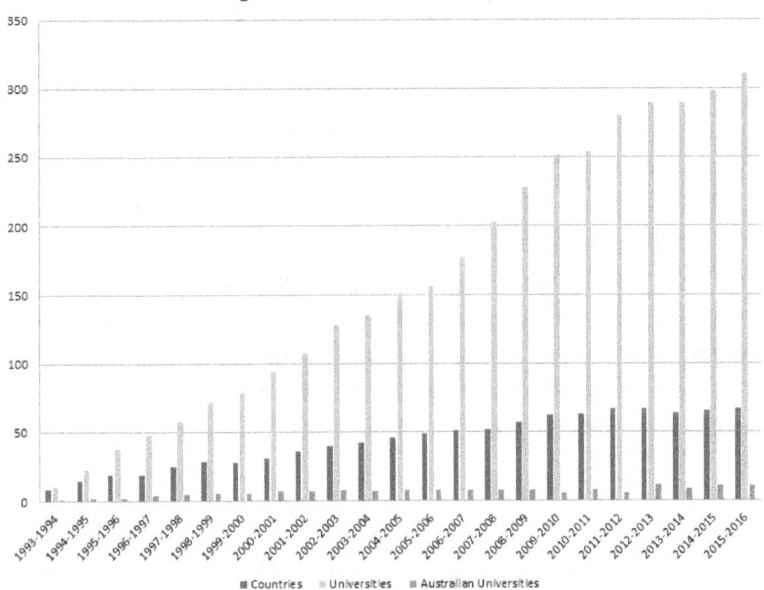

Figure 1-1: Vis Moot Participation

The strong participation of Australian universities was already evident when one of the present authors first participated in the Vis Moot, first as a mock arbitrator in 1999 and the following year as co-

---

[10] Gabriel Moens, *The Quality of Equality: A Study of School Integration and Preferential Admission Programs in the United States* (PhD Thesis, The University of Sydney, 1982).

[11] Source: *Previous Moots*, The Annual Willem C. Vis International Commercial Arbitration Moot <http://www.cisg.law.pace.edu/cisg/moot/mootlist.html>.

coach of a team from Kyushu University in Japan.[12] This chapter's Appendix indicates that Deakin University was one of just 11 university teams (from nine countries) to compete in 1994, joined from the following year by the University of Queensland (where Prof Moens was then teaching). By 1999, four more Australian universities were competing as well, albeit out of total of 72 teams from 29 countries. In recent years up to a dozen Australian universities have competed, including Murdoch University (where Prof Moens also taught), out of around now 300 teams from over 60 countries.

Although the proportionate impact of teams from Australian universities has therefore diminished on quantitative basis, the qualitative impact remains remarkably large. This chapter's Appendix also shows how Australian students continue to punch above their weight in terms of achieving awards, both as teams and for individual oralists. Apart from the quality of the students themselves, a significant factor has undoubtedly been the persistent efforts of Vis Moot team coaches such as Prof Moens, contributing notably to the University of Queensland team winning the competition in 2000 and coming second in 1997.[13] His impact can also be discerned in his coaching of the winning City University of Hong Kong team in 2012 for the ninth Vis (East) Moot, inaugurated in Hong Kong as a parallel competition to attract and cater for interest in the Asian region, as well as in his coaching of its winning team in the (still much larger) Vis Moot competition held in Vienna in 2013.

Undoubtedly, these years of training up Australian law students

---

[12] Luke Nottage, 'Educating Transnational Commercial Lawyers for the 21st Century: Towards the Vis Arbitration Moot in 2000 (Part Two)' (1999) 66/3 *Hosei Kenkyu* [Kyushu University] F1-32 (also available at <http://catalog.lib.kyushu-u.ac.jp/handle/2324/2178/KJ00000745045-00001.pdf>).

[13] Deakin University and later Monash University teams have also stood out, likely due to the efforts of Prof Jeff Waincymer. (One Deakin graduate, Prof Christopher Kee, is also currently a co-director of the Vis Moot and is the author of *The Art of Argument: A Guide to Mooting* (Cambridge University Press, 2007).) The achievements of the students competing since 2009 from the University of Sydney Law School (different from the Law Extension Committee students) have occurred under the dedicated coaching of Prof Chester Brown.

in the intricacies of international commercial arbitration law and practice has seen them expand their influence on legal practice not only in the traditional core venues in Europe and then the United States, but also throughout the newer arbitral venues in Asia. Somewhat perversely, however, some of this training – especially through proliferating arbitration moot competitions – may have contributed to Australian law graduates becoming overly enthusiastic as lawyers pursuing arbitration-related challenges through Australian courts. This chapter tests this possibility by exploring some rather disappointing data on litigation patterns involving the *International Arbitration Act (Cth)* 1974 (IAA, as amended notably in 1989 and 2010),[14] especially over the last decade. We note a rather counter-intuitive increase in IAA-related judgments since the 2010 amendments, quite surprising proportions of cases being filed in federal compared to other courts, and no significant improvements in case disposition times and appeals even in the Federal Court. Accordingly, we recommend further reform of Australia's regime for international arbitration, as well as highlighting some broader challenges for those involved in educating the new generation of Australian jurists in this evolving field.

- **IAA-related Judgments: More or Less?**

In March 2013, we had reviewed all 109 publically available IAA-related judgments that had been handed down since the IAA was amended in 1989, finding the following pattern:[15]

---

[14] See generally Richard Garnett and Luke Nottage, 'The 2010 Amendments to the International Arbitration Act: A New Dawn for Australia?' (2011) 7(1) *Asian International Arbitration Journal* 29 and Richard Garnett, 'Australia's International and Domestic Arbitration Framework' in Philip Evans and Gabriel Moens (eds), *Arbitration and Dispute Resolution in the Resources Sector: An Australian Perspective* (Springer, 2015) 7.

[15] Adapted from Albert Monichino, Luke Nottage and Diana Hu, 'International Arbitration in Australia: Selected Case Notes and Trends' (2012) 19 *Australian Journal of International Law* 181, 185.

Figure 1: Total IAA cases (1989 – 2012)

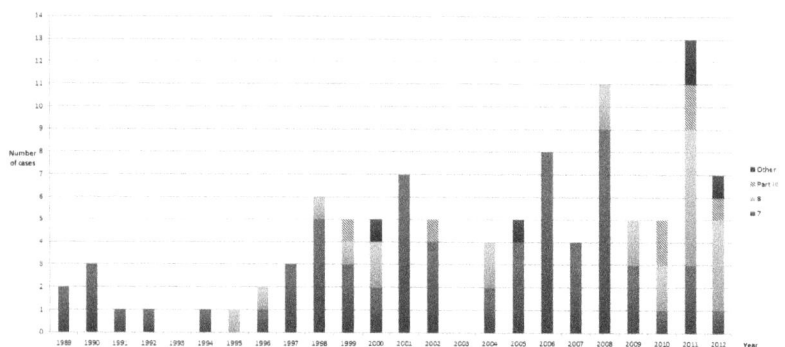

Since 2013, a further 80 judgments have been rendered as follows, dealing with various parts of the IAA (as discussed further particularly in the section starting on page 291):[16]

Figure 2: Total IAA cases (2013 – August 2016)

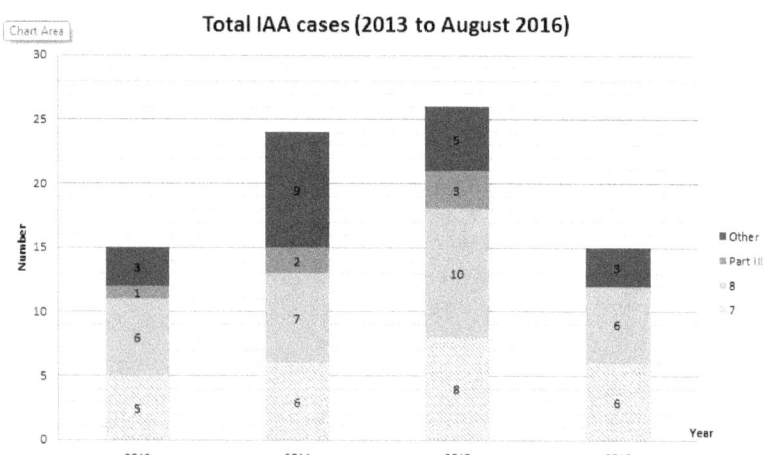

---

[16] The judgments were sourced as at 11 August 2016 from the Westlaw, LexisNexis and Austlii databases by conducting a search of all cases which applied, considered or referenced the IAA. Those indicated as 'Other' made passing reference to the IAA. The complete list of 2013-16 judgments are contained in the online Appendix.

One noteworthy feature is the continued rise in judgments handed down each year, especially in 2014 and 2015. Figure 3 below presents a clearer comparison of the number of notable increase in cases since 2013:

Figure 3: Total IAA cases (2010 – August 2016)

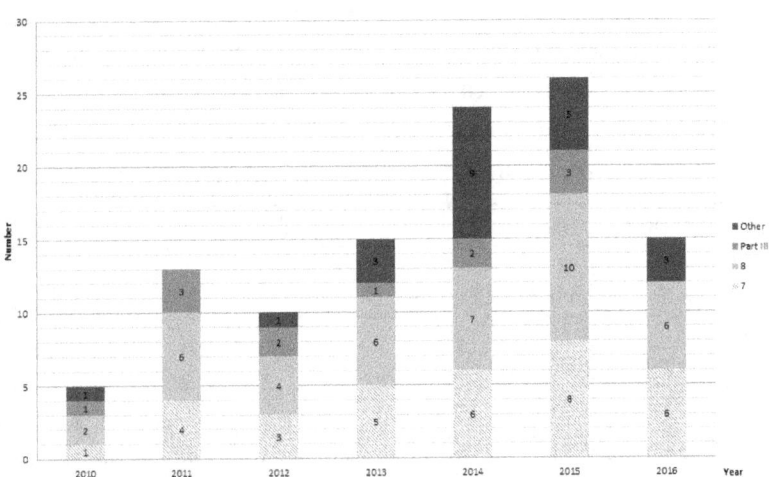

This is unexpected, as one might have expected the 2010 amendments to the IAA to have improved understanding about, and hence the efficiency associated with, international arbitration related matters. One possible explanation is a type of 'availability bias'.[17] Perversely, parties to arbitration agreement and awards – or, more importantly, their legal advisors – may have become more aware of the IAA, including its (longstanding) exceptions to *refusing* enforcement, and therefore more prone to invoking the latter. This may have occurred despite those exceptions being originally designed to be narrowly applied, and although the 2010 amendments indeed aimed to further constrain their applicability in order to promote the effectiveness of

---

[17] Cf generally Luke Nottage, 'Investor-State Arbitration Policy and Practice after Philip Morris Asia v Australia' in Leon Trakman and Nicola Ranieri (eds), *Regionalism in International Investment Law* (Oxford University Press, 2013) 452.

international arbitration.[18] A rough analogy here might be drawn with building a new highway: although designed to reduce congestion, it may lead to more people thinking to travel by car, hence leading to more cars on the road.

An alternative explanation for more reported judgments, which is more optimistic and perhaps more plausible, is that there are simply more underlying disputes and consequently arbitrations since the beginning of the 2010s. After all, arbitral institutions abroad have continued to record increases in case filings in recent years, as indicated by the chart below:

Table 1: Arbitration Case Filings World-Wide (2012 – 2015)[19]

Arbitration Institution:	2012	2013	2014	2015
ICC (International Chamber of Commerce)	759	767	791	801
DIS (German Institution of Arbitration)	121	121	132	134
SCC (Stockholm Chamber of Commerce)	177	203	183	181
VIAC (Vienna International Arbitration Center)	70	56	56	40
SCAI (Swiss Chamber's Arbitration Institution)	92	68	105	100
LCIA (London Court of International Arbitration)	277	301	296	326

---

[18] Garnett and Nottage, above n 14. See eg IAA s 39(2), which requires Australian courts to consider the legislation's objectives set out in s 2D and, pursuant to s 39(2), that 'arbitration is an efficient, impartial, enforceable and timely method by which to resolve commercial dispute' and that 'awards are intended to provide certainty and finality'.

[19] Adapted from Markus Altenkirch and Jan Frohloff, 'Global Arbitration Cases Still Rise –Arbitral Institutions' Caseload Statistics for 2015' (25 August 2016) *Global Arbitration News* <http://globalarbitrationnews.com/global-arbitration-cases-still-rise-arbitral-institutions-caseload-statistics-2015>. We omit their data for International Centre for Settlement of Investment Disputes (ICSID) cases, and recalculate CIETAC cases to include only 'foreign-related' (including international) arbitration case filings, based on <http://www.cietac.org/index.php?m=Page&a=index&id=40&l=en>. We thank Professor Chris Drahozal for pointing us to this article.

ICDR (International Centre for Dispute Resolution)	996	1165	1052	1063
SIAC (Singapore International Arbitration Centre)	235	259	222	271
CIETAC (China International Economic and Trade Arbitration Commission)	331	375	387	437
HKIAC (Hong Kong International Arbitration Centre)	293	260	252	271

This trend may be underpinned by worsening economic conditions in many parts of the world in recent years; earlier, there had also been an uptick in institutional arbitration case filings recorded during and shortly after the Global Financial Crisis (GFC) in 2008.[20] For Australia, there were certainly more *judgments* rendered in 2008; and the recent subsequent increases may be associated with the end of the mining boom in 2011.[21] Unfortunately there is limited data about international arbitrations involving Australian parties, which are most likely to end up in Australian courts.[22] However, the number of Australia-related cases filed in the Singapore International Arbitration Centre grew from just 5 in 2011 to 32 in 2015.[23]

---

[20] Luke Nottage and Richard Garnett, 'Introduction' in Luke Nottage and Richard Garnett (eds), *International Arbitration in Australia* (Federation Press, 2010) 1, 10 (Figure 1). Although economic slowdowns may result in fewer claims because parties cannot afford to pursue them, generally they instead trigger more filings due to more breaches of contract and pressures to recoup losses. See generally eg Luke Nottage and Christian Wollschlaeger, 'What Do Courts Do?' (October 1996) *New Zealand Law Journal* 369 (comparing per capita civil claim filings in New Zealand and Japan, inversely correlated with the business cycle).

[21] Several judgments cited in this chapter involve resource companies or contracts, but the slowdown in Australia's resource sector also impacts on the wider economy, which in turn may lead to more disputes, arbitrations and related court proceedings.

[22] However, occasionally some IAA matters may involve only non-Australian parties and only assets in Australia, such as *ENRC Marketing AG v OJSC Magnitogorsk Metallurgical Kombinat* (2011) 285 ALR 444 (where both parties were non-Australian and the seat was abroad).

[23] See SIAC Annual Reports, available at <http://www.siac.org.sg/75-resources/arti-

Furthermore, although the Australian Centre for International Commercial Arbitration (ACICA) is rare among arbitral institutions in not releasing regular information on its case filings, in 2013 the Secretary-General stated that since the 2010 amendments it had dealt with 30 new cases. In May 2015 it was further estimated that there had been around 40 cases filed since 2010.[24] This means an average of around 8 cases filed each year with ACICA, presumably all or mostly with the seat in Australia. These figures would mark a significant increase compared to the 1 to 4 cases received annually by ACICA over 1998-2009.[25] Figure 2 also shows that in 2015 there was a record number of IAA-related judgments involving arbitrations under Part III, generally applicable only to arbitrations with the seat in Australia.[26] However, there were still only three of these cases, and none involved ACICA.[27] This data suggests that Australia remains a comparatively unpopular seat for international commercial arbitration, although some momentum may be building in recent years.

---

cles-publication/annual-report>. (In 2015, for example, this was similar to the numbers of cases involving parties from South Korea or the US, although in 46 of SIAC's 271 cases the parties came from China and in 91 they came from India.) We are grateful to Natalia Bilan Chen for bringing this development to our attention.

[24] Cited in Luke Nottage, 'International Commercial Arbitration in Australia: What's New and What's Next?' in Nye Perram (ed), *International Commercial Law and Arbitration* (Ross Parsons Centre of Commercial, Corporate and Taxation Law, 2014), also available at <http://ssrn.com/abstract=2393232>, 293. A shorter version of this chapter, initially presented at a Federal Court conference, was also published in 30(5) *Journal of International Arbitration* 465.

[25] Nottage and Garnett, above n 20, 32 (Appendix I).

[26] For an exception, see *ENRC Marketing AG v OJSC Magnitogorsk Metallurgical Kombinat* (2011) 285 ALR 444 (where a German party obtained an order freezing the Russian party's assets in Australia pursuant to Art 17J of the UNCITRAL Model Law as revised in 2006, given force of law by s 16).

[27] *Emerald Grain Australia Pty Ltd v Agrocorp International Pte Ltd* (2014) 314 ALR 299 (arbitration with a Singaporean company under Grain Trade Australia Dispute Resolution Rules), *Hebei Jikai Industrial Group Co Ltd v Martin* (2015) 324 ALR 268 (ad hoc arbitration related to a settlement agreement from an intra-corporate dispute), *Sino Dragon Ltd v Noble Resources International Pte Ltd* [2015] FCA 1028 (UNCITRAL Rules arbitration of an iron ore sales disputes).

- **Applications to Enforce Arbitration Awards or Agreements in Federal or Other Courts**

A second noteworthy feature from Figure 2 above is that there has been a significant increase in the number (and the proportion) of s 8 applications to enforce foreign arbitration awards. Applications for s 7 stays of Australian court proceedings, asserting a valid agreement for arbitration abroad, have also increased but only to the level reported around 2008 (before judgments related to s 7 dropped significantly over 2009-12). This shift may also be driven by the more recent economic slowdown in Australia: award debtors are increasingly resisting enforcement 'at the pointy end', after being subject to unfavourable foreign awards.

In addition, it is interesting to break down the proportions of such s 8 applications, in terms of whether award creditors seek enforcement via the Federal Court or the relevant State or Territory Court:[28]

Table 2: Proportion of IAA s 8 Cases in Australian Federal Courts (2007 to August 2016)

Year	Total no. of cases	No. of s 8 cases	No. of s 8 cases in FCA (and FFCA)	% of s 8 cases in FCA (and FFCA)
2016	15	6	2	33%
2015	26	10	4	40%
2014	24	7	6	86%
2013	15	6	5	83%
2012	10	4	4	100%
2011	13	6	3	50%
2010	5	2	0	0%

---

[28] Either option is permitted, under IAA s 8(2) and s 8(3).

2009	5	2	1	50%
2008	11	2	0	0%
2007	4	0	0	0%
2013-16	80	29	17	59%
2009-12	33	14	8	57%

One might have expected the legal advisors of award creditors to prefer the Federal Court, given its consistently more 'pro-arbitration'[29] or 'arbitration-friendly'[30] rulings in recent years.[31] The average propor-

---

[29] We essentially adopt the definition proposed by Albert Monichino, 'The Future of International Arbitration in Australia' (2015) 5(1) *Victoria University Law and Justice Journal* 1 Part III.D, focusing not simply on whether an international arbitration award or agreement is enforced, but rather whether decisions are reached in accordance with internationally-accepted arbitration norms, case law and authoritative commentary. (Cf eg Dylan McKimmie and Courtney Furner, 'Federal Court of Australia: A Pro-Enforcement Judiciary' (2014) 159 *Australian Construction Law Newsletter* 34, also at <http://acln.com.au/files/ACLN_2014_159_sampleissue.pdf>.) However, we suggest that a pro-arbitration regime is also one where lawyers and courts deal with arbitration-related disputes in a time- and cost-efficient manner, hopefully because they are well-informed by such common understandings. For that reason, for example, we are skeptical about Monichino's view that the failed constitutional challenge to the IAA's UNCITRAL Model Law enforcement regime in *TCL Air Conditioner (Zhongshan) Co Ltd (TCL) v The Judges of the Federal Court of Australia* (2013) 251 CLR 533, and other proceedings related to that matter, exemplify a more pro-arbitration approach in Australia. By adding large costs and delays to the award enforcement proceedings (outlined also in Nottage 2013, above n 24), we see especially the constitutional challenge decision as neutral, at best.

[30] See James Allsop and Clyde Croft, 'The Role of the Courts in Australia's Arbitration Regime' (2015) *Commercial CPD Seminar Series, Melbourne* <http://www.austlii.edu.au/au/journals/FedJSchol/2015/25.html>.

[31] This tendency arguably became apparent from *Comandate Marine Corp v Pan Australia Shipping Pty Ltd* (2006) 157 FCR 45, consolidated eg through *Uganda Telecom Ltd v Hi-Tech Telecom Pty Ltd (No 2)* (2011) 277 ALR 441, *Traxys Europe SA v Balaji Coke Industry Pvt Ltd (No 2)* (2012) 201 FCR 535 (*Traxys No 2*), *Casaceli v Natuzzi SpA* (2012) 292 ALR 143, *Gujarat NRE Coke Ltd v Coeclerici Asia (Pte) Ltd* (2013) 304 ALR 468, *Dampskibsselskabet Nordon A/S v Gladstone Civil Pty Ltd* (2013) 216 FCR 1 469 (*DKN*) and *Armada (Singapore) Pte Ltd (under Judicial Management) v*

tion of cases heard in the Federal Court for 2013-16 compared to that for 2009-2012 do not show much difference, but the former may rise if judgments rendered from September to December this year pick up and are mostly filed in the Federal Court. There is also already a larger proportion if we calculate the average instead from 2012 (64%). In any event, the sample size of foreign award enforcement applications is small, and further diminished when split between Federal Court applications and otherwise, so even one or two cases filed instead in State or Territory courts can make a significant difference to the average proportions. Still, those are worth monitoring. If the proportion of applications to the Federal Court continues to drop, yet the Court is considered to be maintaining its pro-arbitration stance, it could be an indicator that the State and Territory courts are also starting to adopt a similar approach.[32] The latter shift may be indicated in Victoria after the Court of Appeal's 2011 judgment in *Altain Khuder*,[33] for example, or in Western Australia.[34]

Gujarat NRE Coke Ltd (2014) 318 ALR 35 (*Armada*): see James Morrison and Luke Nottage, 'Country Report on Australia For: International Commercial Arbitration – an Asia-Pacific Perspective' (2014) 14/95 *Sydney Law School Research Paper* <http://ssrn.com/abstract=2514124> 3 October 2016, respectively at 6, 18, 32, 2, 19 and 64, and generally Monichino et al, above n 15. See also eg the three judgments in 2015, cited above n 27. Through the 1990s, by contrast, the Federal Court had displayed a less favourable approach towards international arbitration (say compared to New South Wales courts), albeit in an era when Australian courts generally were not so pro-arbitration: see generally eg Richard Garnett, 'The Current Status of International Arbitration Agreements in Australia' (1999) 15 *Journal of Contract Law* 29.

[32] A more pessimistic assessment might be that legal advisors (including perhaps those abroad) are not adequately factoring in this comparison when deciding whether award creditors should file in the Federal Court or otherwise.

[33] *IMC Aviation Solutions Pty Ltd v Altain Khuder LLC* (2011) 38 VR 303 (*Altain Khuder*). For different views on who should bear the burden of establishing whether the award debtor was party to the arbitration agreement under s 8 applications, see Monichino et al, above n 15, and the first-instance decision in *DKN* (2013) 216 FCR 1 469. Compare more recently eg *Esposito Holdings Pty Ltd v UDP Holdings Pty Ltd* [2015] VSC 183, *Sauber Motorsport AG v Giedo van der Garde BV & Ors* (2015) 317 ALR 786, and generally Allsop and Croft, above n 30.

[34] See eg *KNM Process Systems SDN BHD v Mission Newenergy Ltd* [2014] WASC 437 (*KNM*, where Martin CJ awarded indemnity costs against the party unsuccessfully resisting a stay application) and *Cape Lambert Resources Ltd v MCC Australia Sanjin Mining Pty Ltd* (2013) 298 ALR 666 (adopting a broad approach to interpret-

Relatedly, it is interesting to examine patterns in s 7 stay applications, where one party seeks a stay of proceedings initiated in Australian courts, by invoking an agreement to take the dispute to arbitration with the seat overseas:

Table 3: Proportion of IAA s 7 Cases outside Federal Courts (2007 to August 2016)

Year	Total no. of cases	No. of s 7 cases	No. of s 7 cases NOT in FCA (or FFCA)	% of s 7 cases NOT in FCA (or FFCA)
2016	15	6	3	50%
2015	26	8	6	75%
2014	24	6	6	100%
2013	15	5	5	100%
2012	10	3	2	67%
2011	13	4	2	50%
2010	5	1	1	100%
2009	5	3	2	67%
2008	11	9	5	56%
2007	4	4	2	50%
2013-16	80	25	20	80%
2009-12	33	11	7	64%

ing dispute resolution clauses). But see *Samsung C&T Corporation v Duro Felbuera Australia Pty Ltd* [2016] WASC 193 (staying proceedings under IAA s 7, albeit not setting a consistent prima facie standard for reviewing the validity and scope of an alleged arbitration agreement, as do Singaporean courts). For a critique, see Albert Monichino, 'Arbitration Downunder - Two Steps Forward, One Step Back' (2016) 167 *Australian Construction Law Newsletter* 28.

The proportion of s 7 cases filed in the State and Territory Courts is higher, and indeed considerably so since 2013. It may be that legal advisors for the party adverse to arbitration file in those courts because they are aware of the more pro-arbitration stance of the Federal Court. If so, and indeed the State and Territory Courts start to become (or at least are perceived to be) more pro-arbitration as well, we can expect to see a declining proportion as more lawsuits and then s 7 stay applications are filed also in the Federal Court.

- **Case Disposition Times for IAA-related Judgments**

To assist in making such assessments of the different courts, and the extent to which they support and promote international arbitration, it is also worth considering their case disposition times for IAA-related cases. Those also provide a measure of whether the 2010 amendments are indeed proving to be generally effective: if disposition times decrease, it suggests better understanding of the underlying legal principles on the part of both courts and legal advisors.[35] For the latter reason, our study in 2013 compared the case disposition times in the Federal Court (for which data was readily accessible) in the three years before and after the IAA amendments came into force on 7 July 2010. At that stage, we found little change.[36]

Comparing now its disposition times for the subsequent 3 years,[37] we find instead this pattern:

---

[35] Of course, quicker disposition times in this field also needs to be assessed relative to civil litigation generally in the relevant court, which may have introduced more effective case management or other improvements generally.

[36] Nottage, above n 24, 295-6.

[37] The data was sourced from cases identified though searches conducted as at 11 August 2016 on the Westlaw, LexisNexis AU and Austlii databases (for all cases which applied or considered the IAA), then further details of the date of filing and judgment handed down were obtained from the Federal Court of Australia's online search tool, available at <https://www.comcourts.gov.au/public/esearch/disclaimer>.

Figure 4: Months from Filing to Judgment (Unrelated Federal Court Cases, 2007 to August 2016)

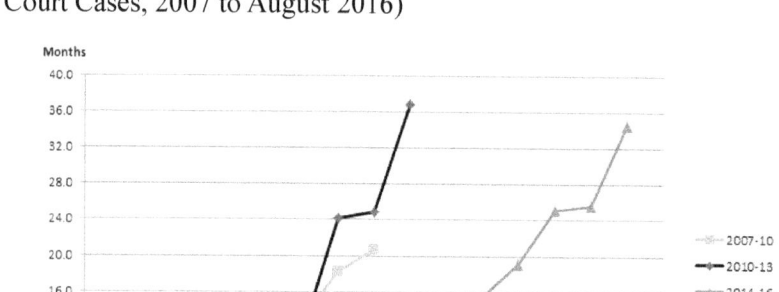

As discussed in the section commencing on page 291, there has been a notable increase in the number of IAA judgments handed down since 2013, and this is reflected in Figure 4. Leaving aside this point of difference (which may cause the 2014-16 case disposition times to appear better than reality in Figure 4 above), there is no marked improvement in the proportionate number of cases which were resolved within either 6 months or 12 months of filing. Specifically:

- across 2014-16, out of the total 15 cases, only 6 had judgments handed down within 6 months of filing (being 40%) and only 10 were resolved within a year (67%); whereas
- across 2010-13, of the total 9 cases, 5 had been resolved within 6 months (55%), although only 6 had judgments handed down within a year (being 67%, which is the same as for 2014-16); and
- across 2007-10, of the total 8 cases, only 2 had judgments handed down within 6 months (so only 25%) but 6 cases had been resolved within 12 months of filing (75%).

Furthermore, since the 2010 amendments there have been a total of 6 cases filed in the Federal Court which, largely due to numerous appeals and related judgments, were in court for over 2 years.[38] In comparison, the longest case to receive judgment in the 3 years prior to the 2010 amendments took only 21 months.[39]

These trends are supported by the more detailed descriptive statistics set out in Table 4 below. These compare the overall distribution in the 3 years before and after the 2010 IAA amendments, and since 2014 to August 2016.

Table 4: Descriptive Statistics for Months from Filing to Judgment (Unrelated Federal Court of Australia cases, 2007 – August 2016)

Statistic	2007-10	2010-13	2014-16
Mean	10.38	11.58	11.32
Standard Error	2.58	4.54	2.77
Median	11.70	3.63	10.33
Standard Deviation	7.31	13.61	10.74
Skewness	-0.09	0.96	0.84
Range	19.87	36.40	34.37
Minimum	0.83	0.37	0.17
Maximum	20.70	36.77	34.53
Count	8	9	15

---

[38] *Castel Electronics Pty Ltd v TCL Air Conditioner (Zhongshan) Co Ltd* (2012) 201 FCR 209, *DKN* (2013) 216 FCR 1 469, *Traxys No 2* (2012) 201 FCR 535, *International Relief and Development Inc v Ladu* [2014] FCA 887 (*Ladu*), *Armada* (2014) 318 ALR 35, *Hopkins v AECOM Australia Pty Ltd (No 4)* (2015) 328 ALR 1*(Hopkins)*.

[39] *BHPB Freight Pty Ltd v Cosco Oceania Chartering Pty Ltd and Another* (2008) 168 FCR 169. A period of 21 months is by no means speedy, but markedly faster than the three years it took to resolve *Traxys Europe SA v Balaji Coke Industry PVT Ltd (No 5)* (2014) 318 ALR 85.

The *average* disposition times for the Federal Court cases across these three time periods are very similar, as are the *median* times from filing to judgment between 2007-10 and 2014-16. (There is a marked decline in the median disposition time for 2010-13, though it would be inaccurate to conclude that this outlier suggests there has been an improvement in case disposition efficiency immediately following the 2010 IAA amendments. As is apparent from Figure 4 above, the distribution of filing to judgment times across 2010-13 is more spread out, but there are a number of cases above the median with a very high disposition time frame, especially compared to before 2010.)

Overall, neither these descriptive statistics nor Figure 4 present a very optimistic picture. While there are a number of Federal Court cases (since the 2010 amendments) which have been resolved within a relatively short timeframe (either in less than 6 months, or within a year of filing), there has been an increase in the number of international arbitration cases which were in the Australian court system for over 2 years, some of which are still ongoing.[40]

- **Choice of Courts and Proportions of Appeals**

Unfortunately, there is no publically accessible data allowing a comparison of case disposition times in State or Territory Courts. However, we can gain some insight from the trends in the court (whether state or federal) in which IAA-related cases are being filed.

As of March 2013, we had also discussed the breakdown of which courts the 109 publically available IAA-related judgments were being filed in, as follows:[41]

---

[40] *Ladu* [2014] FCA 887, *Armada* (2014) 318 ALR 35, *Hopkins* (2015) 328 ALR 1.
[41] Monichino et al, above n 15, 186.

Figure 5: Proportion of IAA Judgments by Court (1989 – 2012)

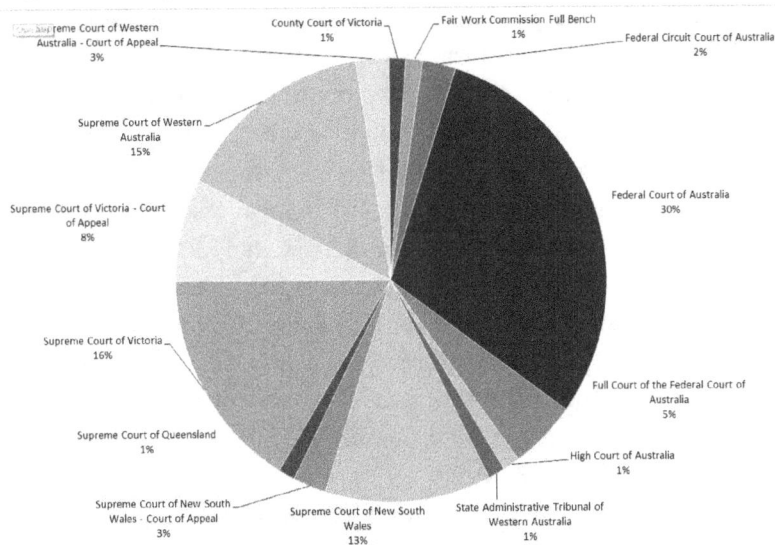

We have re-analysed this data, with Figure 6 showing the proportionate breakdown among various courts since 2013:

Figure 6: Proportion of IAA Judgments by Court (2013 – August 2016)

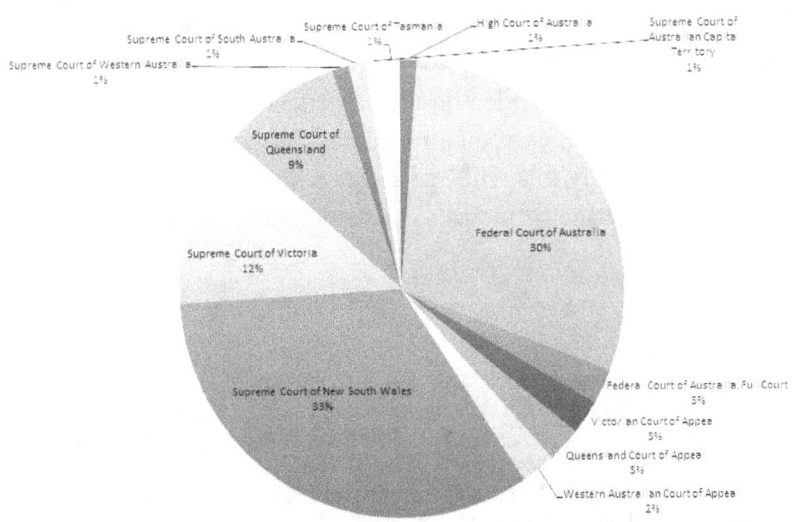

Comparing the two time periods and graphs above, there is only a slight increase in the percentage of cases heard in the Federal Court and Federal Circuit Court of Australia (from 29% to 33%). By contrast, there been a decrease in the overall proportion of initial proceedings heard in the State and Territory Supreme Courts (from 53% across 1989-2012 to 45% across 2013-16). However, it appears that this lower proportion is largely due to an increase in appeal cases heard in these same State and Territory Courts. As of 2012, only 9% of judgments were handed down from the appellate courts of Victoria, Queensland and Western Australia, compared to 13% in the 2013-16 period. Thus, overall, there has been no marked reduction in the number of cases filed in the State and Territory (versus Federal) Courts. Instead, there is a slight overall increase in the number of appeals, both at the State and Territory and Federal levels.

The proportions of cases decided by the Victorian and Western Australian Courts of Appeal are slightly above their pre-2012 averages, while the proportion is unchanged for the Queensland Court of Appeal. (There also remain zero appeals to the New South Wales Court of Appeal, which may therefore present a distinct advantage to initiating IAA-related proceedings in that jurisdiction.) By contrast, the proportion of cases decided by the Full Court of the Federal Court has increased from 4% to 8% (for the post-2012 cases). However, the particular judgments handed down are generally perceived as being pro-arbitration in terms of their outcomes.[42] In an optimist's view of the world, hopefully this will lead to fewer appeals being filed in the future, and consequently reduced disposition times between filing and judgment.

---

[42] See eg Monichino, above n 29; Allsop and Croft, above n 30; Morrison and Nottage, above n 31; and Dean Lewis, *The Interpretation and Uniformity of the UNCITRAL Model Law on International Commercial Arbitration: Focusing on Australia, Hong Kong and Singapore* (Wolters Kluwer, 2016) 115 (describing the Full Court's decision in *Castel Electronics Pty Ltd v TCL* (2012) 201 FCR 209 as 'probably the most internationalist judgment of the courts in Australia').

- **Implications for Improving Australia's International Arbitration Regime**

In a wide-ranging speech on 'Transnational Dispute Resolution' presented in 2016 to the Supreme and Federal Court Judges' Conference, the then Chief Justice of Australia (Robert French AC) remarked that 'judicial adjudication serves larger purposes than the efficiencies, economic benefits and party autonomy served by the arbitral process', but concluded that:[43]

> The Courts themselves, of course, must ensure they are effective actors in the administration of business law by trying to minimize inefficiencies and maximize efficiencies in their processes and to reduce transaction costs. In connection with transnational disputes, there is a common interest in co-operative action to reduce or eliminate disputes as to venue and to provide effective assistance to each other to the enforcement of judgments and co-operation generally.

One of the aims of this chapter has been to contribute to that laudable objective by analysing patterns in court litigation involving the IAA, especially since the 2010 amendments, recognizing also Prof Moens' longstanding interest in and contributions to the field of international commercial arbitration in Australia.

The increase in IAA-related court filings and therefore judgments since 2013 might be explained by a greater number of underlying economic transactions, and consequently more disputes inevitably arising. This may be exacerbated by the economic slowdown both domestically and (especially) abroad. Additionally, however, more filings may be explained (and expected in the future) if outcomes from judicial proceedings are more unpredictable.[44] This can arise firstly

---

[43] Robert French, 'Transnational Dispute Resolution' Speech delivered at the Supreme and Federal Court Judges' Conference, Brisbane, 25 January 2016 <http://www.hcourt.gov.au/assets/publications/speeches/current-justices/frenchcj/frenchcj-25Jan2016.pdf> 15.

[44] Thus, conversely, there is much lower litigation associated with traffic accidents in Japan, for example, thanks to both factual and legal predictability of outcomes for those matters that do occasionally end up in court (eg for more emotional reasons or over-optimism bias). See generally J Mark Ramseyer, *Second-Best Justice: The*

if there is factual uncertainty. However, in IAA-related matters this is less of an issue compared to other types of litigation, and in any event it is unlikely that factual uncertainty in cases has generally increased (compared to pre-2013 cases before Australian courts). Unpredictability in outcomes can be caused, secondly, by differences over the applicable legal principles. It is therefore possible that this remains a problem in Australia in relation to issues relating to the IAA and especially regarding enforceability of arbitration agreements and awards.

One reason could be the legacy of pre-2010 legislation and associated case law, from an era of less concerted judicial support for international arbitration, leaving some residual uncertainty and hence encouraging more court challenges. If so, this case law may eventually 'work itself clean', especially as a result of the generally consistently pro-arbitration judgments emanating from the Federal Court.

However, a further reason for unpredictability in legal principles may be actual (or at least perceived) inconsistencies between the Federal Court and State or Territory Court judgments. The higher-than-average appellate judgments from the Full Court of the Federal Court since 2013 may again help lead the way, since they should be followed by first-instance courts in other jurisdictions unless 'plainly wrong'.[45] However, whether the Full Federal Court decisions can continue to pave the way will depend on the cases that happen to come before the Court, and it is conceivable that those parties averse to arbitration may instead try to litigate before the State or Territory Courts. (The latter judgments may of course end up being appealed to the High Court; but it has hardly ever heard IAA matters, as shown in Figure 6 above.)

Unfortunately, some uncertainty across multiple jurisdictions within Australia seems unavoidable given our constitutional arrangements and entrenched practices, leaving us at a disadvantage compared to unitary jurisdictions such as Singapore and Hong Kong.[46] Accordingly,

---

Virtues of Japanese Private Law (University of Chicago Press, 2015).
[45] See generally *Farah Constructions Pty Ltd v Say-Dee Pty Ltd* (2007) 230 CLR 89.
[46] On a more optimistic view of Australia's role in international arbitration, at the 2016

our courts will have to work even harder to generate uniform interpretations of the IAA and its underlying international instruments. Some positive news comes from a recent quantitative study that found more evidence of this uniformity across judgments in Australia over 2011-15 compared to Hong Kong and even Singapore.[47] However, many of the Australian judgments analysed across this period come from the Federal Court (and not from a broader range of State or Territory Courts). Furthermore, Hong Kong and Singapore benefit from having had previously displayed more uniform, internationalist interpretations of their Model Law-based legislation over earlier eras.

In addition, the recent increase in Australian court filings and judgments may be explained, perversely, by perceived costs and delays associated with Australian court proceedings – despite, for example, the welcome inauguration of dedicated Arbitration Lists in some jurisdictions.[48] (After all, to revert to the analogy of a new highway provided in the section beginning on page 285: it seems that that the 'revamped' IAA route is not only attracting more traffic,

---

Hong Kong International Arbitration Week Rimsky Yuen SC (the Hong Kong Secretary for Justice) commented that Australia was very well-placed to develop a strong footing in dispute resolution as "[l]ike Hong Kong, it has common law and a good judiciary. No one would doubt about the independence of the judiciary of Australia". Similarly, Teresa Cheng (then chair of the Hong Kong International Arbitration Center) noted that Australia offered the benefits of a neutral tribunal, neutrality of rules and laws, and neutrality of the judiciary – the key requirements for a jurisdiction to be chosen as a successful arbitration seat. However, she also noted that Australia is faced with an unfortunate inherent drawback, being its geographical locationdistance: Lara Bullock, 'Australia's Strong, Independent Judiciary Makes it a Suitable Jurisdiction for International Arbitration, Despite a Minor Drawback, According to two Prominent Hong Kong Legal Professionals' *Lawyers Weekly* (24 October 2014) <http://www.lawyersweekly.com.au/news/19808-aus-well-positioned-to-develop-arbitration-seat> 30 October 2016. See also Luke Nottage and Nobumichi Teramura, 'Australia's (In)Capacity in International Commercial Arbitration' *Kluwer Arbitration Blog* (20 September 2018) <http://arbitrationblog.kluwerarbitration.com/2018/09/20/australias-incapacity-international-commercial-arbitration/>.

[47] Lewis, above n 42, 107-29, 203 (Table 2).

[48] Morrison and Nottage, above n 31, 13. The Supreme Court of Victoria also amended its procedural rules on arbitration-related matters with effect from December 2014, as noted by Albert Monichino and Alex Fawke, 'International Arbitration in Australia: 2014/2015 in Review' (2015) *Australasian Dispute Resolution Journal* 192, 207.

but average travel speeds are not changing.) A well-healed and/or aggressive litigant (perhaps like *TCL*), especially with an amenable law firm or counsel, may therefore be more likely to litigate partly to try to encourage a settlement or for other tactical reasons (for example, so the client can protect a wider distributorship network, or just to keep 'face').[49]

Better legal education about the applicable legal principles likely to be applied by the courts in IAA-related matters, as urged by a former President of the Chartered Institute of Arbitrators' Australian branch, may assist to partially deter such litigation. After all, arbitration law is now taught 'at undergraduate level at 21 law schools and at postgraduate level in 10 law schools', as well as via law societies and peak arbitration bodies in Australia.[50] Systematic studies by academics, such as this, should be expanded along with courses in international commercial arbitration like those so ably taught by Prof Moens over many decades.

Nonetheless, better (dis)incentives are arguably even more important. A useful step would be for Australia to follow Hong Kong and other jurisdictions overseas by requiring parties to pay indemnity costs in principle, at least for unsuccessful challenges to international arbitration awards.[51] Unfortunately, despite calls for such reforms for

---

[49] On the never-ending story of *Castel Electronics Pty Ltd v TCL* (2012) 201 FCR 209 and related proceedings, see Nottage, above n 24.

[50] See John Wakefield and Katrine Narkiewicz, 'Australia's New Arbitration Regime: Five Years On' (2015) (2) *Law Society of NSW Journal* 74. Indeed, at Sydney Law School, one of the present authors inherited a well-attended Masters course in 2001 developed by a predecessor, and more recently co-teaches similarly large classes of LLB and JD students. Yet out of all those (probably over 1,000) students, a significant proportion may well have ended up working for law firms now actively engaged in the sometimes ambitious court proceedings attempting to oppose international arbitration agreements, processes and awards.

[51] See *KNM* (above n 34) and May Tai and Simon Chapman, 'Hong Kong Court of First Instance extends indemnity costs principle to actions that delay enforcement of arbitral awards' (31 August 2016) <http://hsfnotes.com/arbitration/2016/08/31/hong-kong-court-of-first-instance-extends-indemnity-costs-principle-to-actions-that-delay-enforcement-of-arbitral-awards/>. The latter notes how Hong Kong courts have applied indemnity costs in principle against unsuccessful parties resisting enforcement of foreign awards (since 2009), bringing setting aside applications (since 2012, discussing

a number of years,[52] the contrary obiter dicta from the Victorian Court of Appeal decision in *Altain Khuder* appears to be influencing even the Federal Court at first instance recently (in another saga involving a persistent litigant incorporated in Hong Kong).[53] Consequently, rather than hoping for uniform principles and applications regarding indemnity costs to emerge nation-wide after many more years of (taxpayer-subsidised) case law development, or through uniform court rules, the government should initiate public consultations about introducing a legislative regime.

---

but not following the Victorian Court of Appeal in *Altain Khuder* (2011) 38 VR 303), resisting stay applications (since 2015), and taking other steps to delay enforcement (since 2016, in *New Heaven Investments Limited & Rondo Development Limited v Yu Guolin*, HCA 115/2013). For recent affirmation of the preference for the indemnity costs principle in Hong Kong (and Singapore) courts, and critique of the Victorian Court of Appeal's *obiter dicta* by a leading Hong Kong arbitrator (and former Judge), see Neil Kaplan 'Making Arbitration Work in a Changing World – A Pacific View: Should We Restrict Challenges by Having an Indemnity Costs Rule?', paper presented at the AMINZ-ICCA International Arbitration Day, Queenstown, 20 April 2018, via <https://queenstowncongress.com/delegates-get-ready-info/presentations/>

[52] Nottage, above n 24; Albert Monichino, 'When High Risk Strategies are Worth a Go' (June 2013) *ACICA News* 2.

[53] See *Sino Dragon Trading Ltd v Noble Resources International Pte Ltd (No 2)* [2016] FCA 1169 at [19]. Despite noting the different approach taken in Hong Kong (albeit judgments through to 2012) and Singapore (at [10]), Beach J agreed with the obiter dicta from the Victorian Court of Appeal in *Altain Khuder* (2011) 38 VR 303 that the unsuccessful party to a setting aside application should not bear a 'reverse onus' to establish that it should not pay indemnity costs. However, Beach J acknowledged that *application* of the conventional principle should still take into account the IAA's objects, the Model Law's limited grounds for challenges, the contractual choice of arbitration, and related 'public policy of discouraging article 34 challenges (and the mirror s 8 proceedings opposing enforcement) that have no reasonable prospects of success' (at [25]). Beach J then went on to find, on the facts, that the successful award creditor was able to prove that several grounds of challenge lacked 'reasonable prospects of success' and so could therefore claim two-thirds of its costs on an indemnity basis. (We thank Greg Nell SC for bringing this judgment to our attention.) Interestingly, at [25], Beach J also noted the obiter dicta recently from Allsop CJ on indemnity costs in *Ye v Zeng (No 5)* [2016] FCA 850, and an earlier extra-judicial speech, even though those remarks seemed to open the way to adopt a broader indemnity costs principle. It therefore remains quite unclear whether, in (likely) future litigation, the Full Federal Court will adopt the approach of Beach J or instead follow the line taken in other jurisdictions such as Hong Kong.

More generally, since Australia is 'coming from behind' compared to other regional jurisdictions that are already currently very popular seats, and additionally will always suffer in that respect due to a geographical disadvantage, our legislature needs to be particularly active in supporting the international arbitration law framework.[54] There are limits to how much can be achieved by the judiciary (through both court decisions and extra-judicial commentary) or by arbitral institutions like ACICA (for example, through revisions of its Arbitration Rules in 2016 and other activities). Although there have been three sets of revisions to the IAA introduced since 2015, they mostly still correct drafting errors or uncertainties rather than grappling with difficult policy issues such as the arbitrability or public policy implications of various provisions in the *Australian Consumer Law* that create further disincentives to Australia-seated international arbitrations.[55]

As the then federal Attorney-General remarked in 2009 when publically promoting amendments to the IAA adopting most of the revised Model Law, as part of an effort also to revamp domestic arbitration in Australia, a key aim was to encourage 'cultural reform' in understandings and practices.[56] However, the unfortunate reality is that changing a culture is not easy and will require persistent efforts at multiple levels. As the Chief Justice of the Federal Court reminded a large audience in his opening keynote address for the ICCA Congress held in Sydney in 2018: 'Arbitration culture, indeed dispute resolution culture, needs to recognise that issues of cost and a lack of efficiency must be addressed'.[57]

---

[54] Proposing a mostly overlapping set of further IAA-related legislative reforms, see Nottage, above n 24; Monichino and Fawke, above n 48, 194-6.

[55] Luke Nottage and James Morrison, 'Accessing and Assessing Australia's International Arbitration Act' (2017) 34(6) *Journal of International Arbitration* 963, especially Part 2.1 (based on Nottage's posting at <http://arbitrationblog.kluwerarbitration.com/2017/05/13/australias-international-arbitration-act-amendments-rejuvenation-thousand-cuts/>), Parts 4 and Part 5.1 (building on and updating Morrison and Nottage, above n 31).

[56] Hon Robert McClelland, cited in Nottage, above n 24, 287. Cf also generally Holmes et al, above n 6.

[57] Hon James Allsop AO, 'Commercial and Investor-State Arbitration: The Importance of Recognising their Differences', paper presented at the ICCA Congress, Syd-

- **Broader Implications for Educators**

This contemporary Australian experience also suggests some significant implications for academics, like Prof Moens, who have diligently and effectively taught international commercial arbitration over many years. Such careers reflect and support an accelerating shift in international arbitration from West to East, especially over the last 10-15 years.[58]

Courses teaching and testing the fundamental principles of arbitration are less problematic. They should more readily lead to students understanding that this procedure is not designed to be 'litigation-lite' but instead something different and innovative, as the federal Attorney-General also declared in 2009.[59] The corollary is that international commercial arbitrators, processes and awards ought not to be readily subject to numerous court challenges. Nonetheless, the post-GFC decline in funding provided by Australian law firms for their lawyers to undertake LLM courses or other further study may have reduced opportunities for them to learn about, or be reminded of, such core principles.

More challenging may be arbitration moot competitions, like the Vis Moot, despite – or perhaps even because of – having been so successfully supported by Prof Moens and his or other students and coaches around Australia for almost a quarter century. On the one hand, a growing suite of moot competitions now provides wonderful 'hands-on' learning experiences,[60] enhancing multiple skills in the

---

ney, 16 April 2018, <http://www.fedcourt.gov.au/digital-law-library/judges-speeches/chief-justice-allsop/allsop-cj-20180416>

[58] See generally Luke Nottage, 'In/Formalization and Glocalization of International Commercial Arbitration and Investment Treaty Arbitration in Asia' in Joachim Zekoll, Moritz Baelz and Iwo Amelung (eds), *Formalisation and Flexibilisation of Dispute Resolution* (Martinus Nijhoff/Brill, 2014) 211.

[59] Hon Robert McClelland, cited in Nottage, above n 24, 287.

[60] See eg the bilingual Intercollegiate Negotiation (and Arbitration) Competition, at <http://www.negocom.jp/eng/>, outlined in 'Beyond Borders in the Classroom - The Possibility of Transnational Legal Education' (2006) 25 *Ritsumeikan Law Review* 183-208 (edited Conference Panel Discussion transcript, with Frank Bennett et al), also at <http://ssrn.com/abstract=1161016>.

best tradition of modern legal education.[61] Yet, on the other hand, such moot problems are deliberately designed to be very finely balanced, to make the competitions particularly interesting for students. They also must be necessarily abstracted somewhat from national contexts when the competitions take place internationally. Consequently, student moot competitors who later go on to be lawyers and encounter real-life arbitration-related issues may too easily come to the idea that challenges and litigation may be worth a try, even if objectively this is misguided. One solution would be to reiterate this risk at and after arbitration moot competitions. Another way is to illustrate how some views are more right than others, for example by publicising sample awards or reasons after completion of the moot.

Nonetheless, there will be limits to such (re-)education. Even if students complete moot competitions and other arbitration courses having got the core message that this is an *alternative* dispute resolution mechanism, once they begin working in law firms they may be tempted to run overly ambitious arguments, especially if their clients are overly ambitious. This may be particularly tempting when combined with a pervasive 'billable hours' model of law firm practice,[62] and a reluctance by some Australian judges to develop a consistent indemnity costs principle regarding failed challenges. Contemporary educators may also therefore need to consider, discuss and act on such broader controversies, mobilising political will and professional support for appropriate reforms.[63]

---

[61] Luke Nottage, 'Teaching Arbitration in Australia: Towards Transnational Associations' (CDAMS Discussion Paper 04/30E, 2005) <www.cdams.kobe-u.ac.jp/archive/dp04-30.pdf>.

[62] See generally Nottage, above n 56 (in Baelz); Luke Nottage, 'Addressing International Arbitration's Ambivalence: Hard Lessons from Australia' in Vijay Bhatia, Christopher Candlin and Maurizio Gotti (eds), *Discourse and Practice in International Commercial Arbitration* (Ashgate, 2012) 11-44 (quoting Western Australian Chief Justice Wayne Martin)

[63] As an innovative antidote recently from the Dispute Institute (formerly IAMA), Schedule 1 of its 2016 Arbitration Rules (<https://www.resolution.institute/documents/item/1844> 21 March 2017) set monetary caps on legal as well as arbitrators' fees that the tribunal can award, even though arbitrators' fees are still otherwise determined in general based on an hourly rate.

APPENDIX: Vis Moot (Vienna) Participation and Awards for Australian Teams

Year	Countries	Universities	Australian Universities	Australian Law Schools
1993-1994	9	11	1	Deakin University (Team Orals - Third Place)
1994-1995	15	23	2	Deakin University, University of Queensland
1995-1996	19	38	2	Deakin University (Best Individual Oralist - Third Place; Team Orals - Second Place), University of Queensland
1996-1997	19	48	4	Deakin University, Griffith University, University of Technology Sydney, Universit
1997-1998	25	58	5	Deakin University, Griffith University (Best Memorandum for Claimant - Third Place), Monash University, University of Queensland (Team Orals - Second Place; Best Oral Advocate - Third Place), University of Technology Sydney
1998-1999	29	72	6	Deakin University (Team Orals - First Place), Griffith University, Monash University, University of New South Wales, University of Queensland (Best Oral Advocate - Third Place), University of Technology Sydney
1999-2000	28	79	6	Deakin University, Griffith University, Monash University, University of Notre Dame, University of Queensland (Best Memorandum for Respondent - Second Place; Team Orals - First Place; Best Oral Advocate - Third Place), University of Technology Sydney
2000-2001	31	94	7	Australian National University, Deakin University, Griffith University, Monash University (Team Orals - First Place), University of Queensland (Best Memorandum for Respondent - Third Place), University of Sydney Law Extension Committee, University of Technology Sydney
2001-2002	36	108	7	Deakin University, Griffith University, Monash University, University of Queensland (Best Memorandum for Client - First Place; Team Orals - Second Place; Best Oral Advocate in the General Rounds - First Place), University of Sydney LEC, University of Technology Sydney, Victoria University Melbourne

A Commitment to Excellence

2002-2003	40	128	8	Bond University, Deakin University (Best Oral Advocate in the General Rounds - First Place), Griffith University, Monash University, University of New South Wales (Best Oral Advocate in the General Rounds - First Place), University of Sydney LEC, University of Technology Sydney, Victoria University of Technology Melbourne
2003-2004	42	135	7	Deakin University, Griffith University, Monash University, Macquarie University, University of New South Wales, University of Technology Sydney, Victoria University Melbourne
2004-2005	46	151	8	Deakin University, Griffith University, Monash University, Macquarie University, University of New South Wales (Best Oral Advocate in the General Rounds - First Place), University of Notre Dame, University of Technology Sydney, Victoria University Melbourne
2005-2006	49	156	8	Deakin University, Griffith University, Monash University (Best Individual Oralist - Second Place), Macquarie University, University of New South Wales, University of Notre Dame, University of Technology Sydney, Victoria University Melbourne
2006-2007	51	177	8	Bond University, Deakin University, Griffith University, Murdoch University, Monash University, University of New South Wales, University of Technology Sydney, Victoria University Melbourne
2007-2008	52	203	8	Deakin University, Griffith University, Murdoch University, Monash University (Best Individual Oralist - Third Place), Macquarie University, University of New South Wales, University of Technology Sydney, Victoria University Melbourne
2008-2009	57	228	8	Deakin University, Griffith University (Team Orals - Third Place), Monash University, Murdoch University, University of New South Wales, University of Sydney (Best Memorandum for Claimant - First Place), University of Technology Sydney, Victoria University Melbourne
2009-2010	62	251	6	Deakin University, Griffith University, University of New South Wales (Best Memorandum for Claimant - First Place; Best Memorandum for Respondent - First Place), University of Sydney, University of Technology Sydney, Victoria University Melbourne

2010-2011	63	254	8	Deakin University, Griffith University, Murdoch University, University of New South Wales, University of Sydney, University of Sydney Law Extension Committee, University of Technology Sydney, Victoria University Melbourne
2011-2012	67	280	6	Deakin University, Griffith University, University of New South Wales, University of Sydney, La Trobe University, Victoria University Melbourne
2012-2013	67	290	12	Deakin University, Edith Cowan University, Griffith University, La Trobe University, Monash University (Team Orals - Second Place), Murdoch University, University of New South Wales (Best Memorandum for Respondent - Third Place), Queensland University of Technology, University of Sydney (Best Memorandum for Claimant - Third Place), University of Sydney LEC, Victoria University Melbourne
2013-2014	64	290	9	Deakin University (First Place Team Orals), Edith Cowan University, La Trobe University, Monash University, Queensland University of Technology, University of New South Wales, University of Notre Dame, University of Sydney, Victoria University Melbourne
2014-2015	65	298	11	University of Sydney (Best Memorandum for Respondent - Second Runner Up) & ten others
2015-2016	67	311	11	Deakin University, Edith Cowan University, La Trobe University, Monash University, Queensland University of Technology, The University of Queensland, University of New South Wales, University of Notre Dame, University of Notre Dame (Sydney), University of Sydney (Best Memorandum for Claimant - First Runner Up), Victoria University, Melbourne

14

TO WHAT DEGREE DOES CUSTOMARY INTERNATIONAL LAW REQUIRE ACCOMMODATION OF A SOURCE COUNTRY'S RIGHT TO TAX HIGH, TAX LOW OR NOT TAX AT ALL?

J. Clifton Fleming, Jr.

- **Introduction**

Because it has been my pleasure to know Gabriel Moens and count him as a friend for many years, I was pleased when asked to contribute to this volume. There is, nevertheless, a seeming incongruity in the fact that Gabriel is an international law scholar while my primary field is income tax law, a subject which is often regarded as purely a domestic creature. This impression is significantly inaccurate. Income tax law, in its cross-border application, is actually based on well-established customary international law principles.[1] This essay will explore the extent to which these principles indicate that the right of a country to

---

[1] There is a small amount of dissent on this point. See Brian J. Arnold, *International Tax Primer*, (Kluwer Law International B.V., 3rd ed. 2016) 3 ("Arguably at least, there is no overriding international law of taxation, arising either from the customary practice of sovereign states or from the actions of some international body such as the UN or the OECD."); H. David Rosenbloom, 'The David Tillinghast Lecture: International Tax Arbitrage and the "International Tax System"' (2000) 53 *Tax Law Review* 137 ("The existence of overarching principles of international taxation . . . qualifies as news."). However, the dominant view is that there is a body of customary international law principles that provides a basic, although limited, structure for international income taxation. See American Law Institute, *Restatement (Third) of the Foreign Relations Law of the United States* (1987), 235-36, 258-66; Reuven S. Avi-Yonah, *International Tax as International Law: An Analysis of the International Tax Regime*, (Cambridge University Press 2007) 5-8; Charles H. Gustafson, Robert J. Peroni, and Richard Crawford Pugh, *Taxation of International Transactions* (Thomson Reuters, 4th ed. 2011) 16-17.

impose a *high tax, low tax, or no tax* on its non-residents' cross-border income must be accommodated by other countries.

- **Significance of the Question**

It is useful to begin with a brief consideration of quantitative data. International commerce is huge. In 2016, the most recent year for which World Trade Organization statistics are available, total worldwide exports of goods and services were greater than U.S. $20 trillion.[2] This was a massive cross-border flow. Indeed, it exceeded the entire 2016 U.S. GDP[3] by more than U.S. $1 trillion and all indications are that it is growing. These facts are relevant to the subject of this essay because a substantial part of this annual cross-border movement of goods and services is composed of international business profits that are an element in every country's income tax base. Not surprisingly, the nations of the world wish to tax these profits in order to help provide the public goods that their residents expect and demand.

- **The Current Legal Regime**

Because the transactions that make up the international stream of commerce involve parties in different countries as well as goods and services that are transferred across international borders, nations will inevitably have competing income tax claims over the resulting profits. Consequently, a legal regime, largely initiated between the two world wars[4] of the twentieth century but subject to continuing evolution, has been developed to address inter-nation conflicts regarding taxing rights over the income produced by the flow of international commerce.

The current regime is based on well-established customary

---

[2] World Trade Organization, *World Trade Statistical Review 2017*, 100, 121 <https://www.wto.org/english/res_e/statis_e/wts2017_e/wts17_toc_e.htm>.

[3] See World Bank, *World Development Indicators Database*, Gross Domestic Product 2016 <https://data.worldbank.org/indicator/NY.GDP.MKTP.CD>.

[4] See Michael J. Graetz and Michael O'Hear, 'The "Original Intent" of U.S. International Income Taxation,' (1997) 51 *Duke Law Journal* 1021.

international law principles. One of these is that each country has the right (but not the obligation) to tax non-residents on all income earned within its borders.[5] Exercise of this right is commonly referred to as inbound taxation or source taxation. A second relevant principle is that each country has the right (but not the obligation) to tax its residents on their worldwide incomes—i.e. the sum of their domestic and foreign-source incomes.[6] Exercise of this right is often referred to as outbound taxation or residence-based taxation.

When these two well-recognized rights are fully exercised, however, they create an inevitable conflict. If Country A (the residence country) applies its residence-based taxation right to profits earned by one of its residents in Country B (the source country), those same profits will be subject to Country B's source taxation right. Allowance of this double income taxation would often mean that the Country A resident would forgo the Country B opportunity and the well-being of

---

[5] See American Law Institute, above n1, §§ 411-12; Avi-Yonah, above n 1, 27; Ilan Benshalom, 'The New Poor at Our Gates: Global Justice Implications For International Trade and Tax Law,' (2010) 85 *N.Y.U. Law Review* 1, 75; Allison Christians, 'Sovereignty, Taxation and Social Contract' (2009) 18 *Minnesota Journal of International Law* 99, 104, 110-11; Manal S. Corwin, 'Sense and Sensibility: The Policy and Politics of BEPS', (2014) 145 *Tax Notes* 133, 138; Jinyan Li, 'Improving Inter-nation Equity Through Territorial Taxation and Tax Sparing' in Arthur J. Cockfield (ed), *Globalization and Its Tax Discontents: Tax Policy and International Investments* (University of Toronto Press, 2010) 117, 120; Wolfgang Schön, 'International Tax Coordination for a Second-Best World (Part I)' Oct. 2009 *World Tax Journal* 67, 72-73. For normative justifications of this rule, see Roy Rohatgi, *Basic International Taxation* (Kluwer Law International, 2002) 12; Stephen E. Shay, J. Clifton Fleming, Jr., and Robert J. Peroni, 'The David Tillinghast Lecture: What's Source Got to Do With It? Source Rules and U.S. International Taxation' (2002) 56 *Tax Law Review* 81, 88-106.

[6] See American Law Institute, above n 1, §412 (1)(a); Avi-Yonah, above n 1, 22-27; Benshalom, above n 5, 75; Christians, above n 5, 104, 110-11; Corwin, above n 5, 138; Schön, above n 5, 90-91. For a normative justification of this rule, see Rohatgi, above n 5, 12; J. Clifton Fleming Jr., Robert J. Peroni, and Stephen E. Shay, 'Fairness in International Taxation: The Ability-to-Pay- Case for Taxing Worldwide Income' (2001) 5 *Florida Tax Review* 299. For a discussion of the connection of source-based taxation and residence-based taxation to the international law concept of sovereignty, see Diane M. Ring, 'What's at Stake in the Sovereignty Debate? International Tax and the Nation-State' (2008) 49 *Virginia Journal of International Law* 155.

both countries might suffer.[7] Customary international law addresses this conundrum by prescribing that Country B's source taxation right takes precedence and that Country A must act to ameliorate the double taxation.[8] In other words, customary international law regards source taxation rights as superior to residence taxation rights.

Speaking broadly, the majority of economically developed residence countries discharge their amelioration obligation with respect to the foreign-source active-business income of corporate residents by exempting that income from residence country taxation.[9] In contrast, this majority of residence countries typically imposes income tax, reduced by a credit for foreign source tax, on (1) all foreign-source passive income, (2) all other foreign-source income of non-corporate residents, and (3) all active business income of corporate residents that bears a low foreign tax.[10] Where the source country tax exceeds

---

[7] Assume the ACo, a Country A resident company, has the opportunity to invest $1 million in either Country A with a 9% pre-tax return or in Country B with a 10% pre-tax return. Both countries tax company income at a 20% rate. If both countries apply their taxes to ACo's Country B return without mitigation, the 40% total tax will reduce the 10% Country B return to 6% (.10 x [1-.40]). If, however, ACo forgoes the Country B investment in favor of the Country A opportunity, only the 20% tax of Country A will apply and ACo will realize a 7.2% after-tax return (.09 x [1-.20]). Since taxpayers focus on after-tax returns, ACo will see a tax-induced incentive to ignore the economically superior Country B investment in favor of the Country A investment. If ACo responds to this incentive, Country B will have lost the benefit of ACo's investment and Country A will have lost the benefit of having its resident pursue a superior opportunity.

[8] See American Law Institute, above n 1, §413 cmt a.; Yariv Brauner, 'An international Tax Regime in Crystallization,' (2003) 56 *Tax Law Review* 259, 265-66, 284. See also Hugh J. Ault and Brian J. Arnold, *Comparative Income Taxation* (Aspen Publishers, 3d ed. 2010) 446.

[9] Rosanne Altshuler, Stephen Shay, and Eric Toder, *Lessons the United States Can Learn from Other Countries' Territorial Systems for Taxing Income of Multinational Corporations* (Tax Policy Center, 2015) 1.

[10] See J. Clifton Fleming, Jr., Robert J. Peroni, and Stephen E. Shay, 'Designing a U.S. Exemption System for Foreign Income When the Treasury is Empty,' (2012) 13 *Florida Tax Review* 397, 412, 427; Staff of Joint Committee on Taxation, JCS-02-05, Options to Improve Tax Compliance and Reform Tax Expenditures 187 (2005). For example, the United States generally does not exempt foreign-source active business income of U.S. corporate residents unless the foreign tax thereon is at least 13.125%. See H.R. Rep. No. 466, 115th Cong., 1st Sess. 626 (2017).

the residence country tax, the credit effectively eliminates the latter tax.[11] However, the residence country does not reimburse its residents for excess source tax by either making a cash payment to the resident equal to the excess source tax or by allowing the resident to credit the excess source tax against residence country tax on residence country income.[12] In the opposite situation where the residence country tax exceeds the source country tax, the foreign tax credit causes the residence country tax to be eliminated up to the amount of the source country's tax but the residence country collects the excess of residence country tax over source country tax.[13] This excess is commonly referred to as a residual tax.[14]

With respect to the types of foreign-source income that residence countries choose to tax, the credit approach to double taxation relief arguably compromises the source taxation right of source countries in two ways. First it deters source countries from exercising their right to tax the income of foreign residents at rates higher than their respective residence country rates. This is because the excess source country tax will encourage foreign residents to pursue opportunities in their residence countries instead of in high-tax source countries.[15]

---

[11] Assume that a Country A resident earns $1 million pre-tax in Country B, that Country A will tax this income at 15% and that the Country B tax rate is 25%. The credit that Country A allows for the $250,000 Country B tax will reduce the $150,000 Country A tax to zero.

[12] In the note 11 example, Country A will not give a credit against its tax on domestic income for, or reimburse its resident for, the $100,000 excess of Country B tax over Country A tax. See Paul R. McDaniel, 'Territorial vs Worldwide International Tax Systems: Which Is Better for the U.S.?,' (2007) 8 *Florida Tax Review* 283, 298; Ault and Arnold, above n 8, 454-51; Gustafson, Peroni, and Pugh, above n 1, 22-23.

[13] Assume that a Country A resident earns $1 million pre-tax in Country B, that Country A will tax this income at 25% and that the Country B tax rate is 15%. The credit that Country A allows for the $150,000 Country B tax will reduce the $250,000 Country A tax to $100,000 and Country A will collect this $100,000 amount from its resident. See Ault and Arnold, above n 8, 447. Gustafson, Peroni, and Pugh, above n 1, 307.

[14] See Gustafson, Peroni, and Pugh, above n 1, 39, 307-08, 485-9.

[15] Assume that a Country A resident can earn $1 million pre-tax on the same amount of capital in either Country A, which will tax the income at 15%, or Country B, which imposes a 25% tax. If the resident pursues the Country B alternative, the credit that Country A allows for the $250,000 Country B tax will reduce the $150,000 Country

Second, where a source country makes a policy decision to attract investment from residence countries by imposing a low source tax rate, the residual tax collected by residence countries, after allowing a credit for the source tax, effectively eliminates the benefit of the source tax reduction that would otherwise be enjoyed by investors from residence countries. This, in turn, defeats the source country's effort to attract foreign investment with a low source tax rate.[16]

In the first situation, the source country's taxation right, which is superior to a residence country's taxation right, is arguably curtailed by the residence country's refusal to reimburse its residents for excess source country tax.[17] In the second case, the source country's supposedly superior taxation right is defeated by the residence country collecting its residual tax.[18] These facts raise an interesting two-part question. As previously noted, customary international law dictates that source country taxation rights are superior to residence country taxation rights. Does this norm include a requirement that when countries tax foreign-source income of their residents, they must respect source taxation rights (1) by reimbursing their residents for payments to high tax countries of excess source tax and (2) by forgoing the collection of residual tax on income earned by their residents in low tax countries? Stated more generally, does customary international law specify

---

A tax to zero but $100,000 of Country B tax will remain uncredited. However, the failure of Country A to reimburse its resident for the $100,000 excess Country B tax will mean that the Country A resident effectively bears a $250,000 tax on the Country B investment and only $150,000 tax if the $1 million is earned in Country A. Thus, there will be a tax bias in favor or pursuing the Country A opportunity.

[16] Assume that a Country A resident can earn $1 million on the same amount of capital in either country A, which will tax the income at 25%, or Country B, which imposes a 15% tax. If the resident pursues the Country B alternative, the credit that Country A allows for the $150,000 Country B tax will reduce the $250,000 Country A tax to $100,000 but Country A will collect that $100,000. Thus, the Country B alternative will bear a total tax of $250,000 ($150,000 paid to Country B and $100,000 paid to Country A) and the tax inducement that Country B sought to create with its 15% tax rate will have been erased by Country A's $100,000 residual tax.

[17] See J. Clifton Fleming, Jr., Robert J. Peroni, and Stephen E. Shay, 'Two Cheers for the Foreign Tax Credit, Even in the BEPS Era, (2016) 91 *Tulane Law Review* 1, 11-12.

[18] See Fleming, Peroni, and Shay, above n 17, 45.

that when residence countries tax foreign-source income, they must accommodate a source country's right to collect excess income tax as well as a source country's right to forgo income tax revenue?

- **The Elements of Customary International Law**

As is well known, a norm has the status of customary international law if it represents a general and persistent practice of states that is followed because states believe they have a legal obligation to do so even though the obligation is not contained in a binding treaty.[19] Obviously, the issue of whether states believe they are under a legal obligation does not arise unless a general and persistent practice exists.[20] Thus, in determining whether customary international law requires residence countries (1) to reimburse their residents for payments of foreign source tax in excess of residence country tax and/or (2) to forgo collection of residual tax on income earned by their residents in low tax countries, the primary issue is whether the countries of the world have established a general and persistent practice of doing either.

- **Obligation to Reimburse**

It is easy to answer the question of whether states follow a general and persistent practice of reimbursing their residents (through a cash payment or a credit against tax on domestic income) for payments of source country tax in excess of residence country tax. They do not. It is simply not done.[21]

The reason why is obvious. If residence countries did practice reimbursement, source countries would know that they could impose high source tax rates without discouraging foreign investment because the treasuries of the foreign residence countries would effectively bear the incidence of the excess source tax. Investors would not feel

---

[19] See American Law Institute, above n 1, §102 (2).
[20] See generally International Law Association, *Statement of Principles Applicable to the Formation of General Customary International Law* (2000) 8.
[21] See Arnold, above n 1, 54; Ault and Arnold, above n 8, 454-57; Brauner, above n 8, 285; Gustafson, Peroni, and Pugh, above n 1, 22-23 McDaniel, above n 12.

a burden.²² Residence countries naturally refuse to tolerate such a raid on the public fisc.

Thus, the general and persistent practice necessary to establish a customary international law reimbursement obligation is lacking. Source countries must look elsewhere for leverage to require residence countries to bear the burden of excess source tax. So far, the search has been unsuccessful.²³

- **Obligation to Forgo Residual Tax**

In addition to eschewing a general and persistent practice of reimbursing residents for excess source country tax, residence countries also fail to follow a general and persistent practice of forgoing residual taxation of foreign income that the residence countries choose to tax. Instead, the general practice is to collect the residual tax.²⁴

This practice draws protests from less-developed country advocates who argue that collecting residual tax deprives poor countries of the capacity to attract badly needed foreign investments with low tax

---

²² If in the note 11 example, Country A gave its resident a $100,000 cash payment or credit against tax on domestic income, the resident would bear only $150,000 of the $250,000 Country B tax. The $100,000 of excess Country B tax would be effectively shifted to the Country A treasury. See also Staff of Joint Comm. On Taxation, JCX-22-06, The Impact of International Tax Reform: Background and Selected Issues Relating to U.S. International Tax Rules and the Competitiveness of U.S. Businesses 13 (2006) ('The foreign tax credit ... limit is intended to ensure that the credit serves its purpose of mitigating double taxation of foreign-source income without offsetting the U.S. tax on U.S.–source income.'); Avi-Yonah, above n 1, 156 ('Every country that has a foreign tax credit must have a limitation....').

²³ Some residence countries allow payments of excess foreign tax to produce fiscal benefits by being claimed as tax credits in earlier or subsequent years in which residence tax exceeded foreign tax payments so that the full potential for foreign tax credits was not realized. However, this may reflect a desire to achieve temporal averaging of tax liabilities rather than to provide reimbursement for excess foreign tax payments. More importantly, there does not appear to be a uniform practice on this point that could be used to establish a reimbursement obligation on the part of residence countries. See Arnold, above n 1, 54; Ault and Arnold, above n 8, 462-64.

²⁴ See Arnold, above n 1, 53-54; Brauner, above n 8, 285.

rates.[1] This is indisputably true but it does not establish that poor countries have a customary international law right to require wealthy countries to forgo collecting residual tax.[2] The general and persistent practice necessary to establish such a right does not exist. Indeed the two model documents that have provided the basis for most of the network of more than 3,000 bilateral double income taxation elimination treaties (i.e. the OECD Model Convention on Income and Capital and the United Nations Model Double Taxation Convention)[3] assume the collection of residual tax when a residence country taxes foreign-source income.[4] Moreover, the world's developed countries have vigorously resisted the attempts of less developed countries to attract investment by unilaterally employing low rates of tax.[5] Thus, the burden is on less developed countries to persuade wealthy countries voluntarily to provide various forms of assistance, including forgoing residual tax through bilateral agreements.[6]

---

[1] See Benshalom, above n 5, 77; David C. Elkins, 'The Merits of Tax Competition in a Globalized Economy', (2016) 91 *Indiana Law Journal* 905, 927; Charles I. Kingson, 'The Coherence of International Taxation' (1981) 81 *Columbia Law Review* 1151, 1159-60.

[2] See Michael Littlewood, 'Tax Competition: Harmful to Whom?' (2004) 26 *Michigan Journal of International Law* 411, 441 ('[I]t seems difficult to categorize the withholding of aid as a violation of sovereignty'); Miranda Stewart, *Redistribution between Rich and Poor Countries* 9 <https://ssrn.com/abstract=3140135> ('Perhaps, the most that can be argued is that rich countries have obligations…to set framework conditions, transition rules and tax policy to support economic development in poor countries.').

[3] See Arnold, above n 1, 135.

[4] See OECD Model Tax Convention on Income and Capital Article 23B; United Nations Double Taxation Convention between Developed and Developing Countries Article 23B.

[5] See generally, Lilian v. Faulhaber, 'The Trouble with Tax Competition: From Practice to Theory,' (2018) 71 *Tax Law Review* (forthcoming).

[6] For an extended discussion, see Yariv Brauner, 'The Future of Tax Incentives' in Yariv Brauner and Miranda Stewart (eds), *Tax, Law, and Development* (Edward Elgar Publishing Limited 2013) 25, 50-54; Karen B. Brown, 'Missing Africa: Should U.S. International Tax Rules Accommodate Investment in Developing Countries?' (2002) 23 *University of Pennsylvania Journal of Economic Law* 45, 68-76; Fleming, Peroni, and Shay, above n 17, 45-49.

- **Conclusion**

Customary international law gives source countries a right to tax foreigners on income earned within the source countries' borders. When those foreigners' residence countries also tax that income, customary international law requires the residence countries to mitigate the resulting double taxation. This is so because the taxing rights of residence countries are regarded as inferior to the taxing rights of source countries. The usual response of the residence countries is to credit the source country income tax against residence country income tax. However, if the source country tax exceeds the residence country tax, the residence country will not reimburse residents for the excess. Although this effectively restrains source countries in the exercise of their taxation rights, customary international law permits residence countries to act in this way. In the opposite situation where residence country tax exceeds source country tax, customary international law allows the residence country to collect the excess even though this compromises the ability of source countries to use low tax rates, or a zero tax, to attract foreign investment.

15

THE INTERNATIONAL HARMONIZATION OF SECURITY RIGHTS LAW: ITS SUCCESSES AND CHALLENGES

Henry Gabriel

- **Introduction**

It is my great privilege to be included in this Festschrift honouring Professor Gabriël Moens, my friend and colleague of many years. Gabriël has brought his immense knowledge of the law and his teaching excellence to thousands of students on four continents, all of whom have gained tremendously from his guidance. His scholarship has influenced the path of the law in many countries, and he has done more than anyone else to introduce a whole generation of Australian law students to international law and arbitration. Normally a Festschrift such as this honors the culmination of an illustrious career, but for Gabriël, although his career has been illustrious, I have no doubt that he is not anywhere near the end of his professional life. I know we can all look forward to the continuance of his work for many years to come.

In this paper, I would like to explore the international harmonization of personal property security rights law and summarize the general principles that are common within the harmonization efforts. I would like to focus on several points. First, I will give an overview of the work of the *United Nations Commission on International Trade Law* (UNCITRAL)[7] and the *International Institute for the Unification of*

---

[7] The United Nations Commission on International Trade Law (UNCITRAL) is a subsidiary body of the General Assembly of the United Nations. UNCITRAL was established in 1966. The commission has a general mandate to harmonise and unify the

International Private Law (UNIDROIT)[8] in the harmonization of the law of personal property security rights. Second, I would like to discuss the generally accepted principles that underlie modern secured finance. Last, I would like to briefly discuss the problems some common-law jurisdictions have had in their attempts to modernize and conform their laws to these generally accepted principles.

I am focusing on the work of UNCITRAL and UNIDROIT as these two multilateral organizations have been the two major sources of model laws and treaties and conventions in secured finance law. There have been some organizational attempts at regional harmonization of secured transactional law,[9] but these projects have not been as wide ranging and as successful as the work from UNCITRAL and UNIDROIT. There have been some very successful recent modernized domestic laws for secured transactions,[10] and we will examine several of them to determine the source of their success.

If we examine the growth and harmonization of private international commercial law, I think it is fair to say that over the last three decades questions of secured transactions have had a dominant role. It is

---

law of international trade. Since its founding, UNCITRAL has prepared a wide range of conventions, model laws and other instruments that deal with the substantive law that governs trade transactions or other aspects of business law which have an impact on international trade. UNCITRAL is made up of 60 member states from five regional groups. Members of the Commission are elected for terms of six years. The terms of half the members expire every three years.

[8] The International Institute for the Unification of Private Law (UNIDROIT) is an independent intergovernmental organisation with its seat in Rome. The purpose of UNIDROIT is to study the needs and the methods for modernising and harmonising private law, particularly commercial law, at the international level. UNIDROIT was created in 1926 as an auxiliary organ of the League of Nations. Following the demise of the League of Nations, UNIDROIT was re-established in 1940 on the basis of a multilateral agreement. This agreement is known as the UNIDROIT Statute, and the membership of UNIDROIT is restricted to States that have acceded to the statute. There are presently 63 member states.

[9] See e.g., John Simpson and Joachim Menze, 'Ten Years of Secured Transactions Reform' (2000) Autumn, *Law in Transition*, EBRD, 20-27.

[10] See e.g., Personal Property Security Act RSO 1990, cP10 (Ontario, Canada); Personal Property Security Act 2009 (Cth) (Australia); and. Personal Property Security Act 1999 (New Zealand).

fair to single out the Cape Town Convention,[11] which along with the United Nations Convention on Contracts for the International Sales of Goods[12] and the New York Convention on the Enforcement on Arbitral Awards,[13] as the three most successful international commercial law instruments in the last fifty years.

Of course, there has been work in other areas such as contracts[14] and arbitration.[15] However, this work has mostly been derivative of existing law. No work in those areas have been revolutionary in the way that secured transactions has evolved.

We should also add that there was a tremendous spurt of development in electronic commerce law. From this there are now internationally accepted bedrock principles in international as well as major domestic law.[16] There is not, however, any new major work in this area currently or on the horizon.

Where the overall harmonization of private international

---

[11] *Convention on International Interests in Mobile Equipment (Cape Town, 2001) – Status* Unidroit – International Institute for the Unification of Private Law <http://www.unidroit.org/status-2001capetown> The Cape Town Convention, also called the Convention on International Interests in Mobile Equipment, has been ratified by 73 countries.

[12] Cyril Emery, *United Nations Convention on Contracts for the International Sale of Goods (Vienna, 1980) (CISG)* 1980 – United Nations Convention on Contracts for the International Sale of Goods (CISG) <http://www.uncitral.org/uncitral/en/> The United Nations Convention on Contracts for the International Sale of goods has been ratified by 86 countries.

[13] Ryan Harrington, *Status Convention on the Recognition and Enforcement of Foreign Arbitral Awards (New York, 1958)* Status <http://www.uncitral.org/uncitral/en/> The United Nations Convention on the Recognition and Enforcement of Foreign Arbitral Awards has been ratified by 157 countries.

[14] In addition to the CISG, there is also the UNIDROIT Principles of International Contracts. For an extended discussion of the importance of these two instruments, see Henry Gabriel, *Contracts for the Sale of Goods* (2nd ed., Oxford University Press, 2009).

[15] See e.g., UNCITRAL Model Law on International Commercial Arbitration (1985), with amendments as adopted in 2006, http://www.uncitral.org/

[16] Henry Gabriel, 'Electronic Commerce in International Commercial Law: Where Have We Ben and Where are We Going' (2011) 14 *International Trade and Business Law Review* 336.

commercial law seems to have lost its steam in the last few years, secured transactions [17] law keeps plugging along, and everyone wants to play. The work on the international harmonization of security rights law has been constant for the last thirty years, and it does not appear to be slowing down.

As I will discuss, there have been several important soft law as well as hard law instruments, and both have and will play important roles in the continuing harmonization of security rights.

- **Why Secured Credit?**

To appreciate the importance of the work in security rights harmonization, one must understand the significance and centrality of secured finance in modern commercial transactions. Quite simply, without external finance, most large transactions in goods and services, both domestic and international, would not take place.

At the heart of the work in the area are two assumptions. First, that capital is global, and second, that the reduction of risks in financing will increase credit and thereby the availability of goods and services.[18] Both assumptions underlie the recent work in the harmonization of secured finance.

Studies conducted by the World Bank, for example, have demonstrated that developing countries whose laws do not permit non-possessory security in moveable property face a serious impediment to economic development. Collateral provides the basis for credit markets that many developing markets lack. Creating and establishing credit is essential to economic development.

The use of collateral is restricted in many countries for lack

---

[17] The use of the term 'secured transactions' is meant to cover all transactions such as pledge and mortgage where the principal aim is to give security, not in the more limited usage of only covering movables as in the American Uniform Commercial Code or Cape Town Convention.

[18] Henry Deeb Gabriel, 'Commentary on the Availability of Credit and the Utility and Efficacy of UNCITRAL's Legislative Efforts in Secured Transactions', in Orkun Akseli (ed.) *Availability of Credit and Secured Transactions in a Time of Crisis* (Cambridge University Press, 2013), p 217

of adequate laws and registries to govern secured transactions. Establishing registries: an essential element of modern secured finance, allow businesses to leverage their assets into capital for investment and growth thereby increasing both the availability as well as the reduction in the cost of credit.[19]

- **Why Harmonization?**

Secured credit may be essential for economic development,[20] but does this also suggest the need for international harmonization? I suggest that it does. What we have witnessed in the last few decades is the rise of global capital moving seamlessly across jurisdictions. With this movement of capital there has developed a set of general principles that have been shown to be the most effective in the financing of assets, both domestically and internationally.

International harmonization, thus, serves two functions. First, it serves to provide easily recognized legal principles of secured transactions among international commercial parties that thereby reduce the transactions costs of operating among different legal systems. Second, the principles of secured transactions themselves have been shown to be efficient and therefore further reduce transaction costs.

---

[19] Elaine MacEachern et al., 'Secured Transactions and Collateral Registries', *Secured Transactions and Collateral Registries*, October 5, 2015, at <http://www.worldbank.org/en/topic/financialsector/brief/collateral-registries>

[20] The key is effective reform and modernization. There have been instances of secured transactions reform in other countries around the world that have not led to increased lending, primarily because the reforms were incomplete; did not feature factors described in this document; or failed to repeal existing laws governing lending. For example, after New Zealand introduced its *Personal Property Securities Act*, there was a sharp rise in lending, with many new security interests being registered. In Eastern Europe, particularly Albania and Romania, the number of security interests registered rose substantially after the reform (security rightsal Code or Cape Tles as in the American Uniform Commercial Code or Captetown Convention. ty, not in the more lim).

- **The Major Instruments that Have Been Developed in the Harmonization of Security Rights Law**

The most prominent instruments for the international harmonization of personal property security rights are the UNCITRAL Legislation Guide to Secured Transactions,[21] the UNCITRAL Model Law on Secured Transactions,[22] and the UNIDROIT's Cape Town Convention on International Interests in Mobile Equipment,[23] but there have been significant other developments as well. For example, the European Bank for Reconstruction and Development published its Model for Secured Transactions in 1994.[24] The Organization of American States promulgated its Model Inter-American Law on Secured Transactions in 2002.[25] The Organization for the Harmonization of Business Law in Africa (OHADA)[26] adopted their Uniform Law on Security Interests

---

[21] *UNCITRAL Legislative Guide on Secured Transactions* UNCITRAL <https://www.uncitral.org/pdf/english/texts> One might also add the United National Convention on the Assignment of Receivables. The United National Commission on International Trade Law's (UNCITRAL) activities in the area of security rights law fits squarely within the broad mandates of the Commission: harmonization and modernization of the law, legal predictability, and the encouragement of economic growth.

[22] *UNCITRAL Model Law on Secured Transactions* UNCITRAL <http://www.uncitral.org/pdf/english/texts>

[23] *Convention on International Interests in Mobile Equipment in Mobile Equipment (2001)* (June 9, 2017) UNIDROIT <http://www.unidroit.org/instruments>

[24] *Model Law on Secured Transactions, European Bank for Reconstruction and Development* 2014 OAS. < https://www.oas.org/dil/>

[25] Organization of American States' Model Inter-American Law on Secured Transactions; https://www.oas.org/dil The purpose of the Organization of American States' Model was to modernize secured transactions law by having OAS member states approve the law. The law was drafted to "foster economic growth in Central and South America, creating a 'regional credit market for the Western Hemisphere.'" See, Buxbaum, 'Unification of the Law Governing Secured Transactions: Progress and Prospects for Reform' and John M. Wilson, 'Secured Financing in Latin America: Current Law and the Model Inter-American Law on Secured Transactions,' (2000) *UCC Law Journal* 43, 107.

[26] Alex Bebe Epale, *The Revised OHADA Uniform Act on Security Law* 2012 Hogan Lovell's. OHADA is an international organization created by treaty signed by fourteen African states. These states realize that while their land is abundant with natural resources, no one will finance these expeditions without a stable legal and commercial framework that would provide for and protect private investment and property, nor

in 1997 and revised it in 2010 and 2012, and the World Bank published its Principles for Effective Insolvency and Creditor Rights Systems in 2015.

We can see two strands in this work. First, there has been the push to harmonize security rights law domestically through soft law instruments and second, there has been the development and ratification of international treaties and conventions to create harmonized principles in cross-border transactions. In both areas, there has been limited success.

- *UNCITRAL Legislative Guide for Secured Transactions & Its Progeny*

One of the more ambitious soft law projects is the UNCITRAL Legislative Guide on Secured Transactions. It is important to recognize that the Legislative Guide is one of the first international instruments to adopt what I will refer to as modern generally recognized principles of security rights law. This is a subject to which we will return as it is an essential linchpin of most international as well as domestic legal development in security rights law.

As with many UNCITRAL projects, the legislative guide began as an inchoate idea that there should be work on secured transactions. As the scope of the project began to crystalize, UNCITRAL moved away from the possibility of an international convention. [27]

This was both a political as well as a practical decision. As to the political dimensions, as I will discuss later, UNIDROIT had already made significant progress on the Cape Town Convention on International Interests in Mobile Equipment, and it was not thought to be prudent to duplicate a convention in the same area as was being done by a sister organization.

There were also the practical concerns of the feasibility of a general convention on security rights in person property. For example, a soft

---

without an independent judicial system to settle impartial disputes. This is an attempt both modernize and harmonize the business law arena in Africa.

[27] See footnote 23, *infra*.

law instrument, such as a legislative guide is not subject to the same pressure to be harmonized with existing domestic laws as are treaties and conventions and other forms of hard law.[28] In the case of a treaty or convention, there is a strong desire by adopting jurisdictions to make the treaty or convention consistent with existing domestic law of the jurisdiction. Yet, the ability to harmonize a new treaty or convention with existing domestic or international law is subject to a variety of difficulties especially when the convention is inconsistent with the jurisdiction's law of property and creditor rights.

The drafters understood that an international convention would conflict with many if not most domestic laws, thereby making its application in transactions overly complex, and for this reason the wide adoption of a convention was thought unlikely.[29] Likewise, the drafters concluded at that time that a model law on Secured Transactions would be unfeasible.[30] These concerns are quite different from the highly specialized and targeted Cape Town Convention, which for reasons I will discuss, has been more successful.

As for the Legislative Guide itself, what is somewhat puzzling is that it purports to be the potential basis for domestic legislative adoption, either as drafted or with minor revisions.[31] This assertion should not be taken too seriously, though, since it was specifically drafted as a set of principles and not a model law suitable for legislative adoption.

The major stumbling block to a model law was the question of whether the common law and civil law rules of property could both be accommodated, and the legislative guide does not bridge that gap. But what the legislative guide does achieve is the setting out of the

---

[28] See Henry Gabriel 'Toward Universal Principles: The Use of Non-Binding Principles in International Commercial Law' (2013) 17 *International Trade and Business Law Review* 241.

[29] See Official Records of the General Assembly, Fifty-Sixth Session, Supplement No. 17 (A/56/17), ¶351, 358, and 359.

[30] See Neil B. Cohen *Should UNCITRAL Prepare a Model Law on Secured Transactions?* 15 Uniform Law Review 325 (2010).

[31] Spiridon V. Bazinas, 'The Utility and Efficacy of the UNCITRAL Legislative Guide on Secure Transactions', *in* Orkun Akseli (ed.), *Availability of Credit and Secured Transactions in a Time of Crisis* (Cambridge University Press, 2013), p. 133.

basic principles for a modern and efficient system of personal property security rights. In this respect, although not, in and of itself, a model for domestic legislation, it is an excellent source for understanding the basic principles of modern secured transactions.

With the Legislative Guide completed in 2007, UNCITRAL followed up the legislative guide with the UNCITRAL Legislative Guide on Secured Transactions: Supplement on Security Rights in Intellectual Property[32] in 2010 and the UNCITRAL Guide on the Implementation of a Security Rights Registry in 2013.[33] Although these two instruments marginally add to the body of UNCITRAL work in secured transactions, their importance is minimal, and to some extent one is inclined to conclude the primary purpose they serve is to have allowed the Working Group to continue working even though the Legislative Guide had been completed.

In 2012, a decade after the work on the legislative guide to secured transactions had begun and five years after it was finished, UNCITRAL began to work on a Model Law of Secured Transactions. During this short interval, the attitudes about the desirability of a Model Law reversed itself from the previous position. The original concerns were reiterated,[34] but:

> [I]t was widely felt that a model law based on the general recommendations of the Secured Transactions Guide would provide urgently needed guidance to States in enacting or revising their secured transactions laws. In addition, it was generally viewed that a model law was sufficiently flexible and could be adapted to the various legal traditions ....[35]

---

[32] 'UNCITRAL Legislative Guide on Secured Transactions: Supplement on Security Rights in Intellectual Property', *United Nations Commission on International Trade Law,* United Nations. 2011.

[33] 'UNCITRAL Guide on the Implementation of a Security Rights Registry', *United Nations Commission on International Trade Law,* United Nations. 2014.

[34] "... the concern was expressed that a model law might be too prescriptive lifting the flexibility of States to address the relevant issues in an appropriate way that would fit their needs and suit their legal traditions." U.N. Doc A/cn.9/743 para. 74.

[35] Ibid para. 75.

In other words, irrespective of the concerns that the developing law of secured transactions favored a specific legal tradition, it was now felt that the development of secured transactions law, both in international instruments as well as domestic enactments, had reached the point of a universal consensus so that a Model Law would have broad acceptability.

The Model Law was completed in 2016. The Model Law retains the general principles of a modern security rights law that are articulated in the UNCITRAL Legislative Guide, and it expands upon the Legislative Guide by providing actual model text for a secured transactions law.

Both the UNCITRAL Model Law as well as the UNCITRAL Legislative Guide to Secured Transactions follow the core principle of modern personal property security rights law; the unitary approach of a "security interest" for all security rights in personal property. Thus, a secured loan, a retention of title sale, and a finance lease are all within the scope of the unitary "security interest".[36] If these UNCITRAL instruments are used as the basis for domestic legislation, these security devices would be governed by a single set of filing, registration and priority rules.

This have become the standard model for modern secured transactions law, and it is likely that these UNCITRAL products may influence future domestic enactments and further harmonize the law of security rights. It is too early to tell what their influence will be, but to the extent that they are used as a template for domestic secured transactions law, this will be a welcome development as this will lead to greater global harmonization of secured transactions law.

- *Half Way Measures*

UNCITRAL's work in security rights also includes a non-soft law instrument. In 2001, the United Nations promulgated its Convention

---

[36] Ibid.

on the Assignments of Receivables.[37] The Convention was quite ambitious, and in many respects, it is more advanced than many of the domestic laws that it would supplement. Given the substantial value of receivables as potential collateral, in many jurisdictions the use of receivables as collateral has only recently or has not been recognized.

The Convention has been quite unsuccessful, and it has never come into force.[38] It is worth examining the likely reasons for this lack of success.

The Convention is somewhat more limited in application than the broader concepts of secured transactions such as those envisaged by the UNCITRAL Legislative Guide and Model Law in that the convention does not bring receivables financing under the general umbrella of secured transactions.

Thus, although it provides for the creation of accounts financing, and sets out the respective obligations of the three parties in the transaction, it does not invoke the necessity of perfection and public notice that would be required under most laws that consider accounts receivable just another asset under their secured transactions law. This, for example, would be the case in the United States, Australia, Canada and New Zealand.

For those countries that already require registration and public notice, the Convention would be a step backwards. For those countries that have not generally recognized receivables financing in their domestic law, the Convention is too far reaching to be compatible with domestic financing. The Convention is firmly placed in the middle of too antiquated and too advanced.

I doubt that it has a future or needs one. Many jurisdictions need to update their domestic legislation to provide for efficient and

---

[37] *United Nations Convention on the Assignment of Receivables in International Trade* UNCITRAL <https://www.uncitral.org/pdf/english/texts>

[38] Liberia has ratified, and Luxembourg, Madagascar, and the United States have signed the Convention. A possible small positive step is that the President of the United States has sent the convention to the United States Senate for ratification. This may or may not happen in the near or not so near future.

functional secured transactions. But the absence of these domestic laws does not necessarily prevent the application of an international convention on secured transactions that is consistent with modern secured transactions. That is the case with the Cape Town Convention on International Interest in Mobile Equipment, which, as we shall see, is a widely ratified international convention based on security rights law that does not reflect the antiquated or inadequate domestic law of some of the ratifying jurisdictions.

But the Receivables Convention falls short because it does not provide for the registry and public notice system that are part of modern secured transactions systems. There may be a need for a convention that provides for the international financing of accounts receivables. It should not be one that is merely a half way measure like the this one.

UNIDROIT has also created some half measures for personal property security rights. In 1988, UNIDROIT promulgated the Ottawa Conventions: the Convention on International Financial Leasing[39] and the Convention on International Factoring.[40] Finance leasing and factoring, of course, are branches of secured transactions, and in some jurisdictions, such as the United States, are subsumed by the general domestic law of secured transactions.

Like the UNCITRAL Receivable Convention, the Finance Leasing Convention is somewhat more limited in application than broader concepts of secured transaction such as those envisaged by the UNCITRAL Legislative Guide and Model Law in that the convention does not bring receivables financing under the general umbrella of secured transactions.[41]

Thus, although it provides for the creation of a three-party finance lease, and sets out the respective obligations of the three parties in the transaction, it does not invoke the necessity of perfection and public notice that would be required in other secured transactions laws that bring finance leases within their scope. For the same reason

---

[39] http://www.unidroit.org/instruments/leasing/convention-leasing
[40] http://www.unidroit.org/instruments/factoring
[41] It only has ten ratifying states and therefore has not been widely used.

that the UNCITRAL Receivable Convention is not a model for future development we should not look to the as a template for development.

The sister convention to the Ottawa Finance Leasing Convention is the Ottawa Convention of International Factoring. As with UNCITRAL's Receivables Convention, this convention is concerned with accounts receivables. Unlike the UNCITRAL Receivables Convention, the Factoring Convention is much more limited in scope. First, it is limited to accounts from business debtors. The UNCITRAL Convention has no similar restriction. Second, and probably more important, the Factoring Convention is limiting transactions where the account debtor is notified of the assignment and thereby does not cover the extensive practice of invoice discounting. For this reason, the utility of the convention is minimal.[42]

Most important, however, the Factoring Convention, as with its sister UNDROIT and UNCITRAL conventions, does not provide for public notice. These three conventions are dated stop gap measures that provide some semblance of security rights, but do not provide the type of third party notice expected of modern secured transactions, and therefore have limited utility and futures.

- *The Cape Town Convention on International Interest in Mobile Equipment*

The most successful international harmonization of personal property security rights is the Cape Town Convention on International Interest in Mobile Equipment.[43] Having come into force in 2001, the Cape Town Convention creates international standards for the registration of ownership, security interests, and leases in certain movable property. As to these secured assets, it also provides remedies for default and it unifies the effect of bankruptcy among the contracting states.

The Convention effectively resolves the widely differing approaches legal systems have for security and title reservation rights. In other

---

[42] It only has nine ratifications and this number is not likely to increase.
[43] *The Convention of International Interests in Mobile Equipment*, opened for signature 16 November 2001 UNIDROIT.

words, the Cape Town Convention directly confronts the major issue that harmonization of security rights across borders presents; that is, how to have a system that is compatible with different legal systems and legal traditions.

The Convention provides a detailed structure for an "international security interest". It also provides, among other issues, for priorities, proceeds, and creditor and third-party rights. The Convention itself does not provide for any specific assets that might be used as collateral. These assets are provided for in separate protocols that proscribe the particular assets.

The Convention itself has seventy-three contracting States; the Aircraft Protocol[44] has sixty-seven contracting states; the Rail Protocol[45] has two ratifications and eight signatures;[46] and the Space Protocol[47] has four signatures. There is currently work on a fourth protocol on mining, agricultural, and mining equipment.

The general structure and the principles of the Cape Town Convention, to a large extent, are consistent with what may be considered the modern principles of secured transactions – a single security system,[48] a registry system, clear priority rules, the concept of perfection, and straight forward enforcement rights.

Consistent with modern security rights law, the security interest created by the convention – the "international interest," covers not only security interests, but also conditional sales contracts and finance

---

[44] *Aircraft Protocol to the Cape Town Convention,* opened for signature 16 November 2001 UNIDROIT. The Aircraft Protocol applies to aircraft which can carry at least 8 people or 2750 kilograms of cargo, aircraft engines with thrust exceeding 1,750 pounds-force (7,800 N) or 550 horsepower (410kW), and helicopters carrying 5 or more passengers. The international registry is in Dublin, Ireland.

[45] *Luxembourg Protocol to the Convention on International Interests in Mobile Equipment on Matters Specific to Railway Rolling Stock,* opened for signature 23 February 2007 UNIDROIT. This protocol covers railway rolling stock. As with the aircraft protocol, the rail protocol is concerned with international interests.

[46] This protocol has not come into force.

[47] *Protocol to the Convention on the International Interests in Mobile Equipment on Matters Specific to Space Assets,* opened for signature 27 February 2012 UNIDROIT.

[48] This is referred to as an 'international interest;' art. 2(2)

leases. In other words, it is a functional definition. Those interests, irrespective of what they are called, are covered by the convention if they function as a security interest and give the creditor a right in the assets upon the debtor's default. This, as we will discuss, is the central element of modern secured transactions law.

There is one major distinction between the Convention and other laws of secured transactions. Where most secured transactions registries are debtor based, the Cape Town Convention provides an asset based registry. This makes sense for the limited scope of the assets that are likely to travel among various jurisdictions.

Moreover, the convention is structured so that it works in conjunction with, although having priority over, otherwise applicable domestic law. In this way, the Cape Town Convention can work harmoniously with various diverse legal systems. It simply supersedes the otherwise applicable domestic law. By doing so, it provides creditors with otherwise unheard-of rights.

By providing a single recognizable legal system, it avoids the problems of having to understand the substantive law as well as the enforcement regimes of many individual countries, many of which may not have anything that resembles real security rights law.

I have suggested that the Cape Town Convention has been successful. This may only partially be true. As I have noted, the Convention itself sets out general principles but does not provide for any specific assets. The three protocols provide for the specific assets covered by the Convention. Only the aircraft protocol has been widely adopted.[49] There are a couple of reasons for this. First, the convention itself as well as the aircraft protocol was a project instituted and supported by the aircraft industry. The aircraft industry could strongly lobby individual governments about the need and usefulness of the convention and protocol. The industry had a well-financed lobbying organization, the Aircraft Working Group that has been able to work closely with governments to push ratification. Moreover, their work has been very strategic. Having achieved ratification by large economies such as the

---

[49] As noted above, neither the rail nor the space assets protocol have come into force.

United States, they were able to extract promises from export credit agencies, such as the American Export-Import Bank for better credit terms for countries that ratified the Convention and protocol.

The reasons for the lack of success of other Protocols are largely due to a lack of support by the affected industries. For example, the least popular protocol, the Space Protocol, is strongly opposed by the satellite industry that claim that it would lead to the financing of new projects more difficult and expensive.[50] Likewise, the rail protocol has not garnered any significant industry support for ratification.

This means these protocols will likely languish for years and only hope for ratification in the future. To ensure success of future revisions and provisions, the Convention must ensure that the given industry supports the Protocol and has the feasibility to lobby States to ratify the protocols.

Although heavily influenced by other laws of secured transactions, it is unlikely that the Cape Town Convention itself will be the source for further harmonization of the law of secured transactions. The Convention is too focused on particular assets – those of high value and generally subject to international mobility. Irrespective, the Convention itself is an example of the movement toward the harmonization of security rights law.

- **The Harmonization of Generally Accepted Principles of Security Rights Law**

I have referred to the "generally accepted universal principles of secured transactions" that developed over the last several decades, and it is time to turn our focus to them.

I have used as a guide a modified set of principles[51] put forth by

---

[50] Satellite Industry Association, 'Global Satellite Industry denounces UNIDROIT Protocol'. *Satellite Industry Association*. SpaceRef.com. 9 March 2012. (last accessed Feb 1, 2017).

[51] 'Secured Transactions Law Reform Project', *Policy Paper* (2016) <https://stlrp.files.wordpress.com/2016/05/str-general-policy-paper-april-2016.pdf

the Secured Transactions Law Reform Project[52], an organization in the United Kingdom that studies secured transactions laws throughout the world with the goal of establishing a basis for the UK law reform using the best models available.[53]

The key features are a single type of security interest for which the same rules of registration priority, and enforcement are applied; the "perfection" of the "security interest" by which the security interest is made valid against other creditors and in the debtor's insolvency, is

---

52 The Secured Transaction Law reform Project was established under the Executive Directorship of Professor Sir Roy Goode to involve interested parties from the professions and the relevant sectors of finance, commerce and industry as participants in the work of considering the effectiveness of the current law, and the ways in which it can be improved. It is guided by a Steering Committee originally chaired by the late Lord Bingham of Cornhill and now by Lord Saville of Newdigate. Professor Goode has now retired as Executive Director and has been succeeded by Professor Louise Gullifer. '*Secured Transactions Law Reform Project: About Us*', Secured Transactions Law Reform Project, November 5, 2015, at <https://securedtransactionslawreform-project.org/>

53 A full list of elements of a modern personal property secured transactions system would include:

- The system should be based on the use of a universal "security interest" with the ability to use any suitable asset to secure an obligation.
- The System should use a definition of "secured transaction" that includes both present and future interest and is identified by substance rather than form.
- The security agreements should be subject to few requirements intended to establish the intent to create a security interest, the identity of the parties, and a description of the assets.
- There should be a notice based on registry filing system based on a central registry with control or possession as alternative bases for notice.
- There should be a clear priority structure.
- Priority should be determined by the date of filing or the date of effective control or possession.
- Pre-filing should be allowed.
- Priority should extend to proceeds.
- Special priority is given to Purchase Money Security Interests.
- Enforcement should be easy and predictable'
- A good faith sale of collateral in the ordinary course of business takes priority over a security interest.
- The secured transactions law needs to be compatible with insolvency laws.

either by registration, possession, or control; registration could be in advance of the creation of the security interest, and the priority of the security interest is governed but the date of perfection subject to an exception for purchase money security interests; and, transactions that serve the same function as a security interest, such as conditional sales contracts, trust receipts, hire purchase agreements, finance leases and assignments of receivables are included and subject to the same rules.

What is clear is that these principles are all consistent with because they are specifically derived from the American Uniform Commercial Code rules on secured transactions.

Based on this American law, the provinces of Canada have adopted similar legislation in their respective Personal Property Security Acts.[54] New Zealand followed suit in 1999, and adopted their PPSA,[55] and Australia followed with similar legislation in 2009.[56]

Although these four countries have adopted similar laws based on similar principles, one should not assume that this is limited to common-law jurisdictions. As discussed earlier, these principles are the core principles of the UNCITRAL Legislative Guide and Model Law. Moreover, they are also consistent with the Cape Town Convention.[57]

---

[54] See e.g., *Personal Property Security Act* RS C 1990.

[55] *Personal Property Securities Act 1999* (NZ). The scheme is like the Canadian Acts in structure and content, with one major exception. This is that unregistered security interests are not void against unsecured creditors, although they are against secured creditors, execution creditors and buyers or lessees of collateral. The New Zealand law is primarily based on the Saskatchewan Personal Property Security Act

[56] *Australian Personal Property Securities Act* 2009 (Cth).

[57] Despite some suggestion to the contrary, the developed and developing international consensus in these principles of security rights law is not part of a plot by American imperialists to inflict upon the world a new American hegemonic economic order. One strong suggestion that it is has been put forth by Gerald McCormack who, using the UNCITRAL Legislative Guides as his target, has suggested that: "In the sphere of secured credit, the UNCITRAL Guide can be considered as an instrument by which the norms set out in Article 9 of the American Commercial Code are writ large across the globe". Gerard McCormack, *Secured Transactions and the Harmonization of Law: the UNCITRAL Experience* (Cheltenham: Edward Elgar, 2011) 76. This is simply nonsense. The Guide's recommendations are closely aligned with the principles of the American Uniform Commercial Code and the Canadian Personal

- **Effectiveness and Difficulty of Harmonization**

How successful have these initiatives been? For some countries such as the United States, Canada, New Zealand, and Australia, the answer is that there has not only been harmonization of the law of security rights, but that these laws have constantly been updated to reflect the change in markets and finance so that the law and current finance practices are carefully aligned.

How successful have the international treaties and conventions been to date? As I have pointed out, except for the Aircraft Protocol of the Cape Town Convention, these treaties on secured transactions have not been widely adopted. Yet, with the work of UNCITRAL as well as regional bodies such as the OAS and OHADA producing the instruments consistent with the principles outlined above, we are likely to get more harmonization beyond the short list of common law jurisdictions that have harmonized their laws of secured transactions consistent with the generally accepted principles.

This is not to say that the adoption of this model of secured transactions is not without its difficulty. Let's look at the definition of a security interest in the American law of secured transactions. This is the starting point for the concept of a unified security interest. Under this statute, a security interest is defined as:

> an interest in personal property or fixtures which secures payment or performance of an obligation.[58]

What exactly is an "interest"? To understand this definition, we can quote the primary drafter Grant Gilmore. Explaining what had been done, he says,

---

Property Security Acts, but that is because the North American model appears to be the most efficient method for a widespread system of secured credit. I pointed out twenty years ago that the United States only exports its good law, and retains for domestic purposes alone its less impressive commercial law. Henry Gabriel, 'The Revision of the Uniform Commercial Code in the United States and Its Implications for Australia' (1998) 24 *Monash University Law Review* 291.

[58] *Uniform Commercial Code*, s. 1-201(b) (35).

It is not suggested that anything useful could have been done to explain the phrase 'an interest ... which secures ... an obligation.⁵⁹

That is hardly an encouraging explanation. But note what it is not. It is not a lien, mortgage, or title right. It is a functional right, not a property right. It is what you have when you have the right to the debtor's property when the debtor does not pay the debt owed.

But for those who assume an "interest" in the debtor's property must create some property right, you would be incorrect. The drafters of the American law of secured transactions knew they were moving into uncharted territory. In anticipation of the hue and cry that was inevitable, it was pointed out that no statute had ever tried to define a mortgage.⁶⁰ A mortgage was what courts say a mortgage is based on history and practice. It worked and it works, and likewise, it was thought, the concept of a security interest would work.⁶¹ It has worked for over sixty years in the United States, but does it work well in other jurisdictions?

I will start with the example of Australia. Specifically, the Australian PPSA adopts the concept of a functional "security interest".⁶² This is the same umbrella that is contained in American law. As such, a

---

⁵⁹ Grant Gilmore, Security Interest in Personal Property, Vol. 1, (Law Book Exchange, 1965).pp. 334-35., 1965

⁶⁰ Ibid.

⁶¹ Ibid.

⁶² *Australian Personal Property Securities Act* 2009 (Cth) s 12(1): "A security interest means an interest in personal property provided for by a transaction that, in substance, secures payment or performance of an obligation (without regards to the form of the transaction or the identity of the person who has title to the property). The scope of the Australian PPSA does not fully track the American law. Thus, for example, consignments, assignments of accounts and chattel paper and leases and bailments for over a year are "deemed" security interest. This is based on the realization that these transactions may or may not actually serve to function as a security right. Article Nine does not assume that consignments and assignments of accounts are "security interests"; instead Article Nine simply says they are governed by the legislation. See *Uniform Commercial Code*, s.9-109. Article Nine also differs from the Australian law in that it only covers those leases that appear to function as security. *See Uniform Commercial Code*, s. 9-203.

conditional sales contract, in other words, a contract with a title retention clause, is specifically covered by legislation.[63] A purported title retention clause does not operate as a condition to the transfer of title; it operates to create a security interest. A title retention clause triggers the operation of the PPSA,[64] and the seller must register the interest or do whatever would otherwise be necessary to perfect the interest.

It is not surprising that such sweeping legislation would be disruptive. The Australian government, to ascertain the effectiveness of the new legislation, commissioned a report to study its effects and possible problems. In 2015, the Government released the report, which weighs in at 542 pages.[65]

One problem articulated in the report is this very question of title retention in a contract. A quick overview of pre-PPSA Australian law will suggest the source of the problem. Prior to the PPSA, one could generally divide security devices into two categories: those where the creditor took an interest in the debtor's property[66] and those in which the creditor retained, by way of contract, some level of title in property.[67] It should be clear that both categories are covered under the PPSA.[68]

What becomes evident from the government report, however, is that some who are deeply steeped in the prior law have trouble with this conclusion. The confusion arises from the language of the PPSA that provides that the creditor has an "interest" in the debtor's property (the

---

[63] Ibid 12(2)(d).
[64] Ibid 12(1).
[65] *Review of the Personal Property Security Act (2009)*. Attorney-General's Department <https://www.ag.gov.au/Consultations/Documents/>
[66] This includes chattel mortgages and company charges. See e.g., Duggan, AJ and David Brown, *Australian Personal Property Securities Law* 2d. ed. (Lexis Nexis Butterworths 2016) 8-9.
[67] This includes conditional sales contracts, hire-purchase agreements and financial leases. Ibid 12-15.
[68] Those closely affiliated with the legislation seem to harbor no doubts on this point. Ibid 15.

interest, of course, being a "security interest"). This, it is suggested, makes sense as a security interest in the case where the debtor has title to the goods and the creditor retains an *in rem* "interest", but this does not make sense, it is suggested, when the creditor, by way of contract, retains some contractual right against the buyer as the contract right would not be effective against third parties.[69]

This seems to me to be a very sensible misunderstanding of the law, but a misunderstanding all the same. Although the statute specifically states it covers retention of title transactions,[70] I suspect that a real concern is the fact that lawyers are having a hard time adjusting to the fact that the legislation carves out a portion of the law of contract and puts it somewhere else; that being, in the Personal Property Security Act.[71]

Why is there a question of whether this "interest" that the secured creditor has in the debtor's property is a real interest in property or a personal interest that might be created by contract? The answer is that Australia's prior law is based on the law of the United Kingdom.[72]

It is this precise point that has cause the greatest difficulty with the adoption of a unitary security rights law in the United Kingdom, and this difficulty may suggest to us a difficulty in further harmonization of the law of security rights.

The United Kingdom, consistent with long developed common-

---

[69] *Review of the Personal Property Security Act (2009)* Attorney-General's Department 43-45. The question is whether all "security interests under the PPSA are effectively in rem rights that would be effective against the world at large, or whether the PPSA is intended to include purely personal rights that are created under contract law. For a further explanation of this, see, Duggan, AJ and David Brown, *Australian Personal Property Securities Law* 2d. ed. (Lexis Nexis Butterworths 2016)

[70] *Personal Property Securities Act 2009* (Cth) s 12(2)(d).

[71] There appears to have been similar resistance in New Zealand when it adopted its PPSA. See: Mike Gedye, 'The New Zealand Perspective' in Gullifer and Aksali (eds), *Secured Transactions Law Reform: Principles Policies and* Practice (Hart Publishing, 2016) 117, 125-28.

[72] This is the common-law dilemma, and this question is simply not addressed in the definition of a security interest or the substantive provisions of Article 9.

law principles, divides secured transactions into two broad categories: real security rights;[73] in which the creditor has a property interest in the debtor's goods, and those transactions that function as security devices but in which the seller does not have an interest in the debtor's assets and merely retains title to the goods until the debtor pays the price.[74] These latter are the conditional sales agreement and the hire purchase agreement.

This practical distinction arose from the Bills of Sale legislation that imposed a registration requirement for chattel mortgages and the Corporations Act which required the registration of a company charge. These create "real rights," and these statutes did not apply to conditional sales contracts.

The English financiers wanted to avoid the registration and enforcement of the requirements of the Bills of Sale Act, and therefore began to rely on the conditional sales agreement. This usage was bolstered when the House of Lords recognized that the Bills of Sale legislation did not apply to a conditional sales contract.[75]

As for the application and complexity of Bill of Sales Acts, there

---

[73] The four devices are the pledge, the contractual lien, the mortgage and the equitable charge.

[74] See e.g., Hugh Beale, Michael Bridge, Louise Gullifer and Eva Lomnicka *The Law of Personal Property Security*, 2d. ed. (2012) Oxford University Press, Oxford, ¶7.03; Robert Bradgate *Commercial Law* (Oxford University Press 3rd ed 2005) 477-534

[75] *McEntire v Crossley Brothers* (1895) AC 457. This is not to assert that the conditional sales contract was a panacea for creditor sellers in England. Under successive versions of the Factors Act and the Court of Appeals case of *Lee v Butler* (1893) 2 QB 318, it became clear that a seller that had retained title under a conditional sales contract would be subject to a good faith purchaser of the debtor-buyer. One might assume as to the actual validity of a conditional sales contract, this has been settled in *Aluminium Industrie Vaassen BV v Romalpa Aluminium Ltd.* (1976) 1 WRL 676, a case so famous that it has spawned the term "Romalpa Clause" for a title retention term. Nothing however, is actually settled in the law. It does appear, however, that it is improper to deem a Romalpa clause an attempt to create a charge under the Companies Act, see e.g., *Clough Mills v Martin* (1985) 1 WLR 111, or presumably otherwise governed by the Bills of Sale Acts.

have been complaints about them for over a century.[76] Irrespective, the Bill of Sales Acts (1878 and 1882, as amended in 1890 and 1891) are still in force and they work in relation to and in an uneasy peace with the Companies Act (and to some extent with the Insolvency Act and the Consumer Credit Act).

To further complicate matters, as with any complicated system that is built up over years of overlapping laws, for consumer protection, the U.K. Consumer Protection Act covers both "real" security interest as well as those quasi-interests such as conditional sales agreements that may have fallen in between the cracks of the legislation covering "real" security rights.[77]

It is a complicated mess, and one does not want to avoid the requirements of the highly technical requirements of these Acts. The consequences can be dour.[78]

It has been suggested that the Canadian reform of personal property security rights arose from the same situation that the U.K. is presently in: the law in Canada had become "highly fragmented" and had evolved into "a complex mix of security devices" and that each device "was subject to a discrete conceptual and legal framework as well as discreet and often highly technical public registration requirements."[79] The same reasons instigated the reforms in New Zealand[80] and Australia.[81]

---

[76] See e.g., Louise Gullifer, 'The English Law of Personal Property Security: Under Reformed?' in Gulifer and Askali (eds), *Secured Transactions Law Reform: Princoples Policies and Practice* (Hart Publishing, 2016) 287, 287-89.

[77] See *Consumer Credit Act* (UK) s. 87(1)(c).

[78] See e.g., *Chapman v Wilson* (2010) EWHC 1746. (a document drafted by a solicitor was held invalid for lack of formality).\

[79] Catherine Walsh, 'Transplanting Article 9: The Canadian PPSAA Experience' in Gullifer and Aksali (eds) *Secured Transactions Law Reform: Principles, Policies, and Practice* (Hart Publishing, 2016) 52.

[80] See generally, Mike Gedye, "'he New Zealand Perspective' in Gullifer and Akasli (eds), *Secured Transactions Law Reform: Principles, Policies, and* Practice (Hart Publishing, 2016).

[81] Duggan, AJ and David Brown, *Australian Personal Property Securities Law* 2d. ed. (Lexis Nexis Butterworths 2016) 18-19.

Why the hesitancy in the U.K.? As I mentioned, it is for the same reason we recently looked at in Australia. Let's look back at the conditional sales contract. It all comes down to the concept of title. If a seller retains "title" to the goods under a contract, that is simply an incident of contract, and it does not create "interest" in the buyer's goods. This is basic contract law, and under the common law of contract, this is not a security interest, but simply a personal right retained by a contracting party. Therefore, it should not require the seller to abide by the formalities of the law of secured transactions. The seller has no interest in the buyer's goods; no lien, no mortgage, hence no security interest.

This is precisely the type of question the functional definition of a security interest avoids.

Might some half way measures satisfy the concerns of the U.K.? We might look back to the Cape Town Convention for an answer.

The Cape Town Convention provides for both title retention as well as the American model of the unitary security interest. The Convention is drafted with the possibility of both "security interests" and "title retention" agreements as the basis for a security right.[82] Moreover, and right to the point, the definition of a "security interest"

---

[82] The Convention also included leases, but that is not relevant to our discussion. See, Goode, Royston Miles, *Convention on International Interests in Mobile Equipment and Protocol Thereto on Matters Specific to Aircraft Equipment*: Official Commentary, (International Institute for the Unification of Private Law (UNIDROIT) 2013) 3d edition, s 2.37. A security interest is an interest created by a security agreement (Article 1(jj)) and includes a security transfer of ownership, a charge in the sense of an encumbrance which binds the asset but leaves ownership with the debtor, a pledge and a contractual lien, which differs from a pledge only in that the asset is delivered to the creditor not as security but for some other purpose, such as storage or repair, so that the contractual provision secures future obligations. All four forms of security interest fall within the scope of the Convention. However, the pledge, being possessory in nature, does not feature significantly in aviation finance. By contrast a contractual lien may be taken to secure charges relating to the aircraft object, such as charges or storage or repair. Non-consensual rights or interests do not fall within the definition of a security interest and are dealt with separately, specifically in Articles 39 and 40. A title reservation agreement (also commonly known as a conditional sale agreement) is an agreement for the sale of an object on terms that ownership does not pass until fulfilment of the condition or conditions stated in the agreement.

itself can cover both interests that assume some title retention by the creditor or a lien type interest in the goods:

> A security interest is an interest created by a security agreement ... and includes a security transfer of ownership, [or] a charge in the sense of an encumbrance which binds the asset but leaves ownership with the debtor ...[1]

This, of course, is a marriage of convenience,[2] but it does provide a way to bridge the question of whether a security interest is analytically more like a mortgage lien or whether it should be treated as property rights by the creditor in the goods. The Convention simply defines a security interest as either, and therefore includes both.

In American, Canadian, and Australian law, all the manifestations of secured finance in personal property are implicitly recognized. Could the simple functional definition of a "security interest" work for example in the Cape Town Convention? I think it clearly could have. But to achieve that, the drafters would have had to risk the possibility that the concept would not be widely understood or accepted.[3]

That was certainly not a risk worth taking. To include this functional definition would require international agreement that concepts such as title and lien are not necessary in a secured transactions law.

This was a leap that American law made seventy years ago, and it has worked well there and other jurisdictions that have followed its path. As we have seen, this is also the approach taken in the UNCITRAL Model Law on Secured Transactions. But for the UNCITRAL Model Law and similar instruments to be adopted, countries will have to move beyond the formal rules of contract and property and take the leap of faith provided for with what I have deemed the generally accepted principles of secured transactions; that means a "security interest" is what a security interest says it is.

---

[1] Ibid.

[2] It is more like a shotgun wedding.

[3] Implicit in my assumption is that the functional unitary "security interest" is a good idea. Some may disagree.

It is an "interest" in the debtor's property to secure a debt. Beyond that, we cannot define it. Yet, this is the standard in which so much energy has been put forth to in the attempt to harmonize personal property security law. How far this harmonization will go internationally is yet to be seen.

16

THE SEVEN HABITS OF HIGHLY EFFECTIVE MOOTERS

Lorraine Finlay

"Remember, to learn and not to do is really not to learn. To know and not to do is really not to know". – Stephen R. Covey *(1989)* [1]

- **Introduction**

Throughout his prestigious academic career Emeritus Professor Gabriël Moens has not only been known for encouraging academic excellence, but also for emphasising the importance of practical legal training. The best example of this has been his long-term support for mooting as an integral part of legal education. As a moot coach his student teams have won the prestigious Willem C Vis International Commercial Arbitration Moot multiple times. He was responsible for bringing the American concept of a dedicated Moot Court into Australian Law Schools by introducing a Moot Court Bench at both the University of Queensland and Murdoch University.[2] As the Dean of Murdoch Law School he was responsible for developing an innovative and world-class moot program that embedded mooting in the curriculum.

Mooting has been used for hundreds of years as a tool for training young lawyers, with the earliest record of law moots dating back to 1428 where it was used by the Inns of Court in England to train young

---

[1] Stephen R. Covey, *The Seven Habits of Highly Effective People: Restoring the Character Ethic* (Free Press, 1989), p 12.
[2] Vernon Nase, 'The Murdoch Moot Court Bench' (2009) 12 *International Trade & Business Law Review* 285, at 285.

barristers in advocacy.³ It has a continued role in modern times, with almost every law school in Australia offering students the opportunity to engage in mooting in some way during their studies. It is "now part of the staple diet of legal education in Australia".⁴

There are, however, different opinions about the value of mooting as an educative tool in law schools. Proponents point to moots giving students significant opportunities to develop their research and writing skills, gain valuable advocacy experience, receive engaged feedback from coaches and judges, and the important role that mooting can play in building the confidence of students in themselves as future lawyers.⁵ However, mooting also has its critics whose claims include that moot court competitions are elitist, inherently artificial and unrealistic, place too little emphasis on written submissions, and focus too heavily on appellate arguments that bear little resemblance to the actual advocacy work young lawyers are routinely engaged in when they first commence legal practice. ⁶

Discussions about the value of mooting have, unsurprisingly, tended to focus on the legal training that mooting provides, whether this be through the gaining of substantive legal knowledge or the development of practical legal skills. What has often been missed from the discussion is a recognition of the character building aspect of mooting and, in particular, its ability to develop general skills that are not unique to law but which are absolutely essential for anybody hoping to build a successful legal career.

My experience as both a mooter and moot coach has certainly

---

³ The Hon. Justice Michael Kirby, *Mooting – Past, Present, Future* (Victoria University of Technology School of Law, Melbourne, 22 August 2001).
⁴ Ibid.
⁵ See, for example, Michael V Hernandez, 'In Defense of Moot Court: A Response to 'In Praise of Moot Court – Not'' (1998) 17 *The Review of Litigation* 69; Darby Dickerson, 'In Re Moot Court' (2000) 29 *Stetson Law Review* 1217; Louise Parsons, 'Competitive Mooting as Clinical Legal Education: Can Real Benefits be Derived from an Unreal Experience' (2016) *Australian Journal of Clinical Education:* Vol. 1, Article 4.
⁶ See, for example, Alex Kozinski, 'In Praise of Moot Court – Not!' (1997) 97 *Columbia Law Review* 178; Bobette Wolski, 'Beyond Mooting: Designing an Advocacy, Ethics and Values Matrix for the Law School Curriculum' (2009) 19 *Legal Education Review* 41.

been that mooting has an important role to play in developing a wide range of legal skills, including research, writing and advocacy skills. It also requires students to gain an understanding of specific areas of law in a far greater depth than is generally expected in a standard law unit. In my view, however, its greatest benefit lies in the way that it develops an individual's character and provides them with non-legal skills that will benefit them in all aspects of their life, particularly their professional life.

In his best-selling book *The 7 Habits of Highly Effective People* Stephen R. Covey spoke of the "Character Ethic" as being the foundation of success. By this, he meant the integration of certain universal principles – "things like integrity, humility, fidelity, temperance, courage, justice, patience, industry, simplicity, modesty, and the Golden Rule"[7] – into habits of daily life that allow people to become more effective in both their personal and professional lives. In a similar way, one of the key benefits of mooting is the way that it teaches students character habits that allow them to become more effective lawyers.

There are a range of essential character habits that mooting builds in students, but perhaps the most important of these include a strong work ethic, resilience, teamwork, strategic decision-making, attention to detail, honesty & integrity, and a global outlook. To this end, I would endorse the observation made by Michael V. Hernandez about his experience of moot courts in America:

> Perhaps the greatest benefit of moot court is intangible but important nonetheless: building character. I have seen people literally transformed for the better by their experiences in moot court. Students who were petrified by the thought of speaking in public, much less making an oral argument before a panel of real judges under adversarial fire, suddenly have come alive in the heat of battle. This transformation does not happen to everyone, but most moot court participants, especially students who receive instruction from coaches, grow noticeably.[8]

---

7 Covey, above n.1, p 18.

[8] Hernandez, above n.5, at 77.

- **A Strong Work Ethic**

There is no getting around the fact that working in law requires a lot of hard work. The hours can be long, and the realities of legal practice mean that lawyers often find themselves required to work additional hours with very little advance warning. The evidence of higher than average working hours is not merely anecdotal or isolated to small pockets of the profession, with recent research undertaken by the Law Council of Australia highlighting long working hours and poor work-life balance as key drivers of dissatisfaction within the legal profession.[9] In a speech to launch Law Week in 2010, the Chief Justice of Western Australia highlighted the potentially detrimental impact of billable hours in particular, noting that the practice has been subject of a number of jokes:

> Many of you may have heard the one about the lawyer in his early 40s who arrived at the pearly gates and protested to St Peter that he had been taken too young and deserved to live longer. St Peter replied that while the lawyer might believe he was only in his early 40s, analysis of his time sheets revealed that he must in fact be in his 90s.[10]

To the extent that workload is driven by an outdated law firm culture that values 'presenteeism' and billable hours over performance and results, this is problematic.[11] On the other hand, while the recent focus within the legal profession on work-life balance and flexible working arrangements is undoubtedly positive, it cannot overshadow the simple truth that, in reality, the law is a demanding profession. The important responsibilities and professional obligations that are placed

---

[9] Law Council of Australia, *National Attrition and Re-engagement Study (NARS) Report* (2013). Accessed at: <file:///C:/Users/20094042/Downloads/NARS%20Report.pdf>.

[10] The Hon Wayne Martin (Chief Justice of Western Australia), *Billable Hours – past their use-by date* (Perth Press Club, Launch of Law Week 2010, 17 May 2010), 4. Accessed at: <http://www.supremecourt.wa.gov.au>.

[11] See, for example, Victorian Equal Opportunity & Human Rights Commission, *Changing the Rules: The experiences of female lawyers in Victoria* (2012), 5; Patricia Easteal, Anne Caligari, Lorana Bartels & Emma Fitch, "Flexible Work Practices and Private Law Firm Culture: A Complex Quagmire for Australian Women Lawyers" (2015) 15(1) *QUT Law Review* 30, at 38.

on lawyers require that they approach their work with a high degree of diligence and commitment. For example, when asked in an interview what advice she would give to practitioners appearing before the Court of Appeal, the-then newly appointed President of the WA Court of Appeal, Justice Carmel McLure, answered:

> It's quite simple, but it's this: never be satisfied with anything but the best you can do for the party you represent. Even if it means, as it almost inevitably will, that you can't charge for all the necessary preparation time. And the preparation time is the time it takes to really come to grips with the reasons below; the framework of legal principles that apply; the legal and factual issues that arise for determination; how the law should apply to the facts and all the evidence relevant to disputed facts. And I add to that: time to contemplate, time to think. If you do all that and you do the best that you can for your client, you'll be a success in your advocacy in the Court of Appeal.
>
> I know there are all sorts of pressures on counsel and really the message is: you're acting for someone else, you have to do the best you can for them. There are no short cuts. You may not be able to charge but that's your obligation. Pride in performance, apart from anything else, can make some client demands or professional obligations on counsel very difficult. The two can be in conflict. But if you follow the path of doing the best you can, the amount of time that will be required in preparation over the long haul of your career will change. It's in your best interests to accumulate a broad knowledge and skill base.[12]

Moot students understand the importance of being prepared, and the need to have a broad base of legal and factual knowledge from which to draw when facing moot judges. Furthermore, unlike law school assignments or exams that can essentially be forgotten once completed, most large moot competitions involve students competing in multiple rounds meaning that even after one moot is completed, there is always more work to be done to prepare for the next moot. Moot students come to understand that no matter how much work

---

[12] Rebecca Lee, 'Pride in Performance: An Interview with the Hon Justice Carmel McLure, President of the Court of Appeal' (2010) 37(3) *Brief* 10, at 11.

you have put in, there will always be more work that can be done to further refine your submissions, develop alternative arguments, or deal with last minute issues or questions that emerge. Any mooter will tell you that preparing for a significant national or international moot competition requires a level of work far beyond what is required for a standard unit studied at law school. While advocacy always involves an element of luck, there is simply no substitute for hard work and preparation. The experience of mooting helps students to truly understand this fact, and to gain a realistic appreciation of the type of work ethic needed to succeed in legal practice.

- **Resilience**

Law is not an easy or relaxing profession. It is both competitive and combative. A lawyer almost inevitably works long hours, faces unrealistic deadlines, has limited ability to control their workload, spends their working life dealing with other people's problems, and measures their time in six-minute billable intervals. The negative impact this can have on mental health is well recorded, with there being a significant body of research over the past decade highlighting the prevalence of depression and other mental health issues within the legal profession.[13] For example, the 2009 *Courting the Blues* report found that "law students and members of the legal profession exhibit higher levels of psychological distress and depression than do community members of a similar age and sex".[14]

Given this, it is fundamentally important for law students and young lawyers to build resilience to help them manage the stress and pressure that they will inevitably face as a practising lawyer. Resilience "is not an innate attribute" but is something that can be learnt and

---

[13] See, for example, Dr Norm Kelk, Dr Georgina Luscombe, Dr Sharon Medlow & Professor Ian Hickie, *Courting the Blues: Attitudes Towards Depression in Australian Law Students and Lawyers* (Brain & Mind Institute, University of Sydney, 2009); Dr Chris Kendall, *Report on Psychological Distress and Depression in the Legal Profession,* (Law Society of Western Australia, March 2011).

[14] Kelk et al., above n.13, p 42.

developed.[15] Indeed, one of the key recommendations of the *Courting the Blues* report was that "law students and legal professionals need to be made aware of, and prepared for, normal forms of stress in the normal workplace".[16]

At first glance, mooting would appear to simply replicate many of the factors that have been identified as problematic in the legal profession. During any moot competition most moot students will have experienced long hours working alone on research, struggling to meet strict deadlines, conflicts with team members, and heightened levels of pressure and anxiety at various times. The very experience of dealing with these issues ultimately serves students well in the longer-term as it helps them to develop the coping mechanisms that they will need in their professional working lives. Indeed, many of the protective factors identified by researchers as important in building resilience in young people are readily identified in the mooting experience. These include building a sense of connectedness through the development of supportive relationships with teammates and coaches; the development of interpersonal skills relating to communication and conflict resolution; the development of cognitive skills relating to problem-solving, decision-making and goal-setting; and the strengthening of confidence and self-esteem gained through developing skills and achieving goals.[17]

Participating in mooting is stressful, competitive and challenging. However, a well-designed moot program and experienced moot coaches will aim to ensure that students participating in a moot are given the support, guidance and encouragement that they need to not

---

[15] Kylie G. Oliver, Phillipa Collin, Jane Burns, & Jonathan Nicholas, 'Building Resilience in Young People Through Meaningful Participation" (2006) 5(1) *Australian e-Journal for the Advancement of Mental Health* 1. Accessed at: <https://researchonline.jcu.edu.au/3691/1/3691_Oliver_et_al_2006.pdf>

[16] Kelk et al, above n.13, 49; Kendall, above n.13, p 7.

[17] See, for example, Oliver et al, above n.15, 1; Helen Cahill, Sally Beadle, Anne Farrelly, Ruth Forster & Dr Kylie Smith, *Building Resilience in Children and Young People: A Literature Review for the Department of Education and Early Childhood Development (DEECD)* (University of Melbourne), p 22. Accessed at: <http://www.education.vic.gov.au/Documents/about/department/resiliencelitreview.pdf>

only survive the experience, but to emerge stronger and more resilient from it.

- **Teamwork**

No lawyer works in total isolation. Being able to work collaboratively within a team is increasingly seen by law firms as a desirable quality in potential employees. However, most law students graduate with relatively little experience in teamwork. The teaching of teamwork skills in law school is generally limited to the occasional group assessment, with much of the teaching and assessment still based on traditional notions of studying law being largely an individual pursuit.

This is a shame, both in terms of future employability and also because of the way that teaching teamwork can enhance a range of professional and interpersonal skills '... including communication, planning and coordination, leadership and cooperation, as well as conflict resolution, problem solving, and creative thinking'.[18] Studies have also shown that small group work results in higher academic achievement and that team building activities help to build 'significantly higher levels of trust, social support, openness, and satisfaction', which itself links back to the earlier discussion about developing resilience in law students.[19]

Mooting is an activity that requires students to engage in meaningful teamwork. The vast majority of national and international moot competitions require students to enter in teams of between 2-5 people. In most cases, these teams are selected through a competitive selection process conducted by each individual law school. Moot students therefore find themselves working collaboratively with a small group of fellow students who they themselves did not select and may not have even known prior to the competition. While individuals may be tasked with independently researching a particular issue or developing a particular argument, preparing for a moot is undoubtedly

---

[18] Janet Weinstein, Linda Morton, Howard Taras and Vivian Reznik, 'Teaching Teamwork to Law Students' (2013) 63(1) *Journal of Legal Education* 36, at 36.
[19] Ibid, 38.

a team effort. It is simply not possible to develop a consistent and coherent set of written and oral submissions if each team member only works individually on discrete areas and the team fails to collaborate across the moot problem. The experience of a moot gives students direct exposure to both the challenges and rewards of working in a team.

- **Strategic Decision-making**

The traditional law school assessment presents students with little opportunity to make the type of strategic decisions that they will routinely need to make as practising lawyers. This observation was also made by Richard E. Finneran, who noted:

> Traditional law school classes are effective at teaching fundamental principles of law and introducing students to the process of legal reasoning, but they do rather little to teach students how to make the innumerable strategic choices that lawyers are faced with every day. It is one thing (and a very valuable thing) to spot all of the legal issues that may inhere in a given factual scenario, but it is quite another to determine, from among those legal issues, which to select and the order in which to present them in order to maximise one's likelihood of success before a court.[20]

Most problem scenarios that are given as either assignment or exam questions at law school are expressly designed to test certain topics that have been covered in class. As a result they tend to raise a limited number of discrete issues that will each generally call for a corresponding 'correct' answer. These answers usually follow a standard format that students are taught when working through practice problems in tutorials. Students generally aren't encouraged to move beyond the material that has been covered in class, or to deviate from the standard answer format that has been taught. Indeed, going beyond the scope of the course material may be detrimental to the final grade if it means that students don't sufficiently address the expected

---

[20] Richard E. Finneran, 'Wherefore Moot Court' (2017) 53 *Washington University Journal of Law & Policy* 121, at 126.

topics covered in the marking guide. It is relatively rare for students to be given a problem question that is complex enough to require any real strategic decision-making.

Moot problems stand in sharp contrast to the traditional law school problem question, both in terms of facts and law. In relation to facts, most moot problems present students with a detailed fact pattern that raises multiple legal issues and that can be interpreted in ways both advantageous and detrimental to each respective side of the argument. In relation to the law, most moot problems are designed to engage with current legal questions that are not entirely settled, and for which there is no definitive 'correct' answer. While students are usually limited to arguing specified grounds of appeal, within those grounds they are not restricted to particular arguments. Students are encouraged to identify issues, consider and weigh up alternative arguments, develop original lines of research, and make strategic decisions about the best way to develop their overall submissions. They will usually be required to consider issues of internal consistency in terms of the way that different arguments fit together and to engage with not only the strengths, but also the weaknesses of their position. Finally, having to answer questions from the Bench during oral arguments requires students to think about where each point that they make will logically lead and to make strategic decisions on the spot. There are few other experiences that students will have during law school that engages this type of strategic decision-making as strongly as mooting.

- **Attention to Detail**

A lawyer is required to display meticulous attention to detail in all aspects of their work. A single word out of place in a contract or missing a deadline by the smallest of margins can spell disaster for a client. While this is a skill that students are always encouraged to improve at law school, students who participate in mooting find it bought into sharp focus due to both the strategic and interactive nature of a moot. The strategic complexity of most moot problems mean that students quickly learn when drafting written submissions that even the smallest details matter. A small fact hidden deep in the moot problem often turns out to have disproportionate legal significance. Selecting precisely the right language when phrasing a difficult point may close off counter-arguments before they even arise or, alternatively, create additional problems that are best avoided. Highlighting a particular fact in relation to one submission may lead to internal difficulties for a later argument. When compiling written submissions most moot teams will prepare numerous drafts and will go over each word that is written time and time again. By the time students actually come to present their oral arguments in a moot competition every submission that is made has been revised, reconsidered and refined countless times.

The interactive nature of a moot competition also encourages mooters to pay keen attention to the details. While students do usually receive feedback from each law school assessment they submit during their studies, this is a largely passive feedback process from the perspective of the student. They are not usually required to respond to the feedback nor to actually engage any further with the assessment once it has been initially submitted. By contrast, moot students know that both their written and oral submissions will be closely examined by both the moot judges and the opposition moot team. Any mistakes or weaknesses will likely be enthusiastically highlighted by opposing counsel, and every point that you raise may be actively tested by the judge. Students are expected to engage with the arguments raised by opposing counsel, and to engage with the questions asked by the Bench. Knowing that you will be subject to this level of scrutiny, and will have to respond to it, tends to focus the mind quite sharply and encourages students to develop a scrupulous attention to detail.

- **Honesty & Integrity**

Lawyers have never rated particularly highly in surveys measuring public perceptions of ethics and honesty. In the 2017 *Roy Morgan Image of Professions Survey* only 35% of respondents rated lawyers as 'very high' or 'high' for ethics and honesty, lower than nurses, teachers, engineers, accountants, public servants and a range of other occupations.[21] The reality of legal practice stands in stark contrast to this public perception, with the professional conduct rules that govern the legal profession in each jurisdiction demanding a high standard of ethics and honesty. A person cannot be admitted to legal practice in Australia unless they meet good character requirements,[22] and professional conduct rules in all Australian jurisdictions emphasise fundamental ethical obligations, including the paramount duty that all lawyers have to the court and the administration of justice.[23]

While Ethics & Professional Responsibility is mandated as one of the *Priestley 11* law subjects required to be taught in Australia as part of any recognised law degree, integrating ethics in a practical way into legal studies is more challenging and tends to be done in a less than comprehensive way. In my experience, mooting can play a role here in giving students practical exposure to ethical issues commonly experienced by advocates.

While moots are generally set in appellate courts, and so don't raise any of the ethical issues that commonly arise when lawyers are dealing with clients or involved in a trial, there are still a variety of ethical concerns raised in the course of appellate advocacy.[24] A good moot coach will ensure that moot students learn to navigate these issues effectively and develop the necessary skills to become an ethical advocate.

For example, the usual preparation process for significant moot

---

[21] *Roy Morgan Image of Professions Survey 2017: Health professionals continue domination with Nurses most highly regarded again; followed by Doctors and Pharmacists* (7 June 2017). Accessed at: <http://www.roymorgan.com/findings>

[22] *Legal Profession Act 2006* (ACT), s 26(2)(b); *Legal Profession Uniform Law (NSW)*, s 17(1)(c); *Legal Profession Act (NT)*, s 25(2)(b); *Legal Profession Act 2007* (Qld), s 35(2)(a)(ii); *Legal Practitioners Act 1981* (SA), s 15(1)(a); *Legal Profession Act 2007* (Tas), s 31(6)(b); *Legal Profession Act 2008* (WA), s 26(1).

[23] See, for example, *Legal Profession Uniform Law Australian Solicitors' Conduct Rules 2015* (NSW) and *Legal Profession Uniform Conduct (Barristers) Rules 2015* (NSW).

[24] See, for example, Lawrence W. Pierce, "Appellate Advocacy: Some Reflections From the Bench" (1993) 61(4) *Fordham Law Review*.

competitions reinforces for students the importance of honesty and candour in advocacy.[25] Students are generally required to prepare submissions for both sides of the moot problem and, as a result, they generally know the strengths and weaknesses of both sides of the case. Prior to the competition itself mooters will participate in a significant number of practice moots before experienced moot judges (who are often themselves practicing lawyers), and during a moot competition will appear before judges who often have a specialised knowledge of the relevant areas of law. The vast majority of mooters will be able to recall a time when they – whether by design or accident – stretched a point in their presentation of the case, were not entirely candid in their discussion of relevant legal authorities, or were less than professional in their responses to either opposing counsel or judges. The vast majority of mooters will equally be able to recall the negative feedback they subsequently received in response from either the judge in question or their moot coach. Such an experience naturally reinforces the importance of civility and honesty in advocacy, and develops in students a greater appreciation for just how far they can extend the law and facts in a particular case before crossing an ethical line.

Ethical and collegiate behaviour is also emphasised and encouraged at all of the major national and international moot competitions. For example, international moot competitions such as the *Willem C. Vis International Commercial Arbitration Moot*, *Philip C. Jessup Public International Law Moot Competition*, *International Maritime Law Arbitration Moot* and the *Manfred Lachs Space Law Moot Court Competition* (amongst others) all offer separate 'Spirit of the Moot' awards for the moot teams that best encapsulate the broader qualities and character that these competitions aim to encourage. While these moots are obviously highly competitive, all moot students will tell you that the overall experience extends far beyond the official results achieved in the particular competition.

---

[25] The Hon. Justice Michael Kirby, *Ten Rules of Appellate Advocacy* (Australian Advocacy Institute – Appellate Skills Workshop, Sydney, 5 May 1995). Accessed at: <http://www.lawfoundation.net.au>

- **A Global Outlook**

This final quality is particularly apt given that this article is part of a collection designed to honour the esteemed academic career of Emeritus Professor Gabriël Moens, who has been known not only for his keen support of mooting but also for his firm belief in the importance of offering global opportunities to law students. This was a defining feature of his time as Dean of Murdoch Law School, where he articulated a global vision for the Law School:

> Murdoch Law School is Australia's Global Law School: it offers global opportunities to students to experience a truly international education enabling them to engage in the international practice of law.[26]

This global focus in legal education is increasingly important given the continued 'internationalisation' of the legal profession, which presents both opportunities and challenges for lawyers. One recognised challenge for law schools is the need to ensure that Australian law graduates are equipped "... with the necessary international and intercultural competencies to work in a global legal context".[27]

Moot competitions offer students unique global opportunities. Most obviously, students participating in international moot competitions will have the chance to travel overseas to be part of the competition. My very first overseas trip was through mooting, when as a law student the moot team that I was part of travelled to Washington D.C. after qualifying for the international rounds of the Philip C. Jessup Public International Law Moot Competition. This still remains the highlight of my time at law school, not only because of the chance to travel overseas but also the opportunity to engage with law students

---

[26] Philip Evans & Gabriël A Moens (eds), *Murdoch Law School: The Search for Excellence* (Murdoch University, 2010), at 10.

[27] Robert French, 'Internationalisation of the Legal Profession' (2013) 227 *Ethos: Official Publication of the Law Society of the Australian Capital Territory* 26, at 27. See also Carmel O'Sullivan & Judith McNamara, "Creating a global law graduate: The need, benefits and practical approaches to internationalise the curriculum" (2017) 8(2) *Journal of Learning Design* 53.

and practitioners from right around the world. Participating in an international moot competition gave me the opportunity to gain an understanding of different legal systems, required me to study law comparatively across different jurisdictions, allowed me to begin developing an international network, and made me aware of global opportunities that I had previously not even considered.

- **Conclusion**

While not every moot student will get the opportunity to travel overseas, they will all find that mooting expands their horizons. Mooting is undoubtedly useful in developing legal research, writing and advocacy skills. In my view, however, the hidden value of mooting lies in the way that it develops character and a range of non-legal skills, specifically a strong work ethic, resilience, teamwork, strategic decision-making, honesty & integrity, attention to detail, and a global outlook. Importantly, these skills are developed while a mooter is still at law school, that is '*before* going into practice, where the interests of a client would be at stake and growing pains are not so readily tolerated'.[28] For these reasons, mooting continues to have an important role to play in any modern law school, where the focus should be not just on graduating students with a technical proficiency in the law but students who are ready to take their place as members of the legal profession, with all of the broader responsibilities that this entails.

---

[28] Hernandez, above n.5, at 78.

17

THE ART AND SCIENCE OF ORAL ADVOCACY: THE WINNER'S PERSPECTIVE

Rajesh Sharma, Harprabdeep Singh and *Eric Ng*

- **Introduction**

Lawyers are known for their gift of the gab. But the tragic truth is that not all lawyers can employ it effectively. It is true that standalone advocacy cannot unilaterally win the case, but effective advocacy can, more likely than not, win the hearts and minds of judges, clients and even audiences. Advocacy is an art as well as a science and no one taught this better than Prof. Gabriël Moens. With good planning, preparation and practice, a law student can be molded into a persuasive lawyer with his/her advocacy skills. Good advocacy skills in mooting require mastery over several areas. In Part I of this Paper, the overall key aspects of a successful moot will cover the case theory, road map, flagging and highlighting key authorities. In Part II, emphasis is laid on answering questions and how to tackle them effectively. Finally, in Part III, the article concludes with an expansion on rebuttal and sur-rebuttal techniques and how to conclude a case. Throughout each Part, acquiring each skill is expounded in a step-by-step method with examples shown from a mooting context which can just as easily be replicated in a real-life court/tribunal scenario.

- **Part I: Overall View of the Entire Case**
  - **Well Begun-Half Done**

Oral advocacy primarily comes into play after the written pleadings are closed. Although oral arguments are a demonstration of oratory skills, the foundation for such arguments are based on a good written pleading which requires a concise use of material facts, in-depth research on the law and creative layers of arguments. If the written submissions are well-articulated, then it becomes relatively easier to make persuasive oral arguments. Therefore, the work put into the written phase must never be underestimated.

The very first minute of the oral arguments sets the tone for the remaining oral submissions. Imagine a mooter standing and saying "Good Morning" when in fact it is 2 pm in the afternoon. In moot competitions, it happens more frequently than one would imagine. This single expression from the mooter may give the impression that he/she is nervous or is not confident. On the other hand, when another mooter stands to speak in the afternoon and then uses the expression "Good Afternoon", he/she will certainly give the impression that he/she is aware of the context i.e. time and is ready to adapt accordingly.

Similarly, when addressing the judge or the panel of arbitrators mooters get mixed up. For example, the classic faux pas includes the use of "Your Excellency" for arbitrators; "Your Honour" instead of "Your Lordship" for the appropriate levels of court and Mr. Chairman/Mr. President in the arbitration context. It is important to show right off the bat that you are confident. Even if you feel nervous, it should not be visible, and the mooter should start the argument as if he/she were prepared and waiting for this opportunity to rise and shine. With a bit of preparation, the early signs of nervousness can be overcome. With a bit of research, it is not hard to determine whether an arbitration panel should be addressed as "Mr. Chairman and members of the tribunal" or "Mr. President and members of the tribunal". Every moot is governed by the applicable rules. Taking an arbitration moot as an example, looking into the rules of arbitration, particular the provisions related to the appointment of arbitrators, the rules would specify the title of the head arbitrator as "Chairman" or the "President".

Going the extra mile makes all the difference in the moot. Using the appropriate address at the start of the oral arguments sets the tone for a flying start and seals a good impression that the mooter is well prepared and certainly in control. This may not be as detrimental in real life but in the mooting context it may cost few marks, marks which can easily be retained from the get-go.

- **Case Theory**

All famous lawyers, or at least the ones worth remembering, are known for their catchphrases i.e. "one liners". Autobiography or anecdotal stories of those lawyers are full of such one liners which show why they were or are successful. The case theory in a moot is that one liner which explains what the case is about or what are the material or core issues for the judge or the arbitration panel to decide. For example, if the Claimant is asking for damages from the Respondent based on a contract then the Respondent may say "Mr. Chairman and members of the tribunal, the Claimant is seeking damages under a contract which my client never entered into". This one liner is challenging the very basis of the claimant's entire argument - the existence of a contract. From the Respondent's perspective if there is no contract then there cannot be any breach, so the question of liability for damages does not arise. From this one liner a judge or an arbitration panel may understand the crucial issue to be decided in this case and gets an early peek into the line of argument which will be taken by the Respondent.

Developing a case theory for a case from either side is no cakewalk. It is probably the single most difficult thing to achieve for two reasons. First, the mooter must understand the entire case to be able to boil it down to a line or two. Second, it is a constant work in progress which takes final shape almost at the final stage of preparation, like a model wearing the last piece of apparel before taking the stage.

A seasoned lawyer may formulate a "case theory" in a relatively shorter period. For nascent lawyers or a mooter, it is a good idea to start thinking about it from the beginning. An easy way to start thinking about it is to ask these simple questions: "what is this case about?" or "why my client should win this case?". The answer to these questions can be used to lay the foundation of the case theory e.g. "This case is about…" or "My client should win because…". As the case theory refers to the whole case, an issue may arise as to how incorporate several distinct issues into a single theory. During preparation, the case theory can be broken down to the micro level first by asking "what is this issue about" or "why my client should win on this issue?". Answers to these questions will help develop a case theory based on one issue which can then be used as building blocks to help at the end to develop a broader and an all-encompassing case theory.

In the arbitration context, the proceedings are typically divided in two or three phases: (1) Jurisdictional phase, (2) Liability phase and the (3) Quantum phase. Having a case theory for each phase is the most preferred option for mooters.

For young lawyers or law students, it is suggested that instead of trying to create a case theory in one or two lines they should first develop it in a greater length, for example, a few lines. As their understanding of the case deepens, they can naturally modify and refine the earlier version of the case theory and distil it through this cyclic process till they develop a satisfying case theory. As such, from the time of writing the memoranda or written pleading stage it is possible and encouraged to develop a tentative case theory which can then be perfected for the oral arguments later.

- **Road Map**

After putting forward the respective side's case theory, a good mooter will provide a "road map" for the decision maker which is basically a skeleton layout showing how he/she will prove his/her points which has been included in the case theory. Re-using the case theory of the Respondent above: "Mr. Chairman and members of the tribunal, the Claimant is seeking damages under a contract which my client never entered into." Using this central argument in the roadmap, he/she may continue and say "In this regard, I will first show you that there is no contract between the parties because there was no offer under law and even if there was an offer that offer was not accepted". This road map shows that the mooter will focus on the basic legal elements for the existence of a contract which is in his/her case the non-existence of a valid legal offer and the non-acceptance of that offer (as an alternative argument), if it exists. If he/she finds that the other requirements of a contract are also lacking such as consideration, legality, capacity, intention etc then those points may also be included in the road map. A road map shows the sequence of the arguments which will be presented by the mooter. This sequencing is important for the logical flow of the arguments. For example, the Claimant cannot argue about damages in a contract without establishing the breach of a contract. Hence, if it is said that "First I will demonstrate that the Respondent is liable for damages and then I will establish that there was a breach of the terms of the contract" then it is indicative of an ill-thought of road map. It is not legally logical to establish damages before establishing breach of a contract (as causation is missing) - one cannot put the 'cart before the horse'.

In a road map, alternative arguments are frequently included. The above example of a road map includes an alternative argument: "In this regard I will first show you that there is no contract between the parties because there was no offer at the first place and <u>even if</u> there was an offer that offer was not accepted". If there is no offer, then there cannot be any contract and the Respondent may win the entire case on that point alone. However, the road map has included the alternative argument which is related to the acceptance of that offer, if any offer exists. Similarly, the Respondent can also use a road map that states, "I will first demonstrate that there is no contract and even if there is a contract it was not breached and even if it was breached my client is exempted from liability". Such a road map gives an idea that the existence of contract will be challenged first and in alternative (if the court/arbitral tribunal considers that there is a contract) then the argument will focus on why that contract was not breached and if that contract was breached why the Respondent is exempted from liability. The road map with alternative arguments shows that a mooter is flexible and ready to deal with various scenarios if the court/tribunal is not with him/her on a point.

- **Flagging of Road Map**

Stating the road map is important but more important is flagging it to flesh it out for effective delivery. In big and complex cases, a lawyer or mooter may present a good road map but if they fail to follow up and use the road map to give an idea to the judge or the arbitration panel as to which point they are arguing, the road map becomes ineffective.

In the example above, the first point in the road map is that there is no contract. A good mooter must always be aware of the road map and he/she make sure to indicate to the judges or the arbitration panel to follow his/her arguments. For example, after stating the road map it can be stated that "Addressing my first argument that there is no contract I have three points to make: 1. There is no offer; 2. Even if there was an offer, it was not accepted and 3. If there was acceptance then that was never communicated." Use of expressions like "Addressing my first argument" flags to the judge and the arbitration panel that now the mooter is focusing on the first issue of his/her road map. The three points to establish that there is no contract is a sub road map for the first issue and it gives an indication as to how this point will be established. These sub points should also be flagged.

It is also important to flag when you move from one argument to another by using expressions like "moving on to my second point"; "going back to my first argument" etc. The importance of flagging is to take judges and arbitrators together with you on your journey of establishing your point. It becomes particularly helpful during heavy questioning. It is often seen in moots that when a mooter is bombarded with questions he/she often forgets or deviates from his/her roadmap. A good mooter will stick to his or her road map and after answering questions will go back to his/her argument by saying "going back to my second point that there was no acceptance...." In this way he/she will be able to complete the arguments related to the points he/she was earlier making. Another method is that while answering questions if all the points on non-acceptance have been put forward then a lawyer or mooter may say "moving on to my third point that the acceptance was never communicated I have two points to make...." The expression "moving on to my third point" is a good example of flagging that the mooter is now moving forward to argue the third point.

When the argument moves from the one big issue to another then the flagging should be done in a different way to attract the attention of the bench and the tribunal. For example, once the issue of contract is argued and the next argument on breach of contract is made then a unique flagging sign should be made in the following way before an arbitration panel: "Mr. Chairman and members of the tribunal, I will now move to my second issue that there was no breach of the contract". The use of expression "Mr. Chairman and members of the tribunal" is aimed to attract the attention of the tribunal on the second issue. Such an expression with a slight pause creates a vacuum of silence and grabs the attention from the tribunal making them alert and engaged in listening to the next issue.

A common mistake among mooters is when they say "if you have no further questions then I will move to my next issue…". In the court context it may work as lawyers have more time but in the moot context, it inevitably backfires. It is often seen that when a mooter uses this expression there is a high likelihood that a member of the tribunal may ask another question before the issue is put to bed. This will take extra time and the mooter ends up incompleting his/her arguments due to a lack of time. It is suggested that the best way is to flag and move from one issue to another and if the tribunal or a judge has any question, they will ask inevitably. It is not suggested that this should be done to avoid questions from the bench or tribunal as it will be explained more in the next section about how to deal with questions. This is suggested with the aim to manage the time appropriately in a moot. A mooter who follows the road map diligently is always able to fight till the end for his/her client.

- **Citing Facts, Cases and other Authorities**

In a moot, the given facts pattern are deliberately designed in a way to see how a mooter may argue his/her case based on a partially favourable and partially detrimental basis. No decent and competitive moot problem will have completely one-sided facts in favour of a singular party. Most international moots have a complex fact scenario, sometimes running between 50 to 100 pages. Therefore, it is important for a mooter to master the facts. This can be achieved by reading the moot problem carefully, and many times, over the period in preparation for the moot. From our experience, we can say confidently that every time a mooter reads the moot problem the reader will find some information which he/she can use to bolster their arguments. This habit of habitual reading of a moot problem may also develop critical thinking skills, analytical abilities and a better use of the facts. For example, in the Vis moot where more than 300 hundred teams take part in the competition every team reads the same moot problem over a period of eight months and yet good teams or mooters use the same facts in a different perspective to their advantage which many other teams may not have even thought about. When reading the moot problem, one must always understand that any information given there must be there for a purpose. Particularly, the answer to clarification questions which are released after the moot problem has been published for some time. Those questions and answers are part of the facts and should be read carefully and moulded into the argument as well.

During the oral arguments phase, it is important to make the life of judges and arbitrators easier. If the fact pattern is complex, then this point becomes more so relevant. It is also true that many judges and arbitrators are not well versed like mooters, so they may miss some important facts. A good mooter always tries to help a judge or arbitrator to understand his/her case by showing facts which are in support of his/her arguments. When citing facts, one must make sure to adopt the trifecta approach - first the page number, then para number and lastly the line number. The sequencing here is important particularly for facts spread across several documents. Through this way, it is easy for a judge or an arbitration panel to first find the page, then the paragraph number on the page and then the line which can be spotted easily. If reference to the facts is done in reverse order then a judge or an arbitrator must wait to hear the page number, which inevitably comes at the end, and by that time he will very likely have forgotten the para number and the crucial line which you want the judge or an arbitrator to read. Therefore, always think about the logical sequence of points and the receptiveness of such by the judge or the tribunal. This may seem like a small thing but in our experience, we can say that it creates a big impact on your argument and has the effect of tipping the winning scales in your moot.

During the oral arguments of a moot, you may have to rely on cases in support of your legal arguments. In our experience, citing a case in a written pleading and using the same case during oral arguments requires a different technique. During oral arguments, it is suggested that emphasis should be made on the year of the decision (recent cases have greater appreciation) and the court which has decided that case (higher court decisions have greater binding persuasion), then the name of the parties may be added in between. Thereafter, the relevant page number should be stated and then the passage of the decision should be quoted. This may take an extra few seconds of your time, but it creates the priceless trust and credibility to win over the audience. It also shows your depth of research. To make your case even more persuasive you may emphasize that the case you are relying on has also dealt with the same law or same rules or the same issues.

When you are relying on any case in a moot which is your strong authority, we suggest you prepare that case like the back of your hand. You must know the facts of the case, the decision - whether the case was decided unanimously or by a majority, the number of judges deciding that case, the names of those judge(s), whether the case has been appealed or the decision (majority or unanimous, number and names of those judges) of the appeal court. In a moot, a common trap question asked by a judge or an arbitrator is when they query about the facts of the case relied on. Not surprisingly, quite often a mooter who is citing the case does not have a command of the facts of that case.

Quite common in an oral argument, mooters rely on a scholarly article or book. Before citing these books and articles, it is preferable to first do some background research to find who the author is. While preparing for the moot, it is almost a reflex action for students to pick what they can get in support of their arguments. They do not check whether the author is a student or an expert. At the time of oral hearings, judges and arbitrators may ask about the author to ascertain if they could rely on the opinion of that writer. If the writer is an expert, only then will there be a favourable impact in relying on that authority.

In citing books, one should first state the name of the author then the title of the book and then page number and then quote the passage on that page. If the book has several edition(s) then you may mention the current edition of the book. This is also important because sometimes authors may change their positions or analysis before the new edition of the book. If that is the case, then you should emphasize on this point clearly to the judges or arbitrators.

When citing an article, you should first name the author followed by the title of the paper, the name of the journal, the year of publication, the page number where the relevant quotation is published and then quote the passage or lines. In cases where the author is not a well-established scholar but if his/her publication is in a very reputable and high-ranking journal then the credibility of the journal will help persuade the judges and arbitrators during your oral hearings.

In well-established and rigorous moot competitions e.g., Vis Moot and Jessup moot you may find that the author of the key book or article is also sitting on the mooting panel. In that situation you should be very careful in citing his/her book or article to him/her. In our experience, we suggest that you should refrain from citing or relying on that authority. This is because first it will be seen as a strategic move of pleasing that particular member of the panel and second if your interpretation or quotation is wrong then that member will certainly destroy your argument or dilute your credibility in front of the entire panel. However, there are some authors who are simply titans in their field and you may have to cite their books or articles while they are also judging you, then you may cite it but follow the general rule that you must know that authority 'like the back of your hand'.

- **Part II: Answering Questions**

  - **Questions from the Judge/Tribunal**

Answering questions in any professional setting is a daunting task. In learning how to cope with this in a moot competition, it is a constant cycle of conquering this issue in every match. After getting into the hearing room, comes the time to perform - deliver the opening speech/submission which one has been preparing for, prepare for a few interjections from the other side's counsel and finally any questions which the decision maker may have. Do all these well and you can be reasonably certain that the decision will be a favourable one. However, it is the final element of this entire process which is probably the most overlooked by mooters.

In the age of scripted speeches, anyone over time can be coached to appear as a great speaker. It is during the question and answer aspect, where moot students who otherwise appear confident and well spoken in their speeches, later crash and burn and wonder why.

The key factors for being a successful orator lies in his/her depth of knowledge, creativity, confidence and temperament. All of these qualities are revealed in how one handles questions. Unfortunately, only a select number of individuals are innately able to conquer the techniques of answering questions gracefully. A quick glance at veteran politicians shows even they have great difficulty, at times, of thinking on their feet and maintaining composure under a barrage of questions despite being well-trained at public speaking.

There are certain core aspects to answering questions which need to be mastered. Maintaining this rigidity would assist mooters in conquering this skill in long-term. After that, bearing in mind a few golden rules would help add fluidity, allowing the speaker to mould this skill based on the audience he/she seeks to convince.

  - **Core Requirements**

The first thing to bear in mind (which honestly applies to any skill one is trying to hone) is that there are no shortcuts, period. Depth of the subject matter and experience are fundamental. Every moot student has to know their subject well for that particular moot. Assuming that is true, the next thing to remember is that you know your subject, at least in relation to that case, better than most, even the judge/arbitrator questioning you. If you stick to your researched points and don't veer off track too much from what you know, you would ordinarily always have the upper hand.

Often, students go into the competition thinking that they will be tested and/or interrogated, which if one applies their mind to it, sets you up psychologically from the outset at a disadvantage because you have already conceded that you are not the one in control. The reality is that the judge/arbitrator is not just questioning you to embarrass/ridicule you, but he/she is also trying to let you into their thought process about your arguments and trying to see if what they are saying makes sense so you could shed some light on it for their benefit (ultimately your benefit if they agree with your view).

Once you see it this way, the questions from the bench become a real-time dialogue between you and the decision maker. In fact, the questions are indicative of where the judge agrees with you and where he/she doesn't, which allows you as the mooter to refine your arguments to address and plug any weaknesses before he/she decides.

Second, prepare for the hearing by researching into your audience. Examine the background (e.g. do they come from a civil or common law background) to get a feel of how he/she thinks and reaches their decisions. It is hard work, but it pays off in the long run. Most judges in moot competitions are "regulars" especially the ones who stand out year after year, finding out how they behave as judges isn't as difficult as one would imagine. One, it teaches you to be meticulous. Two, you get a feel for your audience, so that you can structure your speech and anticipate the type and frequency of questions accordingly.

Third, one of the keys towards a successful dialogue with the audience is to stay one step ahead of them. Moot students can do this by understanding the underlying motivation for the question. In our opinion, there are generally five types of questions.

The first type is the ideal scenario when the motivation is out of curiosity - this is fertile ground for a good dialogue and building rapport with the audience. Any answer to such type of questions can be supplemented with a question of one's own or a comment that shows not only interest but also breadth of research (emphasising the point on depth of knowledge).

The second type is the one dreaded by most moot students, the question is to test you or as we sometimes like to call it, "put you in your place". You can usually identify this type of question based on the tone of the person asking it. The moot student should never lose his/her patience on these types of questions. The best solution is to maintain one's composure, answer the questions quickly and move forward with your submissions.

Then there's the "devil's advocate" question. The purpose of such questions is to act like quick sand, suck you in and not let you off the hook easily. These questions serve no bigger agenda in the case, so the best strategy is to provide a brief answer (rather than being completely dismissive) and get back to the issues that need to be decided in the case.

Occasionally, you will also get questions where the person asking the question wants to impress the moot student with their own mental prowess. These questions tend to operate more like side comments, which are often tangential and irrelevant. Acknowledge the person for asking such a "great" question, thereby achieving the main purpose of such a "question" but bring the discussion back to what you consider to be a "lesser" but more relevant issue for the judge/arbitrator to decide.

Sporadically, the judge/arbitrator starts off the question by stating that "This may be a stupid question...". Be very cautious with such questions. Anyone who is confident and open enough to admit their alleged ignorance on that topic is very likely the one who is truly most knowledgeable on that area and is seeking to obtain an answer through such camouflaged language.

Getting a grasp on all these types of questions is an acquired taste of knowledge and perception. But as we discussed earlier, rigidity is key before flexibility. In general, we would advise moot students structuring their answers in a three-prong method – answer the question, back it up with facts and law, and if necessary, a possible policy analysis.

Using Mr. Singh's personal experiences as a Vis mooter in Hong Kong in 2012, moot students would be able to see below how rigidity is generally favourable with most of the questions from judges/arbitrators.

In the general rounds of the Vis competition, he was frequently asked closed questions such as "Mr. Singh, did your client receive the money from the other side?" Sticking with the general rule, he would answer "Mr. President, No he did not receive the money because [factual proof] which violated [legislation violated]. Further, this is against a fundamental rule in international trade [explain the rule]."

Moot competitions are not murder mysteries, judges/arbitrators would like an answer to their questions first before an explanation/admission/defence. Using this method, the question is acknowledged and answered and depending on the response of the person who asked the question, he may have a follow up question/comment/admission of his/her own which would build a foundation for a dialogue with the tribunal – this is exactly which every moot student wants, to grab the tribunal's attention and keep its entire focus on his or her arguments for the entire period.

All the questions Mr. Singh received were not a bed of roses either and this is where his flexibility kicked in. For example, when he was arguing in the Vis semi-final, a well-known Swiss arbitrator interrupted his speech 30 seconds into his first argument with a blunt question of "Mr. Singh, where is this argument leading to?"

The rigid response would have served no purpose other than to agitate him with a non-answer and possibly alienate the entire tribunal. Mr. Singh responded with a succinct answer, enough to answer arbitrator's question and evince further questions on his answer. He responded with "Mr. Arbitrator, this argument proves the failure to pay the fees rests solely on the Respondent". Immediately, the President of the Tribunal chipped in by saying "How so?" From there, Mr. Singh had gauged his audience and conformed to their needs and structured his arguments accordingly.

Whether it is a follow-up/question in your strong or weak area, the moot student should adopt the rigid way of answering it. As seen further in the golden rules section below, the bench appreciates frankness. If the question is in your weak area, answer it and admit the weakness but use your in-depth knowledge to minimize the damage, for example, by arguing that such weakness is not fundamental or distinguishing it entirely (again fall back on your facts and law).

Moot students in answering questions should focus on the areas which would allow them to continue to engage in a dialogue with the bench (flexibility) while still maintaining the points and key arguments for the case (rigidity). The mixture of both is what the moot student should always seek to master.

- **Golden Rules in Answering Questions**

These golden rules are by no means exhaustive. These rules are more like icing on a cake. The core skills form the foundation for answering questions. By adopting these rules, it gives shape and a better shine to the core skills which have been harnessed by the mooter.

First, always be firm and direct in your use of language. Never use "I think", "I assume", "It could be", "It might be", "It may be". Adopt terminology which reaffirms your belief in your own submissions and has the command of persuasion. "This case has no application" or "That point is incorrect because…".

Second, learn about the power of staying silent. Using filler language is off-putting, annoying and damages the smooth delivery of an argument. Words like "eh", "oh", "hmm", "however". "yes but" which are used habitually shows a lack of mastery over the language. If there is nothing worth saying yet or you are still thinking, stay quiet or ask for a moment, there is no shame or embarrassment in doing so.

Third, do not rebut or try to avoid hypothetical questions by immediately retorting back that "that's not the case". Such an answer betrays the very definition of being a hypothetical scenario. Explain the answer to such a question first and try to link it or distinguish it (as the case may be) after, do not fight it off the cuff because then it seems you are unwilling to assist, or you lack depth of knowledge. The best way to answer the hypothetical question is to bring it back to the law. Even if your answer might be different from the position you have taken in your case. Your answer will demonstrate that you understand the legal position and apply it on a given scenario, but you may indicate that your case is different from the hypothetical scenario.

Fourth, being honest and frank is a virtue. If there is a question to which you do not know the answer to or need time to investigate, then say so. No judge or arbitrator expects any moot student to have a complete knowledge of the law (except on the core points of the case). Babbling or trying to guess the answer potentially not only makes you look foolish but jeopardizes any credibility you may have developed with the bench.

Fifth, humour in a moot competition is a huge risk and one which should be sparingly taken on. Only use it if the mooter is very familiar with the judge/tribunal and knows that using it would build rapport and not destroy it. In the mooting context, a well-executed joke/humorous analogy may work in his/her favour but if it is executed wrongly then you may be doomed.

Sixth, always be professional with your opponent. Disagree with his/her arguments, use their own words but never be petty, misquote or level personal attacks. No one appreciates a bully, least of all a judge or arbitrator.

Mastering the art of answering questions comes down to these core skills that we have identified. The best ones are those who have conquered them with patience, perseverance and hard work over time. Once the mooter has gained rigidity in these core areas, using some of the golden rules identified helps give him/her added flexibility to manoeuvre his way through different legal contexts and audiences.

- **Part III: Rebuttals and Conclusion**

The single hardest part of any advocate's submission is figuring out how to do rebuttals and sur-rebuttals.

Imagine a single match in a moot competition as a boxing match. First you must set the stage with your introduction and get a feel for how the arbitrators will react to your arguments and allow you to set up for the bulk of your argument to follow. The main arguments that you make constitute the most of your fight, the body blows and jabs that set up your argument strategy and which establish your key points to win. If a moot can be analogous to boxing, then the rebuttal and/or sur-rebuttal must be the equivalent of a knockout blow. Like any good knockout punch, a good rebuttal must both be powerful and accurate, targeted with precision, and capable of leaving your opponent floored with no way of getting back up.

The rebuttal should have the following characteristics. A good rebuttal should precisely target key weak areas of the opposing side's argument; it should address areas that are wrong in fact, law, or policy, and it should be short enough to be digestible by the arbitrators and/or judges.

- **Targeting the Rebuttal**

Firstly, the rebuttal should address critical points in the opposing side's argument. For many students, this point is the most difficult to address. Oftentimes, students will have a laundry list of rebuttal points but cannot determine which points would act as the best rebuttal, so rather than critically prune his/her list, the student will simply state all the points. Sometimes, the student will also focus on points that are not relevant to the opposing side's argument, or points that the opposing side does not really have to rely on to make their argument.

Every argument requires the advocate to establish several key points in their submissions. The advocate must establish certain facts, establish several legal points, or at the very minimum, provide explanation for why their side should prevail. A good rebuttal identifies those critical points in the opposing argument, and provides argument or evidence that counters that point, thus collapsing the rest of the argument's structure. Therefore, a rebuttal can be considered to be the equivalent of a knockout punch; a properly done and properly targeted rebuttal can destroy the opposing side's arguments in seconds.

However, to successfully present a rebuttal, the advocate must know not only the strengths and weaknesses of their own arguments, but also the strengths and weaknesses of the opposing argument as well. This proves to be one of the more difficult points for advocates and students to learn, as the focus tends to be on improvement of one's own argument, without paying too much attention to what the opposing side may raise in reply. There is usually very little time to develop good rebuttals on the fly, and it is the rare advocate that has the talent to be able to develop crippling rebuttals off the cuff. Most good rebuttals have already been prepared in advance, in anticipation of what the opposing side will raise, and to prepare such rebuttals, it is imperative that the advocate have a mastery and awareness of not only his argument, but also his opponent's.

There is a secondary benefit in focusing on the opposing side's argument. Usually, the critical weaknesses of the opposing side's arguments are conversely, the strongest areas of attack for the advocate's side. By having an awareness of where the opponent is weak and which points will tear apart their entire argument, the advocate is not only strengthening his own case, but also providing a defensive front for any forthcoming sur-rebuttal from the opponent. Keep in mind that a sur-rebuttal may only address points that arise from the rebuttal.

- **Substance of the Rebuttal**

Having identified what critical points the opposing side must establish, the advocate must now identify the substance of the rebuttal; in other words, the advocate must show what is wrong with the argument of the opponent. This usually requires the advocate to identify whether the opponent has erred in fact, law or policy.

As will have been mentioned above, there are three key layers to an advocate's arguments: facts, law, and policy. Facts are king in a moot court environment, for they are usually indisputable, and therefore can only be interpreted in limited ways. If a fact is useful to an advocate, it is unlikely to be attacked by the opponent, as there is limited evidence with which to counter that fact. Likewise, if the advocate can correctly identify a flaw or fallacy in the opponent's fact pattern, then a rebuttal that points out those flaws can cripple the judge's trust in the opponent's mastery of the facts or the logic being presented. In either case, a rebuttal on factual matters critical to the opponent's argument will almost always be fatal.

However, in the situation of a moot court competition, it is unlikely that there will always be a factual rebuttal available. Most advocates, especially at high levels of a mooting competition, will be aware of the weaknesses of their own argument and will be unlikely to make factual errors which can then be capitalized on by the advocate. However, in most cases, even if there is no factual rebuttal available, there will likely be a legal point of rebuttal open to the advocate. Moot court competitions almost always deal with legal points and situations that are not well settled, to provide avenues of argument for both sides and to provoke engaging discussions. As a result, there will rarely be a situation where one side or the other has an impenetrable legal argument. Issues may remain undecided or decided in *obiter*. Alternatively, considering many moots deal with international law, the case law of one jurisdiction may be contrary to decisions made in other jurisdictions. In some cases, cases from the same jurisdictions may even conflict.

It is the advocate's job to be prepared and to anticipate what legal points the opponent will raise. In many situations there will only be a small subset of sources that will address the points in dispute. By knowing the legal authorities inside and out the advocate can address legal issues raised by the opponent with clarity and show to the arbitrator or judge that the advocate may know the case better than the opponent. If the opponent wrongly or mis-cites a case, the advocate/mooter should be prepared to not only rebut but be able to give the proper reasoning or citation to that case. There may also be the situation where a case, for example, may have been superseded or given negative treatment by a superior court. Alternatively, if the authority was used correctly, but there exists either a contrary source or one that addresses the advocate's point more directly, then that can also be used in the rebuttal.

Finally, the third layer addresses matters of policy, in other words that despite the facts not being in the advocate's favour, and despite the law not being in the advocate's favour, that there still exists persuasive reasons not to decide against the advocate. This is the weakest of the three layers, but it is still effective at times in the form of rebuttal. Whereas the opponent may be correct in law, for policy reasons that law should not be applied in the current situation, or there exists other reasons which advocate against strict interpretation or application of that law. Law typically does not exist in a vacuum. In other words, there are usually reasons for laws to exist, and if those reasons do not match the current situation, that point can be raised in rebuttal. In many cases, policy arguments can be gleaned from HANSARD or the *travaux préparatoires*, which give insight into the negotiation history or the debate surrounding the current drafts of the law and why those laws are in place.

Rebuttal on policy will usually require the advocate to extend beyond the boundaries of normal legal research. Many students are not accustomed to looking behind what the legal sources state and are satisfied to rely on the conclusion stated by those sources without looking into the reasons or the practices that lead to those conclusions. By training the advocate to use their critical faculties to not only know the law, but to also *understand* the law, the advocate can be fully prepared to rebut any argument raised by the opponent.

Overall, the advocate must keep in mind the overarching purpose of the rebuttal; it is the advocate's last chance to get his word in and throw doubt upon the arguments of the opponent. It is the advocate's last chance to either close the door on the opponent or salvage the situation.

- **Structuring the Rebuttal**

Now that the advocate knows how to identify what points of rebuttal are available to him, and what the substance of the rebuttal should be, there is the final step of structuring the rebuttal so that it can be as effective as possible. A rebuttal may be substantively good, but too often students tend to bury their best points of rebuttal or present their points ineffectively, lessening the impact of the rebuttal.

First and foremost, a rebuttal must be as short and concise as possible. As the last word that the advocate will have, the rebuttal must create as large of an impact as possible without boring or losing the judge or arbitrator. Further, novice advocates tend to consider that the rebuttal phase is simply a second chance to reiterate their arguments. Nothing could be further from the truth. At the point of rebuttals, the judges and or arbitrators will have listened to both sides speak at length regarding their issues. There is nothing that a judge wants to hear less than an advocate repeating the same argument that they made half an hour ago with nothing to add or point out.

The conciseness of rebuttals extends to the number of points that need to be addressed. Most students, when first practicing rebuttals, come up with a laundry list of points that they wish to attack in the opponent's arguments. Oftentimes the advocate may come up with 5-6 or even more points of rebuttal. The problem with that is that even the best rebuttal will take at least 20-30 seconds of time to present. With 5-6 points of rebuttal, an advocate will go on for at least 3-4 minutes, which means that even if the advocate has excellent points, most of them will be lost along the multitude of points being raised.

Advocates in moot court competitions should consider themselves limited to 2 points of rebuttal in general, and never more than three points. This goes back to the first point about targeting rebuttals. If the advocate understands the opponent's argument clearly, then there is rarely the situation where the advocate will be able to identify more than 3 points of absolute importance that can be rebutted upon. A good advocate will be able to capitalize on those points to give them maximum effect within as short a time as possible.

Further, structure of the rebuttal must also be tailored to provide maximum impact while drawing attention to the point being rebutted. A good rebuttal can be formed in a three-part structure. Firstly, the advocate should summarize the point being rebutted. In many cases, the advocate will have to provide a reminder of what the opponent has raised. Doing so allows the advocate to ensure that the judge/arbitrator is clear on what point is being rebutted and allows the judge/arbitrator to recall the point being made. Secondly, the advocate must point out what is wrong with the opponent's point. This constitutes the substance of the rebuttal, which, as addressed above, will deal with whether the point is wrong in fact, law, or policy. Finally, the rebuttal must link back to your arguments. This is usually done by a concluding remark going back to the main proposition of your argument.

The three-part structure of the rebuttal is a concise means of getting the point heard. The judge is reminded of the point raised by the opponent, is told immediately after why that point is wrong, and therefore what the counter-proposition by your side is alleging should be the case.

- **Sur-Rebuttal**

If rebuttal is one of the more difficult tasks that an advocate must master to present a successful argument, then sur-rebuttal must be the most difficult task that an advocate can master. Whereas rebuttal can normally be prepared in advance and then tailored over the course of the opponent's arguments, sur-rebuttal requires the advocate to be prepared to anticipate what will arise in rebuttal, and then be able to provide an accurate and concise counterpoint in the space of the minute or two that the opponent is presenting the rebuttal. Since sur-rebuttal must respond only to arguments raised in rebuttal, this leaves very little time for the advocate to formulate a concise and effective response.

Generally, sur-rebuttal is not available to the responding party. However, there may be an agreement, at least in mooting, between the parties to allow for sur-rebuttal, or there may arise an issue during rebuttal that the judge may wish the respondent to address. In either case, the respondent must be prepared and ready to raise points of sur-rebuttal, and therefore must anticipate that even in cases where sur-rebuttal is not allowed, that there will be points that the advocate can address.

While the sur-rebuttal will almost always not be open to further response, the advocate should keep in mind similar principles as when preparing points of rebuttal. Primarily, the sur-rebuttal should address the weakest point in the rebuttal, as that point will usually be where the sur-rebuttal will be most effective. Ideally, even if the rebuttal consists of 3 or more points, sur-rebuttal should remain at 1 or 2 points maximum. Sur-rebuttal, when done effectively, can effectively neutralize rebuttal and leave a lasting image in the minds of the arbitrators/judges, but only if the impact of the sur-rebuttal is powerful enough.

- **Crafting the Conclusion**

Many students focus primarily on the substance of their arguments; finding legal sources, crafting arguments and identifying facts and evidence that will help support their arguments. However, many students ignore the fact that at the end of the process, they will also have to provide a proper conclusion identifying what the arbitrators or judges should take away from the advocate's submissions. In many cases, as advocates run into time management issues and may feel pressure to finish their arguments and sit down, advocates should always keep in mind the importance and the necessity of providing a concise conclusion that will last in the arbitrators/judge's minds as they deliberate.

A proper conclusion provides a review of the arguments that you have made and creates a "soft landing" of sorts for your arguments. Similar to a denouement in writing, a conclusion allows the arbitrator or judge time to process the points in your arguments and gives them a concise review of the points that you want them to take away from your argument. The arbitrator or judge is therefore not left with a question in their minds as to whether your arguments have finished or not, and they have an idea of what the key points are when asking questions of the opposing side or when rebuttal is occurring.

If the advocate/mooter has crafted his introduction clearly and correctly, there will usually be an underlying case theory that has been stated earlier in this paper. The conclusion provides the advocate with another opportunity to remind the arbitrator or judge about the case theory and restate it again as a reminder and for effect. The introduction and conclusion act as bookends for your argument; they provide an overarching case theory which the arbitrators or judges will have in mind as they listen to your arguments, then a conclusion which will nicely sum up the arguments and provide a call-back to your case theory. The bookend effect of this case theory helps your arguments maintain coherence and create a cumulative effect of your arguments. Instead of your arguments being viewed in isolation, they become parts of a larger, more complex and more sophisticated argument. Proper conclusions help reinforce this effect.

Whilst each advocate has his or her own style, conclusions also allow good advocates/mooters to exhibit features of their unique style. Conclusions allow for slightly more dramatic effect depending on the advocate's advocacy skill and their own unique style peculiarities. If the idea of the argument is to provide a lasting image in the mind of the arbitrator or judge, then the conclusion is the opportunity for the advocate to create a "big bang" effect that resonates with the arbitrators or judges. Like the conclusion to a good book, the oral argument should leave the arbitrators or judges satisfied with the whole course of the argument.

The normal structure of a proper conclusion begins with an introductory statement, usually "In sum", or "to sum up", or "in conclusion". Then the advocate will typically provide a brief review of the case, which reminds the judge or arbitrator of the essence of your case. This review usually includes a call back or reminder of the case theory stated in the introduction. The conclusion will then proceed with a succinct restatement of the issues and the points that the advocate wants the judge or arbitrator to take away from the advocate's arguments and what decisions that the advocate wants the arbitrator or judge to make based on those arguments. This includes any remedies that the advocate wants the judge or arbitrator to order. The advocate will usually finish with a polite thank you or other summation to notify the arbitrator or judge that the argument has concluded.

Particularly regarding moot competitions, time pressure is a real and intense factor that many advocates must deal with. After dealing with questions from the arbitrator or judge, and after presenting the bulk of their arguments, many advocates find themselves pressured for time. It is a natural instinct for many advocates/mooters to simply end when their time is up and to fail to provide a conclusion. Even if time has run out, the advocate/mooter should still try to give a proper conclusion, however short, and if the judge or arbitrator allows. In these cases, the conclusion can even be a mere sentence long, but it will still be important to not only signal the end of the advocate's arguments, but also to show that the advocate is calm and steady enough even under time pressure to conclude their arguments.

In sum, while many advocates take conclusions for granted, or tend to ignore them entirely, crafting a proper conclusion takes just as much work as the body of the arguments, and in certain cases, finding a strong, accurate, and effective way of concluding the advocate's arguments may prove harder than the actual argument itself. A proper conclusion, that leaves the arbitrator or judge leaning back in satisfaction, that properly bookends the arguments, and which succinctly states the position in an effective manner deserves as much attention, if not more, than any other element in oral advocacy.

18

SECURING OF PAYMENTS IN WESTERN AUSTRALIA:
THE EFFECT OF CHANGES ARISING FROM THE REVIEW OF THE *CONSTRUCTION CONTRACT ACT* (WA)

Philip Evans

- **Introduction**

The building and construction industry is a vital part of the Western Australian economy. The industry also hosts the largest number of small businesses, accounting for 19 per cent of all small businesses and 17 per cent of all small business employment in WA. In the 2016-2017 period, $20.3 billion worth of work was performed in the building and construction industry. In terms of employment, 140,000 Western Australians are employed in the industry and in terms of business entities, some 42,361 local businesses operate in the building and construction sector.

It is an industry that employs numerous parties with complex contractual arrangements (either express or implied) to deliver its services. At the bottom of the contractual chain there are numerous subcontractors either engaged in the provision of services or supply of goods in circumstances of significant inequalities of bargaining power together with a lack of awareness of basic contractual rights and obligations who are subject to the greatest risk of non-payment.

Subcontracting is the lifeblood of the industry. The 'universal' use of subcontracting in the Western Australian construction industry was referred to in the Report on the Inquiry into the Building Industry of Western Australia where it was noted that the growth of the subcontracting system in Western Australia has brought with it essentially a loss of the traditional master builder and the emergence of the entrepreneurial builder. Some 45 years later there would be little disagreement with this statement.

- **Security of Payment Legislation**

Prior to the introduction of what might be described generally as security of payment (SOP) legislation, where a party to a construction contract was seeking payment for work done or materials supplied, the typical avenues would be confined to an appropriate dispute resolution clause in the contract (usually commercial arbitration) or seeking payment through an action in a court of competent jurisdiction depending upon the amount in dispute.

Under the common law, where there was a dispute relating to payment for work done or materials supplied, the beneficiary of that work had a significant advantage in that they were able to retain any monies owing until a determination by either a court or arbitrator. The difficulties, expense, time and delays inherent in receiving a judgement clearly deterred many from pursuing this course of action and those who did often had to wait months if not years for payment. Sadly, history indicates that by the time of payment many bona fide claimants had become insolvent. Additionally the common law did not provide a party with a right to suspend work when a payment due under the contract was not paid. Also it was not uncommon where there was a written contract for the terms to include 'paid when paid' or 'paid if paid' provisions and lengthy times for payment following the receipt of a payment claim from a contractor.

Submissions to the 2015 Independent Review of the Operation and Effectiveness of the *Construction Contracts Act 2004* (WA) (The CCA Review) conducted by the author, indicated that it was not uncommon for head contractors generally to extend payments to subcontractors for a period ranging from 30 to 90 days. This culture of late or delayed payments does not seem unique to WA with Dun & Bradstreet reporting that the building and construction industry generally has one of the highest rates of payment delinquency. The Royal Commission into Productivity in the Building Industry in NSW indicated that financial losses from late payments constituted 0.34% of turnover and losses from payment defaults in the order of 2.50% of turnover.

The principal objective of security of payment legislation is thus to ensure that parties (particularly at the lower end of the contracting chain) in the industry are paid in full and on time for the work they have done or materials supplied. It is a process designed to 'keep the money' flowing despite possible future actions with respect to the payment issue in dispute. The objective of the legislation was succinctly stated by Bruce Collins QC in the Final Report of the Independent Inquiry into Construction Industry Insolvency in NSW that it is; 'borne out of fairness and a recognition that the head contractor is being paid for the most part for work carried out by others further down the contractual chain.'[1]

The purpose of the rapid adjudication process was more expansively noted by the Hon. Alanah MacTiernan MLA, the then Minister for Planning and Infrastructure, in the Second Reading Speech of the *Construction Contracts Bill 2004* (WA) in 2004:

> The rapid adjudication process allows an experienced and independent adjudicator to review the claim and, when satisfied that some payment is due, make a binding determination for money to be paid. The rapid adjudication process is a trade-off between speed and efficiency on the one hand and contractual and legal precision on the other. Its primary aim is to keep the money flowing in the contractual chain by enforcing timely payment and side-lining protracted or complex disputes. The process is kept simple, and therefore cheap and accessible, even for small claims. In most cases the parties will be satisfied by an independent determination and will get on with the job. If the

---

[1] In August 2012 the NSW Government commissioned an *Independent Inquiry into Construction Industry Insolvency* (conducted by Mr Bruce Collins, QC) to assess the cause and extent of insolvency in the building and construction industry and recommend measures to better protect subcontractors from the effects of insolvency. The report is available from the NSW Department of Finance and Services website at <www.services.nsw.gov.au>.

party is not satisfied, it retains full rights to go to court or use any other dispute resolution mechanism available under the contract. In the meantime, the determination stands, and any payments ordered must be made on account pending an award under the more formal and precise process.

Also in *Re Anstee-Brook; Ex parte Mount Gibson Mining Ltd;* the general object of the CC was described by Martin J as follows:

> It is of fundamental importance, in my view, to understand that the object of this legislation was to attempt to reform earlier unacceptable scenarios of inequality of bargaining power in the construction contract environment. Contractors were highly vulnerable to being hurt by being kept out of funds due to them by an ongoing legal dispute in circumstances where they had performed the contracted work, but had not been paid. It is easy to see how a contractor who is leveraged and pressed for funds may lack the time, opportunity or resources to press its position to a result in a drawn out fight for payment against a well-resourced principal, in a protracted arbitration or contested litigation. The speedy and informal procedures delivered as reforms by the [Act] do not make the adjudicator's decision on the payment of funds final (save as to the capacity to obtain and enforce payment).

- **The *Construction Contracts Act 2004*(WA)**

The CCA commenced operation on 1 January 2005 and is part of national security of payment legislation designed to resolve payment disputes in the construction industry. The main purpose of the CCA is to provide a speedy resolution process by adjudication for resolving payment disputes under Western Australian construction contracts. The CCA provides that payment disputes are determined on an interim basis pending any formal dispute resolution provided in the parties' contract; for example arbitration, or a court process. The CCA also;

- prohibits paid-if-paid or paid-when-paid provisions in construction contracts;
- implies fair and reasonable payment terms into

construction contracts where those terms are not expressed in writing;
- provides a right to deal with unfixed materials when a party to a construction contract becomes insolvent.

Prior to the introduction of the CCA, where there was a dispute relating to payment for work done or materials supplied the beneficiary of that work had a significant advantage in that they were able to retain any monies owing until a determination by either court or arbitrator. The difficulties, expense, time and delays inherent in receiving a judgement clearly deterred many from pursuing this course of action and those who did may have had to wait months if not years for payment.

The 2015 Senate Economic Reference Committee insolvency inquiry clearly indicated that the building and construction industry experiences a disproportionately high rate of insolvency. Additionally the Australian Bureau of Statistics (ABS) data for the four financial years up until 30 June 2016, shows that the building and construction industry insolvency accounted for between 16.17% and 16.51% of all businesses operating in Australia. For the same four financial years, ASIC data shows the building and construction industry resulted in between 20.75% and 24.26% of all companies entering external administration in Australia.

The CCA is administered by the Building Commissioner. In accordance with s 52 of the Act, the Building Commissioner is required to prepare and present an annual report to the Minister for Commerce detailing the operation and effectiveness of the Act for each financial year (the reporting period). The report is submitted to the Minister by 1 November in each calendar year to allow for the outcomes of payment disputes adjudicated under the Act on or before 30 June to be included. Sections of the current report have been reproduced below.

An important provision of the CCA is s 25 which provides that if a payment dispute arises under a construction contract, a party to that contract may apply to have the payment dispute determined by an independent adjudicator registered by the Building Commissioner.

Adjudicators are drawn from a wide range of building professionals including architects, engineers and quantity surveyors and construction law practitioners. Before being registered by the Building Commission, persons must undergo a short training and assessment program run by a number of approved appointers in Western Australia.

To commence an adjudication application under the CCA, the party making the application (the Applicant) for payment, must prepare and serve the application within 90 business days of the payment dispute arising.

Under s 6 of the Act a payment dispute arises if:

- the payment claim has been rejected or wholly or partly disputed; or
- by the time when the amount claimed in a payment claim is due to be paid under the contract, the amount has not been paid in full; or
- by the time when any money or security retained by a party under the contract is due to be paid under the contract, the money or security has not been paid or returned.

Once served with the application, the other party to the construction contract (the Respondent) has 10 business days to prepare and serve their response on the Applicant and the adjudicator appointed to determine the payment dispute. The adjudicator then has 10 business days (or any extension granted by the parties) from receiving the response, or from when the response was due to be received, to make a decision.

The decision is expressed in writing and forwarded to the parties and the Building Commissioner. Prior to the amendments, payments were often delayed as a consequence of the successful party having to seek leave of the court in order to have the judgement enforced in a court of competent jurisdiction. The CCA amendments have now provided a faster means for determinations to be enforced through the courts, by removing the need for leave of the court to be granted and allowing the Building Commissioner to approve the adjudicator's determination.

At the same time it is important to note that in introducing the CCA, it was not the intention of the WA Parliament to provide comprehensive protection to parties unable to look after their own commercial interests. As noted, in part, by the Hon Alannah MacTiernan, the then Minister for Planning and Infrastructure, in the Second Reading Speech ⁰ of the *Construction Contracts Bill* 2004 (WA):

> Apart from these specific unfair practices, the Bill does not unduly restrict the normal commercial operation of the industry. Parties to a construction contract remain free to strike whatever bargains they wish between themselves, as long as they put the payment provisions in writing and do not include the prohibited terms ... This Bill cannot remedy every security of payment issue. Insolvency can be addressed only by commonwealth legislation. Participants in the industry still have to look after their own commercial interests. This Bill will provide the industry with simple and effective tools to clarify rights to be paid and to enforce those rights.

- **The Effect of the 2016 Amendments**

On the 22 November 2016, following the independent statutory review of the CCA, Parliament passed a number of amendments to the act. Most of the amendments commenced operation on 15 December 2016. These amendments included:

- extending the time for making an application for adjudication from 28 to 90 business days;
- amending the definition of a payment claim in the Act to include previously disputed or rejected payment claims (recycling of claims);
- removing the exclusion of 'wholly artistic works' from the definition of construction work in the Act;
- clarifying when a payment dispute arises for the purposes of the Act;

- amending the time measures in the Act for counting days for applications, responses and the adjudication determinations from calendar days to business days;
- narrowing the "mining exclusion" under the Act to exclude only fabricating and assembly of plant used for works for extracting or processing oil, natural gas and minerals from the definition of construction work;
- allowing adjudicators to deal with other adjudication applications simultaneously, if satisfied they can do so without time, cost or efficiency costs to any parties;
- permitting the adjudicator to decide substantial compliance with the section 26(2)(a) of the Act when deciding the validity of an application;
- providing a formal mechanism for applications for adjudication to be withdrawn, and or for adjudicators to issue a determination giving effect to a settlement reached between the parties; and
- providing a faster means for determinations to be enforced through the courts, by removing the need for leave of the court to be granted.

On 3 April 2017, the remaining amendments to the CCA commenced operation. In particular where a construction contract provides that payment shall be made more than 42 calendar days after it is claimed, it will be read as requiring payment within 42 calendar days. The amendments to the CCA applies to all construction contracts executed in WA after 3 April 2017.

In addition to the recommendations relating to structural reform of the CCA, the review report recommended the introduction of a number of polices with respect to matters identified during the review. These included the use Project Bank Accounts (PBA's) on major government projects, unfair contract terms, lack of awareness of the CCA, and poor contact administration knowledge. These will be discussed later in this chapter.

It is now 18 months since the amendments came into force following the review. The review and the subsequent amendments have been described as the most significant impact on the industry in decades. To gauge the effect of the amendments it is appropriate to start from a consideration of the 2016-2017 Building Commissioners' Annual Report.

- **Adjudication Applications**

One measure of the effectiveness of the amendments with respect to resolving payment disputes is to consider the "adjudication activity" since the introduction of the amended Act in December 2016. Table 2.1 of the Building Commissioner's report shows the number of applications for adjudication for the current reporting period against historical reporting periods.

Table 2.1: Applications for Adjudication by Financial Year

Financial Year	Number of Applications	Total Value of Payment Disputes	Mean value of Payment Disputes
2005-2006	29	$10,485,828.12	$361,580.28
2006-2007	36	$15,938,123.77	$442,725.66
2007-2008	86	$98,222,008.65	$1,142,116.38
2008-2009	105	$35,838,998.23	$341,323.79
2009-2010	172	$233,266,050.32	$1,356,197.97
2010-2011	197	$308,553,664.77	$1,566,262.25
2011-2012	178	$183,701,052.55	$1,086,988.48
2012-2013	208	$226,300,887.35	$1,103,906.77
2013-2014	175	$378,903,585.63	$2,165,163.35
2014-2015	235	$580,655,848.46	$2,470,875.95
2015-2016	225	$685,990,359.67	$3,048,846.04
2016-2017	176	$187,563,024.84	$1,065,699.00
Grand Totals	1822	$2,945,419,432.25	$1,616,585.86

It can be seen that the applications for adjudication during the current reporting period (which follows the amendments to the CCA) were down by 21 per cent from the 2015-16 reporting period. Overall the number of applications made during the current reporting period was the second lowest in both number and total value of payment disputes in 7 years.

- **Is There a Relationship Between the Number of Applications and the WA Economy?**

At first sight it would appear that the level of adjudication applications has historically trended with the levels of construction activity in the state with the mining, oil and gas sector (the mining sector) being the most significant user of the adjudication process to resolve payment disputes. The Building Commissioner in his current report opines that the slowdown in this sector is considered to be a contributing factor to the reduction in the number of adjudication applications made during the current reporting period. Whilst acknowledging a downturn in mining activity, at the same time, as at March 2017, Western Australia had an estimated $101 billion worth of resource projects which were under construction, or in the committed stage of development which despite any perceived downturn is nevertheless significant.[2]

When viewed against the applications on an industry wide basis whilst the mining sector originated the greatest percentage value of payment disputes (68.15%) it represented only 13% of the total number of applications for adjudication.

However residential construction in Western Australia has increased in the last two years. With respect to residential construction, from an examination of the Building Commissioner's last two Annual Reports, it can be seen that the use of adjudication to resolve payment disputes is at a five year high by trades in single dwellings, units, multistorey and aged care building. A recent report by the Master Builders Association of WA has indicated that that with respect to residential construction the last three years have seen unprecedented

---

[2] <http://www.abc.net.au/news/rural/2017-04-10/wa-mining-sector-increases-after-three-years-in-decline/8431940>.

growth in new housing construction with over 200,000 new dwellings constructed each year.[3]

Table 2.3 – Applications for Adjudication 2016-2017 (By Industry Sector)

Construction Industry Sector	Applications			
	Number	% Total Apps.	Total $ Amount Payment Disputes	% Value of Payment Disputes
Residential	73	41.5%	$7,639,969.75	4.07%
Public Building	28	15.9%	$31,616,546.65	16.86%
Commercial	30	17.0%	$6,158,411.16	3.28%
Mining/oil and gas	23	13.0%	$127,832,006.12	68.15%
Civil works/ infrastructure	19	10.8%	$7,924,666.50	4.23%
Industrial	2	1.2%	$6,335,985.56	3.38%
Other	1	0.6%	$64,439.10	0.03%
Totals	176	100.00%	$187,563,024.84	100.00%

Whilst perhaps more anecdotal than definitive, there is speculation that a more litigious environment results as a consequence of tight economic conditions. Based on the authors experience as construction lawyer and arbitrator, in tight economic times as opportunities dry up and margins tighten, it is common that disagreements, differences, and consequently, disputes will become more frequent.

As noted in the Western Australian Government Discussion Paper;[4]

> Where a business operates on tight profit margins, financial shocks (such as those stemming from contractual disputes, tender pricing errors or supplier defaults) can wipe out the

---

[3] Master Builders Association of WA, Building and Construction Industry Forecasts, December 2017, <https://www.masterbuilders.com.au/MediaLibraries>

[4] Department of Mines, Industry Regulations and Safety, Government of Western Australia, Security of Payment Reform, Industry Advisory Group Terms of Reference, February 2018, <https://www.commerce.wa.gov.au>

business's profit on a given project and start to erode its capital base. This can lead to financial distress which, in the short term, is often exhibited in late and non-payment of subcontractors and suppliers and, in the longer term, can result in insolvency.

When there is an urgent need for cash flow, businesses in the building and construction industry have been known to tender for work at or below its actual cost. This practice of 'buying work' may stave off financial distress in the short term but usually magnifies the problem in the medium to longer term.

Data from the Australian Bureau of Statistics (ABS) shows that since 2013 the profit margins of businesses in the building and construction [industry], has been lower than the national average.[5]

This issue was also referred to in the Australian Securities and Investments Commission (ASIC) submission to the Senate Economics Reference Committee inquiry into insolvency in the Australian construction industry. The submission noted that in competitive markets contractors will submit tenders with little or no margins and an attempt to gain profit through variations in the work.[6]

Consequently it is difficult to be definitive with respect to the applications for adjudication and the level of construction activity in the state and this is an area which certainly requires additional research in establishing any nexus.

There are also a number of other issues which need to be considered with respect to evaluating the efficacy of the CCA amendments in assisting the resolution or prevention of payment disputes. These include;

- Extending the time for making an adjudication application;
- Increasing the awareness of the provisions of the CCA;
- Increased contractor education with respect to contract administration;
- The limited introduction of Project Bank Accounts (PBA's); and

---

[5] Above n 21, 9.
[6] The Senate Economic Reference Committee, above n2, 21

- The introduction of a WA Building Industry Code of Practice.

- **Extending the time for making an application for adjudication from 28 to 90 business days**

    The CCA Review Report recommended that the time limits in which an Application can be made should remain at 28 days. It was considered that if the provisions of the contract have been followed with respect to the submission of the original payment claim, and if all supporting documentation has been provided to the superintendent or contract administrator, in order to reasonably consider the basis of the claim, then 28 days to prepare an Application under the CCA would be adequate. The majority of submission to the review considered that the current 28 day time limit serves the central purpose of the CCA which is to ensure that the money keeps flowing. Also other submissions indicated that the 28 day time limit should not be altered on the basis that if the time limit for making an application is extended, particularly to 90 days, then the cash flow justification for the rapid adjudication process ceases to be relevant, especially if there is a consequential increase in the response time.

    However the recommendation was rejected and the CCA was amended to increase the time for lodging an application from 28 to 90 days.

    In support of an increase in the time for lodging of an application, a number of submissions, whilst stating a preference was for the adjudication process to remain rapid, commented that industry awareness of the CCA was not 'strong', particularly in regional areas, and that often the 28 day timeframe has passed before an applicant has become aware of the relevant provisions of the CCA. This lack of awareness of the CCA was a common theme throughout a number of the review meetings and was subject to separate comment and recommendation in the Review Report. Other submissions suggested that the 28 day requirement, in being too short, may have had the effect of pre-empting the decision to negotiate a settlement or partake in the alternative dispute resolution (ADR) processes under the contract.

Again whilst there are no definitive statistics available these comments nevertheless suggest that the 90 day period may in fact have an influence on the lower number of applications overall in the last reporting period. The longer time possibly allows for parties in dispute to enter into negotiations and discussions which are usually a precondition in most construction contracts. It is trite to say that a negotiated settlement is preferable to a third party determination. In the event that the dispute is not settled then there is still time to lodge the adjudication application. Whist perhaps conjectural at this time an assumption might be that the longer period is allowing parties to negotiate and settle and thus reduce the need to lodge an adjudication application.

- **Increasing the awareness of the provisions of the CCA**

Throughout the CCA Review it was noted that many issues affecting both contractors and subcontractors did not result principally from significant deficiencies in the CCA's provisions but from a lack of awareness of the CCA and especially its primary objectives. As noted above specifically these are:

- to prohibit or modify certain provisions in construction contracts;
- to imply provisions in construction contracts about certain matters if there are no written provisions about the matters in the contracts; and
- to provide a means for adjudicating payment disputes arising under construction contracts, and for related purposes.

Where parties were aware of the existence of the CCA there was a lack of understanding that adjudication determinations are interim in nature and do not affect the parties' rights under the common law of contract. These rights are preserved allowing subsequent arbitration or litigation. The emphasis on the CCA is on maintaining cash flow.

As noted above, it is in effect a system of pay now, where there is a legitimate entitlement, and argue later.

Additionally many issues raised in the review submissions related to a general lack of understanding of the basic principles of contractual rights and obligations. The Review Report recommended the introduction widespread education and training by all sections of the construction industry as well as additional efforts by the Building Commission to ensure awareness and compliance with the provisions of the CCA as well as basic contract administration training.

The reviewer considered that the introduction, in particular of basic contract administration training courses, would have a secondary befit in reducing contractual disputes generally. A number of studies over the past 10 years have attempted to identify or categorise the causes of construction disputes.[7] Additionally a number of key causal factors contributing to construction disputes have been identified as; [8]

- Poor contract documentation that arise from the organisational system (inadequate or incomplete design information, and ambiguities in contract documentation);
- Scope changes that arise from uncertainty that exists within the project management system (variations due to client, design errors, site conditions); and
- Educational and behavioral adaptations of individuals within the system (poor communication, poor management, skill and experience, and personality traits).

The importance of the need for construction contract administrators to have legal skills and appropriate training was also identified some ten years ago in the Western Australian Government Auditor General's Report, No 6. [9] The report notes in part that benefits of contracting out

---

[7] P, Love, P. Davis and P. Evans, *Prometheus unbound: Unravelling the underlying nature of disputes*. Proceedings of the RICS Legal Research Symposium COBRA, University of Cape Town. Sept 2009; See also Kumararaswamy M. *Conflicts, claims and disputes*. Engineering, Construction and Architectural Management 4 (2). 1997

[8] *The Guide to Leading Practice for Dispute Avoidance and Resolution.* CRC for Construction Innovation report. 2009

[9] WA Auditor General's Report, Maintaining the state road network, Report No 6.

and construction and maintenance can only be achieved where there is a proper understanding of contractual obligations together with effective dispute resolution procedures.

More recently in the context of the Western Australian construction industry, Perth Law firm Jackson McDonald have identified a number of factors which give rise to construction payment claims and noted in particular the failure to properly administer contracts.[10]

In an immediate response to the review recommendations, the state government in December 2016 and January 2017, through the Building Commission, ran free information sessions for building and construction industry participants relating to the amendments to the CCA. Specifically the sessions covered the key changes made by *Construction Contracts Amendment Bill 2016*. Subsequently online versions of these presentations were made available.

In addition, the Building Commission has established on its website a range of materials which have been designed with the aim of assisting parties who wish to lodge a claim for payment under the CCA.[11]

- **The introduction of Project Bank Accounts (PBAs)**

As expected in the CCA Review, a number of submissions referred to payment and operational difficulties generally. Whilst an important provision of the CCA is the rapid resolution of payment disputes, as noted above it was never the intention of the legislation to provide comprehensive protection to parties unable to look after their own commercial interests and it can be appreciated that governments are hesitant in intervening in commercial agreements between parties who should remain free to strike whatever bargains they wish between themselves.

However at the national level, the federal government has ex-

---

June 2009, <http://www.parliament.wa.gov.au/publications>

[10] T. Jacobs, Construction Disputes – why do they happen? <http://www.jacmac.com.au/uploaded/News/publications/201210_Contstruction_Disputes_e-alert.pdf>.

[11] Available at <https://www.commerce.wa.gov.au>

pressed concern at the issue of building and construction insolvency and the relationship with security of payment and on 4 December 2014 the Senate referred an inquiry into insolvency in the Australian construction industry to the Senate Economics References Committee. The Committee report of 3 December 2015 made a number of recommendations regarding the relationship between security of payment legislation and insolvency.[12] One of the recommendations was that uniform security of payment legislation should be introduced to replace the current non-uniform state legislation.[13] On 21 December 2016, the federal government began a review into security of payment legislation in the building and construction industry, to examine in particular the security of payment legislation in all jurisdictions to identify areas of best practice for the construction industry.[14] At the time of writing the review had been completed and the report is currently being considered by the federal government.

In the WA CCA review, a number of submissions suggested that the introduction of a statutory construction retentions trust scheme which would see retention monies go into escrow pending completion of the works. These retention monies would be held by a third party and paid back to the subcontractor at the completion of the defects liability period. It was further submitted that this system would overcome the current disparity whereby principal contractors can earn interest off the retention monies held and delay repayment based on their opinion as to whether the subcontract work is complete.

By comparison, a number of submissions did not support the

---

[12] Senate Economics Reference Committee, above n2, <www.aph.gov.au>
[13] See *Building and Construction Industry Security of Payment Act* 1999 (NSW); *Building and Construction Industry Security of Payment Act* 2002 (Vic); *Building and Construction Industry Payments Act* 2004 (Qld); *Construction Contracts (Security of Payments) Act* 2004 (NT); *Building and Construction Industry (Security of Payment) Act* 2009 (SA*); Building and Construction Industry Security of Payment Act* 2009 (ACT); *Building and Construction Industry Security of Payment Act* 2009 (Tas); *Construction Contracts Amendment Act* 2016 (WA).
[14] The issue of uniform security of payment legislation was considered in the WA CCA Review. The submissions unanimously indicated that if uniform legislation was to be introduced it should be based on the WA Act.

introduction of any form of trust scheme citing legal and practical difficulties in determining which parties in the supply chain are worthy of any legislative protection. It was noted that the imposition of trust arrangements discriminates against the party that assumes the majority of the risk; that is, the builder and principal contractor. It was submitted that the imposition of a trust fund will restrict the ability, particularly in the case of the builder, to use money received from progress payments in a flexible manner, thus depriving them of working capital and forcing them to incur additional financing costs.

Other submissions referred to the specific issue of 'Project Bank Accounts' (PBA's) for use on both government and non-government contracts.

In general terms, a PBA is a payment facility which allows for the direct and simultaneous payment of the head contractor and various participating subcontractors. It is essentially a trust arrangement (deed) intended to assist security of payment issues and thus prevent payment disputes and also isolate funds in the event of head contractor insolvency.

They are essentially interest bearing bank account with trust status into which funds are deposited for the purpose of making payments to the head contractor and subcontractors in the supply chain in a timely manner.[15] As the account has trust status, monies can only be paid to the designated beneficiaries of the account. Thus, the PBA is linked to a trust deed which confines the monies in the account for the designated beneficiaries. The presence of a trust deed ensures once monies are paid into the account they are only accessible to the parties to the trust deed – the main contractor and the members of its supply chain who have agreed to be joined to the deed.[16]

While the introduction of PBA's is a relatively new initiative in Australia, PBA's have been successfully implemented in the United

---

[15] Fenwick Elliot, 'Insight: What We Have Learnt About Adjudication over the Past Twelve Months' (July 2012), <http://www.fenwickelliott.com>

[16] The Guidelines for Deploying Welsh Government Project Bank Account Policy, April 2014. 19 <prp.govwales/docs/prp/toolkit/146404pbaguidancenote.doc>

Kingdom and a number of Australian jurisdictions are committed to their use. [17]

However, PBA's do not seek to alter the existing contractual rights and responsibilities of the parties to a traditional construction contract. They will not prevent a head contractor from experiencing financial difficulty or managing the performance of subcontractors by withholding payments when contractual obligations are not met. Additionally, they do not constrain any party from seeking adjudication under the CCA or from commencing legal proceedings in the event of a dispute.

The research conducted as part of the CCA Review indicated that the usefulness of PBA's appears to be limited to higher value or large one-off projects. It was considered by the author that they are generally unsuitable for the majority of construction projects regulated by the CCA. With respect to any recommendation to amend the CCA to include provisions relating to the use of PBA's, it was considered that the scope and coverage of the CCA is now well settled and any changes by way of introducing the use of PBA's could potentially add legal complexity and possibly restrict the use of the CCA.

Consequently rather than amend the CCA to incorporate the mandatory use of PBA's, in addition to the other amendments to the CCA, the state government introduced PBA's, commencing 30 September 2016, following a three year trial on seven government contracts. These PBA's will be used on the majority of projects administered by the WA Department of Building Management and Works for tendered projects with a construction value over $1.5 million and which utilise an AS2124-1992 contract.[18] Subcontractors performing government work valued at less than this amount have the ability to opt in to the PBA by notifying the head contractor.

---

[17] The Queensland government intends to introduce PBA's on a trial basis commencing 1 January 2018. Details on the operation of PBA's in Western Australia may be found at <https://www.finance.wa.gov.au>

[18] The requirement with respect to the use of AS2124-1992 as a pre-condition is significant. The CCA review report recommended that the AS General Conditions of Contract should be used on all major government projects in order to avoid the problems which occur with the use of bespoke contracts. However this recommendation was not adopted.

The above precondition with respect to the use of PBA's are very restrictive and do not apply to building and construction projects generally or with construction values under $1.5 million. Additionally in the past 18 months in Western Australia there have been a number of builders becoming insolvent or entering into deeds of administration leaving large numbers of subcontractors with little or no prospect for payment for work done[19]. Consequently on 23 February 2018 the WA government announced a review to improve security of payments for subcontractors in Western Australia's building and construction industry, and the establishment of an Industry Advisory Group (IAG).[20]

One of the terms of reference for the new review will be to consider whether statutory trust arrangements should be introduced to protect monies owed to subcontractors in the event a head contractor on the project experiences financial difficulty, and, if so, which model is appropriate for these trust arrangements. Certainly the use of PBA's will be considered in the IAG review.

- **The introduction of a WA Building Industry Code of Practice**

During the CCA Review, in a number of meetings and submissions, issues were raised which at first sight would appear to fall outside the terms of reference of the Review regarding the operation and effectiveness of the CCA. At the same time they were clearly collateral to the review and whilst no recommendations were specifically made with respect to amendments to the CCA with respect to the allegations made or specific conduct complained of, it was nevertheless incumbent upon the reviewer to refer to them in the final CCA Review Report for any future action or enquiry which may be deemed appropriate by the Building Commissioner or Minister for Commerce.

At the lower level of the contracting chain it was evident, as referred to above that there was a basic lack of understanding of contractual

---

[19] Emily Piesse, *Cooper & Oxley Goes into Administration as Contractors Owed Millions* (8 February 2018) ABC News <http://www.abc.net.au/news/2018-02-08/wa-builder-cooper-and-oxley-placed-in-administration/9410034>.
[20] <https://www.mediastatements.wa.gov.au>

principles and rights and obligations under the contract apart from any issues of inequality of bargaining power or economic duress. With respect to what might be described as 'unfair' practices in the construction industry, the submissions of the Small Business Development Corporation, the Subcontractors for Fair Treatment and Master Electricians Australia provided details of practices which appeared to be certainly unethical and in some cases even unlawful. The examples given also appeared to be in breach of any implied common law requirement of good faith in contractual dealing. [21] Some of these practices were also referred to in the confidential submissions and stakeholder meetings. The submission by the Hon Rev Peter Abetz (MLA) refers to some of these practices as follows;

> It is a common reality that some larger well established businesses take advantage of their small subcontractors by deferring payment beyond the agreed terms of trade. These businesses are aware that their small subcontractors depend on them for their livelihood and are not usually in a position to bargain with them effectively or threaten to withdraw their labour.

Unfortunately Western Australia does not have the equivalent of the *Contracts Review Act 1980* (NSW) which confers upon the Supreme, District and Local Courts, powers to review contracts that are 'unjust' (defined in s 4 to include harsh, oppressive or unconscionable conduct).[22]

However, many of the examples given in the CCA review submissions clearly fell within the jurisdiction or provisions of the *Australian Consumer Law* (ACL). The ACL (which forms part of the *Competition and Consumer Act 2010 (Cth)*) sets out a number of rights and responsibilities that serve to guide businesses in their day-to-day dealings with consumers and in particular with other businesses.

---

[21] The issue of good faith in commercial contracts is considered in detail in Elisabeth Peden, *Good Faith in the Performance of Contracts*. (Lexis Nexis, 2003).

[22] The *Misrepresentation Act 1972* (SA) provides criminal sanctions against misrepresentation in certain commercial transactions; to expand the remedies available at common law and in equity for misrepresentation; and for other purposes.

Among other things, the ACL prohibits unconscionable conduct.[23]

Prior to the completion of the CCA review a number of reforms were proposed to the *Competition and Consumer Act*.[24] Submissions to the Harper Review suggested reforms which would assist small business in particular. One of these was to extend the unfair contract term provision to contracts involving small business. This was also the subject of separate review by the Commonwealth government.[25]

These reviews have now resulted in the drafting of the *Treasury Legislation Amendment (Small Business and Unfair Contract Terms) Bill* 2015 which was read for the second time on 17 August 2015. The Bill amended *the Competition and Consumer Act* 2010 (Cth) to extend the unfair contract terms protections to a business with less than 20 employees agreeing to standard form contracts valued at less than $100,000 or $250,000 if the duration of the contract is more than 12 months.[26] It was considered by the Reviewer that this would significantly address some of the concerns raised by smaller subcontractors particularly when faced with unilateral contract provisions or changes by larger organisations.

Again the issue for the Reviewer was should structural changes be made to the CCA to prevent the alleged unfair conduct from occurring?[27] The Reviewer considered that the scope and coverage of the CCA was now well settled and any changes by way of introducing provisions in the CCA dealing with unconscionable conduct or unfair

---

[23] Unconscionable conduct provisions also exist in the *Australian Securities and Investments Commission Act 2001 (Cth)*, which applies to transactions involving financial products and services.

[24] I Harper, P Anderson, S McCluskey and M O'Bryan, *Competition Policy Review Final Report* (Commonwealth of Australia, 2015) (The Harper Review) <http://competitionpolicyreview.gov.au>.

[25] 'Extending Unfair Contract Term Protection to Small Businesses' (Consultation Paper, The Treasury, 23 May 2014) http://www.treasury.gov.au

[26] <http://www.aph.gov.au>

[27] One issue was that the written and oral submissions to the Review were untested. The reviewer did not receive evidence under oath and had no powers of compulsion. Consequently in many instances, the information in the submissions relating to unfair practices reflects opinion or allegations.

terms would potentially add legal complexity and hinder the principal objectives of the CCA with respect to the rapid determination of payment disputes which objectively has been considered generally by stakeholders as being successful in providing a rapid determination of payment disputes?

Consequently rather than introduce additional complexity into the CCA by including provisions dealing with what might be described generically as 'unfair contracting practices', in response to the recommendations contained in the CCA Review Report together with its awareness of a number of current unacceptable practices in the construction industry, the state government, in addition to adopting most of the recommendations regarding amendments to the CCA, introduced a number of other measures to improve both security of payment and contracting practices in the Western Australian construction industry. In addition to proposed legislation to make it an offence to intimidate, coerce or threaten a person or business in the industry, the government indicated it would use the *Building Services (Registration) Act* 2011(WA) as a means of investigating and disciplining registered building contractors who have engaged in unfair behaviour or systematic non-payment of subcontractors. The Minister for Commerce also announced that government intended to introduce a 'code of conduct' for tenderers on state government funded construction projects, and in some cases on private projects, in order to eliminate unacceptable behaviour on building sites and anti-competitive behaviour.

The object of the code is to ensure that when expending public funds, Western Australian government agencies contract with building contractors who conduct themselves in a reputable, fair, safe and responsible manner, both in dealings with the state of Western Australia and within the building and construction industry more broadly. The government acted quickly and within three months of the tabling of the CCA Review Report, on 5 December 2016 the *Western Australian Building and Construction Industry Code of Conduct 2016* (BCI Code) was introduced.[28] The BCI Code applies from 1 January 2017 to new

---

[28] Department of Commerce WA. WA Building and Construction Industry Code of

tendering processes for state projects with a value in excess of $10 million. The code will also apply to 'Private Building Work'[29]. Private building work is defined as work procured by way of a tender process, or if not procured by a tender process, by a contract for Building Work executed, whilst the building contractor is covered by the BCI Code, is also covered by the BCI Code[30]. A building contractor must provide advice in writing when such Private Covered Building Work has a value in excess of $2 million.[31]

The BCI Code is comprehensive and was specifically introduced in order to provide measures designed to protect smaller contractors in both the building and the wider construction industry. These measures include prohibitions on anti-competitive behaviour such as price fixing, sham contracting, harsh or unfair contract terms, and to ensure compliance with the provisions of the CCA. In keeping with its commitment to create greater awareness of measures designed to assist contracting parties in addition to the BCI Code, the Department of Commerce has published implementation guidelines to provide further guidance and information on the obligations contained in the BCI Code. [32]

A significant and important obligation under the BCI Code requires contractors to ensure compliance with the Code in dealing with their subcontractors and also to take reasonable steps to ensure Code compliance by their subcontractors.[33] Most importantly, in view of a number of the submissions to the CCA review regarding breaches of the provisions of the CCA, the Code also reinforces the payment obligations under the CCA by emphasising that contractors must not include any prohibited provisions under the CCA in their contracts

---

Conduct 2016. At <https://www.commerce.wa.gov.au/publications>

[29] This provision is not found in the Commonwealth Building Code which does not apply to subcontractors on private projects,

[30] Above n 43, 4

[31] Above n 43, Clause 26.1

[32] Department of Commerce WA. "Implementation Guidelines". At <https://www.commerce.wa.gov.au/building-and-construction-code-monitoring-unit/implementation-guidelines-1>

[33] Ibid, Clause 8.

and must make 'reasonable and timely' payments and additionally ensure that payment disputes are resolved in a reasonable, timely and consultative way. [34]

In conjunction with the introduction of the BCI Code, a Building and Construction Code Monitoring Unit (BCCMU) has been established within the Department of Commerce.[35] The BCCMU will undertake not only monitoring and compliance activities including investigating alleged breaches but in response to the CCA Review Report recommendations regarding the need for education and awareness programs the Building Commission will also promote awareness of the BCI Code through a range of information and educational activities.

However as with most codes of practice, there are no coercive powers or legal penalties within the provisions of the BCI Code in the event of noncompliance. Nevertheless where the BCCMU believes that a contractor has breached the code, after investigation the contactor will be 'invited' to rectify the breach or the BCCMU may report the breach to the appropriate government agency or body. [36] .Where the BCCMU finds that there has been material non-compliance with the Code this may result in the contractor and its related entities from being awarded future work. [37]

It is possible that future amendments to either the CCA or the BCI Code will occur as a consequence a the recently announced review to further improve security of payments for subcontractors in Western Australia's building and construction industry, through the establishment of an Industry Advisory Group (IAG). One of the proposed terms of reference of the review is whether amendments should be made to the *Building Services (Registration) Act* 2011 to introduce a demerit point system (or other appropriate power) to sanction registered builders that do not pay debts owed to subcontractors and suppliers in a timely manner, or engage in behavior designed to dissuade

---

[34] Ibid, Clause 23.
[35] Ibid, Clause 3.
[36] Ibid, Part 3; Compliance and related matters
[37] Ibid, Clause 30.5(f).

a subcontractor or supplier from enforcing their rights under security of payment legislation.[38]

- **Conclusion**

The CCA Review and the adoption of the review recommendations has had a significant impact with respect to both the resolution of payment disputes and the introduction of more efficient and equitable contract administration processes in the WA building and construction industry. Through amendments to the CCA, the introduction of awareness programs and the introduction of the BCI Code, the state government has indicated its commitment to the provision of protection and assistance for contractors and subcontractors in the construction sector. Its commitment in this area is further exemplified through the recent establishment of an industry advisory group to further consider a number of recommendations made in the CCA Review.

As noted above the Review and the subsequent amendments to the CCA have been described as the sectors 'biggest shakeup' in a decade.[39] Additionally the introduction of the BCI Code will hopefully ensure that when expending public funds, all Western Australian government agencies will contract with building contractors that conduct themselves in a reputable, fair, safe and responsible manner, both in dealings with the State of Western Australia and within the broader building and construction industry.

---

[38] At https://www.mediastatements.wa.gov.au
[39] Above n 18

ABSTRACTS

John Trone, *Lessons from a Teacher*

On many occasions Gabriël Moens has been recognised as an outstanding teacher. This personal appreciation of Gabriël's merits as a teacher is written from the perspective of one of his undergraduate and doctoral students at the University of Queensland.

Nicholas Aroney, *Constitutional Fundamentals*

It is a commonplace that the Australian Constitution cannot be understood without consideration of fundamental doctrines such as the rule of law, judicial review, parliamentary sovereignty, the separation of powers, representative democracy, responsible government and federalism. But in what respects precisely, and to what extent, do each of these doctrines explain the Constitution, and in what ways do they intersect? It is also a commonplace that these doctrines are capable of generating constitutional implications. But if these doctrines suggest contradictory conclusions, which one is to prevail? These are some of the important questions addressed in this article.

Augusto Zimmermann, *The Wrongs of a Bill of Rights for Australia*

The introduction of a constitutionally entrenched bill of rights in Australia would contribute to the elevation of a philosophy that promotes judicial activism but does not necessarily afford the levels of protection needed against arbitrariness and legal uncertainty. What follows is an exposition of basic reasons as to why Australia should not have a constitutionally entrenched bill of rights. Professor Gabriël Moens wrote an important article which convinced me that Australia does not need a constitutionally entrenched charter of rights. Such a legal instrument would not offer the best or most effective way to protect our fundamental rights. To the contrary, not only our delicate federal balance would be further compromised, but also representative democracy and the rule of law could be equally affected.

A. Keith Thompson, *The Spiritual Foundations of Section 51 (XXXI)*

The Australian High Court's interpretation of s 51(xxxi) of the *Commonwealth Constitution* has become unpredictable. The statutory abrogation of the right to sue for personal injury damages at common law is protected, but the abrogation of common law rights adjusted by statute in the past is not. Despite the compensation idea underlying the original version of *Magna Carta*, the Commonwealth is able to take a variety of personal property without just terms if it does not amount to an acquisition under definitions developed since WWII. This article suggests that the High Court needs to revisit its s 51(xxxi) jurisprudence and require the Commonwealth to budget and pay for every acquisition it makes in accordance with a principle that is older than *Magna Carta* because its current jurisprudence does not respect the Rule of Law.

Michael Quinlan, *Born (Again) This Way: Why the Inherent Nature of Religiosity Requires a New Approach to Australia's Discrimination Laws*

Australia has committed to a number of international instruments which recognise the importance of freedom of religion. Whilst Commonwealth legislation seeks to prevent discrimination and vilification on the basis of race, sex, age, disability and sexual orientation, gender identity and intersex status, no such legislation provides protection from discrimination on the basis of religion.

Some may argue that this difference in approach is warranted on the basis that Federal anti-discrimination legislation to date has protected inherent characteristics which are immutable. This chapter does not address the legitimacy of protecting persons from harassment or discrimination because they exhibit characteristics considered to be inherent and immutability. Rather it argues that as a belief in inherency and immutability appears to have been a motivating factor for protecting characteristics to date, equivalent protection of freedom of religion and belief ought to be afforded on the basis of consistency. The chapter questions the assumption that presently protected characteristics are all necessarily immutable and inherent human characteristics whilst religious belief is neither. It argues that religiosity is a natural and inherent characteristic of individuals which has a genetic component and that, for some people, religious faith is at least as immutable as some other presently protected characteristics. The chapter argues that religious freedom is presently treated as a lesser human right in Australia. It concludes that there is a pressing need to revise Australia's approach to anti-discrimination legislation in order to provide more adequate and nationwide protection for persons of faith.

Suri Ratnapala, *Liberal Peace and its Prospects in the Twenty First Century*

The liberal theory of peace as first proposed by Enlightenment philosophers David Hume, Jeremy Bentham and Immanuel Kant holds that individual liberty within nations and free trade among nations provide the surest foundations of peace. Humanity has not and may never achieve these conditions on a global scale. Nevertheless, in the period since the end of the Second World War, the theory has been tested and found credible in parts of the world where liberal democratic systems and cross border trade have flourished. The fall of the Berlin Wall and communism in Europe heralded a period of spreading democracy and trade liberalisation across the world that created an expanding sphere of peace among nations that embraced these values. However, liberal peace is facing serious internal and external threats. Authoritarian tendencies within new and established democracies, the rise of fascism in former communist states and the emergence of faith driven hostility to liberalism pose the most immediate but not the only challenges. This paper explains the logic of the liberal theory of peace, discusses the challenges to liberal peace and prognosticates its sustainability in the face of threats.

Marc De Vos, *Happiness and the Law*

This chapter challenges some of the premises of the literature that promotes subjective wellbeing as a goal for public policy. Having introduced the revival of 'happiness as policy' (Section 1), it tackles the assumption that happiness is a desirable alternative for, or a needed correction of, economic growth and its traditional measure of Gross Domestic Product or GDP (Section 2). It addresses the three core arguments that support the political promotion of happiness: that more economic growth is not the way to promote more happiness (Section 3), that 'happiness' can be sufficiently defined and measured as to make it a reliable policy instrument (Section 4), and that its promotion is morally desirable (Section 5). It highlights the tension between the politicization of happiness and the rule of law (Section 6). It concludes by repositioning the relevance of happiness, arguing for a policy of facilitation rather than determination (Section 7).

Jürgen Bröhmer, *The Use of Force as a Response to Chemical Weapons Attacks – There Might Be Something Brewing in the Laboratory of International Law?*

The law regulating the use of force is the cornerstone of international law and keeping the peace is its prime objective. The Charter of the United Nations has established a set of rules around the use of military force that attempts to restrict the use of force as much as possible. Using military force is legally possible only to self-defend against an armed attack or if authorized by the Security Council. This restrictive regime is challenged when states engage in especially egregious behaviour, for example in massive human rights violations. In this paper, the author examines the April 2018 missile strikes by the USA, France and Great-Britain conducted in response to the use of chemical weapons against civilians by the Syrian government and, in particular, the response of the international community to these military counter-measures. The author asks whether these responses could indicate the possibility of a (beginning) development or shift in international law towards a further exception from the prohibition of use of force when military force is used proportionally as a counter-measure in reaction to the prohibited use of chemical weapons.

Geoffrey Bennett, *Brexit, Art Loans and Frustration*

In June 2016 the United Kingdom (UK) voted in a referendum, by a small majority, to leave the European Union (EU). Amidst the intense debate both in Parliament and the media about the implications of this decision for the economy of the UK the impact on the cultural heritage sector has been largely neglected by those outside that sector. One aspect of this is the impact of Brexit on loans of art between museums and galleries. This article assesses some of the implications and factors that now need to be considered by UK museums and galleries who deal with collections in the EU and what might be done, both immediately and in the future, to deal with these issues.

Bruno Zeller, *The Finality of the Arbitral Award*

This paper analyses what might be called the twilight zone of arbitration that is the intersection of litigation and arbitration especially when the court is asked to set aside an award when not all issues referred to arbitration have been decided. The Victorian Supreme Court in *Blanalko Pty Ltd v Lysaght Building Solutions Pty Ltd* was asked to decide whether an award can be set aside and when and how corrections can be applied to an issue which the arbitrator expressly did not determine. The English Court of appeal in *Michael Wilson & Partners* - where the respondent to the litigation was not a party [but involved] to the earlier arbitration - conclude that "a subsequent litigation is not an abuse of process for being a collateral attack against a previous arbitral award. Importantly the two decisions clarify the relationship between articles 33 and 34 of the Model Law.

Doug Jones, *Overcoming the Tyranny of Distance as an Arbitral Seat*

Nestled within the prosperous Asia-Pacific region is Australia, a nation that has emerged as a competitive seat for international commercial arbitration. This chapter posits that Australia's historical struggles, heightened by the tyranny of distance, have been outmatched by the real capabilities of Australian arbitration. The combination of robust legislation, an independent and supportive judiciary and effective arbitral institutions characterises Australia's pro-arbitration legal landscape, positioning it at the leading edge of international best practice. Today, commercial parties can confidently select Australia as a seat for arbitration, safe in the knowledge of its numerous practical and legal benefits.

Luke Nottage and Diana Hu, *The Joys and Challenges of (Re) educating Australian Jurists in International Commercial Arbitration*

This chapter begins by lauding the major contributions by Professor Moens to the teaching and wider promotion of international commercial arbitration (ICA) in Australia, especially through coaching and other contributions to the Vis Moot competitions since the early 1990s. Yet the chapter notes how ICA-related litigation in Australian courts has grown especially since 2010 statutory amendments, even though they were designed to transform the culture around arbitration to enhance its attractiveness as a cost-effective and speedy form of alternative dispute resolution. Statistical analysis further shows that case disposition times have not significantly improved even in the Federal Court, which otherwise has helped to interpret ICA's key international instruments a more pro-arbitration way. We reiterate that more far-reaching reforms are needed in Australia, including an indemnity costs principle for failed ICA-related court challenges. This should reduce incentives to prolong costs and delays generated by the ever more pervasive 'billable hours' model for legal services delivery. We also speculate that ongoing costs and delays in Australia may be linked to the growth in ICA-related courses and especially moot competitions, leaving a bittersweet challenge for educators.

J. Clifton Fleming, Jr., *To What Degree Does Customary International Law Require Accommodation of a Source Country's Right to Tax High, Tax Low, or Not Tax at All?*

Because it has been my pleasure to know Gabriël Moens and count him as a friend for many years, I was pleased when asked to contribute to this volume. There is, nevertheless, a seeming incongruity in the fact that Gabriël is an international law scholar while my primary field is income tax law, a subject which is often regarded as purely a domestic creature. This impression is significantly inaccurate. Income tax law, in its cross-border application, is actually based on well-established customary international law principles. This essay will explore the extent to which these principles indicate that the right of a country to impose a *high tax, low tax, or no tax* on its non-residents' cross-border income must be accommodated by other countries.

Henry Gabriel, *The International Harmonization of Security Rights Law: Its Successes and Challenges*

This article explores the international harmonization of personal property security rights law and summarize the general principles that are common within the harmonization efforts. I would like to focus on several points. First, this article provides an overview of the work of the *United Nations Commission on International Trade Law* (UNCITRAL) and the *International Institute for the Unification of International Private Law* (UNIDROIT) in the harmonization of the law of personal property security rights. Second, it discusses the generally accepted principles that underlie modern secured finance. Last, it briefly discusses the problems some common-law jurisdictions have had in their attempts to modernize and conform their laws to these generally accepted principles.

Lorraine Finlay, *The Seven Habits of Highly Effective Mooters*

Throughout his prestigious academic career Emeritus Professor Gabriël Moens has not only been known for encouraging academic excellence, but also for emphasising the importance of practical legal training. The best example of this has been his long-term support for mooting as an integral part of legal education. This paper will consider the value of mooting as an educative tool in law schools but will focus on the character building aspect of mooting. While mooting has the obvious benefit of developing legal research, writing and advocacy skills, the paper proposes that its greatest potential benefit lies in the way that it develops non-legal skills such as a strong work ethic, resilience, teamwork, strategic decision-making, attention to detail, honesty & integrity and a global outlook. Discussions about the value of mooting often fail to recognise its important character-building role, with these skills benefiting moot students both in their future legal careers, and all other aspects of their life.

Rajesh Sharma, Harprabdeep Singh, and Eric Ng, *The Art and Science of Oral Advocacy: The Winner's Perspective*

The techniques of oral advocacy focused on in this paper are based on the skills honed, harnessed and later imparted by Professor Gabriël Moens together with the combined experience of the authors. Two authors of this paper have won the Championship in the renowned Willem C. Vis International Commercial Arbitration Moot in Hong Kong in 2012 and Vienna in 2013. Utilizing what they learnt, they are putting into practice principles and techniques of oral advocacy in their professional lives as practicing barristers in Hong Kong. The third author is the former co-coach (with Professor Moens) of both champions and an established academic and moot coach in his own right. Cultivating the experience of all three, using the foundation laid by Professor Moens, this paper has attempted to share the previously unknown tips and strategies of Professor Moens in oral advocacy which can be adopted by any law student whether he/she is a born orator or not. It is our belief that the basic skills of oral advocacy can be learnt which is why the main purpose of this article is to guide law students who intend to practice law either as barristers or solicitors (with higher rights of audience) and who will eventually argue before judges in courts or arbitration tribunals.

Philip Evans, *Securing of Payment in Western Australia: The Effect of Changes Arising from the Review of the Construction Contracts Act 2004 (WA)*

In June 2015 the Western Australian government commissioned an independent statutory review of the operation and effectiveness of the *Construction Contracts Act 2004* (WA), (The CCA). On 22 November 2016 following consideration of the review report, the West Australian parliament passed a number of amendments to the CCA and the amended Act commenced operation on 15 December 2016. This paper considers the effects on the WA construction industry following the passing of the amended act and the introduction of various new policies intended to enhance security of payment and contract administration procedures in the Western Australian building and construction industry. The paper concludes that the adoption of the review recommendations, the subsequent amendments to the CCA and the introduction of the *Western Australian Building and Construction Industry Code of Conduct* have resulted in more efficient and equitable payment practices in the WA construction industry.

List of Publications[40]
Emeritus Professor Gabriël A. Moens

Thesis

- *The Quality of Equality: A Study of School Integration and Preferential Admission Programs in the United States* (submitted for the Degree of Doctor of Philosophy at the University of Sydney, 1982), xi + 365pp

Books

- **Gabriël A Moens** and John Trone, *Lumb, Moens & Trone's The Constitution of the Commonwealth of Australia Annotated*, 9th ed., LexisNexis Butterworths, Sydney, 2016, xlvii + 602 pp
- **Gabriël A. Moens** and Philip Evans, eds., *Arbitration and Dispute Resolution in the Resources Sector: An Australian Perspective*, Springer, London, 2015, xvi + 259 pp (with Foreword by The Hon. Chief Justice Wayne Martin)
- **Gabriël A Moens** and John Trone, *Lumb, Moens & Trone's The Constitution of the Commonwealth of Australia Annotated*, 8th ed., LexisNexis Butterworths, Sydney, 2012, xliv + 576 pp
- Suri Ratnapala and **Gabriël A Moens**, *Jurisprudence of Liberty*, 2nd ed., LexisNexis Butterworths, Australia, 2011, xix + 506 pp
- Philip Evans and **Gabriël Moens**, eds., *Murdoch Law School: The Search for Excellence*, Perth, 2010, 150 pp
- **Gabriël Moens** and John Trone, *Commercial Law of the European Union*, Springer, 2010, exii + 486 pp (with Foreword by The Hon. Michael Kirby AC CMG)
- **Gabriël A Moens** and John Trone, *Lumb & Moens' The Constitution of the Commonwealth of Australia Annotated*, 7th ed., LexisNexis Butterworths, Sydney, 2007, xxxix + 544 pp

---

[40] Articles and comments published in newspapers and magazines are not listed in this List of Publications.

- **Gabriël Moens** and Peter Gillies, *International Trade and Business: Law, Policy and Ethics*, 2^n ed., Routledge/Cavendish, London, 2006, xl + 649 pp
- **Garrick Professor Gabriël A. Moens** and Dr Rodolphe Biffot, eds., *The Convergence of Legal Systems in the 21st Century*, CopyRight Publishing Company Pty Ltd, Brisbane, 2002, 564 pp
- **Gabriël Moens** and John Trone, *Lumb & Moens' The Constitution of the Commonwealth of Australia Annotated*, 6th ed., Butterworths, Sydney, 2001, xxxix + 480 pp.
- **Gabriël A. Moens**, ed., *Constitutional and International Law Perspectives*, The University of Queensland Press, St Lucia, 2000, 271 pp
- **Gabriël Moens** and Peter Gillies, *International Trade and Business: Law, Policy and Ethics*, Cavendish Publishing Pty Ltd, London, 1998, lvii +819 pp
- Suri Ratnapala and **G A Moens**, eds., *Jurisprudence of Liberty*, Butterworths, Sydney, 1996, viii + 312 pp
- R D Lumb and **G A Moens**, *The Constitution of the Commonwealth of Australia Annotated*, 5th ed., Butterworths, Sydney, 1995, l + 676 pp
- **Gabriël Moens** and David Flint, *Business Law of the European Community*, DataLegal Publications Pty. Ltd., 1993, 361 pp (with Foreword by The Rt. Hon. Lord Slynn of Hadley)
- **Gabriël A Moens**, ed., *Academic Freedom Today*, Australian Society of Legal Philosophy, Sydney, 1992, viii + 100 pp
- **Gabriël Moens** and Suri Ratnapala, *The Illusions of Comparable Worth*, Centre for Independent Studies, Sydney, 1992, xvi +106 pp (with Foreword by Charles E. Rice)
- Philip de Lacey and **Gabriël Moens**, *The Decline of the University*, Law Press, Tahmoor, 1990, xvi + 178 pp (with Foreword by Professor Darrell Lumb)

- **Gabriël Moens**, *Affirmative Action: The New Discrimination*, Centre for Independent Studies, Sydney, 1985, xii +112 pp (with foreword by Professor Lauchlan Chipman)
- Ilmar Tammelo and **Gabriël Moens**, *Logische Verfahren der juristischen Begründung* (The Application of Logical Decision Procedures in Judicial Reasoning), Springer-Verlag, Vienna-NewYork, 1976, vii + 111 pp
- **Gabriël Moens**, *Equality for Freedom. A Critical Study of Unresolved Problems of School Desegregation Cases in the United States*, Wilhelm Braumüller Universitäts-Verlagsbuchhandlung, Vienna-Stuttgart, 1976, v + 73 pp (with Preface by Professor Victor G. Rosenblum)

Editor-in-Chief

- *International Trade and Business Law Review* (incorporating *International Trade and Business Law Journal* and *International Trade and Business Law Annual.*, Volumes I-XXI, 1995-2018

Book Chapters

- "The Willem C. Vis International Commercial Arbitration Moot" in *Thomson Reuters' Guide to Mooting* (Anthony E Cassimatis and Peter Billings eds.), Lawbook Co., 2016, 107-144
- "Annotated Text of the *Commercial Arbitration Act* 2012 (WA)" in *International Commercial Arbitration* (Looseleaf set, Eric E. Bergsten ed.), Oxford University Press, 2014 (with John Trone and Philip Evans)
- "Subsidiarity as Judicial and Legislative Review Principles in the European Union" in *Global Perspectives on Subsidiarity* (Michelle Evans and Augusto Zimmermann eds.), Springer, 2014, 157-183 (with John Trone)
- "Domestic Court Proceedings Relating to International Commercial Arbitration in the Resources Sector" in Vol. 3 *Energy between Law and Economics*, United Arab Emirates University, 2013, 1509-1528

- "Law, Legal Theory and Liberty" in *Jurisprudence of Liberty*, 2nd ed. (Suri Ratnapala and Gabriël Moens eds.), LexisNexis Butterworths, 2011, 1-15 (with Suri Ratnapala)
- "The German Border Guard Cases: Natural Law and the Duty to Disobey Immoral Laws" in *Jurisprudence of Liberty* 2nd ed. (Suri Ratnapala and Gabriël Moens eds.), LexisNexis Butterworths, 2011, 271-292
- "Rehabilitating Lawyers. A Short Essay in Honour of Dean and Professor Bintan R Saragih" in *Percikan Pemikiran Huku.m, Ketatanegaraan, dan Kebijakan Publik*, Wildan Akademika dan Universitas Ekasakti Press, 2010, 10-14
- "Commentary on the Arbitration Rules of the Australian Centre for International Commercial Arbitration" in *International Commercial Arbitration* (Looseleaf set, E. Bergsten ed.), Release 2009-6, Issued December 2009, Oceana, Oxford University Press, New York, ii + 88 (with Samuel Ross Luttrell)
- "Teaching of Comparative Law and Comparative Law Teaching" in *Convergence of Legal Systems in the 21st Century* (Garrick Professor Gabriël A. Moens and Dr Rodolphe Biffot eds.), Bruylant Bruxelles, 2006, 265-299 (with Rodolphe Biffot)
- "The subsidiarity principle in European Union Law and the Irish abortion issue" in *Law, Legal Culture and Politics in the Twenty First Century* (G. Doeker-Mach and K. Ziegert eds.), Franz Steiner Verlag, Stuttgart, 2004, 424-438, reprinted in *Law and Legal Culture in Comparative Perspective*, Franz Steiner Verlag, Stuttgart: (G. Doeker-Mach and K. Ziegert eds.), 2004, 406-420
- "Australia: A new approach to international commercial contracts" in *A New Approach to International Commercial Contracts* (J Bonell ed.), Kluwer Law International, 1999, 19-54 (with Lisa Cohn and Darren Peacock)
- "Financing exports: letters of credit" in *International Trade and Business: Law, Policy and Ethics* (Gabriël Moens and Peter

Gillies eds.), Cavendish Publishing Pty Ltd, London, 1998, 387-420 (with Ted Tzovaras)

- "The UNIDROIT principles of international commercial contracts" in *International Trade and Business: Law, Policy and Ethics* (Gabriël Moens and Peter Gillies eds.), Cavendish Publishing Pty Ltd, London, 1998, 79-99 (with David Wagner)
- "Trading blocs: the European Union" in *International Trade and Business: Law, Policy and Ethics* (Gabriël Moens and Peter Gillies eds.), Cavendish Publishing Pty Ltd, London, 1998, 705-728
- "The role of the states in High Court appointments" in *Upholding the Australian Constitution*, Vol. 8 The Samuel Griffith Society, 1997, 17-38
- "Bank confidentiality and governmental control of exchange operations and of their unlawful effects - Australia" in *Money Laundering and Banking Secrecy* (Paolo Bernasconi ed.), Kluwer Law International, 1996, 31-48
- "Law, legal theory and liberty" in *Jurisprudence of Liberty* (G. A. Moens and S. Ratnapala eds.), Sydney, Butterworths, 1995, 1-13
- "The German Borderguard Cases: Natural Law and the Duty to Disobey Immoral Laws" in *Jurisprudence of Liberty* (G.A. Moens and S. Ratnapala eds.), Sydney, Butterworths, 1995, 146-164
- "The wrongs of a constitutionally entrenched bill of rights" in *Republic or Monarchy? Legal and Constitutional Issues* (M.A. Stephenson and C. Turner eds.), St. Lucia, The University of Queensland Press, 1994, 233-256
- "Banking confidentiality and state control of currency transactions and related criminal activities" in *Australian Law and Legal Thinking in the 1990s* (A.E-S Tay and C. S.C. Leung eds.), The University of Sydney, Sydney, 1994, 249-262
- "Mabo and political policy-making by the High Court" in *Mabo:*

A Judicial Revolution (M.A. Stephenson and S. Ratnapala eds.), St. Lucia, The University of Queensland Press, 1993, 48-62

- "Academic freedom: An eroded concept?" in *Academic Freedom Today* (G. Moens ed.), 1992, 57-70
- "Affirmative action and the future of Australia" in *Interdisciplinary Approaches to Peace* (J. D Frodsham ed.), Professors World Peace Academy of Australia, Canberra, 1985, 225-232
- "Die Gestaltungsmethode und ihre rechtslogischen Anwendungen" (The Formation Method and Its Applications in Legal Logic) in *Strukturierungen und Entscheidungen im Rechtsdenken* (I. Tammelo and H. Schreiner eds.), 1978, 83-94

Articles in Law/Business/Management Reviews

- "Maintaining the Attractiveness of Arbitration in a Changing World: The ACICA Arbitration Rules and the SIAC Arbitration Rules" *Sharia and Law Journal*, 2018, 53-84 (with Camilla Andersen and Tracy Albin)
- "The Twenty-Fourth Annual Willem C. Vis International Commercial Arbitration Moot, 2016-2017" XXI *International Trade and Business Law Review*, 2018, 361-406 (with Michael Chen, Geoffrey De Groot, Jessica Downing-Ide, Benjamin Gibbons)
- "The Twenty-Third Annual Willem C. Vis International Commercial Arbitration Moot, 2014-2015" XX *International Trade and Business Law Review*, 2017, 445-532 (with Benjamin Teng, Madeline Rodgers, Matthew Paterson, Samuel Bullen, Sangeetha Badya)
- "The Twenty-Second Annual Willem C Vis International Commercial Arbitration Moot, 2015-2016" XIX *International Trade and Business Law Review*, 2016, 351-447 (with Finian Cullity, Kane Bennett, James Rigby, Ha Neul Sky Kim)

- "How to Mismanage Organisations: A Lawyer's Perspective" Vol. 1, No 1, *Global Journal of Business and Social Science Review*, Jan. 2015, 1-10
- "The Principle of Subsidiarity in EU Judicial and Legislative Practice: Panacea or Placebo?" 41(1) *Journal of Legislation*, 2014-15, 65-102 (with John Trone)
- "The Art of Persuasion", 5 *The Western Australian Jurist*, 2014, 197-212
- "The Legislative principle of Subsidiarity: A Meaningful Restriction upon the Legislative Power of the European Union?" Vol. 2014 – II *Diritto Pubblico Comparato ed Europeo*, 2014, 563-580 (with John Trone and Ermanno Calzolaio)
- "Successful Advocacy for the Willem C Vis International Commercial Arbitration Moot" XVII *International Trade and Business Law Review*, 2014, 204-223 (with Rajesh Sharma)
- "The CEAC Hamburg Arbitration Rules: A European-Chinese Trade-Related Adaptation of the Revised UNCITRAL Arbitration Rules 2010" 79(2) *Arbitration*, April 2013, 138-157 (with Rajesh Sharma)
- "Ninth Annual Willem C Vis (East) International Commercial Arbitration Moot" XVI *International Trade and Business Law Review*, 2013, 433-552 (with Rajesh Sharma, Brar Harprabdeeb Singh, Chan Yin Wai Ada, Chow Yat Sau Jessica, Lau Chirk Yen Jason, Kirpalani Lavesh Prakas)
- "A New Commercial Arbitration Act for Western Australia" *Arbitration & Mediation* (IAMA Journal), June 2013, 41-67 (with Philip Evans)
- "Constitutional, Philosophical and Historical Perspectives of the Capital Punishment Debate in Australia and the United States" 1(2) *Juridica. Acta Universitatis George Bacovia*, 2012, 5-35 (also published in Romanian) (with Keith Thompson)
- "The Validity of Henry VIII Clauses in Australian Federal Leg-

islation" No. 24 *Giornale di Storia Costituzionale*, University of Macerata, Italy, 2012, 133-143 (with John Trone)
- "The Sun Rises in the West: After Dinner Reflections" XV *International Trade and Business Law Review*, 2012, 383-384
- "The Amazing World of Arbitration" XV *International Trade and Business Law Review*, 2012, 152-163 (with Philip Evans)
- "The Seventeenth Annual Willem C. Vis and Seventh Annual Willem C. Vis (East) International Commercial Arbitration Moot, 2009-2010" XIV *International Trade and Business Law Review* (with), 2011, 433-543 (with Prabhjyot Kaur, Lau Ching Kar Karen, Dickie Ham-Dick Mok, Suraj Sajnani, Tse Sau Wai Flora, Rajesh Sharma)
- "The First Amendment to the UNCITRAL Arbitration Rules" XIV *International Trade and Business Law Review*, 2011, 376-386 (with John Trone)
- "Negotiation as a Dispute Resolution Process: Practical and Legal Issues" 10 *Universitas Pelita Harapan Law Review*, 2010, 229-252 (with Philip Evans)
- "The Appointment and Challenge of Arbitrators under the Rules of the Australian Centre for International Commercial Arbitration" Issue 5 *International Arbitration Law Review*, 2009, 84-95 (with Sam Luttrell)
- "The Arbitration Rules of the Australian Centre for International Commercial Arbitration: Distinctive Features", 75(4) *Arbitration*, November 2009, 521-532 (with Sam Luttrell)
- "Reflections on the Role of Mediators and Arbitrators: Can a Good Mediator also be a Good Arbitrator" 6 *Macquarie Journal of Business Law*, 2009, 265-276 (with Philip Evans)
- "Can a Good Mediator also be a Good Arbitrator?" 17 *Asia Pacific Law Review*, 2009, 31-40
- "The Fifteenth Annual Willem C. International Commercial Arbitration Moot, 2007-08" XII *International Trade and*

- *Business Law Review*, 2009, 294-410 (with Samantha D'Silva, Andrew Kirk, Kristian Maley, Vanja Tekić, Craig Williams)
- "The Fourteenth Annual Willem C Vis International Commercial Arbitration Moot 2006-07" XI *International Trade and Business Law Review*, 2008, 313-429 (with Samereh Aljanabi, Marina De Kwant, David Jenaway, Johanna Weaver)
- "The *International Arbitration Act* 1974 (Cth) as a Foundation for International Commercial Arbitration" 4 *Macquarie Business Law Journal,* 2007, 295-324 (with John Trone),
- "The Mysteries of Problem-Based Learning: Combining Enthusiasm and Excellence" 38 *University of Toledo Law Review*, 2007, 101-110
- "The Willem C Vis international commercial arbitration moot 2004-05" IX *International Trade and Business Law Review*, 2006, 215-319 (with Nicholas John Collie, Thomas William Fitzgerald, Katherine Mary Hevron, Madge Puja Mukund and Michael Taylor)
- "The menace of neutrality in religion" Vol. 2004, No. 2 *Brigham Young University Law Review*, 535-574
- "Reflections on commercial dispute resolution" 7 *ADR Bulletin*, 2004, 41-46, reprinted in Vol. 15, No. 8 *World Arbitration & Mediation Report*, August 2004, 242-246
- "An Assessment of Incoterms 2000" 20 *Annual Report of Institute for Legal Research*, 2004, 1-33(with Peter Gillies)
- "The Willem C Vis International Commercial Arbitration Moot 2002-2003" VIII *International Trade and Business Law Annual,* 2003, 311-425 (with Sabine Erkens, Ryan Allan Goss, Andrew Edward Hodge, Marion Alice Jane Isobel, Benjamin John Jackson, Siobhan Maree McKeering, Elena Christine Zaccaria)
- "The subsidiarity principle in European Community Law and the Irish abortion issue" 9 *Jus Gentium*, 2003, 35-71
- "Preferential Admission Programs in Professional Schools:

DeFunis, Bakke and *Grutter*" 42 *Loyola Law Review*, 2002, 411-503
- "The Practice of International Commercial Law in Queensland" VII *International Trade and Business Law Annual*, 2002, 277-296 (with Simon Fisher and Steve Williams)
- "The Willem C Vis International Commercial Arbitration Moot 2000-2001" VII *International Trade and Business Law Annual*, 2002, 325-435 (with Kathryn Louise Brown, Mariel Brooke Dimsey, Martin Ehrenberg, Michael Robert Hodge, Radha Dawn Ivory, Jens Thomas John, Christopher Justin Peters)
- "The Willem C Vis International Commercial Arbitration Moot 1999-2000" VI *International Trade and Business Law Annual*, 2001, 375-476 (with Sophie Maree Devitt, Sarah Catherine Holland, Thomas Jens John, Kateena Anne O'Gorman, Andrew Carl Stumer)
- "A New Approach to International Commercial Contracts: The UNIDROIT Principles of International Commercial Contracts: the Australian Experience" V *International Trade and Business Law Annual*, 2000, 219-254 (with Lisa Cohn and Darren Peacock)
- "The Willem C Vis International Commercial Arbitration Moot 1998-1999" V *International Trade and Business Law Annual*, 2000, 309-415 (with Peter Black, Jonathan Cheyne, Avryl Lattin, Annelies Moens, Carly Roberts),
- "The Willem C Vis International Commercial Arbitration Moot 1996-97" IV *International Trade and Business Law Annual*, 1998, 215-278 (with Joanne Coates, Lisa Cohn, Lisa Ford, Jacqueline Mowbray, Darren Peacock, Dugald Wishart)
- "The Willem C Vis International Commercial Arbitration Moot 1995-96" III *International Trade and Business Law Annual*, 1997, 277-347 (with P Gregory Bashaw, Martha Branigan, Stacy M Cheney, Joseph M Geis, Peter R Jones)
- "Equal opportunities not equal results: 'equal opportunity' in

European law after *Kalancke*" 23 *Journal of Legislation*, 1997, 43-59

- "Church and state relations in Australia and the United States: The purpose and effect approaches and the neutrality principle" Vol.1996, No. 4 *Brigham Young University Law Review*, 787-813
- "The Willem C Vis International Commercial Arbitration Moot 1994-95" II *International Trade and Business Law Annual*, 1996, 229-275 (with Teresa Baldwin, Zeke Bentley, Greg Elphinston, David Kirkpatrick, Frederique Meyer)
- "Judicial law-making in the European Court of Justice" 18 *University of Queensland Law Journal*, 1992, 76-110 (with Ted Tzovaras)
- "Minority situations: In search of peaceful and constructive solutions" 66 *Notre Dame Law Review*, 1991, 1347-1350
- "1992: A challenge to Australian lawyers" *Australian International Law News,* September 1989, 142-184
- "Freedom of movement of goods in the European Economic Community" 17 *Melbourne University Law Review*, 1990, 733-743
- "The 1992 challenge: The right of establishment and the freedom of movement of goods in the European Community" 16 *University of Queensland Law Journal*, 1990, 70-92
- "The pursuit of the legal profession in the European Community" December 1989, No.7, *International Law News. Journal of the International Law Section of the Law Council of Australia*
- "Can you bank on a bank? An examination of the customer-bank relationship in light of the *Cheques and Payment Orders Act* 1986 (Cth)" 15 *University of Queensland Law Journal*, 1989, 183-208
- "The Action-Belief dichotomy and freedom of religion"12 *Sydney Law Review*, 1989, 195-217

- "Ilmar Tammelo: A personal appreciation" 10 *Sydney Law Review*, 1983, 128-142 (with Julius Stone)
- "Die Tegenformulemethode en haar rechstlogische toepassingen" (The Counter-Formula Method and its Legal Logical Applications) *Nederlands Tijdschrift voor Rechtsfilosofie en Rechtstheorie*, 1981, No.1, 55-65 (with Ilmar Tammelo and Popke Brouwer)
- "The integration debate in the United States: The interplay of quality and equality" *Bulletin of the Australian Society of Legal Philosophy*, October 1980, No..17, 4-25
- "Otto Bondy (1904-1976)" 29 Österreichische Zeitschrift für öffentliches Recht und Völkerrecht, 1978, 1-4 (with Julius Stone)
- "Gleichheit als Wesensmerkmal der Gerechtigkeit" (Equality as the Core of Justice) 61 *Archiv für Rechts- and Sozialphilosophie*, 1975, 485-495
- "The Counter-Formula method and its applications in international judicial reasoning" 3 *Syracuse Journal of International Law and Commerce*, 1975, 165-180
- "Die Formen des innerstaatlichen Minderheitenschutzes" (Methods to protect minorities) 32 *Europa Ethnica*, 1975, 2-8
- "Die Gegenformelmethode und ihre rechtslogischen Anwendungen" (The Counter-Formula Method and its Applications in Legal Logic) 1 *Rechtsphilosophische Mitteilungen*, 1974, 1-30 (with Ilmar Tammelo)
- "De rechten van de minderheden op arbeid" (Right of minorities to work) 28 *Tijdschrift voor Bestuurswetenschappen en Publiek Recht*, 1973, 363-372
- "Noot bij vonnis de dato 19 mei 1969" (Review of judgment) *Rechtskundig Weekblad*, 1971, 1955
- "Het juridisch statuut van de tandarts" (The legal status of dentists) 6 *Jura Falconis*, 1969, 87-99 (with Edith Van der Mijnsbrugge)

- "Democratie en rechtsstaat bij Réné Marcic" (Réné Marcic's views on democracy and the rule of law) 6 *Jura Falconis*, 1969, 9-20.

Articles in Specialist and Special Interest Serials

- "The Concept of the Rule of Law: A Western Perspective and its Relevance for the P R China" *Law and Society, Building a Rule-of-Law Society*, Hangzhou, Conference Papers 2017, 32-36
- "The Lure of Arbitration and Alternative Dispute Resolution Education" (Jan-Mar 2015) *CDCorporate Disputes*, 46-49
- "The importance of the 'seat' of arbitration in dispute resolution clauses for finance transactions" (Jan-Mar 2014), in *CDCorporate Disputes*, 46-49
- "How to Mismanage an Organisation: The Peter Principle" (Oct-Dec 2014) *RCRisk & Compliance*, 93-96
- "The Importance of the 'Rule of Law' in the Development of the Australia-China Business Relationship" (2007) *National Observer*, 220-227
- "Intensive law teaching: Flexibility enhancing strategies for law schools" in (1999) *International Law School Deans' Conference on Legal Education for the 21st Century*, 444-457 (also in Chinese: 458-464)
- "The right of freedom of communication: an implied constitutional right?" (1994) 1 *Agenda* 71-79
- "Symptom of a modern malady: The decline of English in school and university" (1993) 20 *Education Research and Perspectives* 94-101 (with Philip R. de Lacey)
- "Comparable worth: An evaluation nightmare" (Winter 1991) *Policy* 21-24
- "The impact of forced amalgamations" (Winter 1990) *Education Monitor* 12-15 (with Philip de Lacey).
- "Sexual harassment and the Sex Discrimination Act 1984" (Autumn 1990) *Policy* 25-28

- "Affirmative action: Success or failure?" (Autumn 1989) *Policy* 15-18
- "Education for minorities: Two competing routes to the mainstream in a climate of confusion" (1986) 6 *Discourse. The Australian Journal of Educational Studies* 45-56 (with Philip de Lacey)
- "Understanding affirmative action: The search for an ideal of equality" *The Teaching of Human Rights* (Human Rights Commission, Occasional Paper no.6, 1984), 82-95

Articles in Journals of Literary and/or Social and Cultural Criticism

- "Belgians" *Multicultural Queensland 2001*, Queensland Government, Brisbane, 2001, 71-72
- "Judicial activism and common sense: An American perspective" (Spring 1998) *Australia and World Affairs* 52-58 (with Marcus R Mumford)
- "The subsidiarity principle and E.C. Directive 93/104" (Spring 1997) *Australia and World Affairs* 51-56
- "Territory rights are not states rights" (Autumn 1997) *Australia and World Affairs*) 49-51 (with John Trone)
- "Medico-legal Issues: the law of kidney transplantation in Australia" (Summer 1997) *Australia and World Affairs* 44-46 (with John Trone)
- "The constitutional protection of human rights" (Spring 1996) *Australia and World Affairs* 48-52, reprinted in Japanese in *International Conference on Comparative Constitutional Law* 1996, 18-21
- "Deciding guilt or innocence" (Winter 1996) *Australia and World Affairs* 46-51
- "International treaties in Australian law: legitimate expectations and the *Teoh* Case' (Winter 1995) *Australia and World Affairs* 57-61 (with John Trone)

- "Assessing Australia's Asian export drive" (Spring 1995) *Australia and World Affairs* 44-47
- "Racist speech and freedom of speech" (Summer 1995) *Policy*, 3-6 (with John Trone).
- "Racial and homosexual anti-vilification legislation" *Dialectic on Anti-Vilification*, Macquarie University, School of Economic and Financial Studies, Centre of Business Law and Ethics, 1994, 1-5
- "Eroding our rights: Towards mind control?" (Summer 1994) *Australia and World Affairs* 21-30
- "Politicisation of the teaching of law" (Summer 1994) *Australia and World Affairs* 52-53
- "International trade and Incoterms" *Res Ipsa*, The University of Queensland Law Society (UQLS), 1994, 78-80
- "Transplantation of organs from living donors: The ethical and legal dimensions" (Winter 1994) *Australia and World Affairs* 51-54 (with Peter K. Donnelly)
- "Section 92 and the implied right to freedom of political communication" (Autumn 1994) *Australia and World Affairs* 46-51
- "The duty to disobey the law: The German borderguard judgment of 3 November 1992" (Summer 1994) *Australia and World Affairs* 43-51
- "Is a bill of rights right?" *Res Ipsa*, University of Queensland Law Society (UQLS), 1993, 72-74
- "Capital punishment: An inhumane way of dying?" (Spring 1993) *Australia and World Affairs* 42-49
- "Will Australia's ratification of the Convention assist children?" *The Convention on the Rights of the Child*, Brisbane, Child, Adolescent and Family Welfare Association of Queensland, 1993, 12-16
- "Judicial activism, expressive activity and the First Amendment" (Winter 1993) *Australia and World Affairs* 46-51

- "An assessment of Australian education" (Autumn 1993) *Australia and World Affairs* 16-24
- "Marine cargo liability: The Amended Hague Rules or the Hamburg Rules?" (Autumn 1993) *Australia and World Affairs* 82-84
- "Courts and social change" (Summer 1992) *Australia and World Affairs* 25-29
- "The completion of the European Community in 1992" (Winter 1992) *Australia and World Affairs* 61-66
- "Diversity or the pursuit of excellence" (July 1992) 23 *Search* 201
- "Neutrality and academic freedom" (June 1992) 23 *Search* 148-149.
- "Diversity demystified: A comment on Dinesh D'Souza's *Illiberal Education*" (1992) 38 *Australian Journal of Politics and History* 270-273
- "Restrictive speech codes" (Autumn 1992) *Australia and World Affairs* 54-56
- "Age discrimination. The case of Dr de Lacey" (October 1990) *Quadrant* 70-73
- "United States of Europe on cards but not this century" (1986) *AFR European Community Survey* (Wednesday, October 22, 1986) 7s.
- "The silent revolution. Affirmative action and the erosion of the rule of law" (December 1985) *Quadrant* 42-51
- "The comparable worth doctrine" (September 1985) *The Optimist* 10-11 (with Philip de Lacey)
- "The new meritocracy. Recent affirmative action developments in universities" (May 1985) *Quadrant* 36-44 (with Philip de Lacey). An edited extract from this article is published in L.J.M. Cooray ed., *Human Rights in Australia,* ACFR, Sydney, 1985, 109-125

- "The excommunication of a heretic. Inside the Human Rights Commission" (March 1985) *Quadrant* 10-15
- "Affirmative action: Strategies for the ethnic communities" *Welfare Service Delivery to Greek People in Australia and Inter-Ethnic Group Relations* (N. Dimitropoulos and M. Ghiotsalitis, eds., 1983), 55-60
- "Recht auf Strafe" (The Right to be punished) (1973) 26 *Der Staatsbürger* n.22, 3

Reviews

1. "Survival and Surpassing" (I. Tammelo) 1972-3 *Rechtskundig Weekblad* 1355.

2. "Wozu Rechtsphilosophie heute" (A. Kaufmann) 1973-4 *Rechtskundig Weekblad* 330.

3. "Kann der Jurist heute noch Dogmatiker sein?" (U. Meyer-Cording) 1973-4 *Rechtskundig Weekblad* 1619.

4. "Das Rassenproblem in den U.S.A." (W. Förster) 31 *Europa Ethnica* 40.

5. "Rassenbeziehungen in den U.S.A." (B. Ruster) 31 *Europa Ethnica* 40.

6. "Grundzüge and Grundverfahren der Rechtslogik" (I. Tammelo and H. Schreiner) 1975 *Rechtskundig Weekblad* 509-512.

7. "Survival and Surpassing" (I. Tammelo) (1976) 7 *Sydney Law Review* 480.

8. "Grundzüge and Grundverfahren der Rechtslogik" (I. Tammelo and H. Schreiner) (1977) 63 *Archiv für Rechts- und Sozialphilosophie* 460.

9. "Le droit et la croissance de la population en Roumanie" (I. Ceterchi and others) (1980) 28 *American Journal of Comparative Law* 135-142 (with K.M. Sharma).

10. "Modern Logic in the Service of Law" (I. Tammelo) (1983) 1 *Journal of Law and Information Science* 296-298.

11. "Australia and the European Communities in the 1980's" (A. Burnett) (April 1984) 1 *Europa* 6-8 (co-authored with S. Norris).

12. "The Rights of Working Women in the European Community" (E.C. Landau) (November 1985), 3 *EC News* 5-6.

13. "Comparative Legal Traditions" (M.A. Glendon, M.W. Gordon and C. Osakwe) (1986) *Lawasia* 157-158.

14. "Justifying Lay Justice" (Z.K. Bankowski, N.R. Hutton and J.J. McManus) (1988) 4 *CIS Policy Report* 6-7.

15. "Australia's Seventh State" (P. Loveday and P. McNab, eds.) (1989) 15 *University of Queensland Law Journal* 267-271.

16. "The Rule of Law. Foundation of Constitutional Democracy" (G. de Q. Walker) (Summer 1989-90) *Australia and World Affairs* 33-35.

17. "South Africa, Namibia and Sanctions" (B. Francis) (Summer 1989-90) *Australia and World Affairs* 60-63.

18. "Business Law" (P. Gillies) (1990) 16 *University of Queensland Law Journal* 144-146.

19. "Galbally! The Autobiography of Australia's Leading Criminal Lawyer" (F. Galbally) (1990) 16 *University of Queensland Law Journal* 146-149.

20. "Commercial Alternative Dispute Resolution" (M.J. Fulton) (1991) 16 *University of Queensland Law Journal* 302-303.

21. "Challenging or Changing the Recipe?" (Review of `Same Difference' by C.L. Bacchi and `Sisters in Suits' by M. Sawer) (Spring 1992) *Policy* 43-45.

22. "The Law Relating to Banker and Customer in Australia" (G.A. Weaver and C.R. Craigie) (1992) 17 *University of Queensland Law Journal* 135-136.

23. "Ninth Justice: The Fight for Bork" (P.B. McGuigan and D.M. Weyrich) (Summer 1992) *Australia and World Affairs* 77-78.

24. "Report of the Australian Human Rights Delegation to China: 14-26 July 1991" (Autumn 1993) *Australia and World Affairs* 73-74.

25. "Tenterfield Revisited. Reforming Australia's System of Government for 2001" (K. Wiltshire) (1993) *Australian Journal of Politics and History* 108-110.

26. "The Attorney General's Lawyer: Inside the Meese Justice Department" (D.W. Kmiec) (1993) 17 *University of Queensland Law Journal* 300-302.

27. "Commercial Arbitration in Australia" (Doug Jones) 6(3) *Construction Law International* (October 2011), 41 (with Philip Evans)

28. "A Private Life – Fragments, Memories, Friends" (Michael Kirby) (2012) Vol. 3 *The Western Australian Jurist*, 271-277

29. "Malice in Media Land" (David Flint), (2012) Vol. 3 *The Western Australian Jurist*, 279-284

Forewords/Prefaces

- "Foreword: The Australian Institute of Foreign and Comparative Law and the Study of International Trade Law", I *International Trade and Business Law Journal*, 1995, iii-viii (with Geoffrey de Q Walker)

- "Academic Freedom: Foreword", *Academic Freedom Today* (ed. G. Moens), 1992) v-vi

- "Foreword", Augusto Zimmermann, *Western Legal Theory: History, Concepts and Perspectives*", LexisNexis Butterworths, 2013, v-vii

- "Foreword", Augusto Zimmermann, *Christian Foundations of the Common Law*, Connorcourt Publications, Perth, 2018, 2018, i-iv.

Reports

- *Human Rights for Australia* (Human Rights Commission, Australian Government Publishing Service, Canberra, 1986) (with A.E.S. Tay)

- *Participation* (The Ethnic Affairs Commission of New South Wales, Report to the Premier, June 1978), 243-279 and 311-321
- Report on the Constitutionality of the *Trade Marks Amendment (Tobacco Plain Packaging) Bill* 2011 (published in 2011 on the website of the Australian Senate) (with John Trone)
- Report on the Plain Tobacco Packaging (Removing Branding from Cigarette Packs) Bill 2009 (published in 2010 on the website of the Australian Senate) (with John Trone)

www.ingramcontent.com/pod-product-compliance
Lightning Source LLC
Chambersburg PA
CBHW052111010526
44111CB00036B/1665